Edited by Veronica Strong-Boag,
Sherrill Grace, Avigail Eisenberg,
and Joan Anderson

Painting the Maple:
Essays on Race, Gender, and the
Construction of Canada

UBCPress / Vancouver

Printed in Canada on acid-free paper ∞

ISBN 0-7748-0692-3 (hardcover)
ISBN 0-7748-0693-1 (paperback)

Canadian Cataloguing in Publication Data

Main entry under title:
Painting the maple

Includes bibliographical references and index.
ISBN 0-7748-0692-3 (bound); ISBN 0-7748-0693-1 (pbk.)

1. Canada – Race relations. 2. Sex discrimination – Canada. 3. Marginality, Social – Canada. 4. Canada – Civilization. I. Strong-Boag, Veronica Jane, 1947-

FC97.P35 1998   971   C98-910985-2
F1021.2.P35 1998

This book has been published with a grant from the Social Sciences Federation of Canada, using funds provided by the Social Sciences and Humanities Research Council of Canada.

UBC Press also gratefully acknowledges the ongoing support to its publishing program from the Canada Council for the Arts, the British Columbia Arts Council, and the Department of Canadian Heritage of the Government of Canada.

Set in Stone by Aitken+Blakeley
Printed in Canada by Friesens
Proofreader: Judy Phillips
Indexer: Patricia Buchanan

UBC Press
University of British Columbia
6344 Memorial Road
Vancouver, BC V6T 1Z2
(604) 822-5959
Fax: 1-800-668-0821
E-mail: orders@ubcpress.ubc.ca
www.ubcpress.ubc.ca

Contents

Acknowledgments

The editors would like to extend their thanks to the Social Sciences and Humanities Research Council of Canada for the funding that made the research, hiring of graduate student research assistants, workshops, conference, and preparation of this volume possible. We would also like to thank the Centre for Research in Women's Studies and Gender Relations at the University of British Columbia for providing management and support during our work; it was always a pleasure to meet at the centre, and we owe special thanks to Jo Hinchliffe and Kristin Schopp for their warmth and practical assistance throughout. As always with research projects as large as this one, there are far too many people to thank individually, but we would like to acknowledge the contributions to our work made by various groups. To the UBC participants in our 1994 workshop; to the participants, from across Canada, in our highly successful 1995 conference; to health care professionals who gave interviews; and to members of the 1995 graduate seminar on 'Race, Gender, and the Construction of Canada' we wish to say: 'Thanks. Your contributions, lively debate, and enthusiasm are what make collaborative research worthwhile.' For permission to reproduce photographs for Figures 1, 2, and 3, it is a pleasure to thank Sharon Pollock and the Vancouver Playhouse Theatre. We also want to offer sincere thanks to Jean Wilson, senior editor with UBC Press, for believing in this book from the start and helping it into the world. And, finally, it is a special pleasure to acknowledge the major contributions made to the research and to this volume by our research assistants – Gabi Helms, Matt James, Paddy Rodney, and Sheryl Reimer Kirkham – who worked alongside us at every stage, from regular meetings to panel discussions, conference organization, and the preparation of this volume. We had great fun together, learned an enormous amount from our collaboration, and benefited greatly from your contemporary perspectives on old issues.

V. S.-B., S.G., A.E., and J.A.
Vancouver

Constructing Canada: An Introduction

Sherrill Grace, Veronica Strong-Boag, Joan Anderson, and Avigail Eisenberg

> In the social sciences, the progress of knowledge presupposes
> progress in our knowledge of the conditions of knowledge. That
> is why it requires one to return persistently to the same objects ...
> Each doubling-back is another opportunity to objectify more
> completely one's objective and subjective relation to the object.
> One has to endeavour to reconstruct retrospectively the successive
> stages of the relationship, because this labour, which is first
> exerted on the person who performs it ... tends to remove its
> own traces.
>
> – Pierre Bourdieu, *The Logic of Practice*

Constructing Community

To speak of the *construction* of Canada today may seem little short of
quixotic. At the close of the twentieth century this country once again
appears to be deconstructing, if not destroying, itself: Ottawa lacks the
political will or skill to hold the country together; Quebec's aspirations
continue to belie national unity, and, if Lucien Bouchard is to be believed,
Canada – by which he means not just English-speaking Canada but Canada
as a country, what Benedict Anderson would call an 'imagined community' – never existed. Other forces, some as long-standing as French
Canada's claim to a special mission in North America, are also eroding the
idea and practice of Canada, while free trade agreements, which facilitate
a postmodern corporate capitalism, and the related, though less understood, phenomenon of globalization threaten to undermine Canada's
claims to distinctiveness and autonomy.

Such challenges recall the early decades of Confederation. Then too,
Quebec, led by the Parti Nationale, asserted its own national interests, and
other provinces seemed almost equally disgruntled. As the Canada that had
evolved from the conquest of Quebec in 1760, the War of 1812, and
Confederation in 1867 appeared to falter, a host of alternative futures

beckoned. Dissolution was rejected, or perhaps only postponed, when Sir Wilfrid Laurier's Liberals promised to harness the nation's future to political compromise and the economic opportunities of the twentieth century. The new century, citizens were told, belonged to them. The unanswered question, however, was: Who really belonged to the narrow community of Canada that was imagined by the *fathers* in the nineteenth century? Today the community we call Canada is still narrow and exclusionary.

Painting the Maple: Essays on Race, Gender, and the Construction of Canada is intended to be a provocative attempt to trace some of the complex ways in which Canada has been and is being constructed. It is a work-in-progress, one in which the first task must be, as Bourdieu reminds us, to recover/rediscover the traces of the constructed relations between generations of people who have laboured to imagine the country and whose efforts (like our own) have covered up their tracks. In the words of Canadian writer Robert Kroetsch, 'We haven't got an identity until somebody tells our story. The fiction makes us real' (63). However, to tell and hear the stories that constitute our reality, we must first recognize the limitations of the dominant story, and no one has exposed that story more efficiently than lawyer, poet, and statesman F.R. Scott in poems like 'The Canadian Authors Meet,' which is as sharply relevant today as it was when it was published in 1957. Scott's poem is a withering satire on the white, middle-class, Victorian attitudes that dominated literary circles and constrained Canadian culture within exclusionary, self-legitimating boundaries. 'O Canada,' Scott laments,

O Canada, O Canada, O can
A day go by without new authors springing
To paint the native maple, and to plan
More ways to set the self same welkin ringing? (248)

This book is an attempt to take up Scott's challenge. Here, many authors meet to ring new bells, to repaint the maple, to tell new stories, and to reimagine Canada.

Painting the Maple has developed out of three years of collaboration by seven students of Canadian culture – four professors and three graduate research assistants – from four fields: English, History, Nursing, and Political Science. We would all describe ourselves as feminists, although we may have somewhat different understandings of what this involves. We met regularly, from the summer of 1993 to the summer of 1996, at the UBC Centre for Research in Women's Studies and Gender Relations, to explore how our separate disciplines have constructed Canada; to foster dialogue and shared understandings; to develop, if we could, a common language; and to uncover, or rediscover, various constructions of our country. This work, conducted alongside a host of other duties, encouraged us to engage in a debate that was never dull and was frequently passionate and tense. There were times when, like the politicians in Atwood's 'Two-Headed Poems,' we asked: 'How can you use two languages / And mean what you say in both?' (69)

Important as talking with each other has been, however, we have also attempted to talk with others through open workshops, conference presentations, seminars, and colloquia. These sessions energized and challenged us. The high point of collaboration was the October 1995 UBC Race, Gender, and the Construction of Canada Conference, which brought together scholars and activists from across Canada and expanded our work-in-progress to include a much wider range of expertise and discipline-based knowledge than was encompassed by our core group. This book is the culmination of successive stages of this three-year collaborative, inter-disciplinary relationship. Some of the chapters that follow are revised texts of presentations given at the conference; others are texts prepared by the core group or by individuals specially invited to contribute.

Contributors include junior and senior scholars with interests in Canadian literature, politics, health policy, society, popular culture, and history. While their essays often reflect disciplinary origins, they go beyond these to embrace the insights and methods of different fields of inquiry. Essays by Lisa Chalykoff, Peter Dickinson, Sherrill Grace and Gabriele Helms, and Christl Verduyn begin with an interest in individual writers' expression of race and gender, but they are equally attentive to how literature helps us make sense of the world around us. Chalykoff, for instance, uses the insights offered in Sky Lee's *Disappearing Moon Cafe* and Denise Chong's *The Concubine's Children* to interrogate the racist assumptions of the 1885 *Report of the Royal Commission on Chinese Immigration*. Grace and Helms argue that Sharon Pollock's play *The Komagata Maru Incident* forces audiences to examine how racism has critically shaped the nation's history. The ways in which the treatment of race and gender in the works of Dionne Brand, Claire Harris, and M. Nourbese Philip are changing both the face of 'CanLit' and the meaning of home – our home and native land – preoccupy Dickinson and Verduyn. Veronica Strong-Boag reassesses the Mohawk-English Canadian poet and performer Pauline Johnson as a woman who challenged the racist and sexist construction of the new nation articulated by the Fathers of Confederation, and Linda Warley examines how the North, First Nations, and Canada are performed and understood at the end of the twentieth century in the popular CBC television drama *North of 60*. Both ignore conventional disciplinary boundaries to uncover other visions of Canada. Similarly, Becki Ross's examination of the concept of 'lesbian nation' employs insights from several disciplines to expand our understanding of how issues of sexuality and nationality are intertwined, simultaneously reinforcing and contradicting each other.

A number of essays converge to show the embedded exclusionary practices of Canadian nationalist policies and practices. Avigail Eisenberg shows the insidious ways in which a discourse based on the concepts of individualism and collectivism hides the culturally imperialist policies of English-Canadians toward Aboriginal peoples and other minorities in Canada. The overt historical project of developing Canada as a white colony, Yasmeen Abu-Laban reminds us, continues in the class, race, and gender biases of a supposedly neutral immigration policy. Exclusionary practices are also deeply entrenched in other Canadian institutions. As Yasmin Jiwani suggests, technologies of communication play a critical role in the production and reproduction of social knowledge, where they legitimize and reaffirm the social order; and, as Jo-Anne Lee and Linda Cardinal argue, we need to understand the role of multiculturalism and feminism within a totalizing and dominating English-Canadian nationalism. By unmasking policy contradictions in health care delivery, Joan Anderson and Sheryl Reimer Kirkham expose the ideologies that underpin the essentializing and marginalizing discourse of multiculturalism and the ways in which this discourse obscures racism. Yet, as Isabel Dyck warns, there are possible pitfalls in conducting even well-intentioned research. White academics researching the lives of people of Colour need to be aware that they may unintentionally contribute to the processes of racialization through which certain groups become inscribed as the subordinate *other*.

As these chapters suggest, the work we have undertaken on race, gender, and the construction of Canada over the past three years has been both collaborative and interdisciplinary. Although we have realized some of the benefits of collaborative interdisciplinary research, we have also had to come to terms with the limitations of crossing disciplinary boundaries. For example, the fact that universities organize knowledge according to discipline-specific departments does not facilitate interdisciplinary teaching or research. In constructing the critical bibliography on race, gender, and the construction of Canada, which concludes this volume, Gabriele Helms, Matt James, and Patricia Rodney regularly wrestled with disciplinary modes of inquiry that resisted integration. But learning has not always been as compartmentalized and disciplined as it is in contemporary institutions; in fact, departmentalized disciplines and curricula, as we know them, are relatively new. So why is it difficult to practise interdisciplinarity and, more to the point, why is it important that we make the effort to do so?

If we narrow our focus to the last fifty years, we can identify three distinct phases of interdisciplinarity in North America.[1] In the period after the Second World War, roughly 1945 to 1960, interdisciplinarity emerged in the academy as a way of building consensus and community. It took the curricular form of 'General Education,' by which was meant the study of shared values cultivated through a shared culture and a common identity. General Education (often called Liberal Education) was usually strategically conservative and ethnocentric. It worked to reinforce unity, to consolidate society, and to resist social, cultural, and historical fragmentation. Between 1960 and 1980, interdisciplinarity became the rallying cry of resistance to tightly unified, homogeneous models of knowledge with their rigid exclusions, hierarchies, and binaries. This interdisciplinarity was counter-hegemonic. It gave us American Studies, Women's Studies, Ethnic Studies, Afro-American Studies, Socialist Studies, Canadian Studies, and so on, and it prepared the way for Postcolonial Studies, Cultural Studies, and Lesbian/Gay/Queer Studies. The current period, roughly 1980 to the present, has seen a dramatic split in intellectual thought between those who call for a return to the 'core curriculum' and to questions of universal, national, or fundamental importance, and those who argue that the actual problems facing society at the end of the twentieth century cannot be solved by specialized knowledge or homogenous, monological methodologies. For this latter group, interdisciplinarity is a *praxis* that brings together scholars within the university and groups outside the university to work on complex common problems and to produce what we think can be transformative knowledge.

The current argument for placing greater emphasis upon interdisciplinary collaboration and integration *within* the academy and *between* the community and the academy arises from an increasingly urgent conviction that contemporary society has problems that must be, indeed can only be, tackled with interdisciplinary methods and expertise. The dilemma of how to construct a modern Canadian nation that is flexible, equitable, and effectively inclusive is precisely this type of problem.

What we have sought to do over the past three years is only a bare beginning. Because we are located professionally within the academy this is where we have started, and by coming together we have struggled to overcome disciplinary, departmental, and institutional barriers to the pooling of our resources. At the most basic level, this struggle has come down to the language we speak. What does the political scientist *mean* by 'construction'? How does what she means differ from what the literary theorist or historian understands by the term? Perhaps most important, in what ways does the 'construction' of identity, values, culture, institutions, and so on determine the formulation of policy that, in turn, affects what the health care professional can or cannot deliver in the community? We have also had to wrestle with the very different discursive practices that, as individuals, we have brought to the seminar table, and it is difficult to see those practices for what they are because, as Bourdieu points out in describing the 'habitus,' they are part of 'embodied history, internalized as a second nature and so forgotten' (56).

The construction of Canada is the development over time of the habitus through the process of imagining community. In order to understand this process and to appreciate the practical import or impact – the institutional and systemic *work* – of the habitus, it is necessary to take discourse seriously. If, as Bourdieu tells us, the habitus 'is what makes it possible for ["the agents of history" – us] to inhabit institutions, to appropriate them practically, and so to keep them in activity' (57), then we must scrutinize the discursive formation of nation to see where, how, and why some discursive practices (stories, texts, voices) install themselves in a narrative of nation and others do not, why some discursive categories appear to be left out altogether and others must fight from the margins for attention.

As Marlene Nourbese Philip observes, 'in a racist, sexist and classist society, the imagination, if left unexamined, can and does serve the ruling ideas of the time' (279). We believe that this collection examines critically the imagining of Canada and challenges us to understand the scope of the work we have yet to do and the means by which we can do it. Each contributor urges us to reexamine the historical, political, social, economic, and cultural bases upon which Canada is built. As always with such endeavours there are caveats. *Caveat emptor:* There are no guarantees here of quick fixes, final conclusions, or stable, centred identities. One purpose of this work-in-progress is to problematize the construction of Canada by *discovering* assumptions, biases, and hegemonic practices. *Caveat lector:* as a work-in-progress, this lesson makes no claim to be complete or all-inclusive; instead, it marks a beginning to a process of inclusion that we now hand on to our readers. *Caveat dictor:* There are many voices here, and this multiplicity of voices mirrors the reality of our experience as living beings. We tune out these voices at our peril.

Imagining Community

The Canada imagined and legitimized in the discourse of the Fathers of Confederation has since been reified through policies, art, literature, and the telling and retelling of Canadian history. For example, in 1870 Sir John A. Macdonald described the rebellious Métis in the Northwest as 'impulsive half-breeds ... [who] must be kept down by a strong hand until they are swamped by the influx of settlers' (Stanley, 95). A year earlier, R.G. Haliburton, a member of the Canada First Movement and a barrister, had articulated this colonizing ethos in terms no less racist but ideologically more revealing. 'A glance at the map of this continent,' Haliburton insisted, 'as well as at the history of the past, will satisfy us that the peculiar characteristic of the New Dominion must ever be that it is a Northern country inhabited by the descendants of Northern races' (2).

By 'Northern races' Haliburton meant northern Europeans and, like many of his contemporaries, he considered geography and climate to be determinants of racial strength and superiority. Because he believed a northern climate provided a superior environment for human development, he elaborated a case for an evolving Canadian supremacy and a national/nationalist identity. For Haliburton, as for so many mainstream thinkers since the 1860s, the arrival of European man was the originary moment for the Canadian nation state. In his widely reprinted essay *The Men of the North and Their Place in History*, he attempts to extend European domination into the foreseeable future (see Berger). This founding ideology is exclusive. Lest there be any misunderstanding, Haliburton reminds 'us' that: 'we are no nameless race of savages, who have no past which we can recall with pride, and no future which we can work out for ourselves and our children. We are the sons and the heirs of those who have built up a new civilization, and though we have emigrated to the Western world, we have not left our native land behind, for we are still in the North' (10).

In the name of national pride, identity, and community, then, Haliburton imagines a Canada that is white, masculinist, heterosexual, Christian, capitalist, and Northern (see Grace). The legacy of oppression and domination passed on to us from the nineteenth century, and so clearly enunciated by Haliburton, informs all levels of our cultural life, from literature, the arts, and policy documents, to scholarly texts, academic hierarchies, and curricula. As an example of this legacy at work in the white Canadian habitus, consider the 1885 Order-in-Council implementing the head tax on Chinese immigrants to Canada. The formulation and implementation of this policy relied on politicians and bureaucrats, but the work of convincing these people and the general public that such blatant injustice was justified was accomplished by portrayals of Asians and their relation to the non-Asian majority in such vehicles as this popular song of the day:

Then let us stand united all,
And show our fathers' might,
That won the home we call our own,
For white man's land we fight,
To oriental grasp and greed
We'll surrender, no never.
Our watchword be 'God save the King'
White Canada forever.[2]

This discursive construction of a racist reality is constantly reproduced in Canada, as stereotypes of Louis Riel; happy, childlike 'Eskimos'; drunken Indians; Chinese 'coolies'; enemy-alien 'Japs'; and so on should remind us.

As we write, a 'new racism' has emerged; 'rich Asians' are now constructed as 'taking over' and 'changing the face' of cities such as Vancouver. These stereotypes operate insidiously to construct the 'other' as a threat to the 'white nation.' At the same time, they work to define and support a raced and gendered elite that sees itself as Haliburton's true heir, and this privileged elite continues to perpetuate and disseminate a set of values and assumptions that help to legitimate policies and practices that, in turn, lead to the many inequities of contemporary Canadian life. As the Canadian philosopher Charles Taylor reminds us, 'our identity is partly shaped by recognition or its absence, often by the misrecognition of others' (25).

Obviously, a gendered and raced construction of history is not unique to Canada. Carolyn Merchant, Edward Said, and George Mosse, among others, argue that Western ideology is built upon values that encourage an aggressive exploitation of nature and the domination of women by men, of 'Orientals' by Westerners, and of the general citizenry by the values of a masculinist elite. When we began our research, we were, as a team, preoccupied with the intersection of race and gender in the construction of Canada. We understood that other constructions and identities, especially those of class and sexuality, have been central to the imagining of Canada, but we wished to focus our investigations in a manageable way and to interrogate an interaction that has been largely ignored in our individual disciplines. Our failure to attend at the outset to the issue of multiple identities, however, proved a continuing problem. One of the first texts we read as a group, bell hooks's *Feminist Theory: From Margin to Center,* highlighted the problem. Hooks provides a powerful account of how feminist theory focuses on the problems and perspectives of white, affluent women, while the concerns of women of Colour, lesbians, and poor women are ignored or are constructed as further types of oppression, which are simply added to the paradigm derived from the experience of privileged white women.

Since hooks's 1984 work, feminist thinkers have made much progress in developing theories that reflect the diversity of oppression. For example, in her study *Justice and the Politics of Difference,* American political theorist Iris Marion Young (39) sets forth five 'faces of oppression' that integrate race, gender, sexuality, class, and other categories. Rose Brewer has given us a way of theorizing the polyvocality of multiple social locations and the simultaneity of oppressions. In Canada, the work of Himani Bannerji and Daiva Stasiulis focuses on the same problem. Stasiulis, for example, argues that we lack 'epistemological frameworks within which to connect race, gender, and class' (178). Like other authors, such as Joy Parr and Roberta Hamilton, she too is particularly critical of 'mechanistic, additive, and non-relational methods': 'In additive models of race, gender, and class, for instance, white women are viewed solely in terms of their gender, while women of Colour are "doubly" or "triply" oppressed by the cumulative effects of race and gender, or race, class, and gender. Such additive models are resistant to acknowledging the relational nature of each social division, the fact that each is positioned and gains meaning in relation to the other' (179). We have attempted to resist additive thinking in our discussion of domination by incorporating a plurality of voices into our readings, the conference, and this volume, but we remain aware that class and sexuality are much more than the add-ons they may at times appear to be in the pages that follow.

Two other perspectives underrepresented in this volume are those of Aboriginal peoples and the Québécois. In both cases, we made efforts to include members of these communities in the dialogue. However, our success was limited for three reasons. First, none of us is a member of these communities or began her/his research with appropriate contacts in place. Building such contacts, while soliciting participation in *our* project, did not prove a strategy destined for success. A better approach would have been to involve members from these communities in the research group from the start. Yet we recognize that such a project would not necessarily be seen as meriting their participation. Second, the difficulties we encountered soliciting participation in our conference from these communities is indicative of the relations among the different communities in Canada. For example, Aboriginal, French-, and English-Canadians have constructed separate intellectual communities that often have little contact with one another. Third, some aspects of our project could well have been anathema to members of these groups. In particular, the implication that the category of 'race' would situate Aboriginal peoples and people of Colour under the same theoretical rubric could well have offended the former, who strive to differentiate the quest for recognition of the inherent right to Aboriginal self-government from the quest of the latter and new 'immigrants' for equal treatment. It may well be that there can be no all-inclusive project; agendas vary, and different groups may define their oppression in different ways.

Practising Community

If, as Kroetsch insists, we must tell our stories to make them real, to invest identity with the force of fact and truth, then the evidence for this process should be easy to locate in current debates about Canadian history and social practice – and it is. Let us briefly consider a few examples of this process in high school history texts; in the so-called fragmentation of history; in the rhetoric surrounding special interest groups; in policies governing health care, employment equity, immigration, and multiculturalism; or, closer to home for academics, the angry polarization that has occurred in recent years over the definition of a liberal education.

The conflict between French and English Canada makes high school history textbooks one of its battlefields, as the fight goes on to instil in the minds of future voters and activists a particular version of what has gone on in Canada's past. The 'sundering of Canadian history,' as Michael Bliss calls it (5), threatens to destroy the country, or at least one accepted vision of it, by inserting the perspectives of those who have thus far been excluded from the history books. And yet the flowering (what Bliss decries as the fragmentation) of historical writing expressed in labour, ethnic, and women's history, or Western, Maritime, and Quebec history, demonstrates both how specialized is the vision of 'master texts' about the exploits of white, central Canadian men and how important and necessary it is to broaden that vision. Similarly, in constitutional politics competing constitutional visions struggle to tell their tale in countless public fora, and before many a parliamentary committee and commission, in the hope that their version of events will be inscribed in the constitutional text. In the constitutional arena, perhaps more clearly than in any other, the traditional vision of Canada appears to be the ideological tool of a ruling elite. The term 'special interest groups' has come to refer to every group except those few that represent white, middle-class (or higher) taxpayers. The practice of identity politics in Canada has resulted in a struggle by the dominant group, no less than by marginalized ones, to strengthen, protect, and advance its identity.

Today's struggles over health care, employment equity, immigration, multicultural policy, and anti-racism, however, indicate that dominant ideas are being challenged. For example, various government documents remind us of the barriers to health care in a system that is supposedly accessible to all. While such documents gloss over racism and sexism and construct issues in neutral terms like 'culture,' they nonetheless remind us that the reality of health care delivery differs from the ideal expressed in public policies. In the 1990s, health reform has emphasized decentralizing health care, increasing sensitivity to local and regional needs, and making health care more accessible to people in their homes. This reform operates on the premise that care closer to home is most preferable because people feel better and get better more quickly in their own environments. In reality, however, families are now assuming major responsibility for health care, and, because they are traditionally expected to be caretakers, women now find themselves assuming increased responsibility for the care of sick family members. The irony in this form of practising community is that such women lose opportunities for paid employment outside the home at a time when many women must work because of economic necessity. Moreover, since work outside the home may make them eligible for public and private pension plans, inability to participate in the paid workforce carries major consequences for later life; these women may well join the swelling ranks of Canadian women who live in poverty in old age (see

J. Anderson; Angus). Moreover, the mounting rhetoric of individual responsibility for well-being rests upon the unacknowledged assumption that, as Peter Li puts it, we are all seen as the architects of our own fortune because it is assumed that equal opportunity is available to all and that our social failures result from personal weaknesses (5).

Employment equity has done little to change the character of authority; people of Colour, the First Nations, and women in general are absent from positions of privilege and occupy the lower tiers of the occupational hierarchy. In the health care industry, for example, structures of dominance in the larger society are reproduced in health care institutions: 'sex, race, economic class, and able-bodied status are important predictors in determining someone's place in the hierarchy [and while] many members of minority races and plenty of poor people are involved in the delivery of health care, very few hold positions of authority' (Sherwin, 228-9). As we know, nursing has remained a woman's profession, and, although the scope of nurses' responsibilities within the health care system has increased, higher education and more responsibilities have not usually granted nurses a greater say in decision making. Women of Colour in nursing are especially disadvantaged: by sexism in health care on the one hand, and by institutionalized racism on the other. To dismantle these disadvantages requires an understanding of sexism, not as added to, but as imbricated with, institutionalized racism.

Our last example of the process by which ideas or beliefs are invested with the force of a truth that is currently being contested is one that has forced us to concentrate on the nature of the Canadian academy. During the summer and fall of 1995, as UBC attempted to manage the controversy created by a crisis in the Department of Political Science, we were reminded once again of the urgency of the situation facing Canadians in general. After several years of graduate student allegations of sexist and racist practices and comments in the department, the issue was brought to a head when an inquiry was called for. That inquiry led to Joan I. McEwen's *Report in Respect of the Political Science Department of the University of British Columbia* and, in its wake, to an escalating series of angry debates that polarized discussion about complex issues. What was at stake for students and for the university as a whole often seemed to be lost sight of.

As a community, the academy institutionalizes the values of the dominant culture. It is not immune from the 'direct' and 'more subtle and pervasive forms of discrimination' in society at large (McEwen, 72). The university is also, indeed perhaps more than other institutions, a critically important site of discursive struggle. Historically, it has created the need for a form of protection that safeguards academic freedom. However, the principles of academic freedom can as easily be used to resist progressive change as to pursue it. Because of the privileged place of universities in liberal societies, their members have the power to distort, as well as to clarify, the concepts, ideas, and arguments that are crucial to the ongoing project of shaping an inclusive community and nation. Its privileges place it in the limelight. And the academy jeopardizes its role in advancing human understanding if it fails to develop policies that effectively address racist and sexist discourses and practices within its own community. Moreover, in failing to reflect the diversity within Canadian society and to embrace a rich plurality of perspectives, it discredits and compromises its own enterprise. Without help from its universities, Canada will continue to be Canada – our home and native land – only for those who are privileged enough to feel at home, who can inhabit and be comfortably inhabited by that habitus that confirms who they are.

The power of words, images, and concepts cannot be underestimated in the construction of Canada. The images of 'Canada First,' the 'true North strong and free,' and the 'two solitudes,' or such terms as 'bilingualism,' 'multiculturalism,' 'anti-racism,' 'First Nations,' and 'academic freedom' name realities in order to insert them into the imagining of community. They map the ongoing struggle to construct the nation. There is an important lesson to be learned from the fact that the writing of a single novel, *Obasan*, focused public attention on a period of racism in Canadian history and that this attention obliged Canadians to learn more about aspects of their history, which, in turn, led politicians to act, through legislation, to redress wrongs. We are able to learn through mediating texts like *Obasan* that Canada is a good deal more than the land Haliburton imagined. But to reimagine the nation we must first free ourselves from the prejudices that F.R. Scott satirizes in 'The Canadian Authors Meet' so that we can 'paint the native maple' in new colours.

Notes

1 In *Interdisciplinarity*, Julie Thompson Klein discusses these phases and reminds us that '*Interdisciplinarity exogenous to the university* must now be given more weight. Exogenous interdisciplinarity originates in the continuous momentum provided by "real" problems of the community, enriching and interrogating *endogamous university interdisciplinarity*, which is based on the production of new knowledge with the aim, more or less explicit, of realizing unity of science' (37-8).
2 This song figured prominently at turn-of-the-century racist gatherings in British Columbia. It is quoted in Peter Ward's *White Canada Forever*, in which Ward examines racist discourse, attitudes, and public policy of a white British Columbia from the mid-nineteenth to the mid-twentieth centuries.

Works Cited

Anderson, Benedict. 1983. *Imagined Communities: Reflections on the Origin and Spread of Nationalism*. London: Verso
Anderson, J. 1990. 'Home Care Management in Chronic Illness and the Self-Care Movement: An Analysis of Ideologies and Economic Processes Influencing Policy Decisions.' *Advances in Nursing Science* 12 (2):71-83

Angus, Jan. 1994. 'Women's Paid/Unpaid Work and Health: Exploring the Social Context of Everyday Life.' *Canadian Journal of Nursing Research* 26 (4):23-42

Atwood, Margaret. 1978. 'Two-Headed Poems.' *Two-Headed Poems*. Toronto: Oxford University Press

Bannerji, Himani. 1995. *Thinking Through: Essays on Feminism, Marxism and Anti-Racism*. Toronto: Women's Press

Berger, Carl. 1970. *A Sense of Power: Studies in the Ideas of Canadian Imperialism*. Toronto: University of Toronto Press

Bliss, Michael. 1991. 'Privatizing the Mind: The Sundering of Canadian History, the Sundering of Canada.' *Journal of Canadian Studies/Journal des études canadiennes* 26 (4):5-17

Bourdieu, Pierre. 1990. *The Logic of Practice*. Trans. Richard Nice. Stanford: Stanford University Press

Brewer, R. 1993. 'Theorizing Race, Class and Gender: The New Scholarship of Black Feminist Intellectuals and Black Women's Labour.' In S.M. James and A.P.A. Busia, eds., *Theorizing Black Feminisms: The Visionary Pragmatism of Black Women*, 13-30. London and New York: Routledge

Grace, Sherrill. 1997. 'Gendering Northern Narrative.' In John Moss, ed., *Echoing Silence: Essays on Arctic Narrative*. Ottawa: University of Ottawa Press

Haliburton, R.G. 1869. *The Men of the North and Their Place in History: A Lecture*. Montreal: John Lovell

Hamilton, Roberta, 1996. *Gendering the Vertical Mosaic: Feminist Perspectives on Canadian Society*. Mississauga, ON: Copp Clark Pitman

hooks, bell. 1984. *Feminist Theory: From Margin to Center*. Boston: South End

Klein, Julie Thompson. 1990. *Interdisciplinarity: History, Theory, and Practice*. Detroit: Wayne State University Press

Kogawa, Joy. 1983. *Obasan*. Harmondsworth, UK: Penguin

Kroetsch, Robert. 1970. 'A Conversation with Margaret Laurence.' In Robert Kroetsch, ed., *Creation*, 53-63. Toronto: New Press

Li, P. 1988. *Ethnic Inequality in Class Society*. Toronto: Thompson Educational Publishing

McEwen, Joan I. 1995. *Report in Respect of the Political Science Department of the University of British Columbia*. Vancouver: UBC

Merchant, Carolyn. 1996. *Earthcare: Women and the Environment*. New York: Routledge

Nourbese Philip, Marlene. 1992. *Frontiers: Selected Essays and Writings on Racism and Culture, 1984-1992*. Stratford, ON: Mercury

Parr, Joy. 1990. *The Gender of Breadwinners: Women, Men, and Change in Two Industrial Communities, 1880-1950*. Toronto: University of Toronto Press

Said, Edward W. 1979. *Orientalism*. New York: Vintage

Scott, F.R. 1981. 'The Canadian Authors Meet.' *The Collected Poems of F.R. Scott*. Toronto: McClelland and Stewart

Sherwin, S. 1992. *No Longer Patient: Feminist Ethics and Health Care*. Philadelphia: Temple University Press

Stanley, George F.G. 1963. *The Birth of Western Canada: A History of the Riel Rebellions*. Toronto: University of Toronto Press

Stasiulis, Daiva K. 1995. 'Diversity, Power, and Voice: The Antinomies of Progressive Education.' In Stephen Richer and Lorna Weir, eds., *Beyond Political Correctness: Towards the Inclusive University*, 165-93. Toronto: University of Toronto Press

Strong-Boag, Veronica. 1997. 'Claiming a Place in the Nation: Citizenship Education and the Challenge of Feminists, Natives, and Workers in Post-Confederation Canada.' *Canadian and International Education* 25 (2):128-45

Taylor, Charles. 1992. *Multiculturalism and 'The Politics of Recognition': An Essay*. Princeton: Princeton University Press

Ward, Peter W. 1990. *White Canada Forever: Popular Attitudes and Public Policy Toward Orientals in British Columbia*. 2nd edition. Montreal and Kingston: McGill-Queen's University Press

Young, Iris Marion. 1990. *Justice and the Politics of Difference*. Princeton: Princeton University Press

Part 1: Parameters of the Nation

Methodology on the Line: Constructing Meanings about 'Cultural Difference' in Health Care Research

Isabel Dyck

Contemporary methodological debates in interpretive social science, and the deconstructive projects of postmodern ethnography and feminist scholarship, signal the complexity of social research in Western postindustrial societies. Any notion of a simple relationship between the researcher, as extractor of data, and the researched, as provider of information, has been eroded. Whose knowledge counts and how knowledge is produced are central issues to consider in surveying and assessing the range of knowledges that express and explain the worlds we live in. Such methodological and epistemological concerns have interested me in my particular position as a white feminist geographer addressing questions of 'cultural difference' at the interface of social science and health care provision. The influence of cultural meanings on the delivery of health care systems is an issue of concern in the context of Canada's multicultural ethic and social reality, but discussion in the social sciences on the politics of culture and the social construction of 'race' suggests that research in this area is likely to be complex.

In this chapter I explore how research concerned with providing improved access to health care for cultural minorities in Canada is implicated in the ongoing construction of understandings of 'difference.' I focus on the research processes of two studies in order to consider how research, even when concerned with challenging homogenizing social categories of difference, may unintentionally contribute to processes of racialization through which certain groups become inscribed as subordinate 'others.' One study concerns the management of chronic illness by first-generation Indo-Canadian and Chinese-Canadian women in Vancouver. I explore the researcher-researched relationship to indicate how the microprocesses of in-depth interviewing are intricately involved in the constitution of social identities and distinctions between 'self' and 'other' within the specificities of place. The second project concerns how student occupational therapists developed competencies relevant to practising in contexts of cultural diversity, with a focus on their interpretation of cultural issues in their fieldwork placements. As in the first study, the microprocesses of research were found to be integral to the negotiation of social identities. In this case, the students drew on personal experiences and narratives on difference to negotiate understandings of both 'whiteness' and 'ethnicity.'

Together the two research projects indicate the problematic nature of the 'field.' Far from being stable, bounded, and detached from everyday social practices, the field places research participants, whether researchers or study subjects, in a relationship within which both actively construct knowledge about themselves and others in an ongoing reconstitution of cultural identities and place; that is, research itself is part of the renegotiation and shifts in meaning about people and places that occur over time and across space. I am particularly interested in analyzing how 'our' gaze, as researchers holding legitimacy and authority in constructing knowledge within a complex layering of research relations, adds to a mosaic of knowledge that constitutes images of 'others.' In framing the analysis I draw on insights from poststructural feminist work, critical 'race' literature, and health geography, as these intersect around the linkage between the interrogation of research methods and identity politics.

To begin, I comment on the discursive construction of the racialized and gendered body, and the power/knowledge nexus central to the representation of the 'other.' Following this is an account of the research processes of the studies, focusing on the dynamics of in-depth interviewing in the first and reflective journal writing by students in the second. In analyzing these dynamics, I discuss the power relations that framed the negotiation of cultural identities in the particular context of the studies, which reflects a history of immigration policy that has increasingly opened up immigration possibilities for non-Europeans in Canada.[1]

Social Research and the Situated Researcher

The embeddedness of research in layers of context is a notion that has been explored by various scholars, particularly in relation to ethnography. It is this layering that has been of interest to me in understanding the politics of diversity that permeated the dynamics of the research projects and added to the challenge of constructing meanings about the lives of others. The researcher-researched relationship, the situatedness of the researcher within intellectual currents, and the location of the research and researcher within wider sets of political and economic relations at a particular historical juncture are all understood to shape how social and cultural realities are perceived and constructed (di Leonardo). These various dimensions of research make researching 'difference' a complex and politically charged enterprise.

In studying others, not only is there the problem of 'us' representing 'them' in the stories we tell, but there is also the problem of what we see and understand being framed by our own location in social relations according, for example, to gender, 'race,' class, and other positionings such as age, religion, caste, and sexuality. The micropolitics of research also influence what story will be constructed and told, particularly if one is using methods highly reliant on intersubjective relationships such as those of in-depth interviewing. Acknowledgments of the power/knowledge nexus in producing accounts have led to attempts to level the playing field of research, although this is a complex challenge and a task that may carry geographical specificity. Furthermore, the researcher brings a theoretical perspective to research that frames both the issues considered appropriate for inquiry and the social categories that inform the analysis.[2]

It is something of this contextuality that I explore here. I reflect on the available academic narratives that framed the design of the research projects and my interpretation of the dynamics of the studies (rather than their results). In situating myself in intellectual currents concerned with the issue of difference, I am necessarily engaged in a politics of contestation that challenges dominant representations of a differently positioned other (see, for example, Bannerji). I also recognize the influence of the different positionings of study participants and researchers on the control of the research and, therefore, on its conclusions. As Haraway has persuasively argued, all knowledge is constructed from a particular subject positioning so that all representations are incomplete and partial. Specifically, I discuss the contributions of feminist scholarship and critical race theory to my approach, particularly with respect to how these ways of thinking collide with dominant versions of the 'problem of culture' in biomedical knowledge and health professional practice.

The Gendered and Racialized Body

A central tension point in feminist scholarship is that of the politics of diversity among women. While the certitude of masculinist knowledge has been eroded by feminist critiques, feminist knowledge has also been shown to be fractured along axes of difference, particularly that of 'race.' The dominance of a 'white' feminist view of a gendered world, and its partiality, has been noted and challenged from the perspectives of both standpoint theory and poststructuralist concerns with the power of discourses and texts in constituting difference and the social identities of 'others' (see Olesen for an overview of research issues related to the diversity within feminist scholarship). The diversity of what constitutes the category 'woman' is remarked upon. Bannerji, for example, comments on the different types of woman that are represented in the non-unitary feminism of Canada and discusses the need for women of Colour positioned outside white feminist discourse to challenge 'the racist typifications or a general objectification of non-white women produced through what Michel Foucault would have called "the gaze," a lens of/for power' (xxvi). The 'gaze' is understood to not only control the objectified subject, but also to be actively involved in the constitution of subjectivity. How the gaze is returned, however, has been approached from different theoretical perspectives and analytical strategies.

Feminist standpoint epistemology, for example, emphasizes the importance of women's experience of a specific subject positioning in claims to 'authentic' knowledge, such as in the case of the particularities of racial oppression for women of Colour (Collins; hooks). However, the valorization of experience in the production of knowledge is also critiqued for its tendency toward essentialism, which diminishes the significance of context, local knowledge, other important axes of difference, and the fluidity of identities (Lemert; McDowell; Ramazanoglu). Dorothy Smith's work has retained the importance of women's everyday experiences in the analysis of women's lives, without discounting 'context' or suggesting an essentialist interpretation. Her institutional ethnography approach, which has been influential in Canadian feminism, employs a historical and cultural materialism that focuses on uncovering the social relations organizing women's experiences in order to understand the various social locations of women. Ng's important unpacking of the category of 'immigrant woman,' for example, shows its social construction within an interplay of class, 'race,' and gender relations. This work has been followed by other feminist analyses of the construction of 'difference' within postcolonial relations intersecting with political economy within the specificity of the Canadian experience (see, for example, Bannerji). Oppositional possibilities to dominant representations are shown, as is the complexity of identities.

A poststructuralist rejection of universalizing categories also explores the fluidity of identities, focusing on their complex and discursive construction in a power/knowledge nexus forged within historically and spatially contingent power relations. Such a perspective is concerned with the microprocesses of power that operate through discursive and material practices in constructing understandings of the body, as a surface of inscription, in particular ways. While a focus on textuality tends to erase the material body, such as in Deleuze and Guattari's body-without-organs, poststructuralist insights have been influential in understanding the interweaving of the discursive and material body in constituting subjectivity. Discursive constructions, including those of dominant cultural interpretations of gender and 'race,' are understood to mediate experiences and to be integral to the embodiment of identity; that is, there is a relationship between the material body and its representation in discourse, an idea that rejects the naturalness of the body in favour of an understanding of its cultural and historical specificity (Butler; Gatens; Grosz).

The 'marking' of the body through discourses about 'race' is a central theme in critical race theory, which rejects essentialist understandings of cultural, ethnic, and racial categories. Writers in the British context, working through an earlier class-based analysis of 'race relations,' are prominent in contemporary analyses of cultural diversity. These analyses include discussion of the social construction of racial categories, the importance of 'race' as an ideology underpinning racisms and processes of racialization, the power of academic narratives in representing and 'fixing' subordinate social identities, and the strategic use and contextual meanings of social identities such as 'black' and 'Asian' (see, for example, Brah; Hall; Modood; Mason; Miles). Work in the Canadian context elaborates such themes, emphasizing the ongoing, contextual shifts in self- and social identities set within cultural transformations located within global flows of information, capital, and people (see, for example, Amit-Talai and Knowles; Bannerji).

Geographers and other scholars sensitive to place bring a further spatial dimension to understanding the interlinking of the local with global processes in the production of subjectivity. They point to variations in how cultural identities are remade in processes of migration in the specific contexts of local resources, sets of relations, and cultures, just as place identities are negotiated and reconstituted along with social change (Anderson; Bhachu; Keith and Pile; Pile and Thrift; Sheth and Handa; Watts). Postcolonial relations are the setting of such a remaking of identities, forged in the present and current global trends but carrying the traces of earlier imperial power relations. Massey portrays the intricate interweaving of the local and broader sets of relations as occurring at multiple geographical scales, shaping places and their identities. The sum of this work suggests that cultures and identities, rather than being fixed or essential, are multitextured, constantly in flux, and under negotiation in the ongoing constitution of people and places.

However, dominant cultural constructions about difference exist in particular places at specific times, bringing attention to the problem of representation in research. The double inscription of gender and 'race' is of concern for women of Colour who have carved out a critical space in the academy (Bannerji; hooks; Mohanty; Spivak). These women have written about the production of their subjectivities within a complex of oppressive relations, which do not readily or usefully separate out in explanation. Generally, in anti-racist research there is interest in how and in what situations representations acquire particular meanings and come to legitimize and control certain definitions and bodies of knowledge about certain groups. In this chapter the representation of the racialized 'other' in health care is my central concern.

Theoretical work on the inscription of the body as gendered and 'raced' has entered discourse on health and health care unevenly. The practice of biomedicine and its body of knowledge has not been concerned with social theory, although it has been the object of critical scrutiny by medical sociologists and medical anthropologists. The body as 'an object of science' contrasts with understandings of the body as discursively and materially constructed within power differentials operating through concrete social practices, or the representation of the body as text (see, for example, Fox; Good; Shilling). Within biomedicine, health professions that adopt a cultural sensitivity model of practice and conventional social research on health and health care, the concepts of ethnicity and 'race,' for example, are predominantly treated as unproblematic categories of difference rather than as 'markers' that act to racialize bodies. Their use as independent, static variables neglects their discursive construction within uneven distributions of power and tends to naturalize difference. Interpretation of health problems and non-adherence to treatment offered in Western health care systems then over-relies on cultural explanations, scapegoating the culture of the patient rather than considering the complexity of the issues at work (Ahmad; Donovan; Pearson; Stein; Stubbs; Jackson).

Incorporating social theory into explanations of minority groups' health and health care suggests that a more nuanced understanding of culture, ethnicity, and 'race' is required if 'culture-blaming' is to be avoided. Furthermore, research needs to take into account the social construction of taken-for-granted social categories, such as 'visible minority,' black, and Asian, and consider the implications of their unproblematized use in framing studies and analyses (Sheldon and Parker; Synnott and Howes). The positionality of the white researcher studying other ways of 'doing' and thinking about health and health care in different places is also at issue (Dyck and Kearns). What does a researcher's 'whiteness' mean in the context of the field, when methods reliant on intersubjectivity and interpretive analysis are used? These issues inform the discussion of the rest of the chapter, in which I focus on the empirical studies and their methods, and their dynamic interplay with the ongoing constitution of cultural identities and place.

The Studies: The Field in Action

The studies were informed by the neglect of issues of racism and the racialization of certain groups in traditional analyses of the problem of culture in health care. Both were predicated on the understanding that the management of differences in cultural meanings around health, illness, and disability in interactions between health professionals and patients or clients shapes the quality and outcome of treatment interventions. However, rather than limiting the analysis to the specificity of the dynamics of health care encounters, the intention of the studies was to locate these encounters within a conceptual framework that recognized a nesting of sociopolitical contexts within which 'race,' gender, and class come to have meaning.

The first project concerned the experiences of first-generation Chinese-Canadian and Indo-Canadian women living with chronic illness (rheumatoid arthritis or diabetes), particularly as this related to their acquisition and use of professional health care knowledge.[3] This research involved observing the clinical encounters of the women with various health professionals and then interviewing the women about the subsequent management of their illness in the context of their everyday lives. We hoped to gain a better understanding of how social practices and relationships at different sites, including the clinic, the home, the neighbourhood, and the workplace, shaped the women's use of the knowledge imparted to them in clinical encounters. The second study differed in that its focus was on the health provider, in this instance occupational therapy students.[4] We were interested in what features of practice students identified as having cultural significance and the types of learning experiences they perceived as important in developing their competency for practice in a multicultural society. During fieldwork placements students kept journals in which they recorded their observations and reflections on these issues, which were then followed up in greater depth in postplacement interviews.

The qualitative methods used in the studies were compatible with current political and epistemological issues informing feminist, anti-racist, and critical health geography research. These approaches have in common a commitment to learning from those who are experiencing the phenomenon of concern and countering, as far as possible, the typical hierarchical researcher-researched relationship. There is, however, considerable 'messiness' to qualitative research, including unanticipated turns of events that may redirect research projects and that may complicate the relationship between the 'storyteller' and the audience (researcher).

Here I aim to show how some of this complexity played out in the research processes of the studies.[5] While the designs and substantive foci of the studies were quite different, and neither initially had been conceptualized around identity issues, it became apparent during analysis that the discursive construction of social identities was integral to the study dynamics. Analysis of the research process provided a further source of data for understanding the construction of the different 'other.' The first of the next two sections focuses on the interview dynamics of women interviewing women, during which difference and identity were negotiated and resistance on the part of some study participants reframed (although it did not transform) the relations of research. The second section concerns the student study participants who, in their reflections on their fieldwork placements, drew on their identities and positioning in society as 'Canadians' in making sense of health care encounters with the 'culturally different' client.

The Interview as a Site of Identity Negotiation

The research concerned with the management of chronic illness by Chinese-Canadian and Indo-Canadian women who had immigrated to Canada as adults was conducted by a team of researchers and research assistants. This was a more complex process than it would have been had white women been interviewing women of Colour, as the interviews were conducted by women of Colour who were trained and in frequent dialogue with the researchers – a woman of Colour and two white women. The research assistants were in the position of being intermediaries who interpreted our purposes and questions to the study participants and then interpreted their stories back to us. How this intermediary work played out indicated a number of bridging points interlinking the 'fields' of university, 'community,' and the participating women's personal social geographies, in which we were all differently and variously located. There was not a separate social and geographical space, comprising a somehow abstracted 'field' out there to be studied. As will be shown, the initial categorization of the participating women, according to broad ethnically defined communities in Vancouver, also belied the complexity and fluidity of identities in a city where there has been rapid demographic change in the decades following changes in immigration policy (Ley, Hiebert, and Pratt).

The research was located in the ongoing programs of research of the investigators, which are concerned with the strategies that immigrant women of Colour employ in meeting their health needs as well as with the adjustment processes of immigrant women more generally. In this work we do not see women as best depicted as victims of cultural change but, rather, as active participants in attempts to deal with health problems, albeit within a variety of social, economic, and political constraints. In devising the research, discussion of our various personal and disciplinary perspectives on the issue of culture and 'race' was an important 'beginning.' It was also an instance of our identities being exposed as multidimensional and shaped by the specificity of our gendered, classed, and 'raced' experiences in the context of our ongoing life stories, which included the salience of 'Colour' or 'whiteness' varying across time and space.

Consensus on how to approach the interviewing was reached in the context of this discussion. We decided to employ research assistants who could use the first language of the women recruited to the study, who came from the same broadly defined Chinese- and Indo-Canadian communities, and who were also immigrants to Canada. While we recognized the diversity within the categories of Chinese-Canadian and Indo-Canadian, we felt some degree of matching in the cultural backgrounds and experience of immigration of research assistants and study participants would facilitate open exchange between the women. Input from the research assistants in analyzing the interview transcripts would aid the understanding of cultural nuances in communication content and style.[6] Although such matching met with some success, the interviews were instructive in revealing the complexity of power relations framing the research encounter. Some interviews flowed in a manner consistent with the ideal of feminist methods, with women talking together as women. There was some reciprocity, and the study participants talked readily about their illness. The women spoke of difficulties they experienced in following advocated treatment procedures and, in some cases, the use of alternate, non-biomedical strategies in managing the effects of their illness. Admission of the researcher to the intimate details of the women's experience of their illness was not automatic, however, but was managed at the boundary between research assistant and researched through identity claims and negotiation. The women drew on various dimensions of identity and experience as they established the grounds from which to construct knowledge. It was here, in particular, that the multistrandedness of identities came into play. The study participants did not identify themselves as 'women of Colour,' as Indo-Canadian, or as Chinese-Canadian. This language of the academy and cultural politics was deferred to other dimensions of 'difference,' such as regional affiliation ('we Punjabis'), or perceived commonalities based on motherhood, or position as a wage-worker in a family with a clearly defined and gendered division of labour. An undifferentiated, 'hyphenated' Canadian or 'immigrant woman' did not exist.

Negotiation of interviewing as a method took place through negotiating definitions of what constituted the research 'site.' Some of the study participants reshaped the typical and anticipated interview setting of women talking privately in their own homes to the researchers or, in this case, the representative of the researchers. For example, one elderly woman did not answer questions or contribute information; rather, her daughter defined her mother's experience and interpreted her actions. Other family members or guests were sometimes present at interviews, participating or sitting quietly to one side as the interview took place. A few study participants elected to be interviewed in the clinic or workplace rather in their own homes. These actions may represent culturally different ways of women talking together and sharing knowledge, or they can be understood as resistance and a way of managing the access of an unknown 'stranger' associated with the dominant power relations of society (as institutionalized in the university). It is clear, however, that women can renegotiate the terms of their participation. Resistance was actively expressed, for example, through being reluctant to make an interview appointment or through imparting little about their lives.

The effect of interpersonal dynamics on the flow of an interview cannot be ignored. Yet to leave the analysis there would be to neglect to consider the location of those dynamics within larger processes of the management and organization of cultural diversity that occur within sets of social relations operating at multiple geographical scales. The negotiation of identity at the scale of the interview site reflects sociocultural changes occurring at the scale of the city, as physical and social transformations of cities and regions take place in the context of international migrations on a global scale. Such negotiation not only reflects such change, but it is also a constitutive act. As women 'placed' each other, they were also negotiating their social positioning within larger sets of relations that inscribe difference and its meanings through material and discursive practices. For instance, the women recruited to the study were defined in terms of dominant, undifferentiated categories, even though we recognized the lack of homogeneity and social construction of the local Chinese-Canadian and Indo-Canadian communities and the categories to describe them. Apart from such categories not necessarily corresponding with self-identification, their uncritical use may contribute to processes of inscription that may construct the different 'other' in a way that engages, and perhaps collaborates, with a 'gaze' that reinforces dominant representations of racialized groups.

In health care research there is an added layering of the research context in the practices and 'expertise' of a system of biomedical knowledge. This institutionalized body of knowledge and practice claims authority and legitimacy in health care and tends to subjugate other health and health care knowledges and practices. The framing of our study within concerns about access to biomedical knowledge, together with the recruitment of the women from the medical clinics they were attending, begins from a power relation within which the women were already subordinated in their position as the distinctive 'other.' In the study, we worked toward diminishing the impact of that power relation on the women through our interviewing strategies, and we met with some success in that we learned much about the complexity of the lives within which some women manage serious and chronic illness.

Identities in Context: Student Health Professionals Talk about Their Health Care Encounters

In this section I discuss a study in which the participants, as student health professionals, are practitioners and representatives of the dominant health care system in Canada. As such they are in a counter-position to the participants of the other study. Again, however, the issue of social identities and their 'fixing' emerged, although this had not been central in planning the research. The students' accounts of their fieldwork placements indicated that their own social location in a multicultural society was an important dimension of their experience and their interpretation of cultural issues in health care. In this study, the students' participation in the research involved them with the 'gaze' in a different way.

The research team consisted of two researchers and a research assistant, all white, and two Canadian-born. The researchers were faculty members in the students' occupational therapy program, so the inherent power relation in this situation was of concern. By working through a research assistant we aimed to protect the students' anonymity and to diminish the effects of the obvious power differential between students and researchers. The openness of many students' discussions of their fieldwork experiences and the program suggests that this strategy was fairly successful.

On entry to the program, half of the class volunteered to be part of the study. The students were mostly typical of the composition of this professional group; that is, predominantly white and female, although there were three males and one of the women students indicated Chinese rather than European ancestry. The majority were in their early twenties. During fieldwork placements at the end of the academic year, the students kept journals in which they recorded events that they considered to be of cultural significance. They were not provided with working definitions, as we wanted to see how they conceptualized cultural issues in practice and what informed their choices regarding which events to record. The majority did not have any background in the current theoretical issues being debated in the social sciences literature on culture, 'difference,' and 'race.' All, however, had had some introduction to the notion of cultural sensitivity in health care: a concern and respect for culturally different norms, values, and ways of approaching health and disability issues.

The journals constituted both a record of events and reflective moments about the students' own positioning in relation to the situations they described. Most indicated uncertainty about what could be explained as due to a client's culture, and there was often a reluctance to accept depictions of clients cast in terms of a group's 'cultural characteristics' or other essentializing notions. In coming to decisions about describing an event as having or not having some cultural significance, students implicitly or explicitly drew on a sense of what constituted 'Canadianness,' although at the same time recognizing diversity within Canadian culture. Although without the language of the politics of diversity, several students recognized the dilemma of potentially 'fixing' difference through attempting to take account of the influence of cultural diversity when working with models of practice reflective of dominant values and conceptualizations of health and disability.

Almost half of the students drew on personal experiences in making sense of the situations they observed, with all but one drawing on their own experiences of growing up in a first-generation Canadian family and their own distinctive cultural heritage. As part of a generation that has grown up in a climate of multiculturalism and an accompanying anti-racist ethic, they constructed understandings of Canada's cultural diversity from their particular subject positionings in ongoing processes of social and cultural transformation. For some, their Canadianness (and other cultural strands that made up their identities) came to be of significance as they were put in a position of interpreting situations where otherness was being negotiated and defined.

While we had framed the study in terms of defining the 'cultural competencies' needed and perceived to be valuable to effective practice from the viewpoint of those delivering health care (the usually 'white' centre), an unanticipated outcome of the journal-keeping was that students repositioned themselves not only as observers of the management of cultural difference in health care, but also as those 'doing' this management. We had expected that the journal entries would consist of accounts of the students' own involvement with clients, including their interpretations and management of difficulties in the therapeutic process, and of how this related to cultural difference. While this type of record was kept, less expected were the many stories concerning other participants in the fieldwork settings. Students referred to interactions between staff and clients of different cultural backgrounds, staff responses when professional models of practice appeared to break down, and instances of culturally specific translations of 'universal' models of practice by health care workers trained in other countries. While students found many of these interactions to be valuable learning experiences, among them were instances of stereotyping and racism, which students rejected as inappropriate.

This type of account brought a further layer to the research in that students became interpreters not only of their own participation in health care, but also of that of other health care workers. In reflecting on situations, the students adopted an almost quasi-research assistant role, observing how others around them constructed and managed cultural difference and its explanation within the overarching framework of the biomedical system of knowledge and practice. They were also necessarily active in negotiating the boundaries of the research in their pre-selection of what would be discussed in the interviews. While the researchers made cultural difference an issue through the focus of the study, students negotiated the meanings of this from their own social locations within Canadian society and as receivers of models of practice with a particular narrative on culture in health care. As participants of the study, they became agents in the development and questioning of knowledge within this particular discursive construction of the racialized 'other.'

Conclusions: The Field, the Particularities of Place, and Identities

The politics of diversity within feminist and anti-racist scholarship problematizes the position of the white academic who, in researching the lives of people of Colour, may, through her or his 'gaze,' objectify and make homogeneous the different 'other.' Recognition of the situatedness of knowledge and the power of representations in contributing to the constitution of subjectivities suggests that researchers should be alert to the power relations permeating the research process and their own positioning in the same sets of social relations as their research participants (Bhavnani; Harding; Nast et al.). Rather than somehow being separate from whom and what they study, researchers bring their own experiences, interests, and narratives about culture and 'race' to interactions in 'the field,' as it straddles the spaces of the academy and 'community.' In this chapter I have attempted to show that during these interactions – whether between researcher and research assistant or researcher/research assistant and study participants – those involved are all taking part in a racializing discourse through which the self- and social identities of different 'others' are negotiated and defined.

Yet this is not a simple process of oppositional categories of 'white' and 'people of Colour' being brought into play, nor is it a discovery and fixing of unitary or primary identities. The research processes explored here highlight the embeddedness of knowledge production within a complex layering of research that constantly unsettled taken-for-granted social categories. The discussions in the first study about our various positionings as team members in the research, the play of identity negotiation in the conversations between women of Colour (research assistants and study participants in this study), and the self-reflection of student study participants concerning their own Canadianness and the uncertainties they felt in using ethnic identifiers to explain it, suggest that identity negotiation may be ongoing but that it is brought into intense focus through this type of research. 'Whiteness' comes under scrutiny as well as the 'ethnicity' of the 'other.'

The research processes explored here highlight the embeddedness of knowledge production within the specificity of a study's research dynamics. In the analysis I have intended to show that the field is not a neutral social and geographical space to study but is constituted, defined, and marked out in a way that is itself constitutive of the ongoing construction of understandings of difference, diversity, and 'race' in conditions of rapid social change. In other words, the field is not just a place to collect 'data' for the purpose of the topic at hand; rather, it is an integral site in an ongoing reconstitution of meanings about social identities and the identity of place. What Canada 'is,' and its particular form in this city and region, is also at stake in this negotiation.

While social identities are malleable and their fixing may be resisted (or, alternatively, used in rewriting the 'other' from the position of those so othered in a politics of identity), the marginalization of certain racialized groups suggests that the power of the 'gaze' is significant in shaping life opportunities and everyday experiences. In addressing the issue of difference in research, the researcher is embedded in the complex relations of power that 'mark' subordinate others. But processes of 'marking' are likely to have a specificity related to how local and wider relations intertwine within the particularities of place. Social categories will have different meanings in different places, so experiences of a racialized body and social identity will vary. Just as 'Indian' in India is a different discursive construction than 'Indian' in Canada (Sheth and Handa), so too the studies here suggest that the reconstruction of cultural identity occurs at the scale of the local and within specific social interactions and social practices. These, in turn, are shaped by migration and resettlement patterns that produce regional differences in the texture of the reality of multiculturalism in Canada.

Health care research studies organized around the notions of culture, ethnicity, and 'race,' therefore, are both located within an academic discourse about difference and are closely connected to our positioning of researchers within particular geographical settings where the 'problem' of culture takes on local significance. Chinese-Canadians and Indo-Canadians constitute the two largest 'visible minority' groups in the Vancouver area, although their internal diversity along class, religion, and region of origin lines, as well as their historical insertion in the area, varies considerably. Relatively little is known about these groups and their health and health care needs, but in order to rectify this we are led into the tricky task of balancing the acquisition of knowledge about particular groups with the dilemma of addressing 'cultural difference' without reinscribing social identities that feed into constructions of 'race.' Both studies discussed here intended to avoid dominant representations and ways of thinking about cultural difference in health care research. Yet it became clear that, if we were not to 'fix' social identities according to 'ethnicity' or 'race,' then the social categories we brought to the research needed to be used cautiously in interpreting the results of the studies.

Thinking about cultural difference in health care research needs to engage with the situatedness of the client, health professional, and researcher (and their knowledges) in a complex set of relations within which difference and its material consequences come to have meaning through the available discourses and narratives about culture and 'race.' Identity has not been a focus of concern in health and health care research. Theory and practice in the health professions have tended not to engage with the issue of racism or with the concepts of race and racialization. The research processes of the studies discussed here indicate, however, that issues of identity permeate epistemological research issues as well as practice issues. While the white researcher is not in a position to 'return the gaze,' he or she is in a position to scrutinize 'whiteness' and its diversity and to consider the implications of theoretical frameworks and social categories that are used to construct knowledge about cultural minority groups. There are considerable difficulties, for example, in working with a notion of culture that is not contextualized within a politics of identity or a discourse of racism and racialization. We need to resituate our own identities within such discourses, as we contemplate the purposes and effects of our research. Before a study begins, both researchers and researched are embedded in a network of inscribed identities and sociopolitical contexts that underlie the social practices and discourses in which we construct understandings of difference. We are all positioned differently in the multicultural reality of Canada, and through our research we contribute to its multiplicity of meanings, whether as observers of political process or as its lived participants. In the important goal of including a wide range of voices as issues of health and health care are reassessed in the context of multiculturalism, there is a paradox: a focus on difference is also party to its construction and the accompanying politics of representation.

Acknowledgments
I wish to acknowledge the contributions of all the participants in the studies to the formulation of the ideas presented here, including my colleague researchers (with whom other chapters are co-authored), the research assistants (Maud Dias, Ranjit Dhari, Sandy Michener, and Marian Ng), and the study participants.

Notes
1 Proudfoot provides an account of the shaping of immigration patterns through government policy since the Immigration Act, 1976. The Canadian Census of 1986 indicated that over 70 percent of immigrants arriving in Canada between 1981 and 1986 were from non-European countries. The changing character of multiculturalism is indicated in Abu-Laban and Stasiulis's discussion of the critiques of multiculturalism policy by various parties, which documents the evolving concerns of multiculturalism over time and its multiplicity of meanings.
2 The literature on these aspects of methodology is extensive. See Atkinson, Clifford and Marcus, Denzin and Lincoln, Fonow and Cook, Haraway, Reinharz, Stacey, Standfield II and Dennis, Todd and Fisher, and Van Mannen for key issues.
3 This research was carried out with co-principal investigators Joan Anderson and Judith Lynam of the School of Nursing, University of British Columbia. The research was supported by grants from the Secretary of State; Multicultural Directorate, Canada; and the British Columbia Medical Services Foundation.
4 Sue Forwell, Clinical Coordinator of the Occupational Therapy Program of the School of Rehabilitation Sciences, University of British Columbia, was co-investigator of this study. The research assistant was a university graduate with professional interviewing skills. The study was funded by a grant from the British Columbia Health Services Foundation. The analysis here addresses issues emerging in the first year of a three-year longitudinal study.
5 It is not the intention here to present the study results. For interpretations of the data, see Dyck (1992, 1995); Anderson, Dyck, and Lynam; Dyck and Forwell.
6 Two of the research assistants had previous experience working with women using

immigrant services, and one worked in community health care. For further discussion of the dynamics of the interviews, see Dyck, Lynam, and Anderson.

Works Cited

Abu-Laban, Y., and D. Stasiulis. 1992. 'Ethnic Pluralism under Siege: Popular and Partisan Opposition to Multiculturalism.' *Canadian Public Policy – Analyse de Politiques* 18:365-6

Ahmad, W.I.U. 1993. 'Making Black People Sick: "Race," Ideology and Health Research.' In W.I.U. Ahmad, ed., *'Race' and Health in Contemporary Britain*, 11-33. Buckingham: Open University Press

Amit-Talai, V., and Caroline Knowles, eds. 1996. *Re-situating Identities: The Politics of Race, Ethnicity, and Culture*. Peterborough, ON: Broadview

Anderson, J.M., I. Dyck, and J. Lynam. 1997. 'Health Care Professionals and Women Speaking: Constraints in Everyday Life and the Management of Chronic Illness.' *Health* 1:57-80

Anderson, K.J. 1993. *Vancouver's Chinatown: Racial Discourse in Canada, 1975-1980*. Montreal: McGill-Queen's University Press

Atkinson, P.A. 1990. *The Ethnographic Imagination: Textual Constructions of Reality*. London: Routledge

Bannerji, H., ed. 1993. *Returning the Gaze: Essays on Racism, Feminism and Politics*. Toronto: Sister Vision

Bhachu, P. 1996. 'The Multiple Landscapes of Transnational Asian Women in the Diaspora.' In V. Amit-Talai and C. Knowles, eds., *Re-situating Identities: The Politics of Race, Ethnicity, and Culture*, 283-303. Peterborough, ON: Broadview

Bhavnani, K-K. 1993. 'Tracing the Contours: Feminist Research and Feminist Objectivity.' *Women's Studies International Forum* 16:95-104

Brah, A. 1992. 'Difference, Diversity and Differentiation.' In J. Donald and A. Rattansi, eds., *Race, Culture and Difference*, 126-45. London: Sage

Butler, J. 1990. *Gender Trouble: Feminism and the Subversion of Identity*. New York: Routledge

Clifford, J., and G.E. Marcus, eds. 1986. *Writing Culture: The Poetics and Politics and Ethnography*. Berkeley: University of California Press

Collins, P.H. 1990. *Black Feminist Thought: Knowledge, Consciousness and the Politics of Empowerment*. New York: Routledge

Deleuze, G., and F. Guattari. 1988. *A Thousand Plateaus*. London: Athlone

Denzin, N.K., and Y.S. Lincoln, eds. 1994. *Handbook of Qualitative Research*. Thousand Oaks, CA: Sage

di Leonardo, M. 1991. 'Introduction: Gender, Culture and Political Economy.' In M. di Leonardo, ed., *Gender at the Crossroads of Knowledge*, 1-48. Berkeley, CA: University of California Press

Donovan, J. 1984. 'Ethnicity and Health.' *Social Science and Medicine* 19:663-70

Dyck, I. 1992. 'Managing Chronic Illness: An Immigrant Woman's Acquisition and Use of Health Care Knowledge.' *American Journal of Occupational Therapy.* 46:696-705

–. 1995. 'Putting Chronic Illness "In Place": Women Immigrants' Accounts of Their Health Care.' *Geoforum* 26:247-60

Dyck, I., and S. Forwell. 1997. 'Occupational Therapy Students' First Year Fieldwork Experiences: Discovering the Complexity of Culture.' *Canadian Journal of Occupational Therapy* 64:185-96

Dyck, I., and R.A. Kearns. 1995. 'Transforming the Relations of Research: Towards Culturally Safe Geographies of Health and Healing.' *Health and Place* 1:139-49

Dyck, I., M.J. Lynam, and J.M. Anderson. 1995. 'Women Talking: Creating Knowledge through Difference in Cross-Cultural Research.' *Women's Studies International Forum* 18:611-26

Fonow, M.M., and J.A. Cook, eds. 1991. *Beyond Methodology: Feminist Scholarship as Lived Research*. Bloomington: Indiana University Press

Fox, N.J. 1993. *Postmodernism, Sociology and Health*. Buckingham: Open University Press

Gatens, Moira. 1992. 'Power, Bodies and Difference.' In M. Barrett and A. Phillips, eds., *Destabilizing Theory: Contemporary Feminist Debates*, 120-37. Cambridge: Polity

Good, Byron J. 1994. *Medicine, Rationality and Experience.* Cambridge: Cambridge University Press

Grosz, Elizabeth. 1994. *Volatile Bodies: Toward a Corporeal Feminism.* Bloomington and Indianapolis: Indiana University Press

Hall, S. 1992. 'New Ethnicities.' In J. Donald and A. Rattansi, eds., *Race, Culture and Difference,* 252-9. London: Sage

Haraway, D. 1988. 'Situated Knowledges: The Science Question in Feminism and the Privilege of the Partial Perspective.' *Feminist Studies* 14:575-95

Harding, S. 1991. *Whose Science? Whose Knowledge?* Ithaca, NY: Cornell University Press

hooks, b. 1992. *Black Looks: Race and Representation.* Toronto: Between the Lines

Jackson, E.M. 1993. 'Whiting-Out Difference: Why US Nursing Research Fails Black Families.' *Medical Anthropology Quarterly* 7:363-85

Keith, M., and S. Pile, eds. 1993. *Place and the Politics of Identity.* London: Routledge

Lemert, C. 1992. 'Subjectivity's Limit: The Unsolved Riddle of the Standpoint.' *Sociological Theory* 10:63-72

Ley, D., D. Hiebert, and G. Pratt. 1992. 'Time to Grow Up? From Urban Village to World City.' In G. Wynn and T. Oke, eds., *Vancouver and Its Region,* 234-66. Vancouver: UBC Press

Lynam, M.J., J.M. Anderson, and I. Dyck. N.d. 'The Intersection of Biomedicine And Women's Standpoint: An Examination of the Processes of Clinical Appraisal.' Unpublished paper

McDowell, L. 1993. 'Space, Place and Gender Relations, Part II: Identity, Difference, Feminist Geometries and Geographies.' *Progress in Human Geography* 17:305-18

Mason, D. 1990. 'A Rose by Any Other Name ... ? Categorisation, Identity and Social Science.' *New Community* 17:123-33

Massey, D. 1993. 'Power-Geometry and a Progressive Sense of Place.' In J. Bird, B. Curtis, T. Putman, G. Robertson, and L. Tickner, eds., *Mapping the Futures: Local Cultures, Global Change,* 59-69. London: Routledge

–. 1994. *Space, Place and Gender.* Minneapolis: University of Minnesota Press

Miles, R. 1993. *Racism after 'Race Relations.'* London: Routledge

Modood, T. 1994. 'Political Blackness and British Asians.' *Sociology* 28:859-76

Mohanty, C. 1988. 'Under Western Eyes: Feminist Scholarship and Colonial Discourses.' *Feminist Review* 30:60-88

Nast, H.J., C. Katz, A. Kobayashi, K.V.L. England, M.R. Gilbert, L.A. Staeheli, and V.A. Lawson. 1994. 'Focus: Women in the Field: Critical Feminist Methodologies and Theoretical Perspectives.' *The Professional Geographer* 46:54-102

Ng, R. 1988. *The Politics of Community Services.* Toronto: Garamond

Olesen, V. 1994. 'Feminisms and Models of Qualitative Research.' In N.K. Denzin and Y.S. Lincoln, eds., *Handbook of Qualitative Research,* 158-74. Thousand Oaks, CA: Sage

Pearson, M. 1986. 'The Politics Of Ethnic Minority Health Studies.' In T. Rathwell and D. Phillips, eds., *Health, Race and Ethnicity,* 100-16. London: Croom Helm

Pile, S., and N. Thrift, eds. 1995. *Mapping the Subject: Geographies of Cultural Transformation.* London: Routledge

Proudfoot, B. 1989. 'The Setting of Immigration Levels in Canada since the Immigration Act, 1976.' *British Journal of Canadian Studies* 4:233-56

Ramazanoglu, C. 1989. 'Improving on Sociology: The Problems of Taking a Feminist Standpoint.' *Sociology* 23:427-42

Reinharz, S. 1992. *Feminist Methods in Social Research.* New York: Oxford University Press

Sheldon, T., and H. Parker. 1992. 'The Use of "Ethnicity" and "Race" in Health Research: A Cautionary Note.' In W.I.U. Ahmad, ed., *'Race' and Health in Contemporary Britain,* 34-47. Buckingham: Open University Press

Sheth, A., and A. Hands. 1993. 'A Jewel in the Frown: Striking Accord Between India/n Feminists.' In H. Bannerji, ed., *Returning the Gaze: Essays on Racism Feminism and Politics,* 45-99. Toronto: Sister Vision

Shilling, C. 1993. *The Body and Social Theory.* London: Sage

Smith, D.E. 1987. *The Everyday World as Problematic: A Feminist Sociology.* Boston:

Northeastern University Press
–. 1992. 'Sociology from a Woman's Experience: A Reaffirmation.' *Sociological Theory* 10:88-98
Spivak, G.C. 1988. *In Other Worlds: Essays in Cultural Politics.* London: Routledge
Stacey, J. 1988. 'Can There Be a Feminist Ethnography?' *Women's Studies International Forum* 11:21-7
Stanfield II, J.H., and R.M. Dennis. 1993. *Race and Ethnicity in Research Methods.* Newbury Park, CA: Sage
Stein, H.F. 1985. 'The Culture of the Patient as a Red Herring in Clinical Decision Making: A Case Study.' *Medical Anthropology Quarterly* 17:2-5
Stubbs, P. 1993. '"Ethnically Sensitive" or "Anti-Racist"? Models for Health Research and Service Delivery.' In W.I.U. Ahmad, ed., *'Race' and Health in Contemporary Britain*, 34-47. Buckingham: Open University Press
Synnott, A., and D. Howes. 1996. 'Canada's Visible Minorities: Identity and Representation.' In V. Amit-Talai and C. Knowles, eds., *Re-situating Identities: The Politics of Race, Ethnicity, and Culture*, 137-60. Peterborough, ON: Broadview
Todd, A.D., and S. Fisher, eds. 1988. *Gender and Discourse: The Power of Talk.* Norwood, NJ: Ablex
Van Mannen, J. 1988. *Tales of the Field: On Writing Ethnography.* Chicago: University of Chicago Press
Watts, M.J. 1991. 'Mapping Meaning, Denoting Difference, Imagining Identity: Dialectical Images and Postmodern Geographies.' *Geografiska Annaler* 73B:7-16

Domination and Political
Representation in Canada
Avigail Eisenberg

Both political scientists and literary theorists might agree that cultural domination and representation go hand in hand. Edward Said shows how English literature has aided Western imperialism through its stereotypes of Africans, Indians, and Chinese as barbaric, primitive, and in other ways very different from Europeans. Said argues that the message conveyed by these depictions is that 'they' are not like 'us' and 'for that reason deserve to be ruled' and need to be civilized (Said, xi).

A similar rationalization for what are sometimes brutal measures of assimilation and domination is found in Canadian literature, which has represented Aboriginal peoples as primitive, uncivilized, and exotic compared to non-Aboriginal peoples. Such depictions are not far removed from the politics of Aboriginal-non-Aboriginal relations. Political policies and debates are generally shaped by assumptions about the cultures and identities of peoples for which they are made. For example, language laws assume the centrality of a language to the cultural survival of a people. Land claims agreements assume the centrality of land to cultural identity. Assimilationist policies assume that it is both feasible and desirable for one cultural community to integrate into another. These assumptions, along with the policies themselves, shape the societies to which they apply. Laws that protect language and culture reaffirm the importance of these aspects of identity. At the same time, they facilitate the expression of linguistic and cultural identity. Insofar as they resonate in the public mind, cultural depictions become the point from which political debate commences and the basis upon which political action is taken.

Two complex examples of how cultural assumptions shape public policy are found in the arguments that individualism is central to English-Canadian culture[1] and that collectivism is central to Aboriginal communities. The insistence upon this distinction reaches its highest pitch in Canadian debates about citizenship and democracy and is highly influential with regard to policies in these areas. Frequently, the question of what constitutes a fair and equitable approach to democratic rights and political representation has been analyzed by depicting Aboriginal peoples as attracted to collectivism and non-Aboriginal peoples as repelled by collectivism and attracted to liberal individualism. This position is generally pervasive in analyses of Anglo-Canadian values, Aboriginal values and Aboriginal politics, and particularly in analyses of politics in Canada's North. The question that follows from this position, and that for years has informed Canadian political analysis, is whether Canada or, more generally, liberal democracies ought to recognize collective rights and values alongside individualism. The fear expressed by critics of cultural rights is that the cost of using such rights to protect cultural identities will be the liberal neutrality and individual rights that otherwise define liberal-democratic ideals (see Fierlbeck). In other words, the special rights of Aboriginal Canadians or any other group are viewed by some as a threat to an otherwise equality-based society (see Crowley). Indeed, any measures aimed at protecting cultural identity are made to appear by some critics to be concessions to illiberal values and compromises of the cultural neutrality that otherwise informs public policies. Defenders of cultural rights often respond to these arguments with scathing attacks on liberalism, which they claim is incapable of protecting minority, and specifically Aboriginal, cultures (see Turpel).

As compelling as the conflict between individualist and collectivist values is as an explanation of cultural conflict, it often obscures more than it reveals about the Canadian experience of Aboriginal peoples. First, it misdirects debate away from the important project of protecting interests that are crucial to individual well-being irrespective of whether they are classified as individualist or collectivist (see Eisenberg). Second, it emasculates the pluralism of both communities and leads one to expect that non-Aboriginal peoples are devoted to individualism (of the same sort) at every turn and that Aboriginal culture (in all its variety) is thoroughly collectivist (see Schouls). Third, it misrepresents the political values of Canadian democracy and representative institutions as individualistic and culturally neutral when they are not. This third consequence of the debate shall be the focus of this analysis. The Canadian representative and electoral system accommodates collective values in numerous ways. Some of its collectivist aspects are, in an important sense, culturally neutral in that they do not directly aid in the domination of one group by another. Others, such as the systemic discrimination in the electoral system that extends privileges to candidates based on culture and gender, and the use of the democratic franchise to coercively assimilate minority cultures, point to a disturbing cultural agenda in which public policy has been used to dominate Aboriginal peoples and other minorities. The historical continuity and consistency of culturally biased policies makes it very difficult to characterize Canadian political values as individualistic; rather, these values are often aimed at advancing the collective cultural dominance of the majority. The existence and effects of cultural domination are either entirely ignored or made to appear exceptional when we accept the contrast between Aboriginal and non-Aboriginal values as collectivist versus individualist. While scholars and policy makers focus on finding grounds to describe and promote Aboriginal claims as collectivist, the assumption that non-Aboriginal peoples are wedded to individualism escapes critical examination.

The first part of this chapter will examine more fully the role played by collectivism and individualism in policies of and debates about political representation and culture in Canada. The second part examines four ways in which political representation in Canada is inaccurately depicted as culturally neutral and individualistic. The final section explores in more depth the insidious effects of using 'individualism versus collectivism' to distinguish the political values of Aboriginal and non-Aboriginal Canadians.

Individualism and Collectivism Defined

In order to examine the values of representative institutions and practices, the first task is to be clear about what counts as individualist and collectivist values. Political individualism requires that representation be based on individual interests and not on the interests of cultures, religious orders, estates, social functions, or classes (Lukes, 78-9). While the interests of, for example, cultures boil down at some level to the interests of individuals, the principle of political individualism requires that governments seek consent from each individual rather than from the heads of the cultures, religious orders, or class-based collectives to which individuals may belong. In this way, liberal individualism purports to be neutral because it holds that the state ought not to serve the interests of a particular culture, religion, gender, or class. Legitimate government must be based on consent that is individually given. The call for 'one person-one vote' and 'one vote-one value' follows from these principles. Every individual's vote ought to count equally according to the principles of liberal individualism. Representation on the basis of cultural or religious membership violates political individualism.

In recognition of the important social bonds among individuals, collectivist schemes may allow representation to be based on group interests and individuals to be delegated by groups to sit in governing institutions. Political systems that allocate seats in government on the basis of cultural identity (such as New Zealand in the case of the Maori) or have different laws for different religious groups (such as India with respect to Hindus and Muslims, or Israel with respect to Jews, Muslims, Christians, and the Druse) are in these ways collectivist. In contrast to those who support political individualism, collectivists might hold that individuals are rightly controlled and disciplined by groups because they rely on groups, for example, for their spiritual well-being or personal identity. Moreover, in order to retain the group's unity, collectivist schemes could require that individuals who deviate from group norms be excluded from the group. Many immigration and citizenship policies exhibit this characteristic, including, most infamously, those of Japan, Israel, and, until recently, Canada (see Abu-Laban). In these ways, collectivist politics is exclusive and is not culturally neutral.

Individualism and Collectivism in Canada
The position that individualism characterizes the political values of the Anglophone majority while collectivism reflects the values of the French-speaking minority (see Arnopoulos and Clift, 36-8; Cook, 146-7; Galipeau, 75; Morton, 71-84; and Trudeau, 1) or, more often, the Aboriginal minority (see Eisenberg, 5-8), is often the central explanation for why some minority groups do not consider Canadian representational institutions to be legitimate. In Canada's North, where Aboriginal peoples comprise a much larger segment of the population than they do in the South,[2] the system of public government is under great pressure to overcome any cultural biases it might contain. Analysts of Northern politics often invoke individualism and collectivism to explain what does or does not work with regard to political representation. For example, the parliamentary form of government is supposed not to work because it 'is premised on the representation of individuals rather than collectivities' (White 1991, 507). This conflicts with the values of Northern Aboriginal cultures, in which 'it is clear that the interests of the group transcend those of the individual' (ibid.). Proposals for the political representation of cultural groups in the Northwest Territories (NWT) legislature are supposed to be unfeasible because they conflict with the individualist values of non-Aboriginal peoples: 'Both [the Canadian government and non-Aboriginal Northerners] are understandably anxious about any deviation from the liberal, individualist representational formula they view as natural and just' (Dacks, 145). Analysis of the conflicts between Aboriginal and non-Aboriginal peoples are often framed by the notions that the non-Aboriginal population is committed to individualism and equality while the Aboriginal population pursues 'rights that are special, rather than universal, and collective, rather than individual' (138-9). As one author expresses the contrast: 'the most significant difference between white and Native values and attitudes' is that 'the Indians as well as the Inuit, place a far higher value on the collectivity and the community' (Whittington, 27).

The importance of individualism and collectivism is echoed in analyses of how electoral boundaries ought to be drawn. The redistricting process in the North is purported to have failed to attract Native participation and to reflect Native values, again because of the divergent perspectives generated by individualism and collectivism. The 1989-90 redistricting process is said to reflect the individualist-egalitarian values perpetuated through a southern, liberal-democratic model of representation. By contrast, 'Aboriginal political culture puts much greater store than does western liberalism on the importance of cultural communities, with the corollary that representation of cultural groups may be more important than that of individuals' (White 1993, 24). Critics of group rights, such as David Bercuson and Barry Cooper, have strongly emphasized the role that individualism does and ought to play in Canada's electoral processes. 'We believe,' they state, 'that Canadian democracy must be based on the principle of one person-one vote, one vote-one value among all electors' (111). The principle of one person-one vote is said to be central to any coherent notion of liberal democracy and is the only tolerable formula for 'a mature federal liberal democracy' such as Canada to adopt. By contrast, 'any attempt to cater to special-interest groups in the drawing of electoral boundaries would violate the political rights of citizens living in a modern liberal democracy' (110-11). They conclude that it is 'of course ... improper to recognize "group rights" in a liberal democracy' (124).

Analysts who reaffirm the cultural abyss between individualistic, non-Aboriginal political values and collectivist, Aboriginal values are sometimes compelled to recognize the numerous ways in which collectivism is entrenched in non-Aboriginal practices. For example, Graham White reaches his conclusions about the influence of individualism on the Northern redistricting process despite judicial decisions, which he examines, that reject the formula of one person-one vote and hold that boundaries ought to be drawn to protect communities (see *Reference re: Electoral Boundaries Commission Act* [1991] 81 DLR [4th] 26 [SCC]). A similar tendency is found in the compelling analysis of Menno Boldt, who argues that the recognition of collective rights breaks a 'long-standing Western-liberal constitutional tradition in Canada establishing the paramountcy of individual rights over collective rights' (54). Despite the numerous examples of collective rights that Boldt recognizes as receiving constitutional protection, he describes the collectivism in the Constitution as ad hoc, as indicative of an *acquiescence* to collective rights and a *confusion* about the status of collective claims in domestic policy (52-3). As does White's analysis, Boldt's analysis treats counter-evidence, which is historically as well as constitutionally significant, as exceptional to the rule that individualism characterizes non-Aboriginal political and social practices rather than as indicative that Anglo-Canadian traditions have significant collectivist aspects.

For policy makers, the conclusion to reach from this literature is that

Canada's representative institutions lack political legitimacy among Aboriginal peoples because of the individualist biases they contain. It follows that, in order to include Aboriginal peoples, political institutions should be reformed to accommodate collectivist values. This perspective follows from White's assessment of the 1989-90 redistricting process, where the 'southern, liberal-democratic model of representation' is blamed for alienating Northern Natives. The Royal Commission on Electoral Reform and Party Financing (RCERPF) appears also to have embraced this train of thought in its finding that parliamentary seats be set aside for a minimum number of Aboriginal representatives.

That individualism is exhibited in various aspects of Canadian political culture and institutions is not disputed here. Nor is it doubted that collectivist values are attractive in various ways to Aboriginal peoples and useful to these and other minorities in protecting their cultures. But the proposition that individualism and not collectivism pervades the Canadian approach to political representation, drawing electoral boundaries, and selecting candidates, and, further, that individualism explains why these institutions and practices fail to attract the participation of Aboriginal peoples, is far more difficult to defend. Even in light of evidence to the contrary, scholars of Canadian democracy embrace the individualist versus collectivist paradigm as a basis for explaining why two cultures fail to see eye to eye. The challenge, then, in overturning the myth that Canadian representative democracy is individualistic lies in also explaining why, in light of clear evidence to the contrary, Anglo-Canadian political institutions are repeatedly cast as individualistic.

Parliament and Party Government
The most obvious place to begin is with the institutional processes and symbolism of parliamentary government in Canada, which, starting with the central procedures of Parliament, are collectivist in uncontroversial and significant ways (Franks, 19-21). The notion of *responsible government* requires that the governing party put forward legislation collectively and accept defeat collectively. If a major piece of government legislation is defeated in the House of Commons, then the government must resign *as a group*. *Cabinet solidarity* requires that if a member of the Cabinet is unable to support a piece of government legislation she or he must leave Cabinet. And *party discipline* exerts considerable pressure on renegade parliamentarians who fail to go along with the decision of the party. The votes of individual members are controlled by their party in the sense that members will be required to leave the party if they do not support its values.

It is interesting to note that in the NWT, which is the only province or territory in which Aboriginal peoples form a majority of the electorate, reforms have been instituted to the practices of parliamentary government that effectively eliminate many of these collectivist practices. NWT elections are carried out without parties, and the legislature operates without party discipline. Without parties, voters are not offered a choice between coherent plans that address the larger political and economic challenges confronting the North. Candidates, who each run as independents, do not have access to the resources that political parties offer, including the power that comes with being elected as a team with a common purpose and united agenda. Since each elected member sits as an independent, nothing compels Members of the Legislative Assembly (MLAs) to pursue a coherent and comprehensive strategy in government (Dacks, 144). Without parties, party discipline, and responsible government, the legislature contains no mechanisms of accountability and, therefore, cannot be used by interest groups, such as those representing cultural communities (e.g., the Inuit Tapirisat of Canada, the Métis Association of the NWT, and the Assembly of First Nations) to advance their particular concerns. In other words, the reforms have reduced the means by which the NWT legislature is able to deal effectively with the distinct cultural interests of the cultural communities in the North. Even though, since 1976, a majority of MLAs in the NWT have been from Aboriginal communities, the absence of a party structure and party discipline has meant that an agenda that addresses Aboriginal interests is not pursued through the legislature. The Northern variations have made parliamentary government less collectivist and, ironically, less capable of addressing communal interests.

One might argue that, despite their collectivist aspects, the practices of parliamentary and party government elsewhere in Canada subscribe to the central tenet of political individualism; namely, cultural neutrality. Although the institution of parliamentary government is clearly a product of a specific culture and historical time, its procedures can be used in principle by any group and, further, can be used to institute policies that protect the interests of any group.

However, the argument *in principle* ought not to obscure the fact that, in Canada, parliamentary institutions have been dominated for over a century by groups that have actively alienated and dominated Aboriginal peoples. This alienation is apparent at a symbolic level where, in all respects, Parliament emulates collectivism by giving expression to the values of British culture and colonial politics. There is a great deal of nostalgia for the traditions and values of Parliament and very little impetus to make the institution more culturally inclusive by, for example, adopting Aboriginal traditions or even by reflecting Aboriginal perspectives on Canadian political history. The art, architecture, rituals, traditions, and procedures of the federal Parliament reflect the history of Canada from a British point of view and unapologetically relay the story of colonial occupation. Members of the legislatures are expected to participate in rituals that symbolize acts of submission, such as bowing to the Speaker and the mace (White 1991, 506). These 'symbols of colonial domination,' as White calls them, doubtless have a profound significance to individuals whose culture was dominated by the colonizers. Moreover, they hardly reflect the individualism that is purported to be the basic value of the institution.

The Right to be Elected and to Vote

The absence of Aboriginal candidates and legislators in Canadian politics, like the absence of women, Chinese, Japanese, Hispanic, black, and Indian Canadians, has given rise to research that has unremarkably concluded that individuals are not treated equitably by electoral processes (see Megyery). This finding is hardly surprising, given the history in Canada of excluding individuals from Parliament on the basis of culture and, further-more, of using the promise of democratic rights to coercively assimilate minorities. For example, Lord Durham's argument against British colonists, who sought to exclude French Quebecers from Parliament, was that including them was a means of assimilating them into British culture. That is, Durham did not recommend that Canadians, both British and French, adopt culturally neutral political values and practices; rather, he prescribed that the French be compelled to abandon their culture and adopt British values in order to enjoy equal political rights.[3] His solution reflects a powerful stream in political thought, historically found in both liberal and socialist traditions, which is that 'national minorities must be dealt with by coercive assimilation or the redrawing of boundaries, not by minority rights' (Kymlicka 1995, 52).

The history of Parliament, as a forum for men of property to deliberate about raising and spending taxes, further shapes the institution's narrow purpose and historical biases in light of the laws and customs that ensured that women and various religious and racial minorities were not property owners.[4] Moreover, legislation that denied full rights of citizenship, includ-ing the right to be elected to Parliament and to vote, is definitive of the political history of Canadian women; Doukhobors; Canadians of Chinese, Japanese, and East Indian descent; and, of course, Aboriginal peoples. The racist and sexist motivations behind legislation that effectively made racial and ethnic origins criteria for membership to the national political com-munity (Carty and Ward, 74) were not mysterious and were often expressed in terms of campaigns for a British-only parliament (Ajzenstat) or for keep-ing Canada 'white forever' (see Ward).

For Aboriginal peoples, democratic rights and citizenship were presented as prizes only to be enjoyed by those who abandoned their Aboriginal identity. 'In order to exercise the federal franchise, Indians were expected to surrender their distinct identity and status and to assimilate into settler society' (Committee on Aboriginal Electoral Equality [CAEE], 8). Many

Aboriginal people rejected the franchise, not because they were repelled by the individual right to vote, but because they recognized in the government's offer the means to their assimilation. The federal government did nothing to dispel their suspicions, nor has it historically presented itself as having a principled commitment to democratic rights and the equal rights of citizenship. The absence of any clear concept of democratic rights was tolerated by the federal government until the postwar period, as may be seen in the fact that the claims of various groups to the franchise varied from province to province (Carty and Ward, 74). And even when the right to vote was granted to the disenfranchised, the means by which votes were collected, counted, and reported sometimes exposed the federal government's less than sincere commitment to the democratic process. For example, even though the Inuit were granted the right to vote federally in 1950, not until 1962 were ballot boxes placed in their communities (CAEE, 8).

Voting rights are not enough to ensure democratic representation in Canada. Minority groups only have a voice in Parliament if they have a voice in parties. Aboriginal people have had little to no voice in Canada's political parties. Not until the 1980s did either the Liberal or Conservative parties establish an Aboriginal association within their party structures. And not until 1982 was there a standing committee on Aboriginal affairs in Parliament (RCERPF, 170; CAEE, 12-3). The exclusion of Aboriginal people and interests from political parties would not exclude them from Parliament if there were more opportunity for individuals to be elected and to contribute to the parliamentary process without being involved in a party, which there is not (except, ironically, in the NWT).

In light of this history, it is no small achievement that policies that explicitly exclude individuals on the basis of gender and culture are today viewed as illegitimate and, specifically, as a denial of the individual egalitarianism that is said to characterize present-day political values in Canada. However, the legacy of these policies and the persistent biases of Canada's governing institutions make it very difficult to conclude that individualism is the predominant value of Parliament. At best, governing institutions offer Canadians the equal opportunity to live a male and Euro-Canadian lifestyle. Not all women or individuals from minority groups will be disadvantaged by such an opportunity. Nor will all men or members of the cultural majority thrive in such institutions. Systemic discrimination does not strictly determine representation on the basis of gender or culture. However, institutions that place at a disadvantage individuals who take maternity/paternity leave, who have significant family responsibilities, who are taught not to be aggressive and assertive, whose first language is not English or French, and who are not financially independent will tend to exclude Canadian women, Aboriginal peoples, and other cultural minorities. The proposal for Aboriginal electoral districts grows out of precisely the observation that, although Aboriginal peoples comprise 3 percent to 4 percent of Canada's population, at any one time only two sitting Members of Parliament (MPs) have been Aboriginal. This cultural visage clearly indicates, prima facie, that Parliament contains biases for certain cultural (and gender-specific) values and against others.

Explicit racism and sexism have given way to systemic biases that favour, in MPs and their staff, certain values, traits, and lifestyles that are culture- and gender-specific. Like policies that prohibited Aboriginal people from serving as legislators, these biases point to a legacy of exclusion that itself undermines the legitimacy of the institution in the eyes of excluded groups. As the Royal Commission on Electoral Reform and Party Financing states in its report, 'our past is replete with symbols of [Aboriginal] exclusion from the Canadian polity. Elimination of discrimination based in law is not sufficient; symbols of inclusion are also needed' (RCERPF, 170).

Electoral Boundaries and Residency Requirements

Canada has historically employed numerous electoral policies to protect the interests of cultural minorities. Electoral boundaries have been drawn to protect 'community of interest' in Quebec until 1970 in order to ensure that English-speaking communities sent representatives to the National Assembly (RCERPF, 178). The practice of sending two elected representatives from each constituency to the legislature (i.e., dual member constituencies) ensured Acadian and Roman Catholic representation in the New Brunswick legislature (RCERPF, 179). More recently, the Supreme Court has ruled that effective representation requires that electoral laws deviate from the one person-one vote formula in order to ensure that minority communities are represented (see *Reference re: Electoral Boundaries Commissions Act*; see Roach).

Measures to protect minority communities through electoral law have been woven into the fabric of Canadian political history. Yet, these measures have rarely been employed to benefit Aboriginal peoples. Outside of the NWT, neither the practice of dual member constituencies nor cultural gerrymandering have been used to protect Aboriginal interests. The explanation for this is only partly innocent. Federally, cultural gerrymandering is useless to the Aboriginal community because its population is too dispersed. Where the Aboriginal population is concentrated, the common practice of drawing electoral boundaries on a north-south axis means that the more populous southern, non-Aboriginal communities comprise the majority within each constituency (CAEE, 10).

Within the NWT, electoral boundaries have been used to protect Aboriginal communities. But the history of using electoral processes for such protection has been short. In the past, electoral boundaries have been drawn to favour the interests of large developers and exploiters of Northern resources rather than the social and economic interests of cultural communities. In the 1970s and early 1980s, the conflict between these interests was particularly intense when the economic promise of Northern resources soared with the price of oil. In light of the dominance of southern economic interests in the North, the Dene, Métis, and Inuit proposed to the federal government that residency requirements to vote in NWT elections be lengthened from one to ten or fifteen years and that the Territories be divided into three different governing units, each of which would contain, respectively, an Inuit, Dene, and non-Aboriginal majority (see Dene National Assembly). The proposal was rejected by the Trudeau government in terms that are worth quoting, since they illustrate so well the government's own strategic use of political individualism and the principle of cultural neutrality. On one hand, the government stated that: 'Legislative authority and government jurisdiction are not allocated in Canada on grounds that differentiate between the people on the basis of race. Authority is assigned to legislatures that are representative of all the people within any area on a basis of complete equality. Jurisdiction is placed in the hands of governments that are responsible, directly or indirectly, to the people – again without regard to race' (Office of the Prime Minister, 280). On the other hand, the government then goes on to state that 'unless the Indian and the Indian claimants are seeking the establishment of reserves under the Indian Act, as in the South, the Government does not favour the creation in the North of new political divisions, with boundaries and government structures based essentially on distinctions of race and involving a direct relationship with the Federal Government' (280).

If the government was committed to the principle that political structures and policies ought *not* to distinguish between individuals on the basis of race, then it would not suggest that Northerners import the race-based system of reserves, which is widely viewed as notoriously unjust to Aboriginal peoples. Moreover, to understand the federal government's position as born out of a hostility to collectivism or an anxiousness about deviating from individualism is to misunderstand entirely the proposals for restructuring the Government of the NWT that it was likely to reject at the time. The cultural conflict between the government and Aboriginal peoples was a conflict over which cultural community would have power over the North. It was not a matter of individualists and collectivists failing to see eye to eye. By taking at face value the government's use of individualist rhetoric, one discounts the possibility that, given the economic promise of the North in the later 1970s and its importance to Canada's defence strategy, the government was willing to use whatever rhetoric it could to secure power over the North.

So far, the Canadian representative system has been shown to reflect collectivist values in at least four respects. First, the liberal ideal that independent and politically equal individuals ought to debate and decide the nation's policy in Canadian legislatures clashes with party discipline, Cabinet solidarity, and responsible government, each of which suggests that the group's interests are more important than those of any particular individual member. Second, the symbols of Parliament reflect a single set of cultural values and practices and ritualize submission to these values, which are predominantly British and colonialist. Third, electoral processes, including the franchise, have explicitly excluded individuals on the basis of race, gender, and class and continue to be systemically biased in favour of certain cultural values and against others so that Parliament has been and continues to be predominantly male and culturally homogenous. Both a collectivist system in which representatives are chosen explicitly on the basis of their culture, class, and gender and an individualist system in which this occurs through systemic biases fail to be culturally neutral and to meet the standards of political individualism because, whether explicitly or systemically, both allow culture, class, and gender to influence whether or not someone is selected to be a representative. Fourth, numerous electoral policies, including electoral districting, have either explicitly privileged certain minority groups by enhancing their chances to be represented or have explicitly denied some groups the right to representation.

Individualism and Cultural Domination
While the cultural values reflected in the representative system have excluded many cultural minority groups in Canada, the treatment of Aboriginal peoples is unique, partly because of the many treaties signed between Aboriginal peoples and the Government of Canada that state or imply that Aboriginal societies will co-exist with non-Aboriginal society and be protected from the latter's influence. In spite of the explicit understandings reflected in the treaties, the Canadian government has vigorously pursued policies to assimilate Aboriginal peoples against their will. The 1969 White Paper represented Indians as 'poor "aspiring whites"' (Weaver, 196), despite an abundance of evidence, all of which suggested that 'Indians ... continued to value their special rights and protected lands ... [and] sought an end to the policies of assimilation' (Weaver, 48; Kymlicka 1989, 144-6). It provided the rationalization for the strategy of the early 1970s – to entice status Indians to exchange their Aboriginal rights for the right to vote. More alarming policies intended to coercively assimilate Aboriginal people include the project to give all Inuit surnames (see Alia) and the residential school system (see Haig-Brown). None of these policies reflects individualist values. Indeed, each displays a pro-

found disregard for individual rights and individual well-being. In the residential school system, for instance, children were removed from their families, forced to abandon their practices, dress, food, and language and to adopt those of the Church and the French or English cultural community. Far from reflecting the state's cultural neutrality, this policy reveals a highly imperialistic government that tried to assimilate a cultural group through the use of methods that are nothing short of cruel.

Moreover, contrary to the impression conveyed by the individualist versus collectivist perspective, non-Aboriginal peoples have not pressed individualist values on Aboriginal communities. For example, no campaign was undertaken to institute freedom of speech or religion within Aboriginal communities or to persuade those communities to adopt the ideals of liberal equality; rather, the policies that have been proposed and pursued have required that Aboriginal peoples abandon their cultural practices and languages and adopt the way of life of non-Aboriginal peoples. In response to these policies, Aboriginal peoples have demanded the recognition of their collective rights, including the collective right to self-government. But the collective measures favoured by Aboriginal peoples are measures that could easily be favoured by any group that finds itself in the position of being powerless, alienated, dominated, and insecure. The defence of so-called 'group rights' is not entirely based on unfamiliar values that are specific to only certain cultures. Such measures are justified on grounds, such as cultural security and individual well-being, that are precious to all people.

Land claims and the Aboriginal demand for the recognition of their inherent right to self-government set Aboriginal claims apart from those of other minority groups in Canada. My purpose here is not to homogenize the needs or claims of all cultural groups; rather, it is to point out that, notwithstanding these cultural differences (some of which may translate into values that are more individualist or more collectivist), the common characterization that Canada's governing and representative institutions are viewed as illegitimate among Aboriginal peoples because Aboriginal peoples subscribe to collectivism while Canadian political institutions reflect individualism is mistaken, and, further, it is insidious.

This characterization is insidious for two reasons. First, when individualism and collectivism are the primary conceptual tools used to describe the enduring conflict between Aboriginal peoples and the Canadian state, the agenda of coercive assimilation and domination can only exist at the margins of explanation. Analytical clarity about the conflict between these two cultures is said to be gained by focusing on a relatively innocent cultural difference; namely, the difference between individualist and collectivist values. Domination and coercive assimilation do not fit the conceptual analysis and, therefore, appear to be anomalous to the government's overall 'individualist' disposition. Instead of explaining the illegitimacy of the Canadian state and the importance of self-government to Aboriginal peoples on the basis of the oppression and domination they have endured at the hands of the state, the clash between individualism and collectivism is said to be at fault. And instead of viewing Canada's imperialism and policies of coercive assimilation as manifestations of cultural values that are strongly collectivist, they are treated as anomalous to an otherwise culturally neutral and individualist liberal state.

Second, the problems of Aboriginal peoples are depicted as created, innocuously enough, by liberal individualism and thus solved by collectivism. Analysis directs us to favour policies that appear to respect collectivist values. So, the reforms to favour are the ones that guarantee legislative seats, that change the adversarial practices of the political or legal system, that draw electoral boundaries to favour community interests and values, and that lengthen residency requirements in order to protect Aboriginal communities. Solutions that require that the government redress Aboriginal peoples for past wrongs, dismantle policies that perpetuate domination and coercive assimilation, settle land claims, and recognize the right to self-government appear unnecessary, irrelevant, and extreme by comparison.

Conclusion

The historical record, as it is relayed today, provides abundant evidence of the political domination of Aboriginal peoples by non-Aboriginal peoples in Canada. The collectivist/individualist explanation for why Aboriginal peoples consider Canadian political structures and institutions to be illegitimate marginalizes this historical record of oppression. It treats as anomalous non-Aboriginal political values and practices that are collectivist and culturally biased, including those that have been employed to secure the cultural dominance of the majority. Like the standard of androgyny against which women have been judged, non-Aboriginal culture becomes the standard against which the distinctiveness of other cultures is characterized.

These abstract terms – collectivism and individualism – also misrepresent the political landscape of Canada in a way that affects public policy and thus shapes political life. They have been used mistakenly to imply that individualist practices and policies predominate in the symbols, rituals, and traditions of Parliament and in the history of electoral processes and democratic rights in Canada. They depict as exceptional the instances in which non-Aboriginal peoples have been resistant to reforming political institutions in ways that would be inclusive of non-English-Canadian cultures. They mislead one to suppose that Aboriginal peoples would be more likely to participate in the political system if collectivist values were imported into it. Such misleading cultural depictions of Aboriginal and non-Aboriginal peoples are the points from which many futile political debates have commenced and the basis upon which the wrong sorts of political action have been taken.

Acknowledgments
I would like to thank Matt James for his research assistance and, especially, for enthusiastically discussing with me many of the ideas in this chapter.

Notes
1 The focus here is primarily on English-Canadian political culture, although some of the observations and arguments are equally relevant to French-Canadian culture.
2 According to the 1986 census, the population of the Northwest Territories is 18 percent Indian, 35 percent Inuit, 7 percent Métis, and 39 percent non-Aboriginal.
3 Durham's stand on assimilation and how it ought to be interpreted is analyzed by Janet Ajzenstat, who also mistakes Durham's assimilationist proposals for a culturally neutral and liberal solution (see, in particular, 242).
4 The legal position of women as property owners is discussed in Davidoff and Hall (275-9). With regard to religious minorities, the British Constitution held that 'membership in the State Church was a prerequisite for full citizenship' until this section was repealed in 1828 (see McCord, 40).

Works Cited
Abu-Laban, Yasmeen. 1998. 'Keeping 'em Out: Gender, Race, and Class Biases in Canadian Immigration Policy.' In Veronica Strong-Boag, Sherrill Grace, Avigail Eisenberg, and Joan Anderson, eds., *Painting the Maple: Essays on Race, Gender and the Construction of Canada,* 69-82. Vancouver: UBC Press
Ajzenstat, Janet. 1984. 'Liberalism and Assimilation: Lord Durham Revisited.' In Stephen Brooks, ed., *Political Thought in Canada,* 239-57. Toronto: Irwin
Alia, Valerie. 1994. *Names, Numbers, and Northern Policy: The Inuit, Project Surname and the Politics of Identity.* Halifax, NS: Fernwood
Arnopoulos, Sheila McLeod, and Dominique Clift. 1980. *The English Fact in Quebec.* Montreal: McGill-Queen's University Press
Bercuson, David J., and Barry Cooper. 1992. 'Electoral Boundaries: An Obstacle to Democracy in Alberta.' In John C. Courtney et al., eds., *Drawing Boundaries,* 110-27. Saskatoon: Fifth House
Boldt, Menno. 1993. *Surviving as Indians: The Challenge of Self-Government.* Toronto: University of Toronto Press
Carty, R. Kenneth, and W. Peter Ward. 1986. 'The Making of a Canadian Political Citizenship.' In R. Kenneth Carty and W. Peter Ward, eds., *National Politics and Community in Canada,* 65-79. Vancouver: UBC Press
Committee on Aboriginal Electoral Equality. 1991. *The Path to Aboriginal Electoral Equality.* Ottawa: Committee on Aboriginal Electoral Equality
Cook, Ramsay. 1966. *Canada and the French-Canadian Question.* Toronto: Macmillan
Crowley, Brian Lee. 1994. *The Road to Equity: Gender, Ethnicity, and Language: Impolitic Essays.* Toronto: Stoddart
Dacks, Gurston. 1990. 'Political Representation in the Northwest Territories.' In J. Paul Johnston and Harvey E. Pasis, eds., *Representation and Electoral Systems,* 137-54. Scarborough, ON: Prentice-Hall
Davidoff, Leonore, and Catherine Hall. 1987. *Family Fortunes: Men and Women of the English Middle Class, 1780-1850.* Chicago: University of Chicago Press
Dene National Assembly. 1978. 'Metro Proposal.' In Robert F. Keith and Janet B. Wright, eds., *Northern Transitions 2,* 265-7. Ottawa: Canadian Arctic Resources Committee

Eisenberg, Avigail. 1994. 'The Politics of Individual and Group Difference in Canadian Jurisprudence.' *Canadian Journal of Political Science* 27 (1):4-21

Fierlbeck, Katherine. 1996. 'The Ambivalent Potential of Cultural Identity.' *Canadian Journal of Political Science* 29 (1):3-22

Franks, C.E.S. 1987. *The Parliament of Canada*. Toronto: University of Toronto Press

Galipeau, Claude Jean. 1992. 'National Minorities, Rights and Signs: The Supreme Court and Language Legislation in Quebec.' In Alain-G. Gagnon and A. Brian Tanguay, eds., *Democracy and Justice*, 66-84. Ottawa: Carleton University Press

Haig-Brown, Celia. 1988. *Resistance and Renewal: Surviving the Indian Residential School*. Vancouver: Tillacum Library

Kymlicka, Will. 1989. *Liberalism, Community and Culture*. Oxford: Oxford University Press

–. 1995. *Multicultural Citizenship*. Oxford: Oxford University Press

Lukes, Steven. 1973. *Individualism*. Oxford: Basil Blackwell

McCord, Norman. 1991. *British History, 1815-1916*. Oxford: Oxford University Press

Megyery, Kathy, ed. 1991. *Ethno-Cultural Groups and Visible Minorities in Canadian Politics: The Question of Access*. Toronto: Dundurn

Morton, F.L. 1985. 'Group Rights versus Individual Rights in the Charter: The Special Cases of Natives and the Quebecois.' In Neil Nevitte and Allan Kornberg, eds., *Minorities and the Canadian State*, 71-84. Oakville: Mosaic

Office of the Prime Minister. 1978. 'Political Development in the Northwest Territories.' In Robert F. Keith and Janet B. Wright, eds., *Northern Transitions 2*, 314-21. Ottawa: Canadian Arctic Resources Committee

Reference re: Electoral Boundaries Commission Act (1991) 81 DLR (4th) 26 (SCC)

Roach, Kent. 1991. 'One Person, One Vote? Canadian Constitutional Standards for Electoral Distribution and Districting.' In David Small, ed., *Drawing the Map: Equality and Efficacy of the Vote in Canadian Electoral Boundary Reform*, 200-19. Oxford and Toronto: Dundurn

Royal Commission on Electoral Reform and Party Financing. 1991. *Report, Reforming Electoral Democracy 1*. Ottawa: Supply and Services

Said, Edward. 1994. *Culture and Imperialism*. New York: Vintage

Schouls, Tim. 1996. 'Aboriginal Peoples and Electoral Reform in Canada: Differentiated Representation versus Voter Equality.' *Canadian Journal of Political Science* 29 (4):729-49

Trudeau, Pierre Elliott. 1992. *Trudeau: 'A Mess that Deserves a Big NO.'* Toronto: Robert Davies

Turpel, Mary Ellen. 1990. 'Aboriginal Peoples and the Canadian Charter: Interpretative Monopolies, Cultural Differences.' *Canadian Human Rights Yearbook* (1989-90) 6:3-45

Ward, Peter. 1978. *White Canada Forever: Popular Attitudes and Public Policy Towards Orientals in British Columbia*. Montreal: McGill-Queen's University Press

Weaver, Sally. 1981. *Making Canadian Indian Policy: The Hidden Agenda, 1968-70*. Toronto: University of Toronto Press

White, Graham. 1991. 'Westminster in the Arctic: The Adaptation of British Parliamentarism in the Northwest Territories.' *Canadian Journal of Political Science* 24 (3): 499-524

–. 1993. 'Northern Distinctiveness: Representation by Population and the Charter: The Politics of Redistribution in the Northwest Territories.' *Journal of Canadian Studies* 28 (3):5-29

Whittington, Michael S. 1990. 'Canada's North in the 1990s.' In Michael Whittington and Glen Williams, eds., *Canadian Politics in the 1990s*, 23-44. Scarborough, ON: Nelson

On the Outskirts of Empire: Race and Gender in Canadian TV News

Yasmin Jiwani

Communication theorists have extensively documented the connections between media and nationalism. Elizabeth Eisenstein's comprehensive treatment of the social implications of print in Europe demonstrates how the printing press eroded the monopoly of the Church and contributed to a growing sense of group identity and awareness. Indeed, the 'Gutenberg Revolution' was instrumental in facilitating the transformation of vernacular languages into national formations, thereby enabling the widespread diffusion of cultural knowledge in ways that far surpassed the local, immediate channels of the oral tradition.

Closer to home, Canadian theorists Marshall McLuhan and Harold Innis have also documented the nationalistic implications of technologies such as print, television, and film. In fact, Innis saw these technologies as essential tools in the building of empires. Such technologies allowed for control over colonies located thousands of miles away. Moreover, they permitted the governing of subject races by enabling the colonizers to alter and codify laws, myths of origins, and genealogies (see, for instance, Goody 1977; Henige 1973, 1982; Said; Tharu). Writers have also commented on the role of communication technologies in spurring decolonization movements (e.g., Fanon) and revolutions in the Third World (Jayaweera; Mowlana; Mowlana and Robinson).

Many of these theorists argue that communication technologies are not 'innocent,' passive, mechanical vehicles but, rather, powerful agents of social change, influencing our stock of knowledge and how we see the world (Berger). As Goody notes, 'The modes of acquiring knowledge affect the nature of that knowledge and the way in which knowledge is organized' (1982, 10) or, as McLuhan popularized it, 'the medium is the message.' Thus, form and content cannot be separated but, rather, work together to promote particular views of the world.

In the context of nationalism, technologies of communication are essential, for they span great distances, uniting some factions and dividing others.

They provide access to and structure for a common stock of knowledge, thereby creating an 'imagined community' (B. Anderson). At the same time, they play a critical role in the production and reproduction of social knowledge, reaffirming and legitimizing the social order. The media then are instrumental in providing a definition of nationness – an identity of 'self' that is constructed in opposition to an 'other' (Hall 1990; van Dijk 1991, 1993).

In the Canadian context, national media play a critical role. From coast to coast, they provide a shared sense of identity in regional, national, and international contexts. They give us a sense of who Canadians are and of how their national interest is affected by developments in other arenas. The national media provide 'images of prescription and description' (Bannerji), defining what is acceptable and unacceptable and how we see and relate to the world(s) within and to those outside.

Nevertheless, the media are 'structured in dominance' (Hall 1980). This is not to imply that the media offer a homogenous fare but, rather, that in the dominant media a hierarchy of discourses prevails (Barthes; White). Hence, not only is the dominant media controlled by elite interests, but, within the dominant discourses that structure media content, the 'us' versus 'them' distinction is pervasive. It is the hierarchical arrangement of these discourses that enables the media to exert hegemonic influence, for by showing that other 'sides' are being represented, albeit in a polarized fashion, the final explanation offered is one that 'appears' to make the best sense of the situation and is grounded in common sense and consensus (Connell; Ellis; Knight).

Nowhere is this more apparent than in the ideological labour that goes into constructing 'the news,' for the news media have a certain legitimacy that is garnered through the use of visual media (i.e., pictures, video footage), their apparent facticity, and their adherence to standards of 'objectivity,' balance, and 'freedom of speech.' The news media are the quintessential weapons of nationalism: they define the nation by contrasting it to other nations, and they provide citizens of the nation with a view to their place in the local, national, and international arena.

Frames, Filters, and Stereotypes: The Currency of the Mass Media

Frames, filters, and stereotypes are the stock in trade of the mass media. However, these 'technics' are institutionally and historically grounded (Darnton; Hall 1990; Tuchman 1976). They lend themselves to a construction of social reality by colonizing that reality into lay language, commonly understood symbols, metaphors, and metonyms (Hartley and Montgomery). By harnessing the unknown to the known, the media represent social phenomena, for to tell a story, one has to use discursive, cultural, and institutional knowledge and conventions in order that it *make sense as a story* (Hall 1980; van Dijk 1993).

Thus, the importance of examining representations lies in what they tell us about the collective imagination; about how social phenomena are made sense of and located; and, more politically, about in whose interests particular representations are produced and reproduced. To begin such an examination, it is necessary first to excavate the historical representations of racialized groups because these representations are part of a common stock of knowledge.

Race and Representation in the Dominant Media

In tracing the evolution of representations of racialized peoples in English language media, the period of British colonialism and imperialism figures as the dominant point of departure. Indeed, the importance of this period is apparent when one realizes that 'from 1815 to 1914, European direct colonial dominion expanded from about 35 percent of the earth's surface to about 85 percent of it. Every continent was affected, none more so than Africa and Asia. The two greatest empires were the British and the French; allies and partners in some things, in others they were hostile rivals' (Said, 41). Canada, having been colonized by both the British and the French, shared and contributed to the production of knowledge about colonized peoples that it either conquered, imported, or attempted to annihilate.

According to Jan Mohamed, Said, and Isaacs, among others, representations of racialized groups achieved widespread circulation during the height of colonialism. Hall (1990) argues that contemporary images of racial groups in the dominant British media are based on the residual 'traces' of representations formed during colonial contact and the expansion of empire (see also Hammond and Jablow; van Dijk 1993). Racial differences achieved a heightened emphasis during this period. The superiority of the colonizers was affirmed and reaffirmed through various discursive practices and forms of knowledge production that underscored the inferiority of subject races (McBratney; Said). Representations that emerged within this context were circumscribed within a 'base grammar of race' (Hall 1990). Such a grammar revolved around three major axes: the superiority of the white race and the inferiority of subject races, the necessary domination and subordination of subject races, and the transference of these inequalities from the realm of history and society to the realm of nature, thus making them seemingly immutable.

Hall notes that the content of this grammar – the particular ways in which it was used to achieve its goal of communicating a particular worldview – consisted of various combinations and permutations of popular stereotypes. Hence, the noble savage of a bygone era stood in opposition to the cunning, debauched savage; the mammy figure of the black female slave stood in contrast to the 'jezebel'; the faithful and loyal Sikh fighter stood in contrast to the lascivious and miserly babu, and so forth. Yet, the dynamic of 'us' versus 'them' was implicitly encoded into these representations, which helped to congeal a sense of national and racialized identity.

These perceptions were not confined to the centres of colonial thought in the motherland of the empire. Rather, they permeated the mutual knowledge and social imagination of the colonizers out in the far-flung colonies, providing them with a rationale for their civilizing mission and protecting them against the wiles of those they needed to subjugate (Huttenback). But what these representations accomplished was the shifting of an 'us' versus 'them' perspective from the immediate European setting to one located outside. As Miles puts it: 'The untamed aggression, sexuality, brutality of the "mythical" wild man previously located in the forested edges of (or within) Europe was given a more precise and specific geographical location in the new world. Moreover, this incarnation of the wild man was also distinguished by skin colour, permitting a conception of the Other as "black" and, therefore, definitively distinct from the European who was white' (24-5).

In the colonies, such perceptions led to the creation of draconian immigration laws that forbade and restricted the movement of people of Colour (K. Anderson; Buchignani and Indra; Huttenback; Roy). Further, the sentiments underlying such representations survived into the next century, where they continued to exert an influence over social and immigration policies. Even in British Columbia, the last 'outpost' of the empire, these representations persisted and were expressed in the formation of anti-Asiatic leagues and other exclusionary bodies.

Even as luminous a character as J.S. Woodsworth was not immune to the racist tendencies current in the period. Writing in 1909, Woodsworth described South Asians in the following manner: 'Owing to his peculiarities the Hindu cannot work with men of other nations; indeed, only with Hindus of his own caste. Their standards of living and manner of life and thought are far *different* than ours. However estimable they may be in India, they are sadly out of place in Canada' (cited in Buchignani and Indra, 46, emphasis added).

Both implicitly and explicitly, the opposition of 'us' versus 'them' underpinned these representations and gave them a potency that still exists today. This oppositional relationship was communicated through various discursive devices that lumped all colonial subjects into monolithic and homogenous groups (Jan Mohamed), examples of which are criminals and deviants (K. Anderson; Chung; Isaacs; Visram), opportunists (Chan), and unassimilable immigrants (Huttenback; Indra 1979). Throughout this literature, the notion of difference is underscored and inflected with negative connotations that imply an extreme version of some trait such as sexuality, inability to adapt, weakness, and so on.

Gender: The Woman of Colour

By the late nineteenth century, as 'race theory' became more fully developed and accepted, gender came into increased focus as being somehow analogous in development and hierarchy to notions of race. Stepan notes: 'Thus it was claimed that women's low brain weights and deficient brain structures were analogous to those of lower races, and their inferior intellectualities explained on this basis. Woman it was observed, shared with Negroes a narrow, childlike, and delicate skull, so different from the more robust and rounded heads characteristic of males of "superior" races. Similarly, women of higher races tended to have slightly protruding jaws, analogous to, if not exaggerated as, the apelike jutting jaws of lower races' (39-40). As were colonized peoples, white women were seen as being emotional and impulsive, weak, and incapable of reason. (Hence, the first wave of feminism began the long journey toward change with the prime motive of proving that gender differences were a result of socialization.) These representations served to justify and legitimize patriarchal domination, and they 'fit' within the ideological schema of 'Adam's world' and notions regarding evolution.

Imperial literature cast *colonized* women in a similar yet different role. On the one hand, colonized women were largely invisible, relegated to the colourful background of exotic colonies where they formed a backdrop to the exploits of the white male colonizer. On the other hand, and where it suited the colonizers, such women were portrayed as being submissive, docile, fecund, dangerous, and knowledgable about the land and its bounty (Jewell; Jiwani 1992b). The polarities apparent in the base grammar of race were also applicable to women of Colour. The mammy stereotype of African slave women equipped the slave owner with a rationale for forcing them to be housekeepers and wet-nurses, whereas the Jezebel stereotype provided him with justification for using rape and other brutal means to force the 'bad girl' into submission (Jewell).

In other colonies, similar constructions prevailed. In 1901, Lord Crewe circulated a memo to his colonial officers urging them not to consort with Native women. The reason behind the directive was that familiarity with Native women diminished the authority of the officers and reduced their effectiveness as administrators (McBratney; Mohanty). So strong was the directive against miscegenation that all kinds of myths were resurrected and disseminated via the popular media to reinforce it (Stam and Spence; Stott).[1]

Representations of women of Colour were highly sexualized. They were seen as being extremely fecund and likely to give birth to numerous offspring who might then challenge or invade the empire. This sexualization was projected onto colonized women who were located in their indigenous lands – the lands considered to be analogous to the bodies of the women themselves – exotic and inviting, ready to be raped, occupied, and conquered (Said). As Stott puts it: 'The landscape of potential Empire becomes the landscape of pornographic fantasies and of sexual terrors. The focus is always on the experience of the white male dominator or explorer, not on the experience of the colonized' (84). Said further elaborates on the rationale underpinning this construction: 'Just as the various colonial possessions – quite apart from their economic benefit to metropolitan Europe – were useful as places to send wayward sons, superfluous populations of delinquents, poor people, and other undesirables, so the Orient was a place where one could look for sexual experience unobtainable in Europe' (190).

The fear of miscegenation survived in the popular imagination and was subsequently reinforced in the media via new communication technologies: radio, television, and film (Stam and Spence). In fact, Stott argues that these same themes of imperialist literature can be seen in recent films outlining the exploits of the white male adventurer Indiana Jones. The dragon lady lives on in popular films such as *Flash Gordon*, and exotic women of Colour provide emblematic backgrounds in James Bond films where, every so often, James deigns to have sex with one of them.

Yet as well as being portrayed as exotic, erotic, and dangerous, women of Colour were also portrayed as hapless victims of oppressive cultural systems. The latter imagery permitted the colonial powers to assume a visage of benevolence and to go into other lands on the pretext of helping indigenous women and civilizing barbaric races (Mani).

Contemporary 'Traces'

There are changes and continuities between these historically inscribed representations and contemporary representations of racialized groups (van Dijk 1991, 1993). However, as with early representations, contemporary images are also aimed at justifying the differential treatment accorded to racialized groups and excluding them via immigration laws from entering the nation (Cottle). This serves to reentrench definitions of 'us' and 'them,' thereby solidifying a sense of national identity.

As with earlier representations, contemporary images derive their meaning from several discursive moves and absences. There is a pronounced absence of representations of racialized people in the national Canadian media. Numerous studies have repeatedly documented this underrepresentation in both television and print media (e.g., Desbarats; Deverall; Erin Research; Generations Research; Granzberg; Indra 1981; Khaki and Prasad; Moore and Cadeau; Peac). The continuing *absence* of people of Colour in the dominant media signifies their invisibility and non-status within the symbolic social order. As Stam and Spence note, such absences signify a discourse of race, as absence is often predicated on exclusion or on a strategy to conceal a racist intent (see also van Dijk 1993).

In their comparative survey of CBC Television and a private broadcasting company, Erin Research found that representations of racialized people were most concentrated in television news items that dealt with crime, war, and terrorism. Further, the highest degree of representation occurred in the foreign news category. People of Colour were only interviewed when the stories dealt with their specific communities (Lazar and Perigoe). As with most news items, attention was only directed to these communities when they were a site of disturbance, thus reflecting their lack of 'fit' within Canadian society – a lack of fit that was normalized through the inclusion of other news items that dealt with government actions, international relations, and human interest stories.

Research dealing with Canadian press coverage of racialized peoples finds that they are largely constructed as immigrant groups and that, as immigrants, they are regarded as a threat to the social order. They are perceived as 'problems,' the only solution to which is the curtailment of further immigration (Ducharme; Scanlon; Thobani 1991, 1992). They are consistently associated with invasion, crime, deviance, cultural differences, and dishonesty (e.g., jumping the immigration queue). This results in a portrayal that clearly marginalizes racialized groups as 'others,' locating them outside the pale of Canadian identity. As 'immigrants,' they are presented as not being authentic Canadians. Yet, the category of authenticity is never interrogated.

Indra's study of the coverage of South Asians in the Vancouver dailies from 1905 to 1976 reveals the longevity of these representations. According to her analysis, in the initial years of South Asian presence in British Columbia (1905-14), the press represented them as being 'fundamentally different from normal members of society. They were shown to be chaotic carriers of a dangerous and foreign culture which threatened the existence of Vancouver as it was then constituted' (166).

Indra further argues that a moral stratification system operated within both dailies, such that some groups were classified as the 'ethnic elite' while others were typified as the 'moral outcasts.' Her analysis of this 'domestic moral community' reveals that Scottish, British, and English ranked at the top, while Americans, Germans, Russians, and French-Canadians scored in the middle range. In contrast, the Chinese, South Asians, Italians, and Aboriginal peoples ranked the lowest. While South Asians are but one among many racialized communities in British Columbia and Canada as a whole, the findings of this study appear to be applicable to the representations of all racialized groups in dominant Canadian media (see, for instance, Dubois; DuCharme; Ginzberg; Khaki and Prasad; Levine; Tator).

In his review of the European, British, and Canadian media, van Dijk observed similar constructions of racialized groups. They were viewed as threats to the cultural order due to their insistence on retaining their own cultures, as threats to the social order due to their violating practices and laws, and as threats to the economic order due to their stealing jobs and taking away scarce resources (van Dijk 1993). In virtually all of these instances, the media were actively engaged in perpetuating the existence of an 'us' versus 'them' relationship, whereby 'they' were seen as invaders taking over the nation or, in the British case, as the 'enemy within.'[2]

Women of Colour: Contemporary Representations

Dominant representations of women reflect changes and continuities from the colonial period. Nevertheless, even contemporary representations cohere around an 'us' versus 'them' dichotomy that ideologically sediments a notion of national identity that is clearly exclusionary. An analysis of contemporary representations reveals the intersecting complexities that surround the construction of race and gender.

As in the literature of imperialism, women of Colour continue to enjoy the media spotlight if they bare their souls and talk about the abuse they face in their own communities. A reading of the 1992 news stories that appeared in the *Vancouver Sun* for the month of July clearly reflects this trend (see Jiwani 1992a).[3] Hence, the *Sun*'s 'Women and the Veil' series dwelt on the oppression of Muslim women at the hands of their husbands and religion. These stories were accompanied by coverage of South Asian men assaulting their wives and evading immigration requirements.

When a group of Muslim women responded to these stories, their response was prefaced by the editor's comments that the young women were in fact raised and educated in the West. This somehow rendered their response more 'intelligible' while at the same time dismissing it by implying that, as they were raised in a 'progressive' environment, they did not really understand the true nature of the situation being covered. This message underscores the media construction of 'others' who are considered non-Canadian.

Women of Colour are also featured in news stories when they are victims of cultural conflict. Unable to reconcile seemingly disparate cultures, they become the darlings of the dominant media. The *Vancouver Sun* relished its role of providing news about South Asian women when it was presented with the opportunity of covering Sarah Kapoor's story (15 August 1992) of cultural conflict. Sarah participated in the *Sun*'s coverage, submitting her own articles. In a sense, Sarah represents the 'bleached ethnic,' and, according to Donald Bogle, the media favour such representations because they downplay race and underscore the necessity of assimilation. Sarah, then, is like 'us' because she, too, is unable to understand the contradictory and oppressive culture of her parents. While Sarah seems to enjoy easy access to the *Sun*'s editors, the Muslim women referred to above had to arrange a meeting and request space in order to have their response printed. The *Sun* did not see fit to solicit an article that would 'balance' its heavy coverage of oppressed Muslim women.

Cultural conflicts, arranged marriages, oppressive cultures, exotic dress and foods – these are the stock in trade of the press's coverage of racialized women. These representations serve to affirm and reaffirm the superiority of the dominant society while underscoring the unbridgeable difference of racialized communities (Youngs 1989). 'They' are thus rendered as unassimilable, unwilling, and unable to become a part of the national self, thereby emphasizing self-identity through exclusion.

It is as 'deviants from "traditional" women's roles' that women of Colour have received the most media attention (Indra, 69). The traditional role for women in general has been one of docility and submissiveness to the patriarchal order. When women challenge that order, they are likely to experience a backlash (Faludi). That backlash may take the form of highly pejorative media coverage, with women being represented as extremists and their messages trivialized, if not dismissed outright.

Representing Reality: Women of Colour as Radical Feminists

The media, as has been pointed out, favour a 'middle-of-the-road' approach that is predicated on the notion of an assumed consensus. Framing issues in a binary manner – constructing them as having two opposing sides – enables the media to persuade the viewer/reader that either extreme is radical and represents fringe elements. However, when one side has more power and is considered to be legitimate (e.g., the government), then the other side is considered to be less legitimate, more radical, and extreme. These representations can be seen in the usual oppositional relationship established between unions and governments/ corporations in television news (Connell; Fiske and Hartley). It is the government side – the side of 'reason' and assumed consensus – that is represented as reflecting national identity. In contrast, the fringe elements are usually constructed as representing those problematic peoples that refuse to 'fit in.'

An illustration of this dynamic is also apparent in the following example of a newscast that was aired on the CBC and CTV late-night news on 31 July 1992.[4] The issue dealt with the withdrawal of the support of prominent women's organizations from the government-commissioned panel on violence. CBC defined the situation as a 'wound in the feminist movement,' while CTV called it a 'rift in the woman's movement.' The 'rift' or 'wound' was ascribed to the panel's lack of representation of women of Colour. News stories, particularly those broadcast on television, tend to embrace a structure that is reminiscent of myths. The focus is on an agent/event that has disrupted the stability of the social order, while the rest of the story is dedicated to examining the actual or potential means by which order may be restored. Where this is not possible, the story is left open-ended, its explanation to be filled in by subsequent newscasts.

In the CBC and CTV stories, the withdrawal of women's groups from the government-commissioned panel on violence constituted such a sign of disorder. The media then proposed explanations and suggested potential solutions. CTV's coverage began with a long shot of a press conference convened by the organizations. The focus shifted immediately to an authoritative white female figure – Mary Collins, the Minister Responsible for the Status of Women – who argued that the groups had in fact been offered various options, which they had declined. Collins represented the voice of reason both in her tone and in her actions (making concessions). Judy Rebick, president of the National Action Committee on the Status of Women (NAC), one of the groups that had withdrawn its support, then explained her side of the story. This was followed by an interview with a black woman front-line worker, Leslie Lekum, who discussed the impact of funding cuts on services for *immigrant* women. The tendency of the media to focus on women of Colour as representing just the interests of immigrant women serves to underscore the popular stereotype that there are no people of Colour who have been Canadians for generations. It also problematizes the notion of Canadian identity.

At no time in the story was it mentioned that NAC is one of the largest women's organizations in the country, representing some 500 other organizations. Nor was it emphasized that the issue of representation was not confined to the lack of women of Colour on the panel (at that point there was only one) but also included the needs of other women (for example, women with disabilities). Other organizations that also withdrew their support were not mentioned. These included the DisAbled Women's Network (DAWN), the Canadian Association of Sexual Assault Centres (CASAC), and the Congress of Black Women. Representatives of these groups were not interviewed. Instead, by personalizing the issue and concentrating on the one black woman, the story effectively displaced the significance of the larger social issue; namely, dealing with the politics of representation. This issue is naturalized as a 'rift' that will heal over time. The concerns articulated by the single woman of Colour interviewed were constructed either as the 'normal' cries of women's groups or as an expression of the needs of a particular group – immigrant women – which is already socially marginalized. More pointedly, the story seemed to pit NAC against mainstream white women in that NAC represented the voices of women of Colour, whereas the panel on violence represented the reasonable and credible voices of mainstream white women.

In the CBC story, the slant is more progressive. Rather than focusing immediately on an accredited figure of authority, the story shifted to Fleurette Osborne, representative of the Congress of Black Women.

Osborne is shown saying, 'We see this also as a reluctance to share some of the power of the people on the panel.' Instead of exploring this issue any further, the camera shifted abruptly to the co-chair of the panel, thus giving access to the authoritative voice of Dr. Pat Freeman Marshall. She countered Osborne's charge by stating, 'It is too late to change the structure of the panel. All this discussion is taking the time and space away from critical discussion of the issues of violence.' There was no further interrogation of Marshall's position. The reality that women are not all the same and, hence, may have different experiences with violence did not even enter the field of debate. Instead, the reporter's voice-over reinforced Marshall's position by outlining that she had offered to appoint 'minority' women as special advisors but that the groups had rejected the offer because they viewed it as tokenism. Marshall's offer was presented by CBC as a sign of concession. However, the report failed to mention relevant background details that might have offered a different explanation.

In the year preceding their withdrawal from the panel, women's groups had been involved with it in an advisory capacity. Moreover, they had also made various other suggestions to the panel, including that its final recommendations be vetted by thirteen different organizations before being presented to the government. The groups had also asked the panel to publicly acknowledge its support of Bill C-46 (concerning sexual assault). The panel had agreed to all the recommendations except the one concerning representation.

The story then shifted to a black woman who was identified as a specialist in anti-racism training. Seated at a conference table, Jennifer Wollcott was shown in her dreadlocks, with the reporter's voice-over commenting: 'She sees all of this as a trend. Minority groups are finally *demanding* power.' Wollcott herself did not use the term 'demand'; rather, she located the issue of representation in a wider context, asking the rhetorical question: 'What's the alternative? For people to keep quiet, for people to be disenfranchised? I don't think that's healthy.' To its credit, the story then moved on to another well-known black woman who was defined as a political commentator – Rosemary Brown. Brown also elaborated on the issue of representation, albeit briefly. She was cut off in mid-sentence by the reporter, who, in a stake-out position, concluded: 'The Canadian panel on violence against women will continue to write its report to present to the government in December. At the same time, the National Action Committee and other national women's groups say they'll do their own work on the issue of violence against women.' Closure is achieved. The status quo has been reestablished. This 'wound' in the feminist movement has been minor enough that it can be ignored and the work to be done continued.

Thus, even though CBC's coverage can be assessed as being relatively progressive in that it included representations of black women who articulated the breadth of the issue, the issue itself was never really resolved and the concerns regarding representation were buried once again.

The oppositions inherent in these newscasts can be identified as follows:

Us	*Them*
White	Women of Colour
Mainstream, government appointed	Marginal, identified as 'immigrant'
Figures of authority and credibility	Front-line workers, have a stake in the process
Maintaining order	Disturbing the order
Voices of reason	Extremists
Conciliatory	Demanding

However, these newscasts also portray women of Colour as being militant – 'demanding' their share of power. It is this militancy that comes across in subsequent news stories, both in the press and on television. The theme of the demanding woman of Colour is also apparent in the kind of coverage given to NAC past-president Sunera Thobani. In virtually every instance, Thobani was shown as being passionate, angry, militant, and demanding. This type of representation is often juxtaposed with equally extreme depictions of far-Right groups (e.g., anti-choice groups or REAL [Realistic, Equal, and Active for Life] women). Thus, in the public's imagination as well as in the media, the two extremes are rendered illegitimate – as irrational movements – which makes it more attractive and reasonable to embrace a moderate perspective. In the case of the above newscasts, that moderate perspective is constituted by the liberal feminism espoused by the minister responsible for the status of women, Mary Collins, and the co-chair of the National Panel on Violence, Pat Freeman Marshall. Both work in the dominant system of power, and their success is used to demonstrate that system's supposed acceptance of equality and equity.[5] Thus, the empire is maintained, and, rather than resolving the 'wound' or the 'rift,' the media have perpetuated it.

Yet what constitutes 'moderate' is itself predicated on the political climate of society. With the present climate tending toward hard-line conservatism, the moderate has become conservative, and the real demands of women of Colour are, as has been said earlier, trivialized if not dismissed.

Conclusion

The media's images of women of Colour as militant and demanding position them outside the boundaries of normative society. As 'bleached ethnics,' or as recipients of the benevolence of the Canadian state, they are only acceptable if they 'stay in their place' – as domestic workers and as submissive wives. As with imperialist fiction at the turn of the century, the message today suggests that it is dangerous to engage with them. Contained in their ethnic exotica, they can be used as signs affirming the tolerance and multiculturalism of Canadian society. Symbolizing all immigrants of Colour, the women remain on the outskirts of the empire, which is the national self.

National self-identity is also maintained by positioning extreme groups at the fringes of society. In this way, the middle-of-the-road, moderate, and reasonable character of the invisible majority is affirmed and taken as symbolic of Canadian identity. This ideological work of producing and reproducing a sense of nation-ness depends on the media being able to identify and portray groups that can be framed as 'extremists' – as not fitting into society.

By creating a double vision that casts both NAC and REAL as extremes, the media conveniently obliterate the differences between them and deflect attention away from the critical role of the state in creating and perpetuating the fragmentation and hierarchical nature of groups in Canadian society. The 'mediated' landscape is levelled and extremes are defined in terms of individual choice rather than in terms of structural inequalities. Thus, the safety and character of empire is maintained and the enemies within are, once more, pushed to the margins and held at bay by the powerful and defining role of the mass media.

Notes

1 Stott, for example, elucidates the literature of this period by drawing on works of Sir Ryder Haggard. Haggard's career as a literary figure began in the 1880s and reached a peak six years later when he finished his stint as secretary to the lieutenant governor of Natal. His writing centres around the recurrent motifs of the literature of the time; namely, a focus on lost races, the search for scientific knowledge (as in the key to immortality), the exploration of strange lands, and encounters with human/subhuman characters. Haggard's numerous writings include: *King Solomon's Mines, Allan Quartermain, She, Ayesha*, and others, many of which have been produced as films. In many of these works, the woman of Colour is represented as a dangerous and exotic creature, possessive, irrational to the point of madness, obsessed, and demonic. The white male explorer, by contrast, is shown to be innocent, honest, virile, and, above all, civilized.

2 These representations are most apparent in news stories dealing with immigration. Typically, the newscast begins with visuals of immigrants and refugees lined up at the immigration counter. Rarely is a white person shown in these long shots. The shots are accompanied by a voice-over, which usually explains unrest in the developing world, the smuggling of bogus refugees, and the vain attempts of illegal immigrants to enter the country. In some instances, the camera may linger on a person of Colour or a woman of Colour who is wearing her traditional dress. The connotations evoked hark back to notions of unassimilable immigrants. Racial and cultural differences are heightened by the medium itself as well as by the manner in which it is used (Jiwani 1993). Thus, racialized groups are constantly portrayed as foreign/different 'others' who fall outside the pale of normative society, unless, of course, their achievements and exotic character

can be used to affirm nationalistic traits such as tolerance.
3 At this time, on an average day the *Vancouver Sun* had a circulation of 460,400.
4 This example is selected from a corpus of seventy-four newscasts tape-recorded between 25 July and 14 August 1992. Stories featuring people of Colour were subjected to an informal discourse analysis. Of the stories that appeared, only two dealt significantly with women of Colour. The present analysis constitutes one such case. The other story dealt with issues of violence against women, with two South Asian-Canadian women being shown addressing a crowd that had gathered outside the law courts in Vancouver. (For full details, see Jiwani 1993.)
5 The kind of oppositional relationship established between Judy Rebick, the then President of NAC, and Pat Freeman Marshall, the co-chair of the Panel on Violence, can be seen in the framing of the recent coverage concerning the charges of sexism and racism in the Political Science Department of the University of British Columbia. In this instance, Pat Marchak, identified with the success story of liberal feminism, is contrasted with Veronica Strong-Boag, who is identified as a proponent of the more extreme 'gender feminism' (see, for instance, Felton).

Works Cited

Anderson, Benedict. 1983. *Imagined Communities*. London: Verso
Anderson, Kay. 1991. 'Race, Place and the Power of Definition.' In Kay Anderson, ed., *Vancouver's Chinatown, Racial Discourse in Canada, 1875-1980*, 8-33. Montreal: McGill-Queen's University Press
Bannerji, Himani. 1986. 'Now You See Us/Now You Don't.' *Video Guide* 8:40-5
Barthes, Roland. 1973. *Mythologies*. London: Paladin
Berger, John. 1972. *Ways of Seeing*. London: Penguin
Bogle, Donald. 1989. *Toms, Coons, Mulattoes, Mammies and Bucks: An Interpretive History of Blacks in American Films*. New York: Continuum
Buchignani, Norman, and Doreen Indra, with Ram Srivastava. 1985. *Continuous Journey*. Toronto: McClelland and Stewart
Chan, B. Anthony. 1981. 'Orientalism and Image Making: The Sojourner in Canadian History.' *Journal of Ethnic Studies* 9 (3):37-46
Chung, Sue Fawn. 1976. 'From Fu Manchu, Evil Genius to James Lee Wong, Popular Hero: A Study of the Chinese American in Popular Periodical Fiction from 1920-1940.' *Journal of Popular Culture* 10 (3): 534-47
Connell, Ian. 1980. 'Television News and the Social Contract.' In Stuart Hall et al., eds., *Culture, Media, Language*, 139-56. London: Hutchinson in association with the Centre for Contemporary Cultural Studies, Birmingham
Cottle, Simon. 1992. 'Race, Racialization and the Media: A Review and Update of Research.' *Sage Race Relations Abstracts* 17 (2):3-57
Darnton, Robert. 1975. 'Writing News and Telling Stories.' *Daedalus* 104 (2):175-94
Desbarats, P. 1982. Address at the *Conference on Visible Minorities and the Media*. Toronto: Multiculturalism
Deverall, Rita Shelton. 1987. *Equal Opportunities to Perform, A Study of the Role of Performers Who Are Members of Visible and Audible Minority Groups in Canadian Communications Media*. Toronto: ACTRA
Dubois, Marie-France. 1993. 'South Asian Women in Canada and Media Discourse: A Feminist Collaborative Analysis.' MA thesis, University of British Columbia, Vancouver, BC
DuCharme, Michele. 1986. 'The Coverage of Canadian Immigration Policy in the *Globe and Mail* (1980-1985).' *Currents* 3 (3):6-11
Eisenstein, Elizabeth. 1980. *The Printing Press as an Agent of Change: Communications and Cultural Transformations in Early Modern Europe*. Cambridge: Cambridge University Press
Ellis, John. 1982. *Visible Fictions: Cinema, Television, Video*. London: Routledge and Kegan Paul
Erin Research. 1991. *Social Trends in CBC Television Programming, 1977-1990: A Content Analysis*. Commissioned by the Canadian Broadcasting Corporation, Ottawa

Faludi, Susan. 1991. *Backlash: The Undeclared War against American Women*. New York: Anchor
Fanon, Frantz. 1965. *Studies in a Dying Colonialism*. Haakon Chevalier, trans. New York: Monthly Review
Felton, Greg. 1996. 'Opinion Piece.' *Vancouver Courier*, 4 February, 11
Fiske, John, and John Hartley. 1978. *Reading Television*. London: Methuen
Generations Research. 1988. *The Portrayal of Canadian Cultural Diversity on Canadian Network Television: A Content Analysis*. Ottawa: Prepared for the Secretary of State
Ginzberg, Effie. 1986. 'Power without Responsibility: The Press We Don't Deserve – A Content Analysis of the *Toronto Sun*.' *Currents* 3 (3):1-5
Goody, Jack. 1977. *The Domestication of the Savage Mind*. New York: Cambridge University Press
–. 1982. 'Alternative Paths to Knowledge in Oral and Literate Cultures.' In Deborah Tannen, ed., *Spoken and Written Language: Exploring Orality and Literacy*, 201-15. Norwood, NJ: Ablex
Granzberg, Gary. 1984. 'The Portrayal of Visible Minorities in Canadian Television During the 1982 Prime-Time Season.' *Currents* 2 (2):23-6
Hall, Stuart. 1980. 'Race, Articulation and Societies Structured in Dominance.' In Stuart Hall, ed., *Sociological Theories: Race and Colonialism*. Paris: UNESCO
–. 1990. 'The Whites of Their Eyes.' In Manuel Alvarado and John O. Thompson, eds., *The Media Reader*. London: British Film Institute
Hammond, Dorothy, and Alta Jablow. 1977. *The Myth of Africa*. New York: The Library of Social Sciences
Hartley, John, and Martin Montgomery. 1985. 'Representations and Relations: Ideology and Power in Press and TV News.' In Teun A. van Dijk, ed., *Discourse and Communication*, 233-69. New York: de Gruyter
Henige, David. 1973. 'The Problem of Feedback in Oral Traditions: Four Examples from the Fante Coastlands.' *Journal of African History* 14:223-35
–. 1982. 'Truths Yet Unborn? Oral Tradition as a Casualty of Culture Contact.' *Journal of African History* 23 (3):395-412
Huttenback, Robert A. 1976. *Racism and Empire, White Settlers and Colored Immigrants in the British Self-governing Colonies, 1830-1910*. Ithaca, NY: Cornell University Press
Indra, M. Doreen. 1979. 'South Asian Stereotypes in the Vancouver Press.' *Ethnic and Racial Studies* 2 (2):166-89
–. 1981. 'The Invisible Mosaic: Women, Ethnicity and the Vancouver Press, 1905-1976.' *Canadian Ethnic Studies* 13 (1):63-74
Innis, Harold. 1951. *The Bias of Communication*. Toronto: University of Toronto Press
Isaacs, Harold. 1958. *Scratches on Our Minds*. Westport, CT: Greenwood
Jan Mohamed, R. Abdul. 'The Economy of Manichean Allegory: The Function of Racial Difference in Colonialist Literature.' *Critical Inquiry* 12 (1):59-87
Jayaweera, Neville. 1985. 'New Technologies and Third World Cultures.' *Cultures: Dialogue between the Peoples of the World* 36:69-87
Jewell, K. Sue. 1993. *From Mammy to Miss America and Beyond: Cultural Images and the Shaping of US Social Policy*. London: Routledge
Jiwani, Yasmin. 1992a. 'To Be or Not to Be: South Asians as Victims and Oppressors in the *Vancouver Sun*.' *Sanvad* 5 (45):13-15
–. 1992b. 'The Exotic, the Erotic and the Dangerous: South Asian Women in Popular Film.' *Canadian Woman Studies* 13 (1):42-6
–. 1993. 'By Omission and Commission: "Race" and Representation in Canadian Television News.' PhD thesis, Simon Fraser University, Burnaby, BC
Khaki, A., and K. Prasad. 1988. *Depiction and Perception: Native Indians and Visible Minorities in the Media*. Vancouver: Ad Hoc Committee for Better Race Relations
Knight, Graham. 1982. 'News and Ideology.' *Canadian Journal of Communication* 8 (4):15-41
Lazar, Barry, and Ross Perigoe. 1989. 'Visible Minorities and Native Canadians in National Television News Programs.' Unpublished manuscript
Levine, Meredith. 1988. 'Canadians Secretly Relieved at Johnson's Fall.' *New Statesman and*

Society 1 (18):8

McBratney, John. 1988. 'Images of Indian Women in Rudyard Kipling: A Case of Doubling Discourse.' *Inscriptions* 3/4:47-57

McLuhan, Marshall. 1962. *The Gutenberg Galaxy*. Toronto: University of Toronto Press

Mani, Lata. 1987. 'Contentious Traditions: The Debate on SATI in Colonial India.' *Cultural Critique* 7:119-56

Miles, Robert. 1989. *Racism*. London: Routledge, Key Idea Series

Mohanty, Chandra Talpade. 1991. 'Cartographies of Struggle: Third World Women and the Politics of Feminism.' In Chandra T. Mohanty, Ann Russo, and Lourdes Torres, eds., *Third World Women and the Politics of Feminism*, 1-47. Bloomington, IN: Indiana University Press

Moore, Timothy E., and Leslie Cadeau. 1985. 'The Representation of Women, the Elderly and Minorities in Canadian Television Commercials.' *Canadian Journal of Behavioural Science* 17 (3):215-25

Mowlana, Hamid. 1979. 'Technology Versus Tradition: Communication in the Iranian Revolution.' *Journal of Communication* 29 (3):107-12

Mowlana, Hamid, and Elizabeth Robinson. 1976. 'Ethnic Mobilization and Communication Theory.' In Abdul Said and L.R. Simmons, eds., *Ethnicity in an International Context*, 16-47. New Jersey: Transaction

Peac Media Research. 1982. *The Role of Non-Whites in English Language Television and Advertising in Canada, Final Report*. Ottawa: Prepared for the Secretary of State

Roy, Patricia. 1980. 'The Illusion of Toleration: White Opinion of Asians in British Columbia, 1929-37.' In Victor Ujimoto and Gordon Hirabayashi, eds., *Visible Minorities and Multiculturalism: Asians in Canada*, 81-91. Toronto: Butterworths

Said, Edward. 1979. *Orientalism*. New York: Random

Scanlon, Joseph. 1977. 'The Sikhs of Vancouver.' In *Ethnicity and the Media*. Paris: UNESCO

Stam, Robert, and Louise Spence. 1985. 'Colonialism, Racism and Representation: An Introduction.' In Bill Nichols, ed., *Movies and Methods*. Vol. 2, 632-49. Berkeley: University of California Press

Stepan, Nancy Leys. 1990. 'Race and Gender: The Role of Analogy in Science.' In David Theo Goldberg, ed., *Anatomy of Racism*, 38-57. Minneapolis: University of Minnesota Press

Stott, Rebecca. 1989. 'The Dark Continent: Africa as Female Body in Haggard's Adventure Fiction.' *Feminist Review* 32 (Summer): 68-89

Tator, Carol. 1984. 'Mail Back Campaign.' *Currents* 2 (2):15-7

Tharu, Susie. 1989. 'Tracing Savitri's Pedigree: Victorian Racism and the Image of Women in Indo-Anglian Literature.' In Kumkum Sangari and Sudesh Vaid, eds., *Recasting Women, Essays in Colonial History*, 254-68. New Delhi: Kali for Women

Thobani, Sunera. 1991. 'News in Black and White.' *Diva: Journal of South Asian Women* 1 (1):56-60

–. 1992. 'Culture Isn't Cause of Violence.' *Vancouver Sun*, 3 January 1992, Opinions Page

Tuchman, Gaye. 1976. 'Telling Stories.' *Journal of Communication* 26:93-7

Ujimoto, Victor K., and Gordon Hirabayashi, eds. 1980. *Visible Minorities and Multiculturalism: Asians in Canada*. Toronto: Butterworths

van Dijk, Teun, ed. 1985. *Discourse and Communication*. New York: de Gruyter

–. 1991. *Racism and the Press*. London: Routledge

–. 1993. *Elite Discourse and Racism*. Sage Series on Race and Ethnic Relations. Vol. 6. Thousand Oaks, CA: Sage

Visram, Rozina. 1986. *Ayahs, Lascars and Princes, Indians in Britain, 1700-1947*. London: Pluto

White, Mimi. 1987. 'Ideological Analysis and Television.' In Robert C. Allen, ed. *Channels of Discourse*, 134-71. Chapel Hill, NC: University of North Carolina Press

Youngs, Tim. 1989. 'Morality and Ideology: The Portrayal of the Arranged Marriage in Contemporary British Asian Drama.' *Wasafiri* 9 (Winter):3-6

Keeping 'em Out: Gender, Race, and Class Biases in Canadian Immigration Policy

Yasmeen Abu-Laban

In 1993, Sunera Thobani, a Tanzanian-born single mother, became the first 'visible minority' president of the National Action Committee on the Status of Women. Thobani's legitimacy in representing Canadian women was publicly challenged in the House of Commons by Ontario MP John MacDougall, who falsely characterized Thobani as an 'illegal immigrant' (Witla, 348). MacDougall's error, with its hostile undertones, painfully illustrates the twisted understandings and assumptions that may infuse our understanding of race, gender, citizenship, national belonging, and immigration.

Thobani's experience raises questions concerning the meaning and place of people, women, immigrants, and the process of immigration in Canadian society. Canada, a settler-colony built upon the back of a pre-existing Aboriginal community by French and British settlers, is defined by immigration. Indeed, currently over 16 percent of Canadians are immigrants – a figure that has been about the same since Confederation (Canada, Statistics Canada, 1991, 8-12). But which potential immigrants get in? How fully are they citizens? What allows the MacDougalls of the world to erect barriers to the full exercise of citizenship rights? Are these processes connected? And if there is a connection, how do we understand it?

In examining these questions, I focus on Canadian immigration policy and the criteria used to define eligibility/ineligibility for formal Canadian citizenship. In doing this, I seek to join two important developments within contemporary social science. First, within feminist scholarship, the complex intersections among gender, race/ethnicity, and class have garnered increasing attention both as social relations that structure and variably impact the lives of men and women, and as forces that have played an important role in the nature of the development of settler societies, such as Canada (see Lorde; Bannerji; Stasiulis and Yuval-Davis). In keeping with this emergent recognition, in this analysis I address biases relating to gender, race/ethnicity, and class in the evolution of Canada's immigration policy, particularly over the post-Second World War period.

Second, over the past decade, across such varied disciplines as sociology, law, philosophy, and political science, citizenship has (re)emerged as an important theoretical concept (see Kymlicka and Norman). *Substantive citizenship* has been the focal point for theorizing citizenship. Substantive citizenship involves pressing issues relating to equality of rights and opportunities; treatment and life condition; and, not least, participatory involvement that ought to come from holding formal citizenship. Despite different emphases, critical approaches to citizenship – such as feminist and Marxist – suggest that in liberal democracies substantive citizenship, with full and equal rights and opportunities, has not followed from formal citizenship (see Marx; Pateman). In short, being a citizen is no guarantee of equality; real equality is hampered by inequities resulting from membership in stigmatized and minoritized groups (see Young).

Despite the many contributions made in the ever-burgeoning citizenship literature, there is a major gap when it comes to discussions of immigration and naturalization.[1] This is an amazing omission because there is a very real association between migration and the question of citizenship. However, because the lens has not been focused on immigration, the question of the extension of *formal citizenship* has not been theoretically integrated into most contemporary citizenship debates; rather, formal citizenship has tended to be treated as a static legal category and, at best, an implicit backdrop to questions relating to substantive citizenship.

In connecting recent developments in feminist scholarship with a more complete understanding of citizenship – one that explicitly links formal and substantive citizenship – I wish to emphasize from the outset that the primary purpose of immigration policy is to deny Canadian citizenship to the majority of the world's inhabitants. Thus, by its very existence, immigration policy – that is, the regulation of the movement and settlement of people – is about excluding. Immigration policy serves an important function in maintaining an inequitable world system (Zolberg, 445) because it involves the denial of citizenship and its attendant rights, particularly the right to enter and legally remain in a country (Yuval-Davis, 61). However, by looking at Canadian power relations and immigration policy in relation to citizenship, it is possible to argue that there is an interrelationship between the criteria used to winnow out potential citizens, as established through state immigration laws and policy practices, and existing inequities based on gender, race/ethnicity, and class among Canadian citizens.

In demonstrating this argument, my analysis highlights why immigration, as well as immigration policy, is of broad relevance in the construction of Canada. Historically, the overtly racist character of immigration policy has influenced the gender and class composition of immigrant groups. While post-1967 immigration policy is distinctive because of the removal of formal racism (Hawkins, 11; Avery, 238), biases relating to gender, race/ethnicity, and class still structure a purportedly neutral and universal policy in a manner that is intensifying as Canada enters the twenty-first century.

Gender, Labour, and the Construction of a 'White Settler Colony'

Immigration policy in Canada includes the acts, regulations, and practices that affect which foreigners are allowed to come to Canada and, ultimately, who may be granted citizenship. In terms of the broad historical perspective, two issues have been of long-standing importance with respect to immigration. Alluding to the historic project of developing Canada as a *'white* settler colony' (Stasiulis and Jhappan, 96-9), the first issue has to do with cultural considerations relating to religion and race/ethnicity, and the second issue has to do with immediate labour needs. For most of Canada's history, Canadian policy has explicitly favoured white Protestants (particularly those of British origin). Although incoming immigrants have not always met the ideal of the model settler and potential citizen, this generally occurred only when there was insufficient labour available in Canada or with regard to countries deemed 'ethnoculturally similar' (Baureiss, 18). Hence, the secure settlement of racialized immigrant minorities and their kin was contingent, not only on the ideological construction of a model settler, but also on the perceived economic needs of the nation. These features have interacted in a complex way with gender and gendered notions of appropriate work roles and, therefore, also highlight the salience of gender in relation to nation and nation-building strategies.

To illustrate these features by way of one historic example, consider John A. Macdonald's national policy, which, as it evolved, emphasized constructing a railway and settling the west. Between 1880 and 1884 Chinese labourers – primarily men – were recruited to work in the most dangerous jobs during the construction of the Canadian Pacific Railway and received little by way of remuneration. Clearly, such conditions were seen as *deserved* for males of certain groups only. As CPR president Thomas Shaughnessy once commented, 'Men who seek employment on railway construction are, as a rule, a class accustomed to roughing it' (cited in Avery, 6). However, following the completion of the railway in 1885, the federal government introduced the Chinese Immigration Act, 1885, which launched the infamous 'head tax' system. Chinese immigration was halted through a series of increasingly high head taxes and then virtually banned altogether in legislation of 1923 (Ferguson, 2; Malarek, 6).

Such intensifying restrictive measures had profound consequences for Chinese families and communities in Canada as well as in China. While a few women were allowed to enter Canada from China between 1885 and 1900 – subsequently some were denounced as prostitutes because in this role they were seen as lessening the threat of miscegenation that single male Chinese workers posed to the dominant white society – generally speaking, the wives and children of Chinese labourers were excluded from entering the country (Das Gupta, 153). Such state practices and policies, which aimed at restricting settlement, were not isolated. Indeed, the historic policies erected vis-à-vis Japanese and South Asian families (Das Gupta, 141-74) actually discouraged the permanent settlement of racialized immigrant minorities.

Socially constructed and gendered notions of men's *public* work and women's *private* work are particularly evident when examining the primarily female migration movement of domestic workers. From the 1900s to the 1960s, a host of programs actively favoured white, single, female European domestics. These were the people who were met with the least restrictive conditions for permanently residing in the country (Bakan and Stasiulis, 317). Indeed, women entering from England and Scotland were actually recruited on the grounds that they were women of 'good stock' who could serve the nation as future wives of white men and future mothers of white children (ibid.).

Generally, this overt racial and ethnic organizing principle structured all immigration intake through the first two decades following the Second World War. During the Depression and the Second World War immigration was restricted, the minimal activity in this area being symbolized by the abolition of the Department of Immigration and Colonization (Cashmore, 419). However, following the Second World War, when Canada emerged as a victorious and potentially prosperous country, immigration was reemphasized as a way of filling immediate labour gaps along the path of economic recovery (ibid.). Here, European (male) labourers, agriculturists, and their immediate families (spouse, unmarried children, parents, or orphaned nieces/nephews) were eligible for entry (*Canada Year Book* 1947, cited in Rawlyk, 290).

Immigration policy was further amplified by Liberal Prime Minister Mackenzie King in a 1947 speech in which he firmly advocated the restriction of immigration from 'the orient' in the name of preserving 'the character of the population'(ibid.). The 'orient' referred to everything in the Eastern hemisphere outside of Europe (Hawkins, 94). In brief, those from 'the orient' were socially constructed as *the Other* – the *them* who were supposedly essentially different from *us* Canadians (see also Said).

In 1952, the Liberal government introduced a new immigration act that became law in 1953. In total, the following reasons were allowed for limiting entry:

(i) nationality, citizenship, ethnic group, occupation, class or geographical area of origin;

(ii) peculiar customs, habits, modes of life or methods of holding property;

(iii) unsuitability having regard to the climatic, economic, social, industrial, educational, labour, health, or other requirements existing, temporarily or otherwise;
(iv) probable inability to become readily assimilated or to assume the
  duties and responsibilities of Canadian citizenship within a reasonable
  time after admission (*Canada Year Book* 1957-8, cited in Rawlyk, 293).

Thus, the minister was given sweeping powers to determine who was and
was not to be allowed into Canada. By interpreting these clauses in various ways, the minister could easily prevent the entry of any applicant. The
act also allowed for a wide range of discretionary powers for officers who
'acted as front line enforcers' of immigration law (Cashmore, 420). The
racial discrimination evident in King's statement and subsequent Orders-
in-Council was, therefore, sustained through the new act, and preference
was given to those immigrating from the United States, Britain, and
Western Europe. The least preferred countries remained those in Asia.

Therefore, in the two decades immediately following the Second World
War, Canadian immigration policy joined with its predecessors in hierarchically ranking peoples of the world. This ethnic/racial ordering clearly
reflected Canada's prevailing white British (and, to a lesser extent, French)
ethnic power structure, itself a legacy of the settler-colonization of the
country. Furthermore, within this global ethnic pecking order, factors
relating to occupation/class (e.g., employability in gendered occupational
categories), as well as a vast array of 'suitability' factors (habits, customs,
potential for assimilation), acted to further differentiate those fit and those
unfit for Canadian citizenship.

The Construction of 'Skills' and the Perpetuation of Inequities

It is true that immigration policy of the post-1967 period does not contain
the overt racism of the policies governing most of Canada's history. Today,
there are immigrants arriving from more diverse countries than was the
case in the past (Canada, Statistics Canada 1994, 39).[2] Yet, Canada's immigration policy still works to produce differential outcomes relating to class,
gender, *and* race/ethnicity.

The post-1967 changes were foreshadowed in the preceding decade.
Beginning in the late 1950s/early 1960s, the economic buoyancy that had
marked the mid-1950s began to deteriorate and regulations governing
unsponsored immigrants (i.e., immigrants without family in Canada)
changed (Cashmore, 422). This was codified into law under the
Conservative government of John Diefenbaker in 1962, when a new regulation combined protecting economic interests, purportedly establishing
more *universal criteria* of admission. This new policy required that an
unsponsored (generally male) applicant be admitted if 'by reason of his

education, training, skills or other special qualifications [the applicant] is likely to be able to establish himself successfully in Canada' (D. Corbett, cited in Satzewich, 78).

This addition had the formal effect of changing previous restrictions on Asian, African, and Caribbean countries regarding unsponsored immigrants. Nonetheless, there were still restrictions placed on these countries vis-à-vis sponsored relatives (Canada, Manpower and Immigration 1974a, 28). Moreover, there is evidence to suggest that the openness of immigration officials toward accepting unsponsored immigrants from previously excluded countries between 1962 and 1966 was about the same as it had been in earlier years (see Satzewich, 93).

The great significance of the 1962 formulation of policy lies in how the focus began to shift toward emphasizing not only the particular occupations that potential immigrants could fill but also their particular skills. Skills, defined by such features as education and training, were a harbinger of a new organizing principle in selecting potential citizens.

Prime Minister Pearson's Liberal government's 1966 *White Paper on Immigration* was the major policy statement on the course that immigration policy should follow. The *White Paper* asserted that 'it is in Canada's interest to accept, and if need be to encourage, the entry of as many immigrants as can readily be absorbed' (Canada, Manpower and Immigration 1966, 5). The *White Paper*, in grappling with the particular question of who should and should not be permanently admissible, sought to 'fairly and effectively' decide this matter (6). Thus, the *White Paper* advocated that 'the answers must involve no discrimination by reason of race, colour or religion, and consequently must be universally applicable' (ibid.).

While this document has been said to have 'unambiguously heralded the total end to racial discrimination in immigration policy' (Canada, Manpower and Immigration 1974a, 32), caution is warranted because the *White Paper* also emphasized another goal; namely, that 'immigration policy must be consistent with national economic policy in general' (Canada, Manpower and Immigration 1966, 7). More specifically, the *White Paper* called for immigrants who are skilled because 'if large numbers of unskilled immigrants come to Canada when the economy is particularly buoyant, the problems of poverty exposed by any economic readjustment will be more severe' (12). Thus, the *White Paper* stressed that 'increasingly we will have to explore new sources of *well-qualified* immigrants' (11). In the buoyant economy of the 1960s, and in the context of dwindling sources of immigration from Europe, the *White Paper* signalled a shift to the long-term need to merge immigration planning with employment policy by arguing that 'a selective immigration policy today must be planned as a steady policy of recruitment based on long-term considerations of economic growth' (12).

The 1966 *White Paper* merged the concept of non-discrimination with a belief that Canada's expanding industrial economy required skilled immigrants. As a result of this, regulations were introduced in 1967 that capitalized on the arguments made in the *White Paper*. The significant features of the 1967 regulations were the stated elimination of discrimination on the basis of race or nationality and the creation of a 'universally applicable point system' (Canada, Manpower and Immigration 1974a, 33-4). The point system was to aid in the selection of applicants by evaluating them according to the same criteria.

The 1967 regulations, including the point system, were enacted through Orders-in-Council because the 1952 immigration act was still in force. It was not until 1976 that a new immigration act was introduced. This act guaranteed that admission should 'not discriminate on the grounds of race, national or ethnic origin, colour, religion or sex' (Canada, Immigration Act 1976, 1197).[3] The Immigration Act, 1976, was preceded and informed by a government-sponsored commission that put out a four-volume work in 1974, referred to as the *Green Paper*. Occurring in an era of stagflation, and with less buoyant economic prospects than there were in the 1960s, this document marks a transition from the arguments that had guided the *White Paper* less than a decade earlier (at least with respect to the clear call for more immigration). Moreover, the *Green Paper* was, arguably, couched in covertly racist concerns about 'the environment' (Richmond, 106). Nonetheless, it is noteworthy that the *Green Paper* observed that the 1966 *White Paper* 'set out more thoroughly than ever before the Government's appreciation of the economic determinants of immigration policy' (Canada, Manpower and Immigration 1974b, 19) and that it upheld the point system as 'the key to welding manpower and immigration policies together as parts of a single endeavor' (22).

The skills discourse, coupled with the point system, forms the heart of the contemporary organizing principle of Canadian immigration policy. The point system seeks to evaluate independent immigrants (i.e., immigrants who are not sponsored by family members and who are not refugees) on the same skills criteria. It has been suggested that the defining characteristics of modern states include 'what have come to be accepted as natural (rational and normal) state functions, of certifying, counting, reporting, registering, classifying and identifying' (Cohn and Dirks, 225). The point system is entirely in keeping with these tenets of the modern state in that it assumes that the 'skills' of applicants – indeed, their entire worth as potential Canadians – are mathematically measurable.

Originally, acceptable applicants were required to obtain 50 out of 100 possible points (Hawkins, 405). Since then, the point system has been subjected to ongoing revision and, as of 1993, applicants must now attain 70 out of 107 points. These are based on: (1) education (16 points maximum);

(2) specific vocational preparation (18 points maximum); (3) experience (8 points maximum); (4) occupational demand (10 points maximum); (5) arranged offer of employment (10 points maximum); (6) age (10 points maximum); (7) knowledge of official languages (15 points maximum); (8) personal suitability (10 points maximum); and (9) current need given the overall number of applicants and desired level of immigration (10 points maximum) (Segal, 48-56).

The Immigration Act, 1976, recognizes three categories of immigrants: family class (where Canadian citizens and permanent residents older than eighteen can sponsor certain relatives who wish to immigrate to Canada); refugees; and independent (which now includes assisted relatives, retirees, investors, entrepreneurs, and self-employed persons). In terms of yearly intake over the 1980s, the independent category has tended to be smaller than the category of family class and larger than the category of refugees. Nonetheless, the independent category is 'the engine that pulls the immigration train' (Islam, 218). While the emphasis on skills in the point system, ironically, affects even refugees, the point system is used explicitly for the category of independent immigrants.[4] However, not every independent applicant is assessed on all the selection criteria. For example, business immigrants (such as entrepreneurs chosen for their ability to create jobs or investors chosen for their ability to infuse capital) are not assessed on such factors as occupation or arranged employment (Canada, Employment and Immigration, *Canada's Immigration Law*, 12). As well, applicants coming in as assisted relatives are given 'bonus points' (Segal, 55).

In comparison with the first two decades following the Second World War, it is evident that the point system has served to further mesh immigration with labour market requirements, labour cycles, and the interests of business. While the adoption of the point system putatively introduces an objective, neutral test linked with seemingly value-free economic considerations, the requirements are not value-free. The so-called indicators of worth are socially constructed and reflect the prevailing Canadian political and economic power structure. This can be seen in the emphasis on knowledge of the French and/or English language and the fact that applicants to Quebec are judged on a different version of the point system, which awards more potential points for knowledge of French. It is also seen in the fact that after age forty-four applicants begin to lose points on age, so that by age forty-nine and above, no points are awarded in this category.

Canada's preference for immigrants who are defined as capable of providing economic benefit has differentially advantaged would-be immigrants in terms of class, gender, and geographic location (and, therefore, race/ethnicity). For example, not all people have the opportunity to meet the educational requirements because education is more accessible, and is available over longer periods, in some countries than it is in others (Law

Union of Ontario, 40). In addition, throughout all countries, women and the poor have been notoriously disadvantaged with regard to educational opportunities.

In addition, the point system's emphasis on certain types of paid skilled work favours work typically performed by men. Women who enter Canada, therefore, usually come as the dependent spouses of male independent immigrants. Indeed, single women, and women in non-marital relationships, are particularly disadvantaged by the point system (Fincher et al., 149-84). Moreover, the category of 'domestic worker,' which consists almost completely of women from the Third World, comes under a separate program not covered by the point system, thereby implying that domestic work does not require skills (ibid.)! In short, the point system reinforces the socially constructed dichotomy between (women's) less valuable private household work and (men's) more valuable public work.

Both Ng (187) and Boyd (60) observe that the point system has systematically structured women's subordination within immigrant families and the labour market, as women are generally the ones who come in as 'dependants' of the (male) independent family member. Moreover, this status of dependent disadvantages immigrant women who need to gain access to state-sponsored official language programs and other social programs designated for independent immigrants (Fincher et al., 149-84). The consequence of immigrant women's dependence on independent fiancés or husbands is heightened in cases of domestic abuse, where 'women face a "choice" of breaking sponsorship and risking deportation or staying silently within an abusive marriage' (Das Gupta, 167).

These long-standing biases inherent in the point system of selection appear even sharper when one considers the federal government's emphasis, particularly under the Mulroney Conservatives, on business immigrants and the introduction in 1986 of the investor immigrant program (Islam, 226). A popular criticism frequently levelled at business immigrants, particularly investors, is that they are buying Canadian citizenship. This criticism implies that it is somewhat more honourable to be *born* with citizenship. Moreover, the theme of buying citizenship masks the degree to which the requirements for independent immigrants are a contemporary form of head tax, given the capital required of investors or the costs associated with the training and education that is likely to make an independent applicant successful (Taylor, 10-11).

In addition to the biases flowing from the requirements for independent immigrants, the fact remains that potential immigrants continue to have differential access to immigration posts abroad, with disproportionately more posts existing in European countries and the United States than in the Third World. For example, in 1992, there were 64 Canadian Immigration Missions: 5 in Africa; 15 in Asia; 13 in Latin America; 19 in Europe (including Moscow); 11 in the United States; and 1 in Australia (Canada, Employment and Immigration 1992). Taking the countries of the Third World (Africa, Asia, and Latin America combined) 51.6 percent of Canadian posts were set aside to cover 79.6 percent of the world's population (world figures derived from Population Division of the United Nations, cited in *The Canadian Global Almanac, 1992,* 427-8)! Moreover, coinciding with this uneven distribution of posts, research also suggests that there are lengthy differences between how long it takes to process applicants in many Third World countries and how long it takes to process those in Western countries (Malarek, 254). The uneven distribution of posts, and the time differences in the processing of applications, suggests that while immigration policy is officially non-discriminatory, there are, nonetheless, sanctioned practices that act in a discriminatory manner with respect to the geographical location and, hence, the ethnic/racial background of potential immigrants.

Finally, as in the two decades following the Second World War, suitability factors remain largely in the hands of individual immigration officers. The point system leaves room for the personal discretion of an immigration officer concerning the suitability of an applicant and, therefore, room for the kind of ethnic and other biases that characterized earlier postwar policy (Law Union of Ontario, 40). The point system, while purportedly universal, is clearly flawed and potentially prejudicial as an instrument for selection.

The Future of Immigration: Reconstructing 'Skills' for a New Era
As Fincher et al. note, in the realm of public policy, immigration policies and practices seem to have been relatively uniquely shielded from the criticisms of their masculinist biases (184). Indeed, far from moving in the direction of rectifying some of the gender biases described above in Canadian immigration policy, current policy debates and policy shifts have moved in the direction of reasserting the need for immigrants with *skills.*

In Canada, immigration has now become far more important an issue in public and political debate than it has been at any other time in the postwar period. Whereas journalist Victor Malarek asserted in 1987 that 'immigration policy has been, and remains, one of the least debated and least understood of the major public policy issues' (ix), by the 1993 federal election, immigration was the topic of partisan debate. This has to do with the addition of the Reform Party to the Canadian party system, coupled with an ongoing breakdown in partisan and elite consensus on the value of multiculturalism policy and its symbolism (Abu-Laban 1994, 242-63).

At its foundation in 1987, the Reform Party criticized immigration policy for altering 'the ethnic makeup of the country.' However, in an effort to be more electable, in 1991 it abandoned this phrasing (Abu-Laban and Stasiulis, 373). However, it is notable that debate over the annual intake of immigrants and the skills of immigrants seems to have replaced the direct references to ethnicity in the Reform Party's more recent attacks. Thus, in 1994, when then Liberal Immigration Minister Sergio Marchi announced that the annual immigration level would remain at 250,000 (Canada, House of Commons, 803), Reform Party immigration critic Art Hanger argued that incoming immigrants were not only too numerous, but they were also unlikely to be of economic benefit because the majority of them were not independent immigrants 'chosen for their human capital, chosen for their skills, their ability to quickly and independently integrate into Canadian life as well as their ability to contribute to the economic needs of this country' (796).

In 1994, the Chrétien Liberals made immigration a topic of major public consultation and, following a somewhat contrived process, later that year came up with a package of adjustments. Proposed changes were premised on the contention that 'our citizenship and immigration program must be more than fair and compassionate, it must be affordable and sustainable' (Canada, Citizenship and Immigration 1994a, viii). In this context, plans for the years 1995 to 2000 are clearly moving toward giving priority to independent immigrants over family immigrants and refugees while, at the same time, lowering the annual numerical intake of immigrants (Canada, Citizenship and Immigration 1994b, 13). The post-1967 immigration policy stress on skills is now taking on new intensity in the context of massive economic restructuring and ascendant neoliberalism. Hence, according to the government, 'immigrants selected for their skills and abilities are more likely to earn higher incomes and spur economic growth' and less likely to make use of social welfare (14-5).

Conclusion

To take a step back from the narrative of early pioneering in Canada is to be reminded that this country is a settler-colony and that immigration, not just natural increase (births outnumbering deaths), has expanded the numbers of its citizens and the range of expropriated and settled territory. The winnowing out of potential immigrants has profoundly shaped the evolving nation.

It is true that, in a context in which the emphasis is on skills, the state's policy of formal non-discrimination has had an impact on the character of contemporary immigration to Canada. Within the parameters of a changing discourse on immigration and immigrants – one that emphasizes skills – Canada has increasingly granted formal citizenship to more non-white immigrants from the Third World than it has in the past. This has made for a much more complex class and ethnic structure within Canada than was the case in an earlier period described by John Porter (Porter, 73; Reitz, 185).

Yet, at the same time, many aspects of substantive citizenship remain linked to being a member of what Porter called the 'charter' (French and British) origin groups. This may be seen in the comparatively low status accorded to multiculturalism in successive proposed constitutional amendments from Meech Lake to Charlottetown, coupled with current attacks on multiculturalism; the underrepresentation of ethnic and 'visible' minorities (particularly females) in the House of Commons; and the popular assumption that 'real' Canadians are white and (originally) European (see also Abu-Laban and Stasiulis, 365-86).

In the final analysis, gender, ethnic, and class biases and hierarchies in immigration policy reflect the Canadian power structure and are unlikely to be completely eliminated until they are expunged from the general population. In this sense, inequalities that govern the process of how formal citizenship is granted, as seen in immigration, are intimately connected to inequalities in substantive citizenship among Canadians. Hence, the socially constructed and historically specific boundaries that serve to grant and deny Canadian citizenship to foreigners do not exist in isolation from the Canadian political community but, rather, reveal its very essence.

Notes

1 Indeed, it is interesting to note that Kymlicka and Norman *explicitly* reject – though they do not explain why – any discussion of citizenship in relation to immigration and naturalization in their otherwise well-documented survey of the literature on citizenship (353). Their deliberate oversight is unfortunate because several interesting empirical and theoretical works have addressed citizenship from the vantage point of immigration and naturalization. For informative accounts of Western industrialized countries, see Brubaker; Layton-Henry; Yuval-Davis; and Soysal. For a fuller discussion of theorizing citizenship and immigration, see also Abu-Laban 1995, Chapter 3.

2 Prior to 1961, some 90 percent of immigrants to Canada were born in Europe, but between 1981 and 1991 this figure fell to 25 percent (Canada, Statistics Canada 1994, 39).

3 This was subsequently reworded to state that admission should not 'discriminate in a manner inconsistent with the *Canadian Charter of Rights and Freedoms*' (Marrocco and Goslett, 19).

4 While the point system does not formally apply to refugees, it is interesting that 'the applicant's age, level of education, job skills and knowledge of English or French are used as guides in determining whether the refugee will be able to cope' (Canada, Employment and Immigration, *Canada's Immigration Law*, 16).

Works Cited

Abu-Laban, Yasmeen. 1994. 'The Politics of Race and Ethnicity: Multiculturalism as a Contested Arena.' In James Bickerton and Alain G. Gagnon, eds., *Canadian Politics*, 2nd ed., 242-63. Peterborough, ON: Broadview

–. 1995. 'The Nation-State in an Era of Regionalism and Globalization: A Comparative Study of the Politics of Migration in the United States and France.' PhD dissertation, Carleton University, Ottawa

Abu-Laban, Yasmeen, and Daiva Stasiulis. 1992. 'Ethnic Pluralism Under Siege: Popular and Partisan Opposition to Multiculturalism.' *Canadian Public Policy* 17 (4):365-86

Avery, Donald. 1995. *Reluctant Host: Canada's Response to Immigrant Workers, 1896-1994*. Toronto: McClelland & Stewart

Bakan, Abigail, and Daiva Stasiulis. 1995. 'Making the Match: Domestic Placement Agencies and the Racialization of Women's Household Work.' *Signs: Journal of Women in Culture and Society* 20 (2):303-35

Bannerji, Himani, ed. 1995. *Thinking Through: Essays on Feminism, Marxism and Anti-Racism.* Toronto: Women's Press

Baureiss, Gunter. 1987. 'Chinese Immigration, Chinese Stereotypes and Chinese Labour.' *Canadian Ethnic Studies* 19 (3):15-34

Boyd, Monica. 1986. 'Immigrant Women in Canada.' In Rita J. Simon and Caroline Brettell, eds., *International Migration*, 47-79. Toronto: Roman and Allenheld

Brubaker, Rogers, ed. 1989. *Immigration and the Politics of Citizenship in Europe and North America.* Lanham, MD: German Marshall Fund and University Press of America

Canada, Citizenship and Immigration. 1994a. *Into the 21st Century: A Strategy for Immigration and Citizenship.* Ottawa: Supply and Services

–. 1994b. *A Broader Vision: Plan 1995-2000.* Ottawa: Supply and Services

Canada, Employment and Immigration. N.d. *Canada's Immigration Law.* Ottawa: Supply and Services

–. 1992. *Mimeo.* (October)

Canada, House of Commons. 1994. *Debates.* 133,013. Wednesday, 2 February 1994

Canada, Immigration Act. 1976. *Revised Statutes of Canada 1976-77.* Ottawa: Queen's Printer

Canada, Manpower and Immigration. 1966. *White Paper on Immigration.* Ottawa: Queen's Printer

–. 1974a. *The Immigration Program.* Ottawa: Information Canada

–. 1974b. *Immigration Policy Perspectives.* Ottawa: Information Canada

Canada, Statistics Canada. 1991. *Immigration and Citizenship*, 1991 Census, Catalogue Number 95-316. Ottawa: Supply and Services

–. 1994. *1991 Census Highlights as Released by the Daily*, Catalogue 96-340E. Ottawa: Minister of Industry, Science and Technology

The Canadian Global Almanac, 1992. 1992. Toronto: Global

Cashmore, Ernest. 1978. 'The Social Organization of Canadian Immigration Law.' *Canadian Journal of Sociology* 3 (4):409-29

Cohn, Bernard S., and Nicholas B. Dirks. 1988. 'Beyond the Fringe: The Nation State, Colonialism and the Technologies of Power.' *Journal of Historical Sociology* 1 (2):224-9

Das Gupta, Tania. 1995. 'Families of Native Peoples, Immigrants and People of Colour.' In Nancy Mandell and Ann Duffy, eds., *Canadian Families: Diversity, Conflict and Change*, 141-74. Toronto: Harcourt Brace

Ferguson, Ted. 1975. *A White Man's Country.* Toronto: Doubleday

Fincher, Ruth, et al. 1994. 'Gender and Migration Policy.' In Howard Adelman et al., eds., *Immigration and Refugee Policy: Australia and Canada Compared.* Vol. 1. Toronto: University of Toronto Press

Hawkins, Freda. 1988. *Canada and Immigration: Public Policy and Public Concern.* 2nd ed. Montreal and Kingston: McGill-Queen's University Press

Islam, Nasir. 1989. 'Canada's Immigration Policy: Compassion, Economic Necessity or Lifeboat Ethics.' In Katherine A. Graham, ed., *How Ottawa Spends: 1989-90*, 209-46. Ottawa: Carleton University Press

Kymlicka, Will, and W.J. Norman. 1994. 'Return of the Citizen: A Survey of Recent Work on Citizenship Theory.' *Ethics* 104 (2):352-81

Law Union of Ontario. 1981. *The Immigrant's Handbook: A Critical Guide.* Montreal: Black Rose

Layton-Henry, Zig, ed. 1989. *The Political Rights of Migrant Workers in Western Europe.* London: Sage

Lorde, Audre. 1984. *Sister Outsider.* Trumansburg, NY: Crossing

Malarek, Victor. 1987. *Haven's Gate: Canada's Immigration Fiasco.* Toronto: Macmillan

Marrocco, Frank N., and Henry M. Goslett. 1992. *The Annotated Immigration Act of Canada.* Toronto: Carswell

Marx, Karl. 1963. 'On the Jewish Question.' In T.B. Bottomore, ed., *Karl Marx: Early Writings*, 3-40. New York: McGraw-Hill

Ng, Roxana. 1988. 'Immigrant Women and Institutionalized Racism.' In Sandra Burt et al., eds., *Changing Patterns: Women in Canada*, 184-203. Toronto: McClelland & Stewart

Pateman, Carol. 1988. *The Sexual Contract*. Oxford: Polity

Porter, John. 1965. *The Vertical Mosaic*. Toronto: University of Toronto Press

Rawlyk, G.A. 1962. 'Canada's Immigration Policy, 1945-1962.' *Dalhousie Review* 42 (3):287-300

Reitz, Jeffrey. 1981. *The Survival of Ethnic Groups*. Toronto: McGraw-Hill Ryerson

Richmond, Anthony. 1988. *Immigration and Ethnic Conflict*. Toronto: Macmillan

Said, Edward. 1979. *Orientalism*. New York: Random

Satzewich, Vic. 1989. 'Racism and Canadian Immigration Policy: The Government's View of Caribbean Migration, 1962-1966.' *Canadian Ethnic Studies* 21 (1):77-97

Segal, Gary S. 1994. *Immigrating to Canada*. 10th ed. Vancouver: Self-Counsel

Soysal, Yasemin. 1994. *Limits of Citizenship*. Chicago: University of Chicago Press

Stasiulis, Daiva, and Radha Jhappan. 1995. 'The Fractious Politics of a Settler Society: Canada.' In Daiva Stasiulis and Nira Yuval-Davis, eds., *Unsettling Settler Societies: Articulations of Gender, Race, Ethnicity and Class*, 97-131. London: Sage

Stasiulis, Daiva, and Nira Yuval-Davis, eds. 1995. *Unsettling Settler Societies: Articulations of Gender, Race, Ethnicity and Class*. London: Sage

Taylor, K.W. 1991. 'Racism in Canadian Immigration Policy.' *Canadian Ethnic Studies* 23 (1):1-20

Witla, William. 1995. 'A Chronology of Women in Canada.' In Nancy Mandell, ed., *Feminist Issues: Race, Class and Sexuality*, 315-49. Scarborough, ON: Prentice Hall

Young, Iris Marion. 1989. 'Polity and Group Difference: A Critique of the Ideal of Universal Citizenship.' *Ethics* 99 (2):250-74

Yuval-Davis, Nira. 1989. 'The Citizenship Debate: Women, Ethnic Processes and the State.' *Feminist Review* 39 (Fall):58-68

Zolberg, Aristide. 1993. 'International Migration.' In Joel Krieger, ed., *The Oxford Companion to Politics of the World*, 444-6. New York: Oxford University Press

Part 2: Constructions of Race and Gender

Documenting Racism: Sharon Pollock's *The Komagata Maru Incident*

Sherrill Grace and Gabriele Helms

To admit Orientals in large numbers would mean in the end the extinction of the white people, and we always have in mind the necessity of keeping this a white man's country.
– Sir Richard McBride,
Premier of British Columbia, May 1914

As a Canadian, I feel that much of our history has been misrepresented and even hidden from us. Until we recognize our past, we cannot change our future.
– Sharon Pollock, 'Playwright's Note,'
The Komagata Maru Incident, March 1978

On 23 May 1914 the Japanese-owned steamer *Komagata Maru* entered Burrard Inlet with 376 passengers who were hoping to settle in Canada. These immigrants were East Indian, the majority of them Sikhs and veterans of the British army. They all carried British passports and were, thus, British subjects legally entitled to enter and settle in this country. However, Vancouver saw itself as a white city in 1914, and it was determined to stay that way (see Figure 1). Two months later, when the *Komagata Maru* sailed back to India, only 24 of the 376 passengers had been allowed to disembark; the rest were blocked by special Orders-in-Council from the Office of Canadian Immigration. One of these 'Orders' (P.C. 24) stipulated that a legal immigrant had to arrive in the Vancouver harbour after a non-stop voyage from his or her port of embarkation, an impossible feat in 1914; the other (P.C. 23) imposed a head tax of $200, which those on board the *Komagata Maru* could not pay. The newspapers of the day ran inflammatory, racist stories, and public sentiment against the would-be immigrants was whipped into a frenzy. Supplies on the ship ran out, and those on board suffered acute deprivation.

The records tell us that one man, Inspector William Hopkinson of the

Figure 1 Cruiser HMCS *Rainbow* guarding the *Komagata Maru*
(Vancouver Public Library, 6229)

Immigration Department, was charged with handling the crisis and that
he urged his already established ring of informers within the local Sikh
community to forewarn him of any effort to assist those on board. A few
weeks after the departure of the *Komagata Maru* on 23 July, some Sikh
informers were assassinated by members of the Sikh community.
Hopkinson himself was murdered on 21 October 1914 by Mewa Singh,
who was arrested, tried, and finally executed on 11 January 1915, by which
time the shameful events of the summer of 1914 were swept aside with the
outbreak of the First World War. The story of the *Komagata Maru* was not
widely reintroduced to Canadians until Sharon Pollock's play opened at
the Vancouver Playhouse in January 1976.[1]

Pollock's *The Komagata Maru Incident* is a powerful one-act play of about
seventy-five minutes duration that sets out to put the historical record
straight by reminding us of this forgotten event in our history and, in the
process, anatomizing the nature and dynamics of racism, not only as a specific episode in the past, but also as a pervasive force in the present. The
play has a fascinating hybrid form: a realistic story is dramatized in a
highly presentational style that draws upon the conventions and aims of
documentary art. An appreciation of this hybrid documentary form is
essential to our understanding of how the play works and to our evaluation of its success.

We have chosen this play for closer analysis because of what it tells us,
through its documentary strategies and hybrid presentational/representa-
tional dramaturgy, about race, gender, and – most important – the

construction of Canada, or of Canada as constructed by the ideologically motivated policies of Euro-Canadians. Early reviewers soon realized that *The Komagata Maru Incident* was not an example of detached theatre. Responses were divided: some reviewers saw Pollock as an 'angry lady' (Wyman) who had written 'a strident, self-serving, leftist propaganda piece' (*Calgary Herald*), and others welcomed the play's 'frontal assault on our smug certainties' (Portman) and its 'direct challenge to WASP complacency' (Hofsess). Before we consider some of the documents consulted by Pollock and the intertexts that inform our understanding of the *Komagata Maru* incident today, we would like to offer some general observations about how the play interrogates racism and sexism and how it exposes the mechanisms through which race and gender support the construction of a white, masculinist construction of Canada.

Among the central elements of the play are its setting – a brothel – its governing theatrical metaphor – the circus – and its three central characters. Pollock's Hopkinson, the immigration inspector charged with getting rid of the unwelcome passengers, is of mixed racial origin.[2] His blond father, whom he idolizes, was British, but his mother, whom he tries to deny and whom he betrays, was Sikh. Evy, the whore with a heart of gold, recognizes Hopkinson for the hypocrite, racist, and fool that he is, but she continues to love and pity him. Pollock gives Evy the lines that unequivocally condemn racism and through her allows us to see how a man like Hopkinson victimizes others and himself because of his racist attitudes and his admiration for white heterosexual masculine identity.

The third character is called 'T.S.' (for 'The System,' perhaps, or for T.S. Eaton), and it is he who holds the entire play together.[3] Dressed in black tails and top hat, with gloves, cane, and goatee, he is the master of ceremonies, the circus magician and barker, the sinister puppeteer and shape-shifting confidence man who 'plays many roles'; he is a politician of mephistophelean proportions. He sets the stage, arouses the characters to action, soft-shoes from one episode to the next, spouts the racist propaganda of government officials, and reminds us constantly that everything we see – *and live* – is theatre, that the Vancouver (or Canada) described in our history books and government policies is a deliberate construction, a product of political legerdemain.

As such a product, of course, Canada can be changed, and this need for and possibility of change is the play's clearest message. Pollock's dramatization of construction, like her staging – in the flesh and blood of 'characters' in live performance – of racism and sexism derives its force from her strategic deployment of documentary evidence within one of the oldest of stage metaphors: the Renaissance idea that 'all the world's a stage' (Shakespeare, *As You Like It* II.vii 139) and life but 'a poor player / That struts and frets his hour upon [it] / And then is heard no more'

(Shakespeare, *Macbeth* V.v 24-6). She has merged the available 'facts' (statistics, dates, recorded events, references to news coverage, government regulations, political speeches) with the 'fiction' of theatre, clothed both in the metaphor of staging (in a brothel, on board a ship/cage), and presented her story as a species of circus sideshow in what we are calling historiographic docudrama.

There is a long and illustrious tradition of documentary art in this country, from the films of John Grierson and the National Film Board (NFB), to the theories of Dorothy Livesay and Stephen Scobie on the documentary poem, to highly successful plays like Rick Salutin's *1837: The Farmer's Revolt* (1976), Theatre Passe Muraille's *Paper Wheat* (1978), and more recent experimental work like *The Book of Jessica* (1989).[4] Radio documentary is a closely related form and many playwrights write for radio as well as for the stage. Pollock comes from this background. In her first major stage play, *Walsh* (1973), and in *One Tiger to a Hill* (1981), she was clearly working within the documentary genre defined by Peter Weiss as the shaping of 'a useful pattern from fragments of reality' (41), but documentary is never merely the shaping, let alone the recording, of fragments of unmediated reality.[5] Documentary is always the result of aesthetic choices, of narrativization, focalization, and subject/object construction. It is a genre, a set of conventions (which will differ depending on the medium) resting on a set of assumptions; it is, in short, *art*.

By calling *The Komagata Maru Incident* historiographic docudrama – instead of 'historiographic metadrama,' as does Richard Knowles – we are stressing the following essential features of the play. First, it is a rewriting of history, a writing up of a neglected story, a writing into the received historical record by means of unmarked documents of elided events and voices. Second, it is drama, drama moreover that flaunts its theatrical and presentational power. Finally, it is the dramatization of an actual historical incident, which occurred in a real place at a specific time, that mixes 'actual' reality (identifiable attitudes toward race and gender, actual immigration policies) with theatrical reality (circus, magician, spectators, objects on display) to illuminate the artificiality of both. This last point cannot be overstressed. The play is not, as the term 'metadrama' (a term borrowed from the theory of the novel and more appropriate for *Blood Relations*) implies, a play about theatre, or acting, or playwriting. It is a play about real life and real events as staged, manipulated, masterminded acts, acts that inscribe, naturalize, validate, and perpetuate the racist, sexist construction of Canada as a country of and for dominant white men, who hold all the cards and make all the rules.

To create her historiographic docudrama, Pollock has done what readers and viewers of the play perhaps intuit without fully appreciating: research.

In preparing to write the play, she examined archives, interviewed individuals, and studied the historical records to see what was happening in the summer of 1914 and how it was being reported.[6] However, most critical studies of Sharon Pollock and *The Komagata Maru Incident* deal exclusively with the play, while few studies of the events of 1914 even mention Pollock's literary rewriting of the incident.[7] The disciplinary boundaries separating Pollock's play from the events of 1914 are, of course, themselves constructions that keep us from recognizing the many intertexts that inform what we mean by the words Komagata Maru and that shape our assumptions about Canada. We would like to follow Pollock across the boundary between what are commonly called 'art' and 'life' in order to examine how the *Komagata Maru* has been given meaning, how that meaning relates to Canada, and what the playwright does with history, document, and drama.

The entry for '*Komagata Maru*' in *The Canadian Encyclopedia* is symptomatic of how the name of the Japanese-owned freighter has come to stand for 'the affair' that developed around it. When we speak of the *Komagata Maru* today, we also speak of racist sentiments, acts of discrimination, and the danger of using government policy to subdue racist fears. The newspapers of the day demonstrate unequivocally the degree of anti-Asian sentiments that permeated life in Vancouver. In Pollock's play, it is T.S. who incorporates the voices of public opinion into his many personae. The headlines of the *Vancouver Sun,* for example, employ a powerful rhetoric of us ('Vancouver citizens') versus them ('Hindu invaders'). The stories regularly employ discriminatory, blatantly racist language, which, for instance, refers to the passengers collectively as 'Hindus' although about 90 percent of them were Sikhs ('Hindus Are Dancing a Religious Can-Can aboard the Komagata – Venerable Old Priest Leads Crowd of Turbaned Tourists in Their Weird and Mystic Dances,' 5 June 1914; '"Poor Old Harman Singh" Knocks Once Again at Dominion's Door to Secure Admission to Canada,' 23 July 1914), while at the same time using euphemisms to disguise the pressures and threats exerted by white men in positions of power ('Searchlights Play on Komagata to Reveal Movements of Hindus and Prevent Smuggling of Arms,' 20 July 1914; 'Arrival of Rainbow Helps Komagata's Passengers to Make up Their Minds,' 22 July 1914). Both news stories and cartoons constructed Canada as white, male, and European – a white man's country (Buchignani, Indra, and Srivastiva, 55).

The 'Roots Issue' of *Rungh* published in 1993, which examines the roots of the South Asian community in Canada, includes an informative piece on the *Komagata Maru* incident that counterpoints an article from the *Province*, a Vancouver daily newspaper, and an editorial from the *Hindustanee*, an English-language newspaper published by the South Asian community and eventually banned by the Canadian government ('When the Ship Came In').[8] A comparison of the discourse in these two contemporary accounts reveals obvious differences in perspectives, but it also reminds us that the Vancouver East Indian community in 1914 was not quietly tolerating the abuse of the passengers but was doing everything in its power to ensure that justice was being served.

The xenophobic attitudes of the public were reinforced by the newspapers, and this feeling of racist sentiment led to a brief revival of the anonymous music hall favourite of 1906 'White Canada Forever' (Ferguson, 30). The idea of Canada as a white man's country was prevalent not only in the media but also in political speeches and government policies; our opening quotation from Sir Richard McBride is only one of many to represent the political atmosphere of the day. H.H. Stevens, leader of the Asiatic Exclusion League (1907) and Conservative Member of Parliament since 1911, was especially vocal in defending his anti-Asian position in an address he delivered to a group of concerned Vancouver citizens on 23 June in the Dominion Hall (Ward, 91). As internal government directives prove, officials had considerable discretion in interpreting rules and laws.[9] On 8 January 1908, the government passed the two Orders-in-Council mentioned earlier to deal with Indian immigration. P.C. 23 raised the sum of money required of a prospective immigrant from $25 to $200. P.C. 24, also called the 'Continuous Journey Bill,' required that an immigrant had to arrive on an uninterrupted voyage from his or her country of birth or citizenship. Such an uninterrupted passage was, in fact, impossible in 1914, for no such ticketing arrangements existed. Agents of the Indian government prevented Gurdit Singh, for example, from leaving on the *Komagata Maru* out of Calcutta; he had to leave from Hong Kong. Although immigration policies did not mention East Indians by name and were not, therefore, openly discriminatory, their restrictive measures made it virtually impossible for them to come to Canada: over 2,600 East Indians had immigrated in 1908, but only six entered Canada in 1909.

A growing number of sociological and historical studies have provided the kind of detailed information on Sikhs in Canada, and especially in Vancouver, that enhances our understanding of the larger context surrounding the *Komagata Maru* affair, including the tireless efforts of the majority to keep Canada a white man's country.[10] In order to indicate the range of approaches to the *Komagata Maru* incident, a brief comparison of the oral history project by Sarjeet Singh Jagpal published as *Becoming Canadians: Pioneer Sikhs in Their Own Words* (1994) with Robert Jarvis's *The 'Komagata Maru' Incident: A Canadian Immigration Battle Revisited* (1992) is worthwhile. Originally compiled by Jagpal for his master's thesis (1991) in the Department of Social and Educational Studies at the University of British Columbia, *Becoming Canadians* is based on an oral history project that presents an 'insider's perspective' in order to 'provide a more balanced account' (12). To Jarvis, however, the incident of the *Komagata Maru* has been 'mythologized by liberal academics and minority propagandists, aided by generous grants from the federal government' (2).[11] It should come as no surprise, therefore, that Jarvis sees William Hopkinson as 'a Canadian martyr and hero' (1) and Mewa Singh, who shot Hopkinson in a corridor of the Vancouver court house, as 'the Sikh terrorist and murderer of William Hopkinson' (43), while for Jagpal and the Sikh community, Hopkinson is the 'corrupt immigration official' and Mewa Singh 'a Sikh martyr' (34).[12] Jarvis's 1992 booklet reminds us that the vision of a white man's Canada, with no non-European immigration, is not a distant memory from the past but is alive and well; racism poses the same threat today as it did in 1914.

On 7 October 1989, the Progressive Indo-Canadian Community Services Society held a conference in Vancouver to commemorate the seventy-fifth anniversary of the *Komagata Maru* incident (Dutton). The goal of the conference was to raise public awareness of Canada's history of discrimination and to expose its systemic nature, not by focusing exclusively on the *Komagata Maru* affair, but by considering the plight of women, First Nations, Japanese-Canadians, and others at the same time. A commemorative dinner on 20 May 1989 organized by the India Cultural Society of British Columbia and a photo exhibition in the Vancouver Public Library were part of the activities. The following year, a plaque was installed overlooking

Figure 2 Komagata Maru commemorative plaque

Vancouver harbour to commemorate 'the 75th anniversary of that unfortunate incident of racial discrimination, and [to remind] Canadians of our commitment to an open society in which mutual respect and understanding are honoured, differences are respected, and traditions are cherished' (see Figure 2). Moreover, the Canadian government issued an apology to the Sikhs for the *Komagata Maru* incident in 1993 (Minhas, 18). Most recently, a short documentary was made by the Komagata Maru Foundation of Canada. These events confirm the important position of Sharon Pollock's play in the historiography and the documenting of the *Komagata Maru*; in a sense, they mark a return to her point of departure and a recognition of the artist's contribution to the ongoing construction of Canada.

The Komagata Maru Incident is clearly intended to remind us of the past construction of Canada and to alert us to the fact that construction of the nation state is an ongoing process about which we can make choices. The circus metaphor and the T.S. figure work exceptionally well, at several levels, to dramatize this theme. Through the circus/T.S. device, complete with background carnival music, Pollock can show us just what a sideshow affair Vancouverites of the day made of the *Komagata Maru*: 'Hurry! Hurry! Hurry! Absolutely the last and final chance to view the Komagata Maru! Anchored in picturesque Vancouver Harbour for two, count 'em, two glorious months! Note the cruiser standing by to the right, see the sun on its guns, what a fantastic sight! Ladies and gentlemen, can you truly afford to bypass this splendid spectacle? Run, my good friends, you mustn't walk, you must run! Cotton candy, taffy apples, popcorn and balloons!' (279) Throughout this spiel, Sophie (the second prostitute) and her client Georg stand, as if at a window, looking out to the harbour and commenting on the scene.

Here, as at so many points in the play, Pollock is forcing us to recognize our role as contemporary spectators: it is *we* who are directly addressed by T.S. at these strategic moments. When T.S. opens the play, it is to us that he speaks. When he touches the characters to life at the beginning, his display of god-like power is for our benefit. When he sets the scene, it is for us: 'Hurry! Hurry! Hurry! Right this way, ladies and gentlemen! First chance to view, the Komagata Maru! At this very moment steaming towards picturesque Vancouver Harbour' (229). And when he addresses *the house*, he speaks to us: 'Mr Speaker; Prime Minister; Honourable Members! Today I am opening my heart to you. I am telling you my fears – fears that affect each and every Canadian today ... I fear for my country, and I fear for my people ... I am not ashamed, nor should you be, to state that this is white man's country!' (249). He even stage-manages Hopkinson's death – to impress us with his skill (286) – before making his final bow.

The dynamic here is powerful and clear. Just as Sophie and Georg, Bill and Evy (and all the other Vancouverites) watch the *Komagata Maru*, so too do *we* watch – we watch them watching each other and are thereby constructed as spectators in a work that presents the very act of spectatorship as an objectification of others that facilitates their dehumanization and mistreatment. Moreover, we are repeatedly caught in the act by ᵀ.S. This reduplication (or *mise en abyme*) effect of watcher being watched is picked up in sharp details such as the face of T.S. reflected in the mirror observing us (in the film version), his prompting when the characters forget their lines, or his demonstration to Hopkinson of how to coerce Captain Yamamoto. But this critique of spectatorship is most powerfully presented through the *mise en scene*, which calls for the East Indian Woman on the *Komagata Maru* to appear in a separate area above the brothel set, behind 'an open grill-like frame' that suggests 'a cage' and 'the superstructure of a ship' (227). This Woman (she is not named), like the Sikhs on the ship, watches those on shore watching them, while we are positioned as voyeurs spying on the brothel and as fairgoers observing the spectacle of one group of people treating another group as if they were caged animals on display (see Figure 3).

Pollock's 'staging [of] the gaze' in *The Komagata Maru Incident* works well

Figure 3 Sharon Pollock's *The Komagata Maru Incident*
(Sharon Pollock fonds, Special Collections, University of Calgary Library)

as an indictment of the overt racist policies of the Immigration Office in 1914 and as a warning to us today that those who forget their history will repeat it.[13] The presentational style, with its foregrounding (another form of staging, after all) of historical facts, events, and documents, blocks a spectator's temptation to dismiss the play as either mere invention or blatant propaganda. This play may be constructed, Pollock tells us, but so is history and so is Canadian identity.

But her analysis of racism does not stop there, and it may be that, in pushing her scrutiny of racialized identity further, she loosens her *pre*sentational grasp and reverts to a more *re*presentational and thus – in the context of this play – more problematic portrayal of the issues. Despite the manipulative omnipresence of T.S., Hopkinson becomes increasingly three-dimensional, individual, and sympathetic as the play moves toward its close and his death. With Evy's revelation that Billy is a victim of his own internalized racism, a racism manifested in his rejection of his East Indian mother – 'And Billy's mother's brown' (269) – and in his denial of his origins, Pollock seems to be saying that racism is a personal, individual problem and that at least some racists – like Billy – are to be pitied because their self-hatred sets them up to be exploited by one group as betrayers of another and, ultimately, of themselves.

There are at least two opposite ways of viewing Pollock's apparent shift from presentational to representational theatrics here. Denis Salter argues that the playwright's 'sentimental attitude' and 'reductive approach' to Hopkinson reduces racism to 'personal neurosis' (xix) and weakens the ethical message and political praxis of the play. When the presentational stylization of docudrama gives way to realism – that is, to a mimetics of character development grounded in a tragic flaw – the spectator is let off the hook. By contrast, Robert Nunn praises the realistic treatment of Hopkinson as a way of involving the audience in the deeper, if self-interested, truth that 'the racist denies a part of his own humanity in denying the humanity of others' (1984b, 75). Where T.S. and the circus trope alienate us and appeal to the intellect, Hopkinson invites emotional identification and pity.

Perhaps this stylistic and ideological ambivalence (presentational versus representational; systemic problem versus personal neurosis) can only be resolved in performance and will differ with each staging, but it is worth remembering that the two modes co-exist in this play from the start. What links them is a set of so-called facts, documents, evidence. Whether those facts are trivialized, played with, manipulated, or embodied literally in a group of actors (one of whom represents a historical figure called William Hopkinson), they are still constructed, the stuff of theatre. They legitimize what Benedict Anderson would call an 'imagined community'; they are signs of what Homi K. Bhabha would describe as a 'narrative of nation,' and they represent what Edward Said has identified as the staging of orientalism.[14] Pollock lays bare that legitimizing, narrating, staging process in an analysis of the role that race and racism plays in the construction of Canada, and, we believe, this analysis is well served by her method, hybrid style, and use of the stage metaphor. Personal atonement and individual death, as imaged in Hopkinson's final words and acceptance of his East Indian roots, solves nothing as long as, so Pollock reminds us, 'The System' is still in place.

But if *The Komagata Maru Incident* succeeds, as we believe it does, in its anatomizing of racism and the construction of Canada, it has less to tell us about gender. As Jill Dolan, among others, has noted, the postmodernist deconstruction of representation in the theatre has left gender bias and asymmetry largely untouched (43). To be sure, Pollock has added three women to this otherwise male story – she has written them back into history – but all three women are stereotypes who serve the central human drama, which is firmly located in Hopkinson. Evy is the whore with a heart of gold and, admittedly, some fine principles. However, that she seems free of racist views (evidenced in her concern for the Sikh in the employment queue, her concern for the passengers on the *Komagata Maru*, and her criticisms of Bill) carries remarkably little dramatic weight because she lacks agency and independence. Bill uses her house as a base for his espionage against the Sikhs; he abuses, demeans, and dominates her, while she forgives and comforts him. Sophie is little more than a silly, shallow woman, out for number one. She parrots the dominant views of society, shrieking at the departing ship: 'We won! We won!' (280). The fact that these two women are prostitutes and that the representational action of the play is set in a brothel is never sufficiently stressed or politicized as a metaphor for the patriarchal system, which it almost certainly is.[15]

If the two white women have little agency beyond their roles as whores on the brothel-stage of their lives, the Sikh Woman on the ship is even more marginalized. Her position as a woman of Colour and single mother turned away from the Canadian door is never explored because she remains, within the presentational mode of the play, the object of our gaze and the objective reminder of *Hopkinson's* identity and history: she is the return of his repressed. Although she gets the final words of the play, the actual words spoken by Mewa Singh on the Canadian gallows, and although these words suggest that she will live to fight racist injustice, her helplessness as a woman is only underscored by T.S., who, with a sly bow, closes the play and, in so doing, reminds us that men like him – politicians, policy makers, city fathers, immigration officials, and so on – remain firmly in control, pulling all the strings. The Woman remains the Other, a sign merely of her own, and her child's, silencing and abjection, in a construction that comes dangerously close to reorientalizing her.

As with the construction of race, one might argue that Pollock's construction of gender centres less on the women than on Hopkinson. Perhaps here we might find some critique of the role played by a masculinist ideology that bolsters the state-supported racism in the play. As we suggested at the beginning, Hopkinson suffers from a hero-worship of his blond, British, imperialist father and the collateral denial of his subaltern identity.[16] Rather than blaming his father for his identity crisis, however, he blames his East Indian mother. That he should be haunted by her, and (as Pollock constructs his story) provoked by her memory to help the *Komagata Maru* and the Woman aboard, does suggest that Pollock sees race and gender as conspiring together to destroy the man who embraces the ideal of white masculinity celebrated by Euro-Canadians and symbolized in the figure of the blond imperialist.[17]

Though less overt and less carefully anatomized than race, a critique of gender is presented in this play, primarily through Hopkinson. Full human agency for women and a dramatic dismantling of gender construction would have to wait for a later play – Pollock's feminist revenge comedy *Blood Relations*. In *The Komagata Maru Incident*, Pollock focuses on the mechanisms of construction – of history, of nation, of personal identity, of imagined communities, and of theatre. What she stages is a politics of recognition that we cannot afford to ignore.

Acknowledgments

A shorter version of this chapter was presented at the Race, Gender, and the Construction of Canada Conference at the University of British Columbia, Vancouver, 20 October 1995; we greatly appreciated the audience's comments and suggestions. We would like to thank Apollonia Steele, Head of Special Collections at the University of Calgary, for her generous assistance with the Sharon Pollock papers, and SSHRC for the funding of this research.

Notes

1 *The Komagata Maru Incident* premiered in Vancouver in January 1976 in a production directed by Larry Lillo with an all-white cast. It was first published in 1978 by Playwrights Co-op in Toronto. All references here are to the reprint of the play in *Six Canadian Plays*. It was adapted for radio as 'The Story of the Komagata Maru' and was aired as part of the CBC school broadcast 'Western Profiles' in 1978, which sought to introduce the notion of the cultural mosaic to children. The script of *The Komagata Maru Incident* was also made into an ACCESS television film in 1984.

2 William C. Hopkinson (1876-1914) was born in Yorkshire. His parents took him to India when his father, a soldier in the British army, was transferred there. In 1904 he became a police inspector in Calcutta, and in 1907 he moved to Vancouver where he worked as an immigration officer and translator. Pollock's portrayal of Hopkinson as of mixed race serves the political message and personal drama of the play. Johnston quotes Fred Taylor, one of Hopkinson's fellow workers, as corroborating Hopkinson's mixed heritage (142-3). See also 'When the Ship Came In' (16) and Narindar Singh (56).

3 Pollock calls her 'Master of Ceremonies' 'T.S.' without further explanation. These initials have been taken to stand for The System, but Pollock has said that T.S. Eaton's initials stuck in her mind (Gilbert 116). Perhaps these possibilities amount to the same thing.

4 For discussion and analysis of Canadian documentary art, see Livesay, and Scobie; for

discussion of Pollock's documentary position, see Bessai, Gilbert, and Nunn (1984a).

5 To be fair, Weiss does not confuse reality and art, but the idea that documentary theatre is made from 'fragments of reality' can be misleading. As Eliot Weinberger argues in 'The Camera People' from *Visualizing Theory*, there is a very 'fuzzy border between "documentary value" and "documentation,"' and this is true of all films (or plays, for that matter) 'no matter how "fictional" ... [their] endless documentation of ... contemporary life' may be (5).

6 Filed with the typescript drafts of the play in the Sharon Pollock Papers at the University of Calgary Library (Box 54: 7-12) are numerous Xeroxes, notes, and quotations from government policies, newspaper articles, and politicians, all of which Pollock gathered during her research for the play. One of these items is the popular song, quoted in the Introduction of this volume (p. 9), called 'White Canada Forever.' In a 22 April 1996 interview with Sherrill Grace, Pollock described her research and her friendship with members of the Vancouver Sikh community who advised her on certain aspects of the play.

7 Johnston's work is the notable exception; he mentions Pollock's play, albeit briefly, in his discussion of Hopkinson's heritage (143).

8 *Rungh* is published in Vancouver; it describes itself as 'an interdisciplinary magazine committed to the exploration of traditional and contemporary South-Asian cultural productions.' The article cited here is 'When the Ship Came In: Remembering the Komagata Maru,' *Rungh* 2 (1993):14-18.

9 Frank Oliver, Minister of the Department of the Interior, wrote to W.D. Scott, Superintendent of Immigration, on 11 April 1908: 'The regulation excluding immigrants who come otherwise than by direct passage from their own country is mandatory, with the provision that if such an immigrant is otherwise desirable the question of his exclusion is to be referred to Head Office and in the meantime he is to be permitted to proceed to destination ... This regulation is therefore intended as a means of excluding those whom it is the policy of the government to exclude, but not to exclude those whom the policy is to admit' (R. Sampta-Mehta, cited in Mangalam 49).

10 The work of white scholars (Hugh Johnston, Peter Ward, Ted Ferguson, James Chadney) has been placed in a broader perspective by Sikhs (Kesar Singh, Narindar Singh, Sarjeet Singh Jagpal, Rajwant Singh, and Sohan Singh Josh).

11 Jarvis's publication is only the tip of the iceberg. The Citizens for Foreign Aid Reform, the publisher of Jarvis's booklet, has set up a 'Canadian Immigration Hotline' to report on crimes committed by immigrants.

12 Mewa Singh was one of four men arrested in July 1914 for carrying revolvers purchased in the United States. Hopkinson tried to befriend him after this incident, once Mewa Singh had given a statement against his friends in order to receive a lesser charge. On 21 October Mewa Singh tried to stop Hopkinson from taking the witness stand in Bela Singh's trial because Hopkinson was expected to support the claim made by Bela Singh, one of Hopkinson's informers, that he had killed two Sikhs and wounded several others in the *Gurdwara* in self-defence rather than on purpose. Only days later Mewa Singh was tried for murder and sentenced; he was hanged on 11 January 1915. As Narindar Singh explains, 'Mewa Singh's courageous action was a classic example of the Sikh tradition of martyrdom. He deeply believed that the very existence of Sikhs and their religion in Canada was threatened, as had been the case when the Muslims ruled India. He was willing to pay the highest price for this cause. The Ross Street Vancouver *Gurdwara* bears Mewa Singh's name and his martyrdom is commemorated annually with a religious service' (55).

13 In Chapter 2 of *Staging the Gaze*, Barbara Freedman provides an interesting analysis of theatre and 'spectator consciousness' as 'a culturally conditioned mode of staging the construction of the real' (50). According to Freedman, it is by 'staging the gaze' (the look that is *returned*) that a play can critique and problematize an audience's assumptions about what is true or real.

14 Anderson, Bhabha, and Said all deconstruct the assumed naturalness of identities, be they national (ourselves) or othered, and Anderson, in particular, shows how the modern

nation-state is a product of its ability to represent itself as both 'a *historical* fatality and as a community imagined through language' (146).

15 That Pollock saw the patriarchal system as implicated in and responsible for the abuses she dramatizes is clear from a note she made to herself in the earliest stages of writing. On the verso of a tentative chronology of events she writes: 'every power scenario is based on patriarchal patterns of submission, domination, seduction, betrayal' (Box 54: 7-11, 23).

16 A subaltern is, literally, a British military term for a commissioned officer beneath the rank of captain. More generally, the term refers to one in a subordinate position, and Gayatri Chakravorty Spivak has shown how the subaltern can be both gendered and classed as well, of course, as racialized. In *The Komagata Maru Incident*, Pollock portrays varieties of subalterneity in Hopkinson, the two prostitutes, the Sikh informers, and the East Indian Woman caged on the ship. The System of the nation-state is predicated upon such subjection.

17 This raced, gendered concept of nordic virility has very deep roots in North American society. Lisa Bloom locates the construction of heroic white American masculinity, as linked to the American state, in the narrative of exploration, and Sherrill Grace traces the roots of the Canadian counterpart of northern manliness to nineteenth-century nationalism. Grace is examining the gendered and raced discourse of North in her SSHRC-funded work-in-progress *Canada and the Idea of North*.

Works Cited

Anderson, Benedict. 1991. *Imagined Communities: Reflections on the Origins and Spread of Nationalism*. London: Verso

Bessai, Diane. 1986. 'Sharon Pollock's Women: A Study in Dramatic Process.' In Shirley Neuman and Smaro Kamboureli, eds., *A Mazing Space*, 126-36. Edmonton: NeWest

Bhabha, Homi K., ed. 1990. *Nation and Narration*. New York: Routledge

Bloom, Lisa. 1993. *Gender on Ice: American Ideologies of Polar Expeditions*. Minneapolis: University of Minnesota Press

Buchignani, Norman, Doreen M. Indra, and Ram Srivastiva. 1985. *Continuous Journey: A Social History of South Asians in Canada*. Toronto: McClelland & Stewart

Calgary Herald. 1979. 'ATP: Proving that Box Office Winners Don't Have to Gamble.' 31 March

Canadian Encyclopedia. 1988. Edmonton: Hurtig

Chadney, James G. 1984. *The Sikhs of Vancouver*. New York: AMS Press

Dolan, Jill. 1988. *The Feminist Spectator as Critic*. Ann Arbor: University of Michigan Press

Dutton, Alan William, ed. 1990. *Beyond the Komagata Maru: Race Relations Today*. Surrey, BC: Progressive Indo-Canadian Community Services Society

Ferguson, Ted. 1975. *A White Man's Country: An Exercise in Canadian Prejudice*. Toronto: Doubleday

Freedman, Barbara. 1991. *Staging the Gaze: Postmodernism, Psychoanalysis, and Shakespeare's Comedy*. Ithaca: Cornell University Press

Gilbert, Reid. 1986. 'Sharon Pollock.' In Jeffrey M. Heath, ed., *Profiles in Canadian Literature*, 113-20. Toronto: Dundurn

Grace, Sherrill E. 1997. 'Gendering Northern Narrative.' In John Moss, ed., *Echoing Silence: Essays on Arctic Narrative*, 163-81. Ottawa: University of Ottawa Press

Hofsess, John. 1979. 'Seduced Not Raped.' *Albertan*, 14 January

Jagpal, Sarjeet Singh. 1994. *Becoming Canadians: Pioneer Sikhs in Their Own Words*. Vancouver: Harbour

Jarvis, Robert. 1992. *The 'Komagata Maru' Incident: A Canadian Immigration Battle Revisited*. Toronto: Citizens for Foreign Aid Reform

Johnston, Hugh. 1989. *The Voyage of the Komagata Maru: The Sikh Challenge to Canada's Colour Bar*. 2nd ed. Vancouver: UBC Press

Josh, Sohan Singh. 1975. *Tragedy of Komagata Maru*. New Delhi: People's Publishing House

Knowles, Richard Paul. 1987. 'Replaying History: Canadian Historiographic Metadrama.' *Dalhousie Review* 67 (213):228-43

Livesay, Dorothy. 1971. 'The Documentary Poem: A Canadian Genre.' In Eli Mandel, ed.,

Contexts of Canadian Criticism, 267-81. Chicago: University of Chicago Press

Mangalam, J.J. 1985. 'The Komagata Maru Affair, 1917.' *Population Review* 29 (1-2):47-58

Minhas, Manmohan Singh. 1994. *The Sikh Canadians*. Edmonton: Reidmore

Nunn, Robert C. 1984a. 'Performing Fact: Canadian Documentary Theatre.' *Canadian Literature* 103:51-62

–. 1984b. 'Sharon Pollock's Plays: A Review Article.' *Theatre History in Canada* 5 (1):72-83

Pollock, Sharon. 1992. *The Komagata Maru Incident*. In Tony Hamill, ed., *Six Canadian Plays*. Toronto: Playwrights Canada

Portman, Jamie. 1977. 'Play Delivers Frontal Assault on Canadians' Smug Certainties. *Calgary Herald*, 26 March

Said, Edward W. *Orientalism*. 1979. New York: Vintage

Salter, Denis. 1989. '(Im)possible Worlds: The Plays of Sharon Pollock.' In Apollonia Steele and Jean F. Tenner, eds., *The Sharon Pollock Papers First Accession: An Inventory of the University of Calgary Libraries*. Calgary: University of Calgary Press

Scobie, Stephen. 1984. 'Amelia, or: Who Do You Think You Are? Documentary and Identity in Canadian Literature.' *Canadian Literature* 100:264-85

Singh, Kesar. 1989. *Canadian Sikhs (Part One) and Komagata Maru Massacre*. Surrey, BC: K. Singh

Singh, Narindar. 1994. *Canadian Sikhs: History, Religion, and Culture of Sikhs in North America*. Ottawa: Canadian Sikhs' Studies Institute

Singh, Rajwant. 1989. *The Sikhs: Their Literature on Culture, History, Philosophy, Politics, Religion, and Traditions*. Delhi: Indian Bibliographies Bureau

Spivak, Gayatri Chakravorty. 1988. 'Can the Subaltern Speak?' In Cary Nelson and Lawrence Grossberg, eds., *Marxism and the Interpretation of Culture*, 271-313. Urbana: University of Illinois Press

Ward, Peter W. 1990. *White Canada Forever: Popular Attitudes and Public Policy toward Orientals in British Columbia*. 2nd ed. Montreal: McGill-Queen's University Press

Weinberger, Eliot. 1994. 'The Camera People.' *Visualizing Theory: Selected Essays from V.A.R., 1990-1994*. New York: Routledge

Wyman, Max. 1976. 'Komagata Maru: The Clash of Symbols.' *Vancouver Sun*, 21 January, 43

Reconstructing Canadian Literature: The Role of Race and Gender

Christl Verduyn

As if there were a moment that I wasn't a woman and a
moment that I wasn't Black, as if there were a moment that she
wasn't white.

> – Dionne Brand, *Bread Out of Stone*[1]

In 'Writing Beyond Race: The Politics of Otherness,' Chelva Kanaganayakam reminds readers that 'the notion of discrimination in literature
is not far-fetched or exaggerated': 'Writing is no less important as an area
of concern than employment, education or immigration,' Kanaganayakam
explains, and 'literary studies in Canada has been in many ways a colonialist discourse that has denied, suppressed or ignored the literature and
experience of the non-white population' (9).

It is necessary to recall that literature takes its place in discussions of
issues of race and gender and their relation to the construction of Canada
because it is still often thought to be exempt from these debates. Culture
has not traditionally been a significant arena of racial contestation. As
Marlene Nourbese Philip has remarked: 'Education, employment, housing,
and police relations have always, and for good reason, garnered most
attention – political, academic, investigative, and personal' (1992, 12). This
is ironic, Philip notes, given that culture has been as much the target of
discriminatory commentary as have individuals. Ironic or not, the fact is
that, as the 1994 Writing Thru Race Conference[2] so clearly showed, literature is not free from considerations of race, any more than, as feminist
analysis has demonstrated, it is uninformed by gender. Thus, when discussing the construction of Canada in terms of race and gender, it is
appropriate to consider literature as well. In Canadian literature, as much
as in any other domain of human experience and expression, race and gender are operative. Moreover, Canada is known both at home and abroad
through and for its writers, particularly its prominent women writers.

In choosing Canadian literature as the avenue through which to share

some observations about race, gender, interdisciplinarity, and 'the construction of Canada,' I have organized my comments around the work of
three writers – Dionne Brand, Claire Harris, and M. Nourbese Philip. I
begin by briefly locating literature and literary studies, as well as myself,
within discussions of race and gender. After outlining a predominant
'CanLitCrit'[3] construct, I turn to the works of Brand, Harris, and Philip.
The choice of these three writers stems in part from the availability of a
useful anthology of their work. Carol Morrell's *Grammar of Dissent* presents
excerpts from each writer's publications along with bibliographic details,
and it is precisely the sort of book that is reconstructing reading lists for
Canadian literature courses. More important, the works of Brand, Harris,
and Philip amply demonstrate the intricacies of the issues being considered here and illustrate my basic point that Canadian literature, its critical
analysis, and its teaching are being reconstructed by questions of race/eth-
nicity and gender. In the process, the image of Canada that this material
conveys is undergoing reconstruction. This observation is shared by a
number of scholars of Canadian literature.

Writers and researchers such as Arun Mukherjee, Himani Bannerji, Enoch
Padolsky, Joseph Pivato, contributors to several recent journal publications,
and others are mindful of the appearances of nation in various forms of cultural expression. Two recent issues of *Essays on Canadian Writing* (*ECW*, 56
and 57), for example, are concerned with Canadian nationhood.[4] In her
introduction to Volume 56, 'Reading Postcoloniality, Reading Canada,'
Diana Brydon points out that while the focus of the volume is academic
and literary, 'the range of discussion involves understanding how
Canadians see themselves and their world and how they are equipped (by
their education and their history) to deal with the difficult moral and practical problems posed by decolonization at the end of the twentieth century'
(1). In his introduction to 'Writing Ethnicity' (*ECW* 57), Winfried
Siemerling notes that 'literary and cultural studies deal with sets of problems that are not reducible to those of the social sciences' (5). But, as Enoch
Padolsky has shown, there is a dialectic between literary criticism and studies in ethnicity or race (22-7). The latter can reply to or integrate insights
from the former.[5] This is not new activity. For example, Marxist and feminist critics, Padolsky observes, 'insist on the connections between literature
and society, and between history and textuality' (28). Postcolonial criticism,
even in its radical poststructuralist mode, also maintains connectedness
with history and society. 'No matter how concerned with rupture, disconti-
nuity, and transgression,' Neil ten Kortenaar asserts in his analysis of race
and nation in Margaret Laurence's *The Diviners*, 'postcolonial criticism of
Canadian literature remains nationalist in inspiration ... Even when the
subject of inquiry is regionalism or ethnicity [or race] or gender, the field of
inquiry remains the nation and determines what will be found' (12).

Contemporary literary criticism in Canada identifies links between concepts and constructs of nation, race, and gender. Recognition of this combination of concerns has had a transforming effect on Canadian literature. In the following, I offer a brief account of some of these changes, drawing on examples from university courses in Women's Studies and Canadian Studies (for which I was an instructor) between 1980 and 1995.

Mentioning Women's Studies and Canadian Studies materializes the integral subtheme of interdisciplinarity. Interdisciplinarity is a key ingredient in the reconstruction of Canada because it allows researchers to look beyond discipline-based knowledge toward knowledge that accrues from the interaction of two or more disciplines. Thus, in the literary domain, for example, interdisciplinarity can involve gender and/or race analysis as well as aesthetic analysis. As a critical approach, interdisciplinarity has been facilitated within both Women's Studies and Canadian Studies, though their institutionalization was not the sine qua non of its practice. Literary studies are, arguably, especially amenable to interdisciplinarity. As a student in the 1970s, confronted with disciplinary options and a concomitant warning not to do a degree in English ('because you'd never find a job'),[6] I reasoned that literary studies at least offered the possibility of working within a nexus of such disciplines as history, psychology, and sociology. With structural analysis being de rigueur in graduate schools in the mid-1970s, there was little room for 'thematic' studies, let alone ones that might take into account the author and the possibility that he might be a she. Questions of race or ethnicity were simply not raised until feminist analysis re-presented gender and reincorporated an embodied subject. Although it was possible to use feminist analysis within the traditional disciplines, it was even more possible within the interdisciplinary framework of Women's Studies. It was here that a generation of women developed Canadian literature courses with gender as a conscious and primary consideration. In my own case, Canadian Studies first facilitated such courses.[7]

From the early l980s on, I was able to offer a Canadian literature course organized around gender, dealing exclusively with women writers (from both Quebec and English Canada). This became the springboard for a vital intersection of gender and race. The catalyst was Joy Kogawa's novel *Obasan*. Embraced by the literary establishment for its superb aesthetic accomplishments, *Obasan* also drew attention to the fact that cultural (read ethnic or racial) differences (read discrimination) were part of Canadian experience and Canadian literary history. This recognition elucidated for me a nagging reservation about poststructuralist feminist theory, which manifested itself in personal uneasiness with the pronoun 'we.' Growing up in an immigrant family, I had a sufficient number of reminders that, even when spoken by women, 'we' was not an all-inclusive pronoun. I mention this not to aggrandize my immigrant experience but to explain my relief when discussions of ethnicity and race joined discussions of gender in the literary arena.

These comments point up the distinction that must be drawn between ethnicity and race, and clarify my involvement in the discussion by identifying the invisible ethnic minority position from which I seek to contribute to it. Race and ethnicity are not to be conflated, nor should they be held entirely separate when considering questions of race and gender and the construction of Canada. But what is the construct that is being revis(ion)ed?

There have been several attempts in recent years to discuss the construction of Canada, partly because of the challenge issued by authors such as Brand, Harris, and Philip. In his 1993 study, *Post-National Arguments: The Politics of the Anglophone-Canadian Novel since 1967*, Frank Davey poses questions pertinent to the discussion of 'what construction of "Canada" and "Canadians" lay behind anglophone-Canadian writers' … imagination of the country, what images, argument, or symbols?'(5)[8] In developing his response, Davey identifies 'national mythologies like "two solitudes" or "survival," national images like [Margaret] Atwood's "ice maidens," beleagured [sic] farmhouses, gothic mothers, [John] Moss's signs of isolation, [Ronald] Sutherland's Presbyterians and Jansenists, and more recently, in Linda Hutcheon's work, national modes of irony and historical metafiction' (6). These are references to what Joseph Pivato terms the Canadian mythopoeic tradition – 'the thematic criticism of [Northrop] Frye, [Doug] Jones, [Margaret] Atwood, [John] Moss and others [which] has dominated the teaching and the reading of Canadian literature' (1991, 24). The major thematic preoccupations of Canadian literary critics can be summed up with such images as Frye's 'garrison mentality,' Atwood's 'survival,' and Stratford's 'ellipse with two centres' (Pivato 1994, 69). This mythopoeic tradition in Canadian letters, Pivato argues, is closely associated with environmental theses of Canadian history that focus on 'man's relationship with the natural world around him: the forest, the climate, the plain, the farm' (1991, 25). This world is often portrayed as a hostile environment, and from this portrayal are derived the familiar themes of survival, isolation, exile, and death in the snow. Pivato establishes a link between environmentalist-thematic interpretations of Canadian history or literature and federalist fidelities. Instead of insisting on a unifying thesis for a national literature, Pivato suggests that critics and readers could opt for a pluralist approach that expands borders and alters the frame of reference, and he argues that Canadian scholarship would gain from the possibilities offered by comparative social history and comparative literature. 'Little time has been devoted to examining how Canadian historical development shared features with other countries – the Protestant ethic, industrialization, urbanism, immigration and ethnic heterogeneity ... Both the view of history and the reading of literature have neglected the institutions, ideas, values, and folklore that immigrants brought from Europe and other countries' (Pivato 1991, 25-6).

Recent accounts[9] and critiques of current CanLitCrit reveal that the constructs widely associated with Canadian literature (nature, the North, isolation, survival, etc.) represent limited conceptualizations of this literary corpus. They are dominant ones and are not without merit.[10] However, they are by no means exclusive, nor are they necessarily the most compelling. Additional and powerful configurations and readings are emerging in the work of writers like Dionne Brand, Claire Harris, and Marlene Nourbese Philip.

'Racism was thé focus of my encounter with Canada,' Brand states in an interview with Dagmar Novak in the 1990 collection *Other Solitudes* (Hutcheon and Richmond, 272). For Brand, writing serves in the struggle against racial stereotyping (ibid., 276). The reality of racism within Canadian experience is a recurrent theme in her writing, as it is in that of Philip, Harris, and others. Sometimes the point is made blatantly, as in Harris's oft-cited poem, 'Policeman Cleared in Jaywalking Case.'[11] At other times, it is the subtext of a story or poem, as in Himani Bannerji's 'The Other Family.'[12] At all times, these writers' texts present an awareness of racism. This awareness extends to Canadian literature in general as well as to criticism and publishing. Thus, Harris confronts 'Canadian literature as it has been defined, as in Anglo-Saxon, male' (cited in Williamson, 121), while Philip locates racism in Canadian publishing and criticism (1992, 281): 'The currents of racism in Canadian society run deep, they run smooth, lulling white Canadians into a complacency that will see racism anywhere else but in Canada. Racism is as much the determining factor in the brutal and deadly confrontation between the police and African Canadians as it is in the traditional approach of arts councils and related institutions to African-based aesthetics and African Canadian artists' (Philip 1992, 12).

Philip names two political realities – being black and being female (1992, 65). These are inseparable and are understood both as political and historical realities. As a result, gender cannot be considered a separate concern, as has sometimes been the case, even in feminist analyses of (Canadian) literature. While Canadian feminist critiques have done much to deconstruct CanLitCrit, and the images of Canada it delivers, by inserting women writers' views and expressions into the formulation of Canadian experience, for writers like Philip this is not enough. Race and class are necessarily interwoven and must be approached and analyzed as such.

Brand's writing is distinct in its exploration of the intersections of race and gender. 'The difference is that I'm a lesbian,' Brand comments in an interview with colleague Makeda Silvera. 'I rejected that construct that also constructs women ... I'm talking about distancing myself as a human being from concepts or constructs of womanhood that are laid down largely through the rule of men' (Silvera, 358-9). For Brand, male constructs of womanhood are linked to those of country and nationhood, and they 'invigorate the morality in anti-colonial arguments' (360). Such linkages are not unfamiliar in the writing that dominated the Quebec of the Quiet Revolution, where the vision of an independent country and nation was frequently evoked by male authors through the use of stereotypical images of the female body.[13] The generation of feminist writers that emerged from this period not only reappropriated the representation of women's bodies and experiences, but it also distanced itself from the nationalist agenda.[14] A similar process would seem to be unfolding in English-speaking Canada.

Whether as object of reproach or of approach, the country or nation is a recurring figure in writings by women of racial or ethnic minority identification in Canada today. Nourbese Philip dedicates her collection of essays and writings on racism and culture, *Frontiers*, to Canada itself, 'in the effort of becoming a space / of true true be/longing' (5). Only in belonging can one feel part of the country and assume its nationality, she maintains. In the absence of a sense of belonging, there is only being 'othered.' Philip's challenge to the country is to transform this othering into 'm/othering.' 'Canada *needs* to m/other us,' she asserts. 'Her very salvation depends on m/othering all her people – those who be/long(ed) here when the first Europeans arrived – the Native peoples; as well as those, like the African, who unwittingly encountered History and became seminal in its development' (1992, 23-4).

The vital combination of race and gender in the writings of these three authors constructs a politicized and historicized vision of Canada at the same time that it secures the interdisciplinary nature of their work. 'My poems have always been poems that document something social, something historic, so there has been a mix of documentary poems and at times more lyrical poems,' Brand observes (Silvera, 366). For Brand, the sociopolitical and historic are essential ingredients in aesthetic expression. 'To read [Brand's] poetry,' Himani Bannerji remarks, 'is to read not only about her but also about her people, her identification with their struggles both in the metropole of Canada and the hinterland of the Caribbean' (1993, 38). Brand's is 'a kind of poetry which is "usable" in the business of everyday life, which is not transcendant [sic] over it' (Bannerji 1993, 38). Bannerji is drawing out Brand's resistance to poetry conceived as 'pure' art, apart from the quotidian.[15]

The valorization of the 'ordinary, everyday' that Bannerji discerns in Brand's work opens onto the consideration of the recently identified area of life writing. This newly acknowledged genre and critical practice have ushered in a whole range of literary subjects, styles, and practitioners and, in tandem with explorations of race and gender, is radically changing the frame of Canadian literature and the profile of Canada it presents. These writings are redefining what and who makes up Canadian literature. An excellent example is *Sharing Our Experience*, edited by Arun Mukherjee. This collection of letters was a project of the Canadian Advisory Council on the Status of Women for an anthology containing 'the living personal history of many women who, because of their ethnicity or racial origin, believe it important to share their thoughts and feelings.'[16] The letters' 'aura' of authenticity was more than textual effect for Mukherjee. 'The "truth" of these autobiographical accounts,' Mukherjee comments in her introduction, 'hits with a far stronger force than the "truth" of art where one is always conscious of the fictionality of art and the artistry of the artist' (1993, 11). It is not coincidental that life writing should be gaining critical momentum just as writings by authors previously marginalized as 'ethnic' or 'minority' are receiving recognition. As Francesco Loriggio observes in 'History, Literary History, and Ethnic Literature,' writing by ethnic (and racial) minority authors brings to literature an everydayness that is aesthetic strategy. These writers do not need to *imagine* exclusions, exceptionalities, or modernism's ruses because these have been inherent to their being, Loriggio explains. In the prose of their everyday lives lies the force of history (Loriggio, 35).[17] Life writing overrides the dichotomy of life and art, as it overrides generic categories such as the novel or the poem, valorizing literary efforts perceived to be outside or on the periphery of CanLit. The letters that make up *Sharing Our Experience* cause Arun Mukherjee – 'a person who makes her living by teaching literature to university students,' as she notes (1993, 11) – to rethink what is privileged as literature and who are recognized as writers. The letter-writers' success in drawing Mukherjee into their worlds leads her to redraw the lines around literature. 'In the end,' Marlene Kadar states, 'life writing problematizes the notion of Literature' (Kadar, 12). Out of problematization, however, new possibilities arise.

As boundaries shift, creative reference points are also being altered. 'My imaginative life doesn't take place here,' Nourbese Philip states (cited in Williamson, 230). 'I've never written a poem about winter and how cold or hard I find it.' Philip's work images[18] her island past, 'there [where] family was the whole village, if not island, / and came in all shades of black' (cited in Morrell, 117). When she depicts Canada, she chooses 'the hot heavy days' of 'July Again,' when 'front porches blossom, / from spinning wheel to begonia, / roman candles to petunias, / like the colonies' (122-3).

For Dionne Brand, as well, creative inspiration is found 'in another place, not here.' This line from *No Language Is Neutral* (Brand 1990b, 34)[19] became the title of the author's recent first novel, *In Another Place, Not Here* (1996), which opens with Elizete and Velia's (the main characters) first encounter: 'one afternoon as I [Elizete] look up saying to myself, how many more days these poor feet of mine can take this field, these blades of cane like razor, this sun like coal pot ... I see she. Hot, cool and wet, I sink the machete in my foot, careless, blood blossoming in the stalks of cane, a sweet ripe small wash me faint. With pain. Wash the field, spinning green mile after green mile around she. See she sweat, sweet like sugar' (3-4). This is a decidedly non-northern landscape, and the language that conveys it to readers is non-standard English. Brand's use of the Trinidadian, or demotic, speech, like Philip's and Harris's use of nation language,[20] constitutes a concrete sign of the very real changes taking place in Canadian literature.

It is beyond the scope of this essay to detail the various stages in the introduction of nation language to Canadian literature,[21] but it is important to register this development and its significance. Major Canadian publishers are now prepared to publish works that incorporate non-standard English. Perhaps more important, Canadian writers are prepared to share various nation languages with readers, for, as Brand reports, the decision to do so is complex: 'In the beginning I refused to use it because I really didn't want any Canadian to exoticize it [the Trinidadian]. And then when I finally used it I wanted to use it well. I really wanted to bring something else to it – because of its innate lyricism, some hear it and they say, "ohh ... " And I really didn't want all that patronizing shit. I wanted it to be taken seriously' (cited in Morrell, 368).

Beyond the risk of exoticization or, alternatively, degradation of one's language, lies the anguish of living in a 'foreign' language. This is powerfully captured by Nourbese Philip's poem 'Discourse on the Logic of Language,' in which English is portrayed as 'a foreign lan lan lang / language / l/anguish / anguish / – a foreign anguish / ... english / is a foreign anguish' (Philip 1989, 56-8). The foreign/ness of language is a theme that recurs in conjunction with the foreign/ness of landscape. 'Maybe this is where the metaphorical Canadian landscape comes in,' Philip speculates in a twist on the familiar 'Canadian theme' of the 'vast, empty' spaces of wilderness, 'the nothingness, the void, where you go to the frontier and seemingly there's nothing beyond it' (cited in Williamson, 231).

What writing by authors like Philip, Brand, and Harris shows is that there *is* something beyond the familiar frontier. Rich sources of imaginative traditions and myths are found beyond national borders. If 'nature' (wilderness) and the North have gripped Canadian literary expression and still-framed the images of the country, then creative inspiration flows increasingly from southerly locales. The effect of this border-crossing is an internationalization of Canadian literature. Critics like Joseph Pivato welcome this development. In *Contrasts* (1991), Pivato identifies intellectual isolationism as a central weakness of environmentalist theses of Canadian history and writing (25). He regrets lost opportunities to explore experiences that Canada shares with other nations, such as the Protestant ethic, industrialization, urbanism, immigration, and ethnic and racial heterogeneity (25-6). Writing like Brand's, Harris's and Philip's addresses these lacunae and, in the process, radically alters the frame of reference and the image centred within it. 'I don't consider myself on any margin, on the margin of Canadian literature,' Brand asserts. 'I'm sitting right in the middle of Black literature, because that's who I read, that's who I respond to' (1990, 14). Transposed to the construction of Canada, this is a differently centred expression, indifferent to the 'frontier' or 'geographical determinism' of the mythopoeic thematic tradition (see Pivato 1991, 25). It is a construct that stretches toward Central America and the Caribbean and across to Africa, in a definite departure from what Harris calls the 'bedrock determination to keep Canada Euro-centric' (cited in Williamson, 115).

Discussions of race challenge a Euro-centric construction of Canada. In conjunction with the challenges raised by gender analysis, these discussions facilitate a departure from constructions of Canada as a blank white page, empty and pure, a vast expanse of innocence, an icy cleansing place for the soul (Manguel 1994, 22-5). By overriding national frontiers and by relating less to geographical identification and more to peoples' traditions, this writing constructs culture as being just as crucial as nature.[22] As Cyril Dabydeen suggests, in his preface to *A Shapely Fire: Changing the Literary Landscape*, this writing redefines 'the conventional understanding of nationhood: from one viewed solely in terms of physical place to that which is based on a concept of the landscape of the mind, wherein place and psyche become intertwined in nation-building' (9-10). My readings corroborate Dabydeen's observation. Canada may be constructed in psychological or emotional terms, with vast physical spaces transforming into psychic spaces that are often much smaller, though no less intense. In Andrée Dahan's *Le Printemps peut attendre* (1985), for example, Quebec society is encompassed within a school located on the outskirts of Quebec City. Elsewhere, claustrophobic basement apartments in urban settings abound, an extreme example appearing in Sharda Vaidyanath's 'Pioneer Days,' where the protagonist retreats daily to the safety of a broomcloset until her husband returns from work (Mukherjee 1993, 117-23).

As Arun Mukherjee notes, Himani Bannerji's long prose poem 'Doing Time' portrays Canada as a prison for those who are not white and who are also women; Dionne Brand's female narrators see themselves as women in enemy territory; and for many Aboriginal writers, Canada is occupied territory (see Silvera, 424). These constructions locate different geographies, articulate different mythologies, and require readers to break through 'the sound barrier.' In her theory-fiction piece of the same title,[23] Himani Bannerji provides a sample of the results of such relocation. Bannerji begins with an epigraph from the Indian classical epic, *The Mahabharata*. Only later in the text does she share her awareness that many readers will not understand the reference. 'Western scholars of classical Indian literature would know,' Bannerji writes, 'but how many are they in number?' (cited in Scheier, 34). The author reminds readers that her cultural references cannot be taken for granted, as can, 'for example, the Bible, or even references to the peripheries of classical Greek literature' (34). She underscores the point that an array of mythologies circulates beyond the barrier of the familiar, which obstructs *hearing* (reading). These mythologies may be less familiar to some, but they are no less within the realm of writing in Canada.

Canada is being reconstructed through the writing of authors like Brand, Harris, and Philip. In practical terms, this has reshaped the lists of books I and others invite students to read under the rubric of Canadian literature. These lists can now comprise an array of new names and writing styles. Arun Mukherjee's *Sharing Our Experience* has met with enthusiastic student response. Critical classics such as Atwood's *Survival* or Frye's *Anatomy of Criticism* are noted en route to the study of books such as Mukherjee's *Oppositional Aesthetics* or Pivato's *Contrasts* (1991) and *Echo* (1994). These changes to the framework of Canadian literature, as I encountered it in the 1970s, are 'making a difference,' to play on the title of the most recent anthology of Canadian 'multicultural' literature, a 500-page volume by Smaro Kamboureli (1996). Writing by authors like Dionne Brand, Claire Harris, and M. Nourbese Philip is altering the way in which Canada is constructed, with the result that readers increasingly understand it as a country with complex gender, race, and ethnic dimensions that must be debated. This literature portrays Canada as a nation of both urban and rural cultures whose artistic inspirations flow from south, east, north, and west. This new 'construct' of Canada comprises not just, or even primarily, physical or geographical dimensions but also psychological or emotional dimensions and political passions – as is expressed in the writings of Canadians who identify with ethnic or racial minorities.

Notes

1 Cited in Morrell, 172. In this chapter, quotes from Brand, Harris, and Philip are found in Morrell, unless marked otherwise.
2 Organized through the Writers' Union of Canada, the conference generated public controversy for its policy of restricting attendance at daytime discussions and events to First Nations writers and writers of Colour.

3   Popular short-form expression for Canadian literary criticism.

4   Issue 58 (Fall 1995), guest-edited by Diana Brydon, is entitled 'Testing the Limits: Postcolonial Theories and Canadian Literatures.' Issue 57 (Winter 1995), 'Writing Ethnicity,' is guest-edited by Winfried Siemerling. Issue 54 is 'The Gender Issue.' A new issue, debate, or concern may be said to have 'penetrated' the critical centre when established journals start to devote special volumes to them.

5   Padolsky demonstrates this in his article through an analysis of Joy Kogawa's *Obasan* that draws upon social science models of acculturation.

6   So I did my undergraduate degree in French and Spanish (languages and literatures) and an MA and PhD in Lettres françaises.

7   Generated by 1960s nationalist enthusiasms, Canadian Studies programs by and large predated Women's Studies programs. At Trent, Canadian Studies was established in 1972 and Women's Studies in 1987.

8   It is thus disappointing that Davey bases his study on books selected because they have been important to particular Canadian audiences and have offered some portrayal of Canada as a 'semiotic field.' 'This criterion excludes from direct examination some recent novels of Canadian ethnic communities,' Davey reasons, 'which are of considerable importance, such as Nino Ricci's *Lives of the Saints*, Moyez Vassanji's *The Gunny Sack*, and Rohinton Mistry's *Such a Long Journey*, novels which contain few if any significations of Canada or of Canadian polity' (7). Davey allows that 'their lack of such significations, however, itself has political implications which contribute to the general suggestions of this study' (ibid.). But this would seem to be the canon at work. Davey's choice of novels 'that have been widely acclaimed, circulated, and studied' (ibid.) is not a neutral qualifier.

9   In addition to the Davey article and work by Joseph Pivato, see contributions to the twentieth anniversary issue of *Essays on Canadian Writing* (51-2) as well as essays by Arun Mukherjee, Francesco Loriggio, and so on.

10   The point here is not to take away (from) these concepts but to add to them.

11   In which the poet probes a real-life incident, wherein a white police officer arrests a young black woman for jaywalking. The young woman is stripsearched and jailed in what is an excessive and racist reaction to a minor and widely committed 'offence': jaywalking!

12   Where a non-white mother and daughter consider a drawing of their family unit, produced by the young daughter at her majority-white school. The daughter ends up adjusting the picture.

13   In a novel as famous as Hubert Aquin's *Prochain Episode*, the much-sought-after, elusive female character is known only as 'K,' the English pronunciation of which articulates the first half of the French pronunciation of the word 'Quebec.'

14   See Smart, 'The (In?)Compatibility of Gender and Nation in Canadian and Québécois Feminist Writing,' in which she concludes that 'there has been no real intersection between nation and gender' in contemporary Quebec feminists' writing.

15   This holds true for many writers, to be sure. Bannerji characterizes Brand's particular poetic practice as a commitment to socialist reconstruction, best illustrated by the poem 'Anti-poetry' in *Chronicles of the Hostile Sun*, which explores the limits of poetry in the face of everyday social injustices (Bannerji 1993, 39).

16   This was the wording of the original conception of the project, developed by the Canadian Advisory Council on the Status of Women under the auspices of the Social Development Committee and published in 1993.

17   For more on this important feature of life writing, see Kadar. Life writing, Kadar explains, humanizes and makes less abstract the 'self-in-the-writing.' At its most radical, life writing as a critical practice enhances reading as a means of 'emancipating an overdetermined "subject"' (Kadar, 12).

18   For a lengthy and fascinating play on the words 'image' and 'imagination,' see Philip's introduction to *She Tries Her Tongue, Her Silence Softly Breaks*, 'The Absence of Writing or How I Almost Became a Spy.'

19   The last entry in the section entitled, like the collection as a whole, 'No Language is Neutral' (34). The line continues, 'a woman might touch / something between beauty and nowhere, back there / and here, might pass hand over hand her own / trembling life.'

20 I share Teresa Zackodnik's preference for identifying as 'nation language' what others may refer to as Caribbean dialect or vernacular: 'Designations such as "demotic," "dialect," and "vernacular," impart the notion that this is somehow not a language but a bastardization or degeneration of standard English,' Zackodnik succinctly explains. See Zackodnik (1995). The important implication of the expression nation language is that it is a distinct language. For more on nation language, see Brathwaite.
21 See Kaup for some use of nation language in the work of writers Austin Clarke, M. Nourbese Philip, and Dionne Brand.
22 Philip (1992, 14), citing Oliver Sacks. Silvera and Brand are discussing the question of where they write, but I see a metaphorical sense in Brand's comment that space is not all that important to her.
23 'The Sound Barrier: Translating Ourselves in Language and Experience,' anthologized in Scheier, Sheard, and Wachtel, 26-40.

Works Cited
Aquin, Hubert. 1985. *Prochain Episode*. Montreal: Cercle du livre de France
Bannerji, Himani. 1990a. 'The Other Family.' In Linda Hutcheon and Marion Richmond, eds., *Other Solitudes: Canadian Multicultural Fictions*. Toronto: Oxford
–. 1990b. 'The Sound Barrier: Translating Ourselves in Language and Experience.' In Scheier, Sheard, and Wachtel, eds., *Language in Her Eye: Writing and Gender*. Toronto: Coach House
–. ed. 1993. *The Writing on the Wall: Essays on Culture and Politics*. Toronto: TSAR
Brand, Dionne. 1990a. 'The Language of Resistance.' *Books in Canada* 19 (7):13-6
–. 1990b. *No Language Is Neutral*. Toronto: Coach House
–. 1990c. 'Interview with Dagmar Novak.' In Linda Hutcheon and Marion Richmond, eds., *Other Solitudes: Canadian Multicultural Fictions*, 271-7. Toronto: Oxford
–. 1994. *Bread Out of Stone*. Toronto: Coach House
–. 1995. 'In the Company of My Work.' In Silvera Makeda, ed., *The Other Woman: Women of Colour in Contemporary Canadian Literature*, 356-80. Toronto: Sister Vision
–. 1996. *In Another Place, Not Here*. Toronto: Knopf
Brathwaite, Edward Kamau. 1984. *History of the Voice: The Development of Nation Language in Anglophone Caribbean Poetry*. London: New Beacon
Brydon, Diana. 1995. 'Reading Postcoloniality, Reading Canada.' *Essays on Canadian Writing* 56 (Fall 1995):1-19
Dabydeen, Cyril. 1987. *A Shapely Fire: Changing the Literary Landscape*. Oakville, ON: Mosaic
Dahan, Andrée. 1985. *Le Printemps peut attendre*. Montreal: Quinze
Davey, Frank. 1993. *Post-National Arguments: The Politics of the Anglophone-Canadian Novel since 1967*. Toronto: University of Toronto Press
Harris, Claire. 1984. 'Policeman Cleared in Jaywalking Case.' *Fables from the Women's Quarters*. Toronto: Williams-Wallace
–. 1993. 'I Dream of a New Naming.' In Janice Williamson, ed., *Sounding Differences: Conversations with Seventeen Canadian Women Writers*, 115-30. Toronto: University of Toronto Press
Hutcheon, Linda, and Marion Richmond, eds. 1990. *Other Solitudes: Canadian Multicultural Fictions*. Toronto: Oxford University Press
Kadar, Marlene, ed. 1992. *Essays on Life Writing: From Genre to Critical Practice*. Toronto: University of Toronto Press
Kamboureli, Smaro. 1996. *Making a Difference: Canadian Multicultural Literature*. Toronto: Oxford University Press
Kanaganayakam, Chelva. 1994. 'Writing Beyond Race: The Politics of Otherness.' *Toronto Review* 12 (3):7-l7
Kaup, Monika. 1995. 'West Indian Canadian Writing: Crossing the Border from Exile to Immigration.' *Essays on Canadian Writing* 57:171-93
Kogawa, Joy. 1981. *Obasan*. Toronto: Lester and Orpen Dennys
Loriggio, Francesco. 1990. 'History, Literary History, and Ethnic Literature.' In J. Pivato,

ed., *Literatures of Lesser Diffusion*, 21-45. Edmonton: Research Institute for Comparative Literature

Manguel, Alberto. 1994. 'Contemplating Canada.' *Imperial Oil Review* 78 (Summer):22-5

Morrell, Carol. 1994. *Grammar of Dissent*. Fredericton: Goose Lane

Mukherjee, Arun, ed. 1993. *Sharing Our Experience*. Ottawa: Canadian Advisory Council on the Status of Women

–. 1994. *Oppositional Aesthetics: Readings from a Hyphenated Space*. Toronto: TSAR

–. 1995. 'Canadian Nationalism, Canadian Literature and Racial Minority Women.' In Makeda Silvera, ed., *The Other Woman: Women of Colour in Contemporary Canadian Literature*, 421-44. Toronto: Sister Vision

Padolsky, Enoch. 1990. 'Establishing the Two-Way Street: Literary Criticism and Ethnic Studies.' *Canadian Ethnic Studies* 22 (1):22-37

Philip, Marlene Nourbese. 1989. *She Tries Her Tongue, Her Silence Softly Breaks*. Charlottetown: Ragweed

–. 1992. *Frontiers: Essays and Writings on Racism and Culture*. Stratford: Mercury

–. 1993. 'Writing a Memory Of Losing That Place.' In Janice Williamson, ed., *Sounding Differences: Conversations with Seventeen Canadian Women Writers*, 226-44. Toronto: University of Toronto Press

Pivato, Joseph, ed. 1990. *Literatures of Lesser Diffusion/Les littératures de moindre diffusion*. Edmonton: Research Institute for Comparative Literature

–. ed. 1991. *Contrasts: Comparative Essays on Italian-Canadian Writing*. Montreal: Guernica

–. 1994. *Echo: Essays on Other Literatures*. Toronto: Guernica

Libby Scheier, Sarah Sheard, and Eleanor Wachtel, eds. 1990. *Language in Her Eye: Views on Writing and Gender by Canadian Women Writing in English*. Toronto: Coach House

Siemerling, Winfried. 1996. 'Writing Ethnicity,' *Essays on Canadian Writing* 57:1-32

Silvera, Makeda, ed. 1995. *The Other Woman: Women of Colour in Contemporary Canadian Literature*. Toronto: Sister Vision

Smart, Patricia. 1994. 'The (In?)Compatibility of Gender and Nation in Canadian and Québécoise Feminist Writing.' *Essays on Canadian Writing* 54:12-22

ten Kortenaar, Neil. 1996. 'The Trick of Divining a Postcolonial Canadian Identity: Margaret Laurence between Race and Nation.' *Canadian Literature* 149:11-35

Williamson, Janice, ed. 1993. *Sounding Differences: Conversations with Seventeen Canadian Women Writers*. Toronto: University of Toronto Press

Zackodnik, Teresa. 1995. '"I Am Blackening in My Way": Dionne Brand's *No Language Is Neutral*.' *Essays on Canadian Writing* 57:194-211

'In another place, not here': Dionne Brand's Politics of (Dis)Location

Peter Dickinson

> Poetry is here, just *here*. Something wrestling with how we live,
> something dangerous, something honest.
> – Dionne Brand, *Bread Out of Stone*

I had originally thought that I would begin this chapter on Dionne Brand by locating myself within it, charting a course through the stormy waters of identity by offering a catalogue of the subject positions on which I randomly float: white Anglo-Scots gay male academic currently navigating between freelance writing in Vancouver and a research fellowship at the Université de Montréal. But, as Adrienne Rich points out in her essay 'Notes toward a Politics of Location,' this kind of Dedalusian game of mapping – a game that Rich admits to playing herself as a child – presumes a fixed centre, 'from which the circles [expand] into the infinite unknown' (212). It is this 'question of feeling at the center that gnaws' at Rich throughout her essay. 'At the center of what?,' she asks (212). And if, as Rich implies, my centre 'will not hold,' what does that say about the margins that I have constructed in my overly Cartesian universe, in my work on nationalisms and sexualities in contemporary Canadian literatures, in this essay? Brand offers a suitably destabilizing and dislocating response when she says: 'I don't consider myself on any "margin," on the margin of Canadian literature. I'm sitting right in the middle of Black literature, because that's who I read, that's who I respond to' (1990a, 14).

Clearly, then, a more fluid definition of the 'politics of location' is required before beginning any study of Brand's work: something more responsive to the shifting parameters of her identity as a black woman, lesbian, writer, documentary filmmaker, academic, scholar, archivist, and cultural activist; something akin to that articulated by Chandra Talpade Mohanty in 'Feminist Encounters: Locating the Politics of Experience.' In this essay, Mohanty sketches the outlines of 'the historical, geographical, cultural, psychic and imaginative boundaries which provide the ground for political definition and self definition for U.S. feminists in 1987' (31). According to Mohanty, these intersecting boundaries open up a 'temporality of struggle,' a site of political 'engagement' that 'suggests an insistent, simultaneous, non-synchronous process characterized by multiple locations,' at the same time as the 'reterritorialization' of said boundaries allows for 'a paradoxical continuity of self,' a 'mapping and transforming [of] political location' that 'suggests a particular notion of political agency, since ... location forces and enables specific modes of reading and knowing the dominant' (41, 42).

In what follows I want to examine the various national and sexual boundaries that both give shape to and delimit, at once legitimate and circumscribe, the production, distribution, and reception of Brand's work in this country as well as the ways in which Brand 'reterritorializes' these boundaries in her writing, (dis)placing or (dis)locating the national narrative of subjectivity, for example, into the diaspora of cross-cultural, -racial, -gender, -class, and -erotic identifications. In so doing, I will discuss how Brand elaborates both 'a temporality of struggle' and 'a paradoxical continuity of self' that are not only multiply located, but also multidirectional; how, in other words, Brand, as writer, inscribes her national and sexual experiences in historically defined representational forms, and how I, as reader, accede to those representations through a negotiation of my own historical and experiential contexts. The chapter is divided into two parts: in the first, I present an overview of recent feminist and postcolonial reconsiderations of the 'politics of location,' focusing on how publishing and media technologies in this country frequently contribute to the 'unlocatability' of Brand's work as distinctly 'Canadian'; in the second, I 'perform' a preliminary speech act reading of her critically acclaimed poetry collection, *No Language Is Neutral*, suggesting that a politics of location must also, in some senses, be accompanied by an ethics of listening.

As Caren Kaplan summarizes, 'The term "politics of location" emerged in the early 1980s as a particularly North American feminist articulation of difference, and even more specifically as a method of interrogating and deconstructing the position, identity, and privilege of whiteness' (139). Initially used by Adrienne Rich in a series of related essays exploring the effects of racism and homophobia on the women's movement in the United States (most of which have since been published together in *Blood, Bread, and Poetry*), the term, in seeking to account for the production and proliferation of multiple and manifold identities in an era of diaspora and displacement, as well as hegemonic Western interest in those identities, has since '[become] its own academic reification' (Kaplan, 138), at once deconstructing and naturalizing the boundaries between centre and margin.

Central to Rich's conception of a politics of location is her awareness of the impossibility of a 'global' vision of feminist solidarity, which, as she sees it, is merely a creation 'of white Western self-centeredness,' and which, moreover, is frequently founded on a deliberate confusion between what Rich identifies as competing 'claims to the white and Western eye and the woman-seeing eye.' 'Marginalized though we have been as women,' she asserts, 'as white and Western makers of theory, we also marginalize others because our lived experience is thoughtlessly white, because even our "women's cultures" are rooted in some Western tradition' (1986d, 219). Yet, as Kaplan points out, such a deconstructive move toward change – what Rich elsewhere refers to as a simultaneous process of 'demasculinizing' and 'de-Westernizing' (1986d, 225) – is inherently flawed from the outset because it mistakenly conflates 'Western' and 'white,' thereby 'reinscribing the centrality of white women's position within Western feminism' (141).

If Kaplan politely chastises Rich for failing to consider adequately her own identificatory investments in theorizing and receiving difference, Michele Wallace vehemently denounces Rich's role as a 'gatekeeper' of American feminism, 'somebody who defines the inside, thus keeping me out' (48-9). Describing herself as 'unlocated' and 'schizophrenic' as a black feminist writer and critic in the United States, Wallace advances a theory of location that contrasts sharply with that espoused by Rich. As Wallace puts it, 'when it came to writing, it turned out to be very much a problem of spanning several locations at once, none of which I was able to call home' (50). At the same time, however, she is careful not to discount or elide her sometimes intense feelings of fragmentation and of 'writing in silence' (49). In so doing, she articulates a politics of *un*location that seeks to legitimize 'the multiplicity of positions and allegiances that characterizes the contemporary diasporic or marginal subject' (Kaplan, 143). For Wallace, then, a politics of location is entirely a matter of 'process,' by which she necessarily means 'more than one process, more than one location, perhaps three or four, none of which connect in any self-evident manner. Or perhaps it is because I haven't found the connections yet. Perhaps this is the level at which my work can be in dialogue with itself without superimposing a premature closure or a false unity' (49).

Brand likewise forestalls 'premature closure' and 'false unity' in her work by embracing 'the dialogue between self and other in herself' (Zackodnik, 206). Unlike Wallace, however, Brand is willing to extend this dialogue to include Rich as well. In *Listening for Something*, her latest documentary feature, and one of the last films to be produced out of the National Film Board of Canada's Studio D, Brand engages the American writer in an extended conversation about the nation-state, citizenship, global capitalism, revolutionary socialism, racism, feminism, sexuality, and the positioning of themselves and their work in relation to each of these subjects.

Their ongoing dialogue, shot in grainy black and white, is intercut with lush colour sequences, in which the camera roams across the landscapes of the United States, Canada, and Tobago, visually locating the viewer as Rich and Brand read from their respective poetry.

It is interesting to note that Rich begins her contribution to *Listening for Something* in much the same way that she opens her essay 'Notes toward a Politics of Location': by critiquing Virginia Woolf's celebrated claim, in *Three Guineas*, that women have no country. As Rich puts it in the film, the challenge of growing up as a middle-class white woman in the racially divided southern United States was precisely to refuse such transcendent avenues of escape and to locate herself materially within the historical flux of her country, her city, her home.

And yet, a central paradox within Rich's formulation of a politics of location concerns the fact that her radical rethinking of the United States feminist movement, of 'how this *location* affects me, along with the realities of blood and bread within this nation' (1986a, 183), was actually occasioned by a trip to Sandinista-governed Nicaragua in the early 1980s. Understanding the meaning of 'being here' meant 'going there,' to reconfigure the title of one of her essays about the visit.[1] Or, as Kaplan succinctly puts it, 'Rich completely rewrites her "home" in terms of "away"' (141).[2] The irony is of course that a politics of location – at least as it is initially elaborated here by Rich – does not necessarily travel well as a theory of transnational feminist liberation. Nor does such cultural relativism adequately account for the various historical, material, and situational contingencies attendant upon the diasporic conditions of enslavement, migration, and decolonization, which more often than not contribute to a sense of displacement and exile, of feeling 'away' while 'home' and vice versa, or of feeling 'in between' the two. Gloria Anzaldúa has referred to this liminal space, this 'vague and undetermined place created by the emotional residue of an unnatural boundary,' as a 'borderland' (3).[3] Homi Bhabha, in his introduction to *The Location of Culture*, has recently labelled this realm 'the *beyond*,' a term that signals 'neither a new horizon, nor a leaving behind of the past' but, rather, 'a sense of disorientation, a disturbance of direction,' a term, moreover, that 'captures something of the estranging sense of the relocation of the home and the world – the unhomeliness – that is the condition of extra-territorial and cross-cultural initiations' (1, 9). 'The diaspora has made the world "home,"' according to Claire Harris, but this 'home' is less a tangible locale than a 'space between two worlds,' a 'place of paradox,' a 'limbo' to which poets like Harris and Brand find themselves confined (125). For her part, Brand has enumerated the politics of her particular *dis*locations in *Chronicles of the Hostile Sun* in terms of a further set of spatial paradoxes. Despite having lived *here* – in Canada – 'all [her] adult life,' what seems to matter most is that Brand was born down *there* –'in the Caribbean.' Having one's papers in order, owning a Canadian passport – these things are virtually meaningless in the face of an obdurate national psychology that, official government policies notwithstanding, continues to reinforce in Brand and her fellow immigrants the feeling that they are 'stateless anyway' (1984, 70).

What Brand seeks to convey with this statement, and throughout the collection from which it emerges, according to Leslie Sanders, 'is not "home" but rather "other people's experience" and "other places." As a black West Indian and a citizen of that "Third World," her poetic offering legitimately is "other," but it is also conscious of being so, it is consciously oppositional. And it is "here," not "there"' (26). Although Sanders for the most part persists in analyzing Brand's writing in terms of its imaginative figuring – 'as race, place and heritage' (22) – of the West Indies, she also 'dares' to claim Brand as a 'Canadian' writer. She does so by recuperating Brand's trope of 'statelessness' within and through Marshall McLuhan's paradigm of the 'borderline': 'statelessness as an imaginative reality is particularly possible and fruitful in this country of resonances. Claiming Brand as a Canadian writer is part of daring the identity McLuhan posits is truly Canadian. Similarly, by becoming a Canadian writer, Brand is extending the Canadian identity in a way McLuhan would recognize and applaud' (20).[4]

Sanders's use of the verb 'becoming' is, I believe, telling here, since Brand's race, gender, and sexuality necessarily preclude full participation in national citizenship and, thus, prevent her from ever 'being' a Canadian writer. In this sense, then, Brand remains a 'borderline case.' Or, as Carol Morrell suggests in her introduction to *Grammar of Dissent*, Brand, together with fellow Trinidadian-Canadian poets Harris and Marlene Nourbese Philip, represents 'a particular kind of exiled woman': 'Of African descent, their cultural and linguistic history has been foreshortened: much of Africa was lost when their ancestors were forcibly brought to the New World. Having themselves voluntarily emigrated to Canada, they have become distanced from their childhood experiences of family and community in Trinidad. In Canada, because of what they call subtle but systemic racism, these women do not readily fit in. To many Canadians they "are" the colour of their skin. Each has had some of her writing rejected by Canadian publishers as not being "Canadian enough"' (9). The link between the Canadian publishing industry and nationalist sentiment that Morrell alludes to in passing at the end of this quotation bears further investigation, I believe, especially as it has an impact on the 'statelessness' of a writer like Brand, for whom Canada is both home and 'enemy territory' (1988, 97). For, as Kaplan astutely notes, when it comes to the interpretation of texts, the politics of location cannot be separated from the politics of 'production and reception'; that is, the need to '[historicize] the relations of exchange that govern literacy, the production and marketing of texts, the politics of editing and distribution, and so on' (139).

In constructing itself as 'The Canadian Publisher,' McClelland & Stewart helps define and foster, to a certain extent, literary nationalism in this country. As Arun Mukherjee has recently put it, mainstream publishing houses mirror 'the "soul" of the nation, its history and traditions, which are also conceived in terms of a nation's unified "spirit"' (433). But what does this say about the legions of small, independent presses in this country (The Women's Press, Sister Vision, Williams-Wallace, Mercury, Gynergy, Ragweed, Press Gang, Theytus, Fifth House, TSAR, Goose Lane, Polestar, etc.) that have made it their mandate to publish the work of 'racial minority women' writers like Dionne Brand?[5] If large established houses like McClelland & Stewart reflect the 'soul' of Canada (a soul that, needless to say, is overwhelmingly male and white), if such official channels of 'print-capitalism' might be said to help operationalize what Benedict Anderson has called 'imagined nationness' (46), then the 'alternative' presses (dare we call them *counter*-presses?) enumerated above would seem to reflect Canada's dark, outered, and exotic 'Other.' As Mukherjee remarks, the dominant discourse here is not one of nationality but of 'ethnicity': 'Many Aboriginal and racial minority women writers have spoken eloquently about how their writing has been turned down time and again because it was not deemed "Canadian," but "ethnic," that is emerging from and speaking to a minority group. When published by small, usually "ethnic" presses, the establishment – reviewers and academics – othered it in multiple ways: it was exotic; it was "Black," or "Native," or "South Asian"; it was about "immigrant" experience. The category Canadian has been denied to these writers, their work seldom seen as contributing to "Canadian" life.' (430)

This would perhaps explain why early reviews of Brand's work – which, up until the 1990 release of *No Language Is Neutral*, was published almost exclusively by Williams-Wallace, a small press specializing in writings by Afro-Caribbean women – are so clearly drawn along lines of race and gender. As Mukherjee implies, critical print review media in this country often work hand in hand with the publishing industry to institutionalize dominant views of what it means to write 'as a Canadian.' In the case of two 1983 reviews of Brand's poetry, this process of institutionalization is also one of 'othering.' Douglas Fetherling, for example, opens his *Books in Canada* review of Brand's *Winter Epigrams* by admitting that 'Brand's name is a new one to me, and I know only what the little blurb reveals, that she "is a Toronto Black poet" who's published three earlier titles' (38). By the end of his review, however, Brand is no longer 'a *Toronto* Black poet,' but a 'West Indian' one: 'To this West Indian poet, the winter is not the stuff of the Gilles Vigneault song nor a Calvinist visitation meant to test people; it's a strange and terrible ordeal' (38). Brand's collection thus becomes, in

Fetherling's estimation, testimony not to the poet's facility with a satirical and ironic form that dates back to ancient Greece, but to her inability (or unwillingness) to write about that most Canadian of experiences – winter – in a manner representative of the literary traditions of the 'two founding nations' (France and England).[6] For her part, in a *Quill & Quire* mini-review of *Primitive Offensive*, Catherine Russell concludes that much of the book has 'a threatening tone,' Brand's 'African theme' producing a poetic language that likewise becomes 'primitive in its violence and nakedness.' In the end, Russell sighs, 'Brand's persistent reworking of her anguish is ... exhausting. One craves a pair of bongos at least to carry one through the onslaught' (76).

In an interview with Beverly Daurio, also published in *Books in Canada*, Brand responds to the representation of her work in reviews as follows: 'Reviews are equally racist. Work by peoples of colour has to prove universality; a white writer is never asked to prove that. The other things you look for in a review are words like "anger." Reviewers always talk about the anger of Black writers' (14). Thus, in her review of Brand's recent novel, *In Another Place, Not Here*, we find Joan Thomas, in the *Globe and Mail*, praising Brand's 'apparently effortless facility with language' but reacting against the 'bitter tone' that 'seems to be the point of view of the novel': 'there is no hope of a future that transcends the tragedies of the past,' laments Thomas of the book's ending, 'anger is the end of the road' (C10). But in seeking transcendence, and by imposing her own sense of closure onto the text, Thomas ignores the deliberately unfinalizable quality of Brand's novel. Divided into two parts, set in two different locales (Toronto and an unnamed Caribbean island), focalized through two different protagonists (Elizete and Verlia), alternating between first and third person narration, using language that combines both a lush participial demotic and a standard English idiom, travelling back and forth in time and space, playing off the themes of home and exile, and complicating dichotomies of race and gender with issues of sexuality and class, *In Another Place, Not Here* repeatedly confounds readerly expectations. Unfortunately, Brand's reframing of intra- and extratextual centre-margin relations in this way tends to get lost on the CanLitCrit establishment, which for the most part still operates under the aegis of an either/or equation of literary nationalism: does she write about Canada or not? And if so, *how* does she write about it?

'Where is here?' Northrop Frye famously queried on the eve of Canada's centennial celebrations (220). But for Brand, 'Here is not a word with meaning when it can spring legs, vault time, take you ... her away [...] here is nothing to hold on to or leave a mark, here you ... hold on to your name until it becomes too heavy and you forget it' (1996a, 199). Because Brand's 'here' is necessarily mediated, provisional, evanescent – in a word, 'unlocatable' – her work remains marginal/marginalizable in academic discussions of Canadian literary canons. In this regard, we begin to see how 'national' publishing, reviewing, and teaching priorities further complicate the issue of a politics of location with regard to Brand's work: different notions of location, of what it means to be 'here' and write about 'there,' for example, give rise to contradictory political practices and agendas.

I want to conclude this chapter with a brief textual analysis of Brand's 1990 collection of poetry, *No Language Is Neutral*. More specifically, adapting the speech act theory that implicitly informs Judith Butler's *Gender Trouble* and Homi Bhabha's 'DissemiNation,' I want to assess the extent to which Brand's strategic use of 'lesbian' parataxis and 'Caribbean' demotic forms in the text's two long poems, 'hard against the soul' and the title sequence, 'No Language Is Neutral,' locates minority utterance in (performative) opposition to hegemonic patriarchal and nationalist discourses. I only regret that, due to my inability to quote at length from either of these extraordinary pieces, this assessment must necessarily be a foreshortened and partial critical exercise.

Although neither explicitly mentions him in their texts, it seems to me that both Butler's and Bhabha's senses of 'the performative' – as applied to the elaboration of gender and cultural differences, respectively – owe something to the definition of the term put forward by J.L. Austin in *How to Do Things with Words* (first published in 1962). In this posthumously published book, Austin distinguishes between two categories of linguistic utterance: 'constatives' and 'performatives.' Whereas the former category is made up of utterances that describe a situation or state a fact that can be assessed as 'true' or 'false,' the latter category consists of utterances that actually perform an action in words, one that is neither true nor false but, rather, 'felicitous' or 'infelicitous,' sincere or insincere, well invoked or misinvoked (Austin, 12-8). In other words, performatives are not just utterances that 'say' something; they also 'do' something (133). And, as Austin demonstrates with his analysis of the performative function of the phrase 'I do' in a marriage ceremony (5-11 and passim), the *location* in which it is spoken has a significant impact on the production of meaning put into play by a given *locution*.

Despite the fact that he later reverses his own binary opposition between constatives and performatives in favour of a three-tiered iterative/iterable system of 'locutionary,' 'illocutionary,' and 'perlocutionary' acts (see Austin, 94-108), Austin's internal hierarchy of performatives has been the subject of much deconstructive scrutiny. In 'Signature, Event, Context,' for example, Jacques Derrida criticizes, among other things, Austin's refusal to discuss all those performatives labelled 'non-serious' and '*parasitic*'; that is, utterances 'said by an actor on the stage, or ... introduced in a poem, or spoken in soliloquy' (Austin, 22).[7] And, in the final chapter of *Bodies that Matter*, Butler challenges the 'centrality of the marriage ceremony in J.L. Austin's examples of performativity,' once again emphasizing the importance of location: 'from where and when does such a performative draw its force, and what happens to the performative when its purpose is precisely to undo the presumptive force of the heterosexual ceremonial?' (224-5).[8] Moreover, Butler, like Derrida before her, critiques Austin for attributing the 'binding power' of the performative speech act solely to the intentional will or authority of the speaker. As she notes, the issue of power is much more complex here: 'If the power of discourse to produce that which it names is linked with the question of performativity, then the performative is one domain in which power acts *as* discourse' (1993, 225). Nevertheless, the absent presence of Austin at the end of Butler's earlier book is here invoked (or misinvoked) by name precisely to reassert that 'genders can be neither true nor false, neither real nor apparent, neither original nor derived' (1990, 141). (Austin is even more of a presence in Butler's *Excitable Speech: A Politics of the Performative* [1997].)

How, then, does gender 'perform'? What exactly does it 'do'? Or, to quote Butler, 'In what senses is gender an act?' 'As in other ritual social dramas [like marriage, for example],' she notes by way of reply to her own question, 'the action of gender requires a performance that is *repeated*. This repetition is at once a reenactment and reexperiencing of a set of meanings already socially established; and it is the mundane and ritualized form of their legitimation' (1990, 140). This *'stylized repetition of acts'* – what Butler (once again following Derrida) refers to elsewhere as 'citationality' (1993, 12-6 and passim) – 'moves the conception of gender off the ground of a substantial model of identity to one that requires a conception of gender as a constituted *social temporality'* (1990, 140-1). Within the 'social temporality' of Brand's 'hard against the soul,' its 'temporality of struggle,' to reinvoke Mohanty's phrase, the reiteration and re-membering of lesbian desire is thus partly performed through the stylized, paratactical repetition of the homonym 'hear/here.' In the space of a single stanza or even line, one word is called forth and responded to by the other, as in section IV of the poem, for example, where a lover's voice floats up out of sleep and is answered by a warm embrace. It is *here*, in 'these gestures,' according to the speaker of the poem, that we *hear* the beginnings of time (Brand, 1990b, 39). And time's surcease.

Similar tropes of recitation and repetition abound throughout this suite of poems, most notably in the first section, with its successive incantations of 'this is you girl,' each used to introduce a new stanza, and to catalogue an increasingly vivid progression of concrete images that supplement the opening deictic (6-7). The concept of addressivity is of equal importance in this regard. Indeed, the prominent position afforded the pronoun 'you' throughout the collection, and its frequent placement alongside or in conjunction with one or another of the 'hear/here' word pairings (as in 'I hear you / I am here for you'), suggests that Brand's poetry is part of a larger dialogue, that the negotiation and articulation of her identity takes place in a 'dialogic of differences' (Zackodnik, 206).

Of course, gender and sexuality are not the only provisional identities being performed here, as the citational locations/locutions of that word, and its auditory complement, elsewhere in the collection demonstrate. As Brand's text points out, there are no easy equivalencies to be made in terms of the discontinuous 'social temporalities' of gender and race. However, it is interesting to note the degree to which race, in contemporary cultural criticism, is taken as *the* one identity category that defies performative description and theorization; that is, notwithstanding narratives of passing, racial difference is interpreted as 'readily knowable,' and therefore 'readable,' because the signs of difference are always already there, made visible to the naked eye (see Martin, 110).[9] In other words, races are either 'true' or 'false,' not 'felicitous' or 'infelicitous.' But once again to revert to Austin, this is to conflate performance in its literal or *literary* (i.e., theatrical) sense with linguistic performativity, a discursive equation that Butler, in *Bodies that Matter*, admits to being partly responsible for by earlier 'citing drag [in *Gender Trouble*] as an example of performativity, a move that was taken then, by some, to be *exemplary* of performativity' (1993, 230; see also 1990, 137-8). As Butler goes on to clarify, 'If drag is performative that does not mean that all performativity is to be understood as drag' (1993, 230-1). Thus it is with Brand's frequent use of Caribbean demotic illocutions in her poetry, the presence of which, in 'No Language Is Neutral' in particular, must not be read reductively as a sign of the text's performance of a kind of racial drag or parodic minstrelism. Indeed, the 'rudiments' of Brand's grammar in this context (which is by no means 'rudimentary'), her 'grammar of dissent' in the words of Carol Morrell, are deeply rooted in history, combining a cultural 'morphology' of silent subjection ('rolling chain and copper gong') with the whispered 'idioms' of unfettered colloquy ('talking was left for night and hush') (1990b, 23).

What we are hearing here, in this text, is an act of resistance, performed through the Creolization of a dominant language (English) and resulting in the creation of a 'variable, distinct speech community' (Winer, 12). African peoples, forcibly relocated to the Caribbean by European slave-trading powers in the eighteenth and early nineteenth centuries, were prevented from communicating with each other in their original tribal tongues and so put together a new, hybrid language, one that deliberately 'contaminated' the official patron discourses of their colonizers (English, French, Dutch, Spanish, etc.) with African idioms and speech patterns. Or, as Brand puts it, 'Hard-bitten on mangrove and wild bush,' men and women suddenly found themselves 'spitting out the last spun syllables for cruelty' because there was a 'new sound forming, / pushing toward lips made to bubble blood' (1990b, 23). Teresa Zackodnik has recently analyzed the interplay between standard English and what she (after Edward Brathwaite) calls Caribbean nation language in Brand's poetry, connecting it with related issues of identity and place: 'Dionne Brand's poetry exhibits this ambivalence [toward place and language], yet also moves toward a notion of the exiled self as place and belonging, and a conception of the language that will voice her experience as a multivoiced discourse in both standard English and Caribbean nation language' (194).[10] Of course, neither language is neutral here; as Brand well knows, each is thoroughly marked by and imbricated in the other: 'Each sentence realized or / dreamed jumps like a pulse with history and takes a / side' (34).

As sociolinguist John Roy has pointed out, in many Caribbean Creole, or nation, languages, 'tense marking is optional'; what is of greater grammatical importance is aspect – that is, whether a given verb phrase describes an event that has already occurred or whether it describes 'a state that exists at the moment of speech' (146, 147). Within the context of Brand's 'No Language Is Neutral,' and within the larger framework of Austin's theory of performative utterances, it is worth pausing over her rather idiosyncratic use of the verb 'to do' throughout the poem. Consider, as but one example, the following two lines: 'Silence done curse god and beauty here, / people does hear things in this heliconia peace' (1990b, 23). In the first instance ('done curse god'), the aspect marked is 'completive,' done, as a 'preverbal marker,' having 'the dominant sense of completion of an activity, event or process' in Lise Winer's schematization of English Creoles in Trinidad and Tobago (27). But as Winer goes on to note, when combined with another auxiliary verb (in Brand's case, the non-stative 'curse'), the meaning of done becomes more ambiguous, either 'emphasizing the end-point of an event,' 'viewing the event as a completed whole,' or assessing 'the situation as having been achieved at some previous point in time, but as still continuing' (28). In the second instance ('does hear things'), the aspect marked is 'habitual' or 'present imperfective,' which 'refers to a repeated activity, a relationship between a dynamic situation and a bounded period of time during which this activity occurs' (26). In both instances, however, the aspect is clearly not marked as 'perfective'; that is, we are meant to hear that the racial history Brand is performing for us here is not something in the past, that the Caliban-like cursing informing this passage, and the poem and text from which it emerges, necessarily continues in the present, relocated to metropolitan centres like Toronto and Vancouver, teeming with 'race conscious landlords and their jim crow flats, oh yes! / here!' (Brand 1990b, 31).

Eliding the degree to which racial identities, like gender and erotic identities, are also performative (at least in terms of linguistic speech acts) is to presume that whites are not also racialized in accounts of cultural difference, that whiteness is the free-floating signifier, the undifferentiated, performative ground against which all other (i.e., non-white) hues of the rainbow must figure themselves in fixed and static opposition:[11] 'White. She had thought that it was a style, a way of living well that perhaps anyone could acquire,' writes Brand of Verlia in *In Another Place* (1996a, 136). One consequence of this stylization of whiteness as normative, according to Brand and Linda Carty in '"Visible Minority Women": A Creation of the Canadian State,' is that all non-whites become 'quantitatively aberrant and qualitatively homogeneous' (169). Moreover, as Brand points out in a paper she delivered at the 1994 Writing Thru Race Conference in Vancouver, the construction of 'whiteness' as synonymous with 'Canadianness' carries with it further powers of social legitimation and exclusion: 'The European nation-state of Canada built itself around "whiteness," differentiating itself through "whiteness" and creating outsiders to the state, no matter their claims of birthright or other entitlement. Inclusion in or access to Canadian identity, nationality and citizenship (de facto) depended and depends on one's relationship to "whiteness"' (1994, 173-4).

The performative slippage between racial and national identities (not to mention class and sexual ones), between whiteness and Canadianness, that Brand highlights here is also articulated by Bhabha – albeit in a much different context – in his highly influential essay, 'DissemiNation.' Like Butler's theories of gender performativity, Bhabha's conception of 'national ambivalence' would also seem to be predicated on the iterative/iterable premises of speech act theory. In posing the question 'How do we conceive of the "splitting" of the national subject?' Bhabha distinguishes between the 'accumulated temporality' of the pedagogical (or constative, to put it in Austinian terms), which 'founds its narrative authority in a tradition of the people,' and the 'repetitious, recursive strategy,' the '"in-between"' temporality of the performative, which 'interrupts the self-generating time of national production' through 'its enunciatory "present"' (1990, 298-9). In so doing, Bhabha is 'attempting to discover the uncanny moment of cultural difference that emerges in the process of enunciation' (312), a process 'that arises from the ambivalent splitting of the pedagogical and the performative,' and from which 'there emerges a more instantaneous and subaltern voice of the people, a minority discourse that speaks betwixt and between times and places' (309).

However, in speaking betwixt and between times and places, something inevitably gets lost. 'Between my stories / and the time I have to remember,' writes Brand in 'No Language Is Neutral,' 'between me and history,' a verse can still go missing, a chapter may yet disintegrate and turn to dust (1990b, 26). In the 'blood-stained blind of race and sex' (27), some narratives emerge more clearly than others, and some stories never get told at all. Hence Butler's claim that the repetition of a performative 'act' of gender is always, in some senses, 'a provisional failure of memory' (1993, 244, n. 7); and hence Bhabha's reworking of Ernst Renan's notion that the act of national identification also requires a 'syntax of forgetting,' or 'forgetting to remember': 'To be obliged to forget – in the construction of the national present – is not a question of historical memory; it is a construction of a discourse on society that *performs* the problematic totalization of the national will' (1990, 310, 311). In the construction of the 'national [and sexual] present' of Brand's 'No Language Is Neutral,' the here and now of 'race conscious landlords and their jim crow flats,' 'this place where you are a woman and your breasts need / armour to walk. Here' (1990b, 33), there is an acknowledgment that 'truth' is unimportant, that 'nostalgia' feeds a lie, and that memory is but a 'fiction.'

But if Brand's 'syntax of forgetting' seems to suggest here, in 'No Language Is Neutral,' a process of fragmentation, a splitting in two in terms of national identity (with 'one branch [falling] silent' and the other 'argu[ing] hotly for going home' [1990b, 31]), a continuation of the 'statelessness' elaborated in *Chronicles of the Hostile Sun*, in 'hard against the soul' her language of re-membering, her navigation of 'the thick soil of / who we are' (41), her tracing of 'the map to coming home, the tough geography' (40), implies a provisional alignment of racial, gender, and erotic identities within a single, coherent location – the lesbian body. It is only here, the final lines of the poem suggest, that the speaker finds a true vision of herself ('my eyes followed me to myself' [51]), or more properly the multiplicity of her *selves*. What others deny exists, or label *terra incognita*, is instantly recognizable to Brand. This is a place she has been before she tells us in the very last line of the poem. And to which she will no doubt return.

According to Morrell, Afro-Caribbean-Canadian writers like Brand, Harris, and Nourbese Philip frequently adopt an essentialist subject-position in their work as a tool 'for political intervention': 'This strategy allows them both a community and a coherent sense of self – however fictive or imaginative – from which to act and write' (10). Brand's invention here, at the end of *No Language Is Neutral*, of a 'mythic' space from and through which to speak, her 'reterritorialization' of the shifting boundaries of her identity (as a black woman, as a lesbian, as a black lesbian) in order to map out 'a paradoxical continuity of self,' thus returns us once again to Mohanty and the politics of location or, more properly, the politics of the locational *and* the locutional. In her essay 'Travels in the Postmodern: Making Sense of the Local,' Elspeth Probyn 'explore[s] a central problematic within feminist cultural theory' – first articulated by Gayatri Spivak – that is, 'Whether the subaltern can speak' (177). She does so by organizing her thoughts 'around three current metaphors: locale, location, and local' (177). 'Locale,' in Probyn's schema, refers to both a discursive and non-discursive place that is the setting for a particular (gendered) event, 'home being the most obvious example.' 'Local' would appear to be the more spatialized locale's temporal equivalent, that which 'directly issu[es] from or [is] related to a particular time.' Finally, 'location' is more methodological in meaning, corresponding to the 'sites of research' through which knowledge is ordered and sequenced (178). Roughly, then, we may classify the three terms as follows: locale = experiential; local = contextual or historical; and location = institutional. The feminist cultural critic's task thus becomes, according to Probyn, to 'make sense' of the local (i.e., the historical and contextual) '[with]in and against' the opposite extremes and conflicting pulls of locale and location. 'Interwoven through these concerns,' Probyn concludes, 'is the very immediate question of whether the subaltern can speak. This question requires that we be continually vigilant to the necessity of bringing to the light the submerged conditions that silence others and the other in ourselves' (186).

'In another place, not here, a woman might touch / something between beauty and nowhere' (Brand 1990b, 34). In another place, not here, a woman might, in other words, be heard. As Brand's textual play on the homonym 'here/hear' demonstrates, any radical rearrangement of hegemonic figure/ground indices of identity first of all requires us to replace the standard feminist and postcolonial equation of the politics and poetics of location concerning who can and cannot speak with one that looks more closely at who is listening; it also requires us to examine carefully the nature and intent of this listening, to determine how privileged (white) groups 'can know the difference between occasions for responsive listening and listening as an excuse for silent collusion with the status quo of racial and neocolonial inequalities' (Roman, 79). 'Quite here, I hear from you' is the anaphoric phrase used by Brand throughout 'Phyllis,' another poem included in *No Language Is Neutral* (1990b, 11-3). Echoing her here, within the 'locale' of my body, and the 'location' of the academic institution, I am striving to hear, to make some sense of the 'local' languages of race, gender, class, and sexuality and the role each plays in the construction of Canada as a nation.

Notes

A slightly different version of this essay forms a chapter of my book *Here Is Queer: Nationalisms, Sexualities, and the Literatures of Canada*, forthcoming from the University of Toronto Press.

1 See her '"Going There" and Being Here,' in *Blood, Bread, and Poetry*, 156-9. Other essays in this volume dealing with Rich's experiences in Nicaragua, particularly as they affected her subsequent formulation of a 'politics of location' vis-à-vis United States feminism, include 'North American Tunnel Vision' and 'Blood, Bread, and Poetry: The Location of the Poet.' It is interesting to note that at the end of the latter essay 'poems by Dionne

Brand' are listed among those writings that Rich turns to 'for signs of [the] fusion I have glimpsed in the women's movement, and most recently in Nicaragua' (1986a, 187). Rich may be referring here to a series of epigrams that Brand wrote to Ernesto Cardenal, Nicaraguan priest, poet, and former Sandinistan politician; see Brand 1993.

2 For a sustained critique of the concept of 'home' as it figures in feminist cultural criticism, see Biddy Martin and Chandra Talpade Mohanty, 'Feminist Politics: What's Home Got to Do With It?'

3 On how 'Anzaldúa's location in the borderland leads her to deny that there is any place that can be called home' (250), and on how her text 'can be read as oppositional to binaries such as home and exile, center and margin, power and passivity, dominant and dominated, personal and political, public and private histories' (236), see Inderpal Grewal, 'Autobiographic Subjects, Diasporic Locations.' Having said this, however, and, moreover, having acknowledged that Anzaldúa writes from multiple locations precisely in order to 'enable' cross-cultural feminist coalitions, Grewal nevertheless stresses that 'the term "borderlands" has become specific to Chicano culture, thus designating the specific locations of Mexican-Americans' (248).

4 In his essay, 'Canada: The Borderline Case,' McLuhan asserts that 'Canada is a land of multiple borderlines, psychic, social, and geographic' (244), a condition that contributes to what he calls 'Canada's low-profile [national] identity' (246), which, far from being a hindrance in the 'global village,' 'nourishes flexibility' and 'approaches the ideal pattern of electronic living' (247, 248).

5 I borrow the locution 'racial minority women' from Arun Mukherjee; see her 'Canadian Nationalism, Canadian Literature and Racial Minority Women.'

6 For a much different reading of *Winter Epigrams*, one that traces 'the line of ... tradition' in which Brand is writing to the Caribbean (1983, 18), see Edward Brathwaite 1985.

7 Critics like Mary Louise Pratt and Shoshana Felman, however, have since made use of Austin's theories to examine the operation of just such a class of performatives in literature. See Pratt, *Toward a Speech Act Theory of Literary Discourse*; and Felman, *The Literary Speech Act: Don Juan with J.L. Austin, or Seduction in Two Languages*.

8 Eve Kosofsky Sedgwick also invokes Austin and 'the weird centrality of the marriage example for performativity in general' to make much the same point regarding 'sexual orthodoxy' in her essay 'Queer Performativity.' See especially pp. 2-4.

9 On the intersections between race and gender in narratives of passing, see Valerie Smith. Butler introduces sexuality into the admixture of competing identities with her readings of Jennie Livingston's film, *Paris Is Burning*, and Nella Larsen's novella, *Passing*. See Butler 1993, 122-40 and 167-85, respectively.

10 See also Brathwaite, *History of the Voice: The Development of Nation Language in Anglophone Caribbean Poetry*.

11 I am borrowing the figure/ground metaphor from Biddy Martin here; see Martin 1994, 110 and passim. She is, in turn, borrowing it from Butler; see Butler 1990, 123 and passim. Toni Morrison has recently provided a much needed corrective to this prevailing view vis-à-vis American fiction in *Playing in the Dark: Whiteness and the Literary Imagination*.

Works Cited

Anderson, Benedict. 1991. *Imagined Communities: Reflections on the Origins and Spread of Nationalism*. 2nd ed. London: Verso

Anzaldúa, Gloria. 1987. *Borderlands/La Frontera: The New Mestiza*. San Francisco: Aunt Lute

Austin, J.L. 1975. *How to Do Things with Words*. 2nd ed. J.O. Urmson and Marina Sbisà, eds. Oxford: Clarendon

Bhabha, Homi K. 1990. 'DissemiNation: Time, Narrative, and the Margins of the Modern Nation.' In H. Bhabha, ed., *Nation and Narration*, 291-320. New York: Routledge

–. 1994. *The Location of Culture*. New York: Routledge

Brand, Dionne. 1984. *Chronicles of the Hostile Sun*. Toronto: Williams-Wallace

–. 1988. 'At the Lisbon Plate.' *Sans Souci and Other Stories*. Toronto: Williams-Wallace

–. 1990a. 'The Language of Resistance.' Interview with Beverly Daurio. *Books in Canada* 19 (7):13-6

–. 1990b. *No Language Is Neutral*. Toronto: Coach House
–. 1993. *Winter Epigrams and Epigrams to Ernesto Cardenal in Defense of Claudia*. Toronto: Williams-Wallace
–. 1994. *Bread Out of Stone*. Toronto: Coach House
–. 1996a. *In Another Place, Not Here*. Toronto: Knopf
–, dir. 1996b. *Listening for Something ... Adrienne Rich and Dionne Brand in Conversation*. National Film Board of Canada, Studio D
Brathwaite, Edward Kamau. 1984. *History of the Voice: The Development of Nation Language in Anglophone Caribbean Poetry*. London: New Beacon
–. 1985. 'Dionne Brand's Winter Epigrams.' *Canadian Literature* 105:18-30
Butler, Judith. 1990. *Gender Trouble: Feminism and the Subversion of Identity*. New York: Routledge
–. 1993. *Bodies that Matter: On the Discursive Limits of 'Sex.'* New York: Routledge
–. 1997. *Excitable Speech: A Politics of the Performative*. New York: Routledge
Carty, Linda, and Dionne Brand. 1993. '"Visible Minority" Women: A Creation of the Canadian State.' In Himani Bannerji, ed., *Returning the Gaze: Essays on Racism, Feminism and Politics*, 169-81. Toronto: Sister Vision
Derrida, Jacques. 1982. 'Signature, Event, Context.' Trans. by Alan Bass. *Margins of Philosophy*, 307-30. Chicago: University of Chicago Press
Felman, Shoshana. 1983. *The Literary Speech Act: Don Juan with J.L. Austin, or Seduction in Two Languages*. Trans. Catherine Porter. Ithaca, NY: Cornell University Press
Fetherling, Douglas. 1983. 'Resurrecting the Long Poem: From Robin Skelton's Old Cornish Ballads to the Pornography of Winter in Montreal.' Rev. of *Wordsong*, by Robin Skelton; *What Place Is This?*, by Rosalind MacPhee; *God's Geography*, by Don Gutteridge; *Split Levels*, by Judith Fitzgerald; *Winter Epigrams and Epigrams to Ernesto Cardenal in Defense of Claudia*, by Dionne Brand. *Books in Canada* 12 (8):37-8
Frye, Northrop. 1971. 'Conclusion to a *Literary History of Canada*.' In *The Bush Garden: Essays on the Canadian Imagination*, 213-51. Toronto: Anansi
Grewal, Inderpal. 1994. 'Autobiographic Subjects and Diasporic Locations: *Meatless Days* and *Borderlands*.' In Inderpal Grewal and Caren Kaplan, eds., *Scattered Hegemonies: Postmodernity and Transnational Feminist Practices*. Minneapolis: University of Minnesota Press
Harris, Claire. 1986. 'Poets in Limbo.' In Shirley Neuman and Smaro Kamboureli, eds., *A Mazing Space: Writing Canadian Women Writing*. Edmonton: Longspoon/NeWest
Kaplan, Caren. 1994. 'The Politics of Location as Transnational Feminist Practice.' In Inderpal Grewal and Caren Kaplan, eds., *Scattered Hegemonies: Postmodernity and Transnational Feminist Practices*, 137-52. Minneapolis: University of Minnesota Press
McLuhan, Marshall. 1977. 'Canada: The Borderline Case.' In David Staines, ed., *The Canadian Imagination*, 226-48. Cambridge, MA: Harvard University Press
Martin, Biddy. 1994. 'Sexualities without Genders and Other Queer Utopias.' *Diacritics* 24 (2-3):104-21
Martin, Biddy, and Chandra Talpade Mohanty. 1986. 'Feminist Politics: What's Home Got to Do with It?' In Teresa de Lauretis, ed., *Feminist Studies/Critical Studies*, 191-212. Bloomington: Indiana University Press
Mohanty, Chandra Talpade. 1987. 'Feminist Encounters: Locating the Politics of Experience.' *Copyright* 1:30-44
Morrell, Carol. 1994. 'Introduction.' In Carol Morrell, ed., *Grammar of Dissent: Poetry and Prose by Claire Harris, M. Nourbese Philip, Dionne Brand*, 9-24. Fredericton: Goose Lane
Morrison, Toni. 1992. *Playing in the Dark: Whiteness and the Literary Imagination*. Cambridge, MA: Harvard University Press
Mukherjee, Arun P. 1995. 'Canadian Nationalism, Canadian Literature and Racial Minority Women.' In Makeda Silvera, ed., *The Other Woman: Women of Colour in Contemporary Canadian Literature*, 421-44. Toronto: Sister Vision
Pratt, Mary Louise. 1977. *Toward a Speech Act Theory of Literary Discourse*. Bloomington: Indiana University Press
Probyn, Elspeth. 1990. 'Travels in the Postmodern: Making Sense of the Local.' In Linda

J. Nicholson, ed., *Feminism/Postmodernism*, 176-89. New York: Routledge

Rich, Adrienne. 1986a. 'Blood, Bread, and Poetry: The Location of the Poet.' In *Blood, Bread, and Poetry*. 167-87. New York: Norton

–. 1986b '"Going There" and Being Here.' In *Blood, Bread, and Poetry*, 156-9. New York: Norton

–. 1986c 'North American Tunnel Vision.' In *Blood, Bread, and Poetry*, 160-6. New York: Norton

–. 1986d 'Notes toward a Politics of Location.' In *Blood, Bread, and Poetry*, 210-31. New York: Norton

Roman, Leslie G. 1993. 'White is a Color! White Defensiveness, Postmodernism, and Anti-racist Pedagogy.' In Cameron McCarthy and Warren Chrichlow, eds., *Race, Identity, and Representation in Education*, 71-88, New York: Routledge

Roy, John D. 1986. 'The Structure of Tense and Aspect in Barbadian English Creole.' In Manfred Görlach and John A. Holm, eds., *Focus on the Caribbean: Varieties of English Around the World*, 141-56. Amsterdam: John Benjamins

Russell, Catherine. 1983. Review of *Primitive Offensive*, by Dionne Brand. *Quill & Quire* 49 (9):76

Sanders, Leslie. 1989. '"I am stateless anyway": The Poetry of Dionne Brand.' *Zora Neale Hurston Forum* 3 (2):19-29

Sedgwick, Eve Kosofsky. 1993. 'Queer Performativity: Henry James's *The Art of the Novel.*' *Gay and Lesbian Quarterly* 1:1-16

Smith, Valerie. 1994. 'Reading the Intersection of Race and Gender in Narratives of Passing.' *Diacritics* 24 (2-3):43-57

Thomas, Joan. 1996. 'Poetry Fires Hot Brand Novel.' Review of *In Another Place, Not Here*, by Dionne Brand. *Globe and Mail*, 29 June 1996:C10

Wallace, Michele. 1989. 'The Politics of Location: Cinema/Theory/Literature/Ethnicity/Sexuality/Me.' *Framework* 36:42-55

Winer, Lise. 1993. *Trinidad and Tobago: Varieties of English Around the World*, Amsterdam: John Benjamins

Zackodnik, Teresa. 1995. '"I Am Blackening in My Way": Identity and Place in Dionne Brand's *No Language Is Neutral.*' *Essays on Canadian Writing* 57:194-211

'A Red Girl's Reasoning': E. Pauline Johnson Constructs the New Nation

Veronica Strong-Boag

In the late nineteenth and early twentieth centuries, Canadians struggled to make sense of a colonial past, the Riel Rebellions, Native protest, feminist agitation, and the looming presence of a southern rival. The artists and writers who matured in these turbulent years offered some answers. Among this Confederation generation, E. Pauline Johnson is a unique example of a Euro-First Nation poet and non-fiction and short story writer. While well known in her own day, Johnson is largely remembered for producing Canada's best-selling book of poetry, *Flint and Feather* and, in particular, for writing 'The Song My Paddle Sings,' which has been reproduced in a host of texts as a celebration of a northern nation.[1] More significantly, she developed a nationalist narrative in which Indians, Euro-First Nations, and women reject inferiority and claim an equal place. The daughter of a Mohawk-English union, Johnson publicly challenged the exclusionary nationalist narratives of her day.

Pauline Johnson articulates a racialized femininity that embodied and unsettled many of the middle-class conventions of late nineteenth-century Canada. Hers is one version of what Judith Butler has described as 'performative accomplishment' (1990, 271; 1993). Like today's performance artists,[2] Johnson 'wore' gender, race, and class in ways that could be both transgressive and reinscriptive. As she sought secure footing among the prejudices of her age, her messages seem sometimes ambiguous and ambivalent. In identifying her as a performer who highlighted issues of race and gender in her ongoing conversation with European Canada, I do not dismiss these conditions as in any way 'unreal' or as less significant because they are constructed in daily discourses. They remain critical sites of power and oppression in the real world. I wish rather to emphasize their construction, whether consciously or unconsciously, by Johnson and her audiences.[3]

In her efforts at communication, Pauline Johnson became one of those writers who, as postcolonial critics like Edward Said have suggested, endeavoured 'to rechart and then occupy the place in imperial cultural forms reserved for subordination, to occupy it self-consciously, fighting for it on the very same territory once ruled by the consciousness that assumed the subordination of a designated inferior Other.'[4] To be sure, sometimes her arguments seem dispersed, fragmentary, and often undeveloped. As critics Bill Ashcroft, Gareth Griffiths, and Helen Tiffin point out in *The Empire Writes Back*, such limitations are typical of early postcolonial texts, which came 'into being within the constraints of a discourse and the institutional practice of a patronage system which limits and undercuts their assertion of a different perspective' (6). A reconsideration of Johnson as social critic and her work as a subversive narrative reveals a 'conscious effort to enter into the discourse of Europe and the West, to mix with it, transform it, to make it acknowledge marginalized or suppressed or forgotten histories' (Said, 216). Unlike some writers of Aboriginal ancestry who have chosen in the first instance to speak to a Native community, Pauline Johnson performed largely for European Canada (Silvera). So far as we can tell, few listeners and readers were Native. Through stage and published work, she tried to translate Aboriginal and Mixed Race experience into public images that settlers could value. In the process, she outlines a hybrid nationalist identity that denounces oppression and incorporates the inheritance of Native peoples and the recognition of women.

The Making of a Canadian Postcolonial Performer

Born in 1861 in southwestern Ontario to an activist Mohawk father, George Henry Martin Johnson, and an English-born woman from an abolitionist family, Susanna Howells, Pauline Johnson was reared in comfort on the Grand River's Six Nations territory. There, a respectable middle-class enthusiasm for canonical Romantic poets like Byron or Shelley mingled with a passionate commitment to protecting Indian people from the assaults of unprincipled Europeans.[5] Such views situated Johnson and her family within the mainstream of the liberal nationalism of her day.[6] Her elite family entertained leading individuals, from the governor general and Iroquois chiefs on down, exposing her to many of the burning questions of the day. Johnson's family, with its biculturalism, its liberal nationalism, and its middle-class privilege, provided a highly unusual vantage point from which to view the volatile mixture of influences that was to become modern Canada. It sharply distinguished her and, ultimately, her writing from the group of nationalist poets – Duncan Campbell Scott, Archibald Lampman, Isabella Valancy Crawford, Bliss Carman, Charles G.D. Roberts, and Wilfred Campbell – with whom she is commonly compared.

The Johnson household prepared its children to straddle the Aboriginal and European worlds, which, through trade and settlement, still remained closely connected for many nineteenth-century Canadians. As an interpreter and forest warden for the Department of Indian Affairs and a translator for the Anglican Church in the mid-decades of the century, Johnson's father[7] moved among different communities. His two sons and two daughters might have hoped to do the same. They were, as Pauline Johnson remembered in her short story, 'My Mother,' 'reared on the strictest lines of both Indian and English principles. They were taught the legends, the traditions, the culture, and the etiquette of both races to which they belonged; but above all, their mother instilled into them from the very cradle that they were of their father's people, not of hers'(1987, 69). Despite such injunctions, status and nationality for the Iroquois are traced through the mother, not the father. Her identity as a Mohawk could not come in the traditional manner but only from the federal Indian Act.

In the nineteenth century, the Grand River Mohawks remained a powerful and proud part of the Six Nations Confederacy, which had established Canada's most populous and prosperous Native community near Brantford in 1847 (Weaver 1994, 182; 1972). The territory itself was multinational, harbouring European-Canadians, blacks, the members of the Iroquois Confederacy, and a number of smaller allied tribes. During the nineteenth century a decisive split emerged between 'culturally conservative Longhouse people and the more acculturated Christians' (Weaver 1994, 183). The Longhouse faction championed traditional language, rituals, and governance (Shimony; Weaver 1972). Such views evoked little support among Anglican Mohawks like the Johnsons, who initially felt optimistic about their relations with the dominant society. The flourishing state of the Christian Grand River community in the last decades of the nineteenth century seemed full of promise to Iroquois Christians who hoped to contribute to the emergence of a Native-European union (see Weaver 1994). Such optimism would later dissipate in rancour and despair. However, until the end of her life Pauline Johnson sought to express the positive vision of an inclusive nationality espoused by her family and others like them.

Johnson's access to the Mohawk community was limited by the fact that her English mother was never fully integrated into the Grand River territory. Close ties to her mother's relatives, schooling by a governess and in a city high school, and Pauline's residence throughout her twenties in Brantford's middle-class neighbourhoods, further undermined the influence of George Johnson and his father, John Smoke Johnson, both of whom were well-known Mohawk leaders, and that of her extensive Native family. Pauline Johnson stood on the periphery of even Grand River's Native community and 'its well-integrated system of values and morals' (Weaver 1994, 215).

Given her incomplete immersion, Johnson's performances as a Native woman, or 'Indian Princess,' always encountered problems of authenticity. One solution, as revealed in the deerskin dress she often wore, was to fabricate a synthetic pan-Indian stage presence that necessarily relied as much upon popular European fantasies of the Native as it did upon direct Aboriginal inspiration. Her reference to whites, such as William Lighthall and Charles Mair, for assistance in putting together a realistic stage presence (by whose standards?) captures her problems most poignantly.

Upon George Johnson's death in 1884, his widow and daughters, Pauline and Evelyn, permanently left the Six Nations territory and resettled in Brantford, a bustling industrial market centre.[8] Their shift from prominence in the Mohawk community to a socially inferior position in town mirrored the general decline in the situation of Mixed Race and Native peoples in Canada. The move also reinforced European cultural influences. Pauline attended and performed in theatrical amateur entertainments in Hamilton and Brantford and continued writing. Like many daughters of the middle class, she experimented with verse whose forms and themes often reflected the conventional sentiments of Victorian Canada.

Throughout Johnson's life she claimed the literary traditions of Great Britain to be as much her own as were those of the Six Nations. The result is a cultural hybrid who juggles influences from both sides of her family as she seeks to bridge Canada's racial divide. In a world that typically thinks in terms of dualisms, Mixed Race individuals are troubling. As one contributor to the 1994 volume *Miscegenation Blues: Voices of Mixed Race Women* points out, those of plural ancestry 'embody some of the most unresolved contradictions in current human relations' (Green, 291). In their hands, 'nationality' can become 'unstable, mobile, and heterogeneous – a fluid process of negotiation rather than a rigid imposition of meaning' (Donaldson, 116). In the heyday of Euro-Canadian nation-building Johnson faced an uphill struggle. Neither she nor her audiences could always be sure what she was expected to, or would, perform. Hers was a life-long search for a credible and profitable means of enacting her own and Canada's hybridity.

The difficulty and loneliness of Johnson's position encouraged her to develop a style that made direct application to her listeners and readers. Much like other performance artists, she communicated in ways that are 'intensely intimate,' with an 'emphasis on personal experience and emotional material, not "acted" or distanced from artist or audience' (Forte, 255). Her efforts at emotionally direct communication, at the establishment of empathy, especially through the use of melodrama and comedy, encouraged a recognition of women's and men's, of Natives' and non-Natives', shared humanity. Once she forged such bonds with her audience, Johnson could hope to create new space for First Nations and women in Canada's settler society.

As her long days at home from the age of eighteen until she gave a public recital in Toronto in 1892 at age thirty further reveal, a strong-minded Euro-First Nation spinster faced many handicaps in creating space for herself during the high age of British imperialism and paternalism.[9] While discrimination has always existed, the European-Canadian assessment of Indians had been deteriorating from an earlier emphasis on their 'fundamental humanity to one based on the theological and sociological theories which relegated them to the sub-human' (MacDonald, 103). Those of joint Native and European heritage also fared badly. The collapse of the Prairie resistances in 1870 and 1885 doomed the hopes of Louis Riel and others for recognition of the Euro-First Nations community. By the late 1880s, prospects for those claiming Native heritage looked bleak.

Native Canadian writers emerged to address the ongoing crisis of their relationship with the dominant society. Penny Petrone charts evidence of resistance from an Indian and Euro-First Nations elite armed with a formal education and command of English. While protest came from many tribes, the Iroquois, with their long history of alliance with the British Empire, were especially prominent.[10] Not all Aboriginal participants in debates about the future of North America voiced opposition to European encroachment. One commentator has suggested that the handful of Native writers publishing in the United States at the turn of the century were basically assimilationist. 'Their characters accept white values and cultural traits, often rejecting the traditional way of life' (Larson, 36). There is also the question of resistance offered by the Aboriginal performers who peopled Wild West shows, burlesque halls, and popular entertainments of every kind in Europe, North America, and all around the world during these years. Their performances, constructed by themselves and the managers, negotiated complicated terrains of complicity and protest that are difficult to appreciate or evaluate.[11] In whatever fashion they confronted their common vulnerability, Native writers and performers contributed to the growth of pan-Indian sentiments in these years (Larson). In their preoccupation with relations with white society, they provide a critical backdrop for Pauline Johnson, the first Euro-First Nation or Native woman to assume a major public role in Canada.

The mid-nineteenth century also saw the birth of a generation of Canadians deeply influenced by the feminist movement. Johnson matured in a community debating women's roles, especially their right to higher education, paid work, and political power. Brantford and its surroundings produced, along with Native activists, Emily Stowe, Canada's first female school principal and, later, the founder of the country's first suffrage society (Bashevkin, Chapter 1), and a crowd of pioneer female journalists. For a woman of ambition, Ontario in these years appeared full of promise. Johnson's uncertain position, an unmarried daughter in a widow's family, gave her particular reasons to rethink the situation of her sex and to join other women in asking questions of the new nation.

While the recurring racism of turn-of-the-century feminism has been described by scholars, the politics of gender and race are fluid and never uncomplicated (Bacchi; Valverde). A number of American suffragists had a special interest in the history of Native peoples. They were impressed by the presence of powerful women in the Iroquois Confederacy. For some feminists, Indian society appeared to supply 'an alternative to American patriarchy,' suggesting that male domination was neither inevitable nor omnipresent.[12] Pauline Johnson draws the same comparison in the *London Daily Express* in 1906:

> I have heard that the daughters of this vast city cry out for a voice in Parliament of this land. There is no need for an Iroquois woman to clamour for recognition in our councils; she has had it for upwards of four centuries ... From her cradle-board she is taught to judge men and their intellectual qualities, their aptness for public life, and their integrity, so that when he who bears the title leaves his seat in council to join the league-makers in the happy hunting grounds she can use her wisdom and her learning in nominating his fittest successor ... The old and powerful chiefs-in-council never attempt to question her decision ... There are fifty matrons possessing this right in the Iroquois Confederacy. I have not heard of fifty white women even among those of noble birth who may speak and be listened to in the lodge of the law-makers here. (1987, 232)

Other Iroquois activists, desirous of outside, especially feminist, support, also emphasized the authority of their matrons.[13] As such arguments make clear, the politics of race and gender were not always at odds. In an age of multiple and overlapping protest movements, Johnson was well equipped to make critical connections between the politics of race and gender.

The decision to confront prevailing prejudice is far from easy. One Mohawk writer, Beth Brant, has recently reminded us:

> To write or not to write is a painful struggle for us. For everything we write can be used against us. *For everything we write will be used against us.* And I'm not talking about bad reviews. I'm talking about the flak we receive from our own communities as well as the smug liberalism from the white 'literary' enclave. Writing is an act of courage for most. For *us*, it is an act that requires opening up our wounded communities, our families, to eyes and ears that do not love us. Is this madness? In a way it is – the madness of a Louis Riel, a Maria Campbell, a Pauline Johnson, a Crazy Horse – a revolutionary madness. A love that is greater than fear. A love that is as tender as it is fierce. (17)

It is just such a counter-discourse, essentially feminist and postcolonialist, that Johnson was to articulate on platforms in theatres, schools, and churches across the country after she entered the uncertain world of the paid recitalist in 1892. In these performances, she staged a femininity that was simultaneously and ambiguously raced. In a white ball gown, she offered herself as the epitome of upper-class Victorian womanhood. Minutes later, she would reappear as a passionate Aboriginal woman clad in leather and feathers.

Johnson's Indian ancestry enhanced her marketability, an appeal she capitalized on in her presentation as an archetypal 'Indian Princess' – someone, in other words, like Pocahontas in the American story, or Molly Brant in the case of the northern colonies, who acts to redeem European men, saving them from the wilderness and the wilderness for them.[14] Here is both affirmation and repudiation of the middle-class conventions of gender and race. Johnson's ultimate dependence on the patronage of the dominant society required this ambiguity.

For the rest of her life she orchestrated a public career that fed on melodrama, jingoism, and commercialism, together with a commitment to writing verse and stories that would both win the praise of literary critics and address the oppression of Native peoples and women. Her oral skills proved the key to earning a living, while her ability to publish poems and stories nourished her appeal to audiences and her claim to middle-class respectability.[15] While the results were uneven, as she herself painfully acknowledged,[16] Johnson persevered in struggling to translate her views into forms that would be simultaneously acceptable to both a cultural elite and popular audiences. In the process she extended Native American women's long-standing role – first exercised as mistresses, wives, and guides – as 'mediators of meaning between the cultures of the two worlds.'[17] Over the course of the twentieth century, Canadian audiences would find that Aboriginal performers, such as Grey Owl (in reality the transplanted Britisher, Archibald Belaney) and Buffy Sainte-Marie,[18] served in some measure as critical 'symbols in the Canadian-history enterprise' (Emberley 18; Francis). In many ways, the reality faced by Aboriginal peoples is beside the point. Indian performers are often valued inasmuch as they can confirm Canada's particular relationship to the northern landscape and, ultimately, its difference from the United States. In the face of growing racism, however, Native roots jeopardized Johnson's efforts to parlay a talent for public expression and poetry into a living. As a public woman and as an Indian artist, she was to live on society's periphery, able finally neither to marry nor to guarantee her security.[19]

Marginality was further reinforced by Johnson's role as an interpreter and champion of a peripheral culture. Advocates and creators of Canadian literature had to fight hard to find a hearing. Only too often they found themselves on the defensive in the face of British and American aspirations to imperial domination and the colonialism of Canadians themselves. In her life and her work, Johnson had to negotiate many identities in the dominant culture's commercial and aesthetic markets. She had to sell to the very society she critiqued her need for respectability and sympathy juxtaposed with a message that potentially unsettled conventions of race and gender.

Talking Race

Challenging a dominant narrative that held that 'to the majority of English speaking people, an Indian is an Indian, an inadequate sort of person possessing a red brown skin, nomadic habits, and an inability for public affairs'(Johnson 1900, 440) took courage. This boldness was recognized by her contemporaries. According to the nationalist poet, Charles Mair, the effect of Johnson's 'racial poetry ... upon the reader was as that of something abnormal, something new and strange, and certainly unexampled in Canadian verse. For here was a girl whose blood and sympathies were largely drawn from the greatest tribe of the most advanced nation of Indians of the continent, who spoke out "loud and bold," not for it alone but for the whole red race, and sang of its glories and its wrongs in strains of poetic fire' (cited in Foster, 179). As one of a tiny group of North American Native women who challenged racism on stage and in writing, Johnson was a lonely figure.[20]

Her earliest contributions to public life – in 1884 at the reinternment of the Seneca orator, Red Jacket, and, two years later, at Brantford's unveiling of a statue to the Mohawk chief, Joseph Brant – identify heroic liberal figures who match any in the contemporary European nationalist lexicon.[21] Here are Natives of giant stature. Their merits and those of First Nations and Euro-First Nations peoples in general do not, as Johnson argues, meet with deserved respect. The history of Indian-White contact is the history of recurring ignorance and injustice. Pauline Johnson's inaugural recital in Toronto in 1892 electrified listeners with 'A Cry from an Indian Wife,' a passionate indictment of the crushing of the Prairie tribes in 1885, an encounter still fresh in memory and one that had sharply divided the country. Early 1890s articles, such as 'The Iroquois of the Grand River' and 'A Glimpse of the Grand River Indians,' construct more realistic portraits to counter prejudices that fail to make critical distinctions among the tribes or to recognize their merits (cited in Keller, 111-12) .

Johnson regularly pillories the prejudice that consigns all people of Aboriginal background to inferiority. In 1892, her powerful rejoinder to contemporary racism, 'A Strong Race Opinion on the Indian Girl in Modern Fiction,' catalogues and dismisses racist stereotypes that relegate Indian women to the losing side in war and in love (cited in Keller, 120-1). Poems like 'The Cattle Thief' and 'Wolverine' likewise reject the dehumanization that accompanies genocide. Audiences are asked to think of the Native characters as individuals with heroic qualities, more than a match for the erstwhile victors, who are, in turn, not in reality 'plucky Englishmen' but 'demons,' 'robbers,' and 'dogs' (Johnson 1972, 10-4, 22-6). In a nice reversal of conventions, the white intruders are reduced to non-humans. Johnson herself is not immune to racist constructions. In ways that are reminiscent of eugenic thinkers but also evoke older Native rivalries, she accords the Iroquois, the Cree, the Sioux, the Haida, and the Squamish superiority over other Aboriginal tribes. Faith in elite Natives armed her in struggles against those who sought to dismiss her and those she represented.

Throughout her life Johnson wrote and performed works that starkly detail the ruin inflicted by newcomers and their governments. One short story, 'As It Was in the Beginning,' takes residential schools to task. Another, 'Her Majesty's Guest,' depicts the brutality of liquor-sellers, enemies who had, on three occasions, physically attacked her own father (Johnson 1989). Poems like 'Silhouette,' 'The Corn Husker,' and 'The Cattle Thief' dramatize the starvation that dogged the tribes in these years (Johnson 1972, 103, 7-9).[22] In face of injustice, cattle rustling is readily justified. As Johnson explains, in a revealing use of the first person, 'When *you* pay for the land you live in *we*'ll pay for the meat we eat' (1972, 13 [author's emphasis]). In other passages, the hypocrisy of conquerors who 'had come with the Bible in one hand, the bottle in the other' is exposed.[23] Here are hard lessons about complicity and betrayal that audiences were not used to hearing.

In the early poems 'Ojistoh' and 'As Red Men Die,' Johnson attempts to create sympathy with dramatic portraits of idealized Native women and men who are every bit the equal of those found in the Scottish and English ballads with which listeners might be more familiar (1972). In deference to her audiences and no doubt to her need to earn a living, no poem portrays violence directed at newcomers. First Nations men and women are for the most part noble, long-suffering, generous, and open to reasonable overtures. In poems like 'Wolverine' and 'The Cattle Thief' (1972), and short stories like 'Catharine of the Crow's Nest,' they, rather than the European intruders, demonstrate humanity (1987). While Johnson sometimes despairs, as when she laments her 'dear dead race' in her story 'A Red Girl's Reasoning' (1987), she also insists on the 'innate refinement so universally possessed by the higher tribes of North American Indians'(1987, 103). She argues further that if you 'put a pure-blooded Indian in the drawing room ... he will shine with the best of you' (cited in Keller, 112). The Natives' 'adaptability to progress'(1987, 104) makes them fully capable of entering the modern world. Her portrait of heroic and thoughtful Native figures stands in stark contrast to the 'disappearing race' chronicled in the poems of her more powerful contemporary, Duncan Campbell Scott of the federal Department of Indian Affairs.[24] Johnson's faith in the ultimate competitiveness of non-Europeans also helps explain her enthusiasm, in the poem 'The Man in Chrysanthemum Land,' for Japan's defeat of Russia in the 1904-5 war (1972, 158-9).[25] Like other liberal and anti-racist critics of her day, she interpreted that conflict as the belated triumph of non-Europeans over their would-be white masters (Martin).

In 1909, Johnson retired to British Columbia, a province that had by then become the centre of Indian protest.[26] Her assistance to Squamish chief Joe Capilano in 1906 when he and other representatives of BC tribes petitioned King Edward, like the long hours they spent together in Vancouver while he narrated the stories of his people and the assistance she gave to his son in public speaking, were in keeping with long-demonstrated sympathies. Johnson's relationships on the west coast also reflected the ties that increasingly connected Native peoples of different communities in the twentieth century.

The Legends of Vancouver (1911), published at the end of her life, reaffirms Johnson's persistent efforts to remap the Euro-Canadian imaginative landscape. As she reminds readers, the twin peaks that rise to the north of the city are not 'the lions,' so-named by a foreign-born settler with a mind for the exotic or the patriotic but 'without the love for them that is in the Indian heart' (1926, 3). The mountains have a far older indigenous history as 'the sisters' of Indian legend. Her retelling of Squamish stories unnames the land colonized by Europeans and evokes a powerful human landscape preceding their arrival.[27] The Native inheritance is located at the centre of human history in British Columbia and Canada. In such writing, Johnson suggests, as Edward Said has said of other resistance writers, that indigenous peoples have 'a history capable of development, as part of the process of work, growth, and maturity to which only Europeans had seemed entitled' (213).

Speaking of Women

While she tends to locate oppression primarily in racism, and she is most emphatic about its particular ill effects, Johnson remained sensitive to how women are damaged by the convergence of racial and sexual prejudice. She explains her double vision: 'I am a Redskin, but I am something else too – I am a woman'(1987, 13). Indeed, as A. LaVonne Ruoff has observed, Pauline Johnson's writing resembles that of many other female writers in the nineteenth century. In her stories 'the heroine encounters mistreatment, unfairness, disadvantage, and powerlessness which result from her status as female and child. The heroine accepts herself as a female while rejecting the evaluation of female with permanent children. In the course of the narrative women are rejected as sexual prey and a pragmatic feminism is embraced' (Johnson 1987, 19). The Mohawk writer Beth Brant has argued further that Pauline Johnson, in 'breaking out of the Victorian strictures of her day ... drew a map for all women to follow' (60-1). Unlike

Euro-Canadian writers, Johnson identifies racism rather than patriarchy as the chief obstacle to the fair treatment of women.

Race could also be significant in empowering women. Johnson frequently roots her commitment to equality in Native traditions. In one story, 'The Lost Salmon Run,' a Squamish elder outlines this in describing her reception of a granddaughter: 'Very good luck to have a girl for first grandchild. Our tribe not like yours; we want girl-children first, we not always wish boy-child born just for fight. Your people, they care only for war-path; our tribe more peaceful ... I tell you why: girl-child may be some time mother herself; very grand thing to be mother' (1926, 37-8). Much the same argument about the value of women is made when Johnson points to the power of Iroquois matrons. These are influential figures who contest and, often, dominate the landscape.

Johnson's female characters, like her performances, are distinguished by passionate feeling. Polite conventions about heterosexual relations, with their common emphasis on female passivity and male initiative, are rare. A series of love poems, particularly those appearing after her own unhappy affairs, evoke female passion. The canoe figures significantly as an expression of, and vehicle for, women's desires for love and mastery. Her early work, 'The Song My Paddle Sings,' launches this preoccupation with lines like 'I wooed you long but my wooing's past; My paddle will lull you into rest' and its reference to the river as a 'bed' and its waters as a 'breast.' Here, the heroine triumphs in the rapids that 'roar,' 'seethe and boil, and bound, and splash,' 'but never a fear my craft will feel' (1972, 29-31). In a later poem, 'The Idlers,' she again uses the first person to conjure up a memory of perfect passion. The male object of her erotic gaze is explicit:

Against the thwart, near by,
Inactively you lie,
And all too near my arm your temple bends
Your indolent rude
Abandoned attitude
And again
Your costume, loose and light,
Leaves unconcealed your might
Of muscle, half suspected, half defined;
And falling well aside
Your vesture opens wide,
Above your splendid sunburnt throat that pulses unconfined.
(1972, 59-61)

Disappointment eventually quells this optimism. Sleeplessness and despair dominate the poems 'Re-voyage,' 'Wave-Won,' and 'In the Shadows.' Days were now 'haunted' and 'dreary.' Even the speaker's 'arm as strong as steel' brings no salvation (1972, 65 and 67).

By the time of Johnson's second volume of poetry, *Canadian Born* (1903), loss provides the major theme in 'Thistle-Down,' 'Through Time and Bitter Distance,' and 'Your Mirror Frame' (1972, 99, 105-6, 117-8). The author's lack of repentance about her feelings is perhaps, however, best captured in the poem 'In Grey Days':

> Deep human love for others
> Deep as the sea
> God-sent unto my neighbour –
> But not to me.
> Sometime I'll wrest from others
> More than all this
> I shall demand from Heaven
> Far sweeter bliss.
> (1972, 131)

Such depiction of women's physical and emotional responses is unusual in the Canada of her day. In talking of passion and in embodying the very results of miscegenation, she was a controversial figure for her audiences. Were her presentations to be taken as proof that women sui generis had sexual desires? Or were they rather an expression of her Native heritage – in other words, a demonstration of inherent primitivism or even degeneracy? Just who was performing what? Such questions had to be negotiated afresh with each new set of listeners and readers.

Passion was not the only strong emotion requiring interpretation. Betrayal, violence, and death recur in Johnson's work. From her early narrative poem, 'Ojistoh,' in which a Mohawk woman murders a would-be rapist, to the later story 'As It Was in the Beginning,' again recounted in the first person, in which the Euro-First Nation heroine takes revenge on an unfaithful priest and a still more unfaithful lover (1987), she champions a stern code in which women are neither to be seized nor taken for granted. When Charles McDonald, in the short story, 'A Red Girl's Reasoning,' refuses to recognize the customary Native marriage between his wife Christie's parents, an issue which bitterly divided real-life Canadians in these years,[28] she responds, 'Why should I recognize the rites of your nation when you do not acknowledge the rites of mine?' (1987, 117).

If heterosexual relations spell trouble, Pauline Johnson joined other women writers in crediting her sex with strong maternal feelings. Remarkable mothers stand out in stories such as 'Catharine of the Crow's Nest,' 'The Next Builder,' 'Mother o' the Men,' and 'The Tenas Klootchman' (1987). In the first, an Indian woman, Maarda, shows newcomers the meaning of generosity when she rescues a white foundling. In the stories written for an American boys' magazine and published in 1913 as *The Shagganappi*, good women civilize sons, inspiring them to higher levels of honour and achievement. In her account of her own mother's life, Johnson lovingly portrays a woman who devotes herself to her children (1987). Ultimately it is women's maternalism that provides an important point of connection between the races. In 'A Cry from an Indian Wife,' the narrator describes her own agony at seeing her family and nation going to war. She nevertheless comments:

> Yet stay, my heart is not the only one
> That grieves the loss of husband and of son;
> Think of the mothers o'er the inland seas;
> Think of the pale-faced maiden on her knees;

These reflections, with their direct appeal to the enemy, cast doubt on 'the glories of war' and conjure up a common humanity (1972, 18).

Inspired by their capacity for nurture, women in general emerge, as did the Native women who make peace by marrying tribal enemies in poems such as 'Dawendine,' as the chief promise of a more just and peaceful world (1972, 118-21). In the story 'The Envoy Extraordinary,' the character 'old Billy' sums up these sentiments: 'these mother-wimmen don't never thrive where there's rough weather, somehow. They're all fer peace. They're worse than King Edward an' Teddy Roosevelt fer patchin' up rows, an' if they can't do it no other way, they jes' hike along with a baby, sort o' treaty of peace like' (1987, 138). This faith in women's special nature was a commonplace that Johnson, like a host of her feminist contemporaries, used to contest misogynist conventions.[29] Such shared assumptions added to her appeal for the US *Mothers' Magazine*, in which she regularly published.

While Pauline Johnson self-consciously chose to speak as 'One of Them'[30] – as the Iroquois and, by extension, as all Native women of Canada – and their lives lay close to the centre of much of her writing, she maintained close friendships with non-Native women. Her first poem, appearing in the American magazine *Gems of Poetry* in 1884 is dedicated 'To Jean,' a white girlhood friend. During her itinerant career, she relied on women's work and emotional support. The suffragist Nellie McClung met the recitalist in the mid-1890s and her response captures the response of many. In her autobiography she recollects that 'at her first word, we felt at home with her ... [this] charming, friendly woman' (1945, 35). That initial regard initiated a now lost correspondence of almost twenty years' duration.

The significance of female friendships is described in Johnson's short story, 'Mother o' the Men.' Here Mrs. Lysle (we never learn her first name) chooses to accompany her North-West Mounted Police husband to the

Yukon. 'But there are times even in the life of a wife and mother when her soul rebels at cutting herself off from all womenkind, and all that environment of social life among women means, even if the act itself is voluntary on her part.' Later on, 'during days when the sight of a woman's face would have been a glimpse of paradise to her,' she 'almost wildly regretted her boy had not been a girl – just a little sweet-voiced girl, a thing of her own sex and kind' (1987, 182, 187). The author of these words had good reason to value her own sex. Her death from cancer in Vancouver in 1913 was made immeasurably easier by the life she had fostered among women. A host of correspondents encouraged her spirits. Efforts by the Women's Canadian Club, the Women's Press Club, and the Imperial Order Daughters of the Empire ensured no financial worries. A female world anchored her to the end.

What all this begs, of course, is the question of Johnson's own feminism. Certainly her maternalism is characteristic of the women's movement of her day. So too is her recognition of female strength and capacity (Prentice et al.). But as a recent reminder explains, 'Native women are feminist in a way that women of other culture groups, other religions, rarely understand ... Where differences arise between mainstream feminists and Native women they centre around causes of oppression and particularly racism. Whereas mainstream feminists see the primary cause of their oppression as patriarchal society, Native women are more inclined to see their oppression as arising from racism and colonialism' (Grant, 43). Johnson seems to fit this definition. Her poems and stories draw clear links between the treatment of women and the racism of the dominant society. Oppression rarely appears a simple relationship between sexes or races. Her female characters must first reject racialization to be recognized as fully human.

Creating a New Nation

While endeavouring to chart her course as a Native and as a woman, Pauline Johnson had to locate and define herself as a Canadian at a time when this identity was far from sure. This preoccupation, which is central to her writings, also revealed how far she had moved from the insistence of other Christian Iroquois on their status as allies of Great Britain rather than as citizens of Canada. Nationalisms in various forms competed for adherents and legitimacy (Berger). As the first post-Confederation collection of Canadian verse, *Songs of the Great Dominion* (1889), indicates, poets were among those who sought to capture the essence of what it meant to grow up in the northern half of the continent. A contributor to that influential volume, Pauline Johnson never gave up the effort to articulate a founding tradition of narrative and metaphor in the wider context of British cultural and political imperialism. Her championship of a cultural and racial 'hybridity' rooted in the northern landscape recalls her own family's efforts on the Grand River. Although Johnson has little to say about French Canada, she shifts the question of racial partnership away from the prevailing Eurocentrism to include Natives.

Membership in a family of Mohawk United Empire Loyalists (UELs) gave a special twist to Johnson's preoccupation with the nature of an identity separate from that of the United States and Great Britain. The patronage of British governor generals, literati, and salon hostesses, invaluable in establishing the credentials and the respectability of the Euro-First Nation poet, deepened her appreciation of and dependence on the centre of empire. Her early initiation in the English cultural canon kept her an enthralled captive. Lines in her poem 'My English Letter' provide eloquent testimony to this fascination. Referring to England as the 'Motherland,' and it is indeed the birthplace of her own mother, Johnson writes of exile:

> Although I never knew the blessed favour
> That surely lies in breathing English air.
> Imagination's brush before me fleeing.
> Paints English pictures, though my longing eyes
> Have never known the blessedness of seeing
> The blue that lines the arch of English skies.
> (1972, 76)

Such nostalgia seems typical of what Ashcroft, Griffiths, and Tiffin identify as the 'second stage of production within the evolving discourse of the post-colonial,' or 'the literature produced "under imperial license" by "natives" or "outcasts"'(5).

Like other elite Natives, Johnson has an ambiguous relationship with empire. As the descendant of British allies and the daughter of an English mother, she seeks to claim the culture of the imperial centre without accepting its denigration of the periphery. She rejects the racism while sharing some of the sentiments of imperialist contemporaries. Like the political economist and humorist Stephen Leacock, who thunders in his essay, 'Greater Canada: An Appeal,' 'the Empire is ours too, ours in its history of the past, ours in its safe-guard of the present' (36), Johnson repudiates inferiority for Canada, Britain's legitimate heir. A unique blending of Old World and New World, it, not the 'old land,' is the 'beloved of God' (1972, 172, 79). Unlike Anglo-Canadian imperialists, however, she includes Native peoples as full participants in the imperial project. The hybrid empire she envisions is pluralistic and meritocratic.

Johnson's relationship with the rising power to the south is, in contrast, much less positive. Kinship with William D. Howells, the American man of letters, seems to have been disappointing. His dismissal of her work and apparent slighting of his Aboriginal cousins went hand in hand with the greater difficulty Johnson encountered with US audiences who tended, like some American literary critics at the end of the twentieth century, to appropriate her as a home-grown product.[31] Their relative rudeness, beginning with her 1896-7 tour south of the Great Lakes (it was claimed that they 'treated Pauline as if she too were a circus freak, though they were a bit awed by her obvious refinement and talent' [Keller, 234]) enraged her and helped confirm the benefits of the continuing British connection. Johnson also had a front seat on the American Indian wars of the late nineteenth century, and she shared with many Canadians the faith that matters were better north of the 49th.[32] When she envisions Canada's future, she insists that 'the Yankee to the south of us must south of us remain' (1972, 80).

For Pauline Johnson, like some contemporaries, British justice provides the critical imperial inheritance (Dean). The rule of law will allow Canada to escape American unrest and corruption. Revealingly, the United States is frequently 'othered' or, in a curious way, even orientalized in the accounts of Canadian imperialists like Johnson. A rebellious colony, the US had repudiated its British inheritance and is thus susceptible to racial degeneration and despotism. In contrast, in Canada, the traditions of British law, with their promise of equality to all, supply an essential bulwark against the tyranny of the majority and allow minorities to survive. Johnson sums up her hope for a pluralistic future in a story entitled 'The Brotherhood': 'The Mohawks and the palefaces are brothers, under one law ... It is Canadian history' (1913, 220). Similar aspirations concerning the rule of law fuelled the continuing appeal by Native peoples to the courts, the Crown, and, eventually, the League of Nations and the United Nations, where they attempted to speak as the allies, not the conquered, of Great Britain (Drees).

Johnson identifies one institution as central to the maintenance of law and order and as symbolic of the significance of fair play among races. As Keith Walden has suggested, the North-West Mounted Police (NWMP) quickly emerged after their creation in 1873 as a major icon of the new nation (4). The NWMP, later the RCMP, provided an essential guarantee and evidence of Canada's regard for law and of its fundamental difference from the US. Johnson's 'The Riders of the Plains' typically loomed as larger-than-life figures who, while few in number, were brave enough 'to keep the peace of our people and the honour of British law.' 'Felons,' 'rebels,' and the lawless, all of whom were only too likely to originate south of the border, have no place in the land of the Lion and the Union Jack (1972, 103). Although no disillusionment is found in Johnson's surviving work, Natives, in general, quickly learned, especially after 1885, that the Mounties were at least as much keepers as protectors.

For Johnson, fair dealing by national authorities not only upheld the principles of British justice, it also helped guarantee Canada itself. She insists that the Indian heritage is a key ingredient of national survival. At the dedication of Brant's memorial in 1886, she writes:

So Canada thy plumes were hardly won
Without allegiance from thy Indian son.
. . . .
Then meet we as one common brotherhood
In peace and love, with purpose understood.
. . . .
Today the Six Red Nations have their Canada.
(Van Steen, 45-6)

Her tours across the country with their introduction to other First Nations offered her the opportunity to confirm their special relationship to the Dominion. In regard to the Sioux, her heroic hunters of the Plains, she explains: 'King Edward of England has no better subjects; and I guess it is all the same to His Majesty whether a good subject dresses in buckskin or broadcloth' (cited in Van Steen, 263). The appeal of Squamish chief Capilano to the same monarch in 1906 is the right of an ally and an equal.

While European newcomers may offer the advantage of British law, First Nations also bring important qualities to a biracial partnership. There is, of course, the courage and loyalty that stood at the core of Johnson's own family history, but there is also, contrary to the racist depictions of Natives as savage, a special proclivity for peacemaking. She employs a youngster in one story to speak for the newcomers in acknowledging 'brotherhood with all men ... We palefaces have no such times ... Some of us are always at war. If we are not fighting here, we are fighting beyond the great salt seas. I wish we had more of ... your Indian ways. I wish we could link a silver chain around the world; we think we are the ones to teach, but I believe you could teach us much (1913, 213).

The peaceful inclinations credited to the original inhabitants of North America resemble the higher sentiments ascribed to women. Indeed, Indian women in her stories and poems are often the special champions and expressions of intergroup harmony. Whether nature or nurture creates this phenomenon is never clear. Today it seems best explained as part of the idealization of the oppressed that characterizes much resistance writing. The essential moderation of Johnson's appeal is reaffirmed by her associated message of the need for mutual forgiveness. She leaves it to a character to explain: 'Forgive the wrongs my children did to you, And we, the red-skins, will forgive you too' (cited in Van Steen, 263).

European settlers are also encouraged to reconsider their bloody history of contact with other peoples. Her poems 'Wolverine' and 'The Cattle Thief' testify eloquently to ignorance, irrationality, and violence, and their cost in Native lives. In one story, a formerly jingoistic hero reconsiders the Boer War and recants old allegiances. The death of a good friend makes him realize that 'the glory had paled and vanished. There was nothing left of this terrible war but the misery, the mourning, the heartbreak of it all' (1913, 211). Such reflections suggest Johnson's affinities with the liberal critics who questioned Britain's attack on the Boers (Schoeman; Koss; Page). The same critique of British morality informs her condemnation of the Christian churches' treatment of Natives. It also explains her contribution to the international condemnation of official France's anti-semitism in the Alfred Dreyfus affair. In 'Give Us Barrabas,' she exposes supposedly civilized Europe as diseased, 'leprous,' without claim to moral authority (1972, 118-8).[33] In her writings, Native peoples supply Canada with ready sources of indigenous virtue.

The key to Johnson's understanding of the best course for the new nation is inclusiveness and partnership – between Native and British and between female and male. The highly visible women who crowd narratives are ultimately 'sisters under the skin.' In articulating key values, they are not passive bystanders in history but forces to be reckoned with. Their courage, loyalty, generosity, and persistence will anchor a young nation into the future. Pauline Johnson's Canada, like the 'land of the fair deal' proposed by Nellie McClung, charts an important place for women in the creation of civil society.

Superior qualities justify adoption into the Canadian 'tribe,' but Johnson also hopes that the fact of being 'Canadian-born' will itself create shared sympathies and qualities. The title poem of her second volume of verse suggests that offspring of aristocrats and common folk can grow up, like the members of the NWMP, in harmony and equality, the products of an essentially beneficent northern environment. The 'glory' of a 'clean colonial name,' of fresh beginnings, is enough to make 'millionaires' of all (cited in Van Steen, 271). In the new Dominion, Euro-First Nations individuals are well equipped to claim citizenship as their 'blood heritage' (ibid.). In one story, where a member of the British elite is typically required to draw the appropriate moral, a governor general repudiates the prejudices of lesser men in defending a Euro-First Nation boy: 'The blood of old France and the blood of a great aboriginal race [Cree] that is the off-shoot of no other race in the world. The Indian blood is a thing of itself, unmixed for thousands of years, a blood that is distinct and exclusive. Few White people can claim such a lineage. Boy, try and remember that as you come of Indian blood, dashed with that of the first great soldiers, settlers and pioneers in this vast Dominion, that you have one of the proudest places and heritages in the world. You are a Canadian in the greatest sense of the great word ... you are the real Canadian' (cited in Van Steen, 272-3).

As these remarks suggest, the issue of race was important – and dangerous.

Race could confer virtue and intermarriage, even among great 'races,' and it could compromise the purity increasingly valued by the racial theorists of the day. Hybridity might combine the best; it might also bring with it degeneration. In opting for hope, Johnson denies the prejudices of the age. The hybrid Canada she attempts to will into being is to repudiate the corrupt heritage of European racism.

Johnson's hopes appear especially rooted in the West, where she spent many of the later years of her life. 'Booster' poems, such as 'The Sleeping Giant' on Thunder Bay; 'Calgary of the Plains'; 'Brandon'; 'Golden of the Selkirks'; and, the most rambunctious of all, 'A Toast' (dedicated to Vancouver), celebrate the erasure of past differences (1972, 110, 158-9, 133, 96, 121-2). In the future, individuals and races are to be taken on their own merits. Such cities, like Canada itself, do not care who you have been, only what you may contribute to an emerging identity.

The nation described by Johnson struggles with racism and sexism. The future of Native and Euro-First Nations peoples absorb her, to the exclusion of any examination of how non-British Europeans and others might fit in. Confronted with the vulnerability of First Nations communities in her day, Johnson had no hope of taking back the country, of returning Europeans to their own homelands. However she might celebrate the virtues of Native peoples, she has to deal with the ongoing reality of injustice, of conquest and settlement, with no other explanation than, as one of her characters says, 'perhaps the white man's God has willed it so' (1972, 19). Her hopes rest with a renewal of the old partnership that had united the British and the Iroquois in the War of American Independence and with a recognition of women's value. In her attention to the injustices suffered by women and First Nations, Pauline Johnson voices something more than the 'sentimental nationalism' some critics have seen (Doyle, 50-8). In her hands, 'nationalism' becomes 'one of the most powerful weapons for resisting colonialism and for establishing the space of a postcolonial identity' (Donaldson, 8).

A Postcolonial Liberal Inheritance

We know little of how Pauline Johnson's audiences received her views and almost nothing of her reception by First Nations listeners. For the most part, only one part of a conversation has survived. To be sure, there are clues. A veteran of the 1885 Prairie campaign, in near tears upon hearing 'A Cry from an Indian Wife,' confessed, 'When I heard you recite that poem, I never felt so ashamed in my life of the part I took in it' (cited in Keller, 60). A host in a small Manitoba town was heard to say, by way of introduction, 'Now, friends, before Miss Johnson's exercises begin, I want you all to remember that Injuns, like us, is folks' (121). The liberalism of the supposed 'colour blindness' embodied in these remarks suggests one influential source of support for Johnson. Her appeal to a tolerance and fair-mindedness based on a faith in a universal humanity convinced at least some receptive listeners. A few in her audiences understood some part of the message about First Nations, women, and Canada that she tried to deliver.

It is also clear that part of Johnson's appeal was her apparent lack of threat. Some listeners and readers, like one 1892 reviewer, enjoyed the fact that 'speaking through this cultured, gifted, soft-voiced descendant' was the 'voice of the nations who once possessed this country, who have wasted away before our civilization' (cited in Francis, 113). Representatives of dead or dying competitors for resources are easy to patronize, especially when they promise the illusion of a stronger national connection with the natural landscape. As Daniel Francis suggests in *The Imaginary Indian*, 'Having successfully subdued the Indians, Whites could afford to get sentimental about them' (123). Such scepticism is, however, only part of the story. It does not capture the common ambivalence and the outright opposition of some white Canadians to the abuses of European and male power. Johnson always had sympathizers. Her subversion of traditions that consign women and Natives to subordination and anonymity are significant, nourishing recurring liberal hopes for a more pluralist and egalitarian society. In her own way, like other resistance writers and performers at the turn of the century, Pauline Johnson prepared society to 'relinquish or modify' the idea of domination (Said, 200). Today she has literary heirs in Euro-First Nations writers like Beatrice Culleton, Maria Campbell, Beth Brant, and Lee Maracle who, too, name injustice and call for an equal partnership in a reformed nation (Lundgren; Brant).

Acknowledgments

My thanks to the 'Race and Gender Group,' whose discussions have been supported by a SSHRCC Strategic Grant 1992-5. Thanks too for the comments of Gillian Creese, Julie Cruikshank, Margery Fee, Carole Gerson, Nitya Iyer, Jane M. Jacobs, Kathy Mezei, Dorothy Seaton, Donald Smith, Wendy Wickwire, Donald Wilson, and members of the audience at a talk based on this chapter that I gave to Native Studies and Women's Studies at the University of Toronto on 22 April 1996. I would also like to thank Lorraine Snowden for her research assistance.

Notes

1 This chapter employs the terms 'Indian,' 'Native,' 'Aboriginal,' and 'First Nation' to refer to the original human inhabitants of North America, excluding the Inuit peoples of the North. Turn-of-the-century Canada regularly referred to individuals and populations who are a product of Indian-French unions as Métis and to those who are a product of Indian-British unions as 'mixed bloods.' 'Half-breed' was used to refer to both groups. In order to avoid the racism embodied in such usage, I have used the term Euro-First Nation to refer to such individuals and groups. 'European' is used in reference to individuals, Canadian and otherwise, whose families originate in the continent of Europe. So far as I have discovered, Pauline Johnson chose to refer to herself as Iroquois, Mohawk, Indian, and 'red' or 'redskin.'

2 For a fascinating discussion of contemporary women performing artists, see Forte. I would

also like to thank Dr. Merlinda Bobis (herself a performance artist) of the Faculty of Creative Arts, University of Wollongong, Australia, for her assistance in making this connection to Johnson.

3 For the limits and opportunities of 'performance,' see the essays in Diamond, especially the 'Introduction' by Diamond and Rebecca Schneider, 'After Us the Savage Goddess.'

4 Said (210). See also Turner, who provides a useful exploration of selected Canadian texts that attempt to create 'new discursive space' for a postcolonial nation. Turner focuses on Euro-Canadian writers, and Johnson is not a concern.

5 Her father, for example, was active, to the point of being assaulted by non-Natives, in efforts to protect Indian timber and Indians from the liquor trade. See Keller and also Barron.

6 The classic feminist figure of this international liberalism was Lady Ishbel Gordon, Countess of Aberdeen, disciple of William Gladstone and founder of the National Council of Women of Canada in 1893. See Saywell and Strong-Boag.

7 On the role of children of Indian/European unions, see Brown (204-11). George M.H. Johnson was the son of Helen Martin (d. 1866), the daughter of the Mohawk George Martin and Catherine Rolleston (a woman of German background who was captured during a raid on Pennsylvania settlements), and John Johnson (1792-1886), hero of the War of 1812 and the speaker of the Council of the Six Nations. See also Smith (1987) for an important account of the efforts of one outstanding Euro-First Nation individual to find accommodation between the Native peoples and European settlers in early nineteenth-century Ontario.

8 On the development of Brantford's middle class, see Burley. Unfortunately, this study makes no mention of Native peoples and pays little attention to the role of women. See Johnston, especially Chapter 10, for greater, although still limited, attention to the Iroquois Confederacy.

9 On British imperialism and patriarchy in these years, see Ramusack and Burton (469-81).

10 See, for example, the writers (Dr. Peter Martin or Oronhyatekha [1841-1907], Frederick Ogilvie Loft [1861-1934], Levi General or Deskeheh [1873-1925], and John Ojijatekha Brant-Sero [1867-1914] – all closely associated with the Grand River reserve) who regularly challenged prejudices. Brant-Sero, for example, campaigned to win recognition of the Iroquois as the first United Empire Loyalists, founders of Canada itself. (See Petrone, Chapters 2, 3, 4.)

11 See, for example, the case of the dancer described in McBride. My thanks to Trudy Nicks of the Royal Ontario Museum for drawing this volume and the issue in general to my attention. See also the related situation of the Australian Aborigines discussed in Poignant. My thanks to Kay Schaffer of the University of Adelaide for giving me a copy of this volume.

12 Landsman (274). See also Wagner. For a critical assessment of women's power in Iroquois society, see Tooker.

13 See Levi General or Deskeheh as cited in Petrone (104).

14 On this myth, see the now classic article by Green (1975, 698-714). See also Larson (Chapter 2, 'The Children of Pocahontas').

15 Her efforts to combine European and Native traditions are also seen in the work of contemporary writers like Lee Maracle. See Lundgren (69).

16 See the comments in her letter to a friendly critic, cited in Petrone (82-3).

17 Kidwell (97). On the role of the wilderness and the function of Native guides, see Jasen (especially Chapters 4 and 5).

18 See Smith (1990). Buffy Sainte-Marie is a folksinger and songwriter born at the Piapot Reserve in Saskatchewan in 1941.

19 See Keller on Johnson's failed romances and recurring financial problems.

20 Somewhat later, Iroquois women such as the American activists Minnie Kellogg (1880-1948) and Alice Lee Jemison (1901-64) would also assume major public roles as critics of European prejudice. Kellogg was born at the Oneida Indian Reservation in Wisconsin and educated at Stanford, Barnard, and Columbia's School of Philanthropy. She married a non-Indian lawyer and became an activist in the Society of American Indians and a

powerful writer. She was the author of *Our Democracy and the American Indian* (1920). Alice Lee Jemison was born in New York State, graduated from high school, married a Seneca steelworker, and worked at various jobs while active as an outspoken critic of the American Indian Bureau. See Hauptman (1981, 12 and passim). See also Hauptman (1986, and passim; 1985). At least one powerful speaker from another tribe also appeared somewhat earlier. See Sarah Winnemucca (1844?-1891), the American Northern Paiute woman who produced the autobiography *Life among the Paiutes: Their Wrongs and Claims* (1883). See Canfield. Unfortunately, we do not know whether Pauline Johnson knew of such women.

21 See, for example, her characterization of Red Jacket's thought as 'liberal, and strong, / He blessed the little good and passed the wrong / Embodied in the weak' (cited in Van Steen, 47).
22 See Carter and Andrews.
23 'My Mother' (1987, 64-5). See also her poem, 'The Derelict' (1972).
24 See Titley. See also the more sympathetic view of Scott's treatment of Indians in Dragland.
25 Death and disappearance are also major themes for contributors to the section, 'The Indian,' in Lighthall.
26 On British Columbia in these years, see the important studies by Barman and Tennant.
27 On 'unnaming,' see Ashcroft, Griffiths, and Tiffin (141). On similar efforts by other Native writers, see Petrone (Chapters 2 and 3).
28 See Van Kirk (49-68).
29 See, for example, the arguments in McClung (1915).
30 Her nom de plume (1900, 440-2).
31 See, for example, the otherwise excellent 'Introduction' by A. LaVonne Ruoff (Johnson 1987).
32 See Prucha. On Canadian assumptions of superiority, see Owram.
33 On the significance of the Dreyfus affair as a touchstone for the liberalism of the day, see Wilson and Feldman.

Works Cited

Andrews, Isabel. 1975. 'Indian Protest Against Starvation: The Yellow Calf Incident of 1884.' *Saskatchewan History* 28 (2):41-51
Ashcroft, Bill, Gareth Griffiths, and Helen Tiffin. 1993. *The Empire Writes Back. Theory and Practice in Post-Colonial Literature.* London and New York: Routledge
Bacchi, Carol Lee. 1983. *Liberation Deferred? The Ideas of the English-Canadian Suffragists, 1877-1918.* Toronto: University of Toronto Press
Barman, Jean. 1991. *The West Beyond the West. A History of British Columbia.* Toronto: University of Toronto Press
Barron, F.L. 1983. 'Alcoholism, Indians and the Anti-Drink Cause in the Protestant Indian Missions of Upper Canada, 1822-1850.' In I.A.L. Getty and A.S. Lussier, eds., *As Long as the Sun Shines and Water Flows: A Reader in Canadian Native Studies*, 191-202. Vancouver: UBC Press
Bashevkin, Sylvia. 1985. *Toeing the Lines: Women and Party Politics in English Canada.* Toronto: University of Toronto Press
Berger, Carl. 1971. *The Sense of Power: Studies in Ideas of Canadian Imperialism, 1867-1914.* Toronto: University of Toronto Press
Brant, Beth. 1994. *Writing as Witness: Essay and Talk.* Toronto: Women's Press
Brown, Jennifer. 1980. *Strangers in Blood: Fur Trade Company Families in Indian Country.* Vancouver: UBC Press
Burley, David G. 1993. *A Particular Condition in Life: Self-Employment and Social Mobiliiy in Mid-Victorian Brantford, Ontario.* Toronto: University of Toronto Press
Butler, Judith. 1990. 'Performative Acts and Gender Constitution: An Essay in Phenomenology and Feminist Theory.' In Sue-Ellen Case, ed., *Performing Feminism: Feminist Critical Theory and Theatre*, 270-82. Baltimore and London: Johns Hopkins University Press
–. 1993. *Bodies That Matter: On the Discursive Limits of 'Sex.'* London: Routledge
Canfield, Gae Whitney. 1983. *Sara Winnemucca of the Northern Paiutes.* Norman:

University of Oklahoma Press
Carter, Sarah. 1990. *Lost Harvest: Prairie Indian Reserve Farmers and Government Policy.* Montreal and Kingston: McGill-Queen's University Press
Dean, Misao. 1991. *A Different Point of View: Sara Jeannette Duncan.* Montreal and Kingston: McGill-Queen's University Press
Diamond, Elin, ed. 1996. *Performance and Cultural Politics.* London and New York: Routledge
Donaldson, Laura E. 1992. *Decolonizing Feminisms. 'Race,' Gender, and Empire Building.* Chapel Hill and London: University of North Carolina Press
Doyle, James. 1994. 'Sui Sin Far and Onoto Watanna: Two Early Chinese-Canadian Authors.' *Canadian Literature/Literature canadienne* 140 (Spring):50-8
Dragland, S.L. 1974. *Duncan Campbell Scott: A Book of Criticism.* Ottawa: Tecumseh
Drees, Laurie Meijer. 1995. 'Introduction to Documents One through Five: Nationalism, the League of Nations and the Six Nations of Grand River.' *Native Studies Review* 10 (1):75-88
Emberly, Julia V. 1993. *Thresholds of Difference: Feminist Critique, Native Women's Writings, Post-Colonial Theory.* Toronto: University of Toronto Press
Feldman, Egal. 1981. *The Dreyfus Affair and the American Conscience, 1895-1906.* Detroit: Wayne State University Press
Forte, Jeanie. 1990. 'Women's Performance Art: Feminism and Postmodernism.' In Sue-Ellen Case, ed., *Performing Feminisms: Feminist Critical Theory and Theatre,* 251-69. Baltimore and London: Johns Hopkins University Press
Foster, W. Garland. 1931. *The Mohawk Princess: Being Some Account of the Life of TEKAFHON-WAKE (E. Pauline Johnson).* Vancouver: Lions' Gate
Francis, Daniel. 1993. *The Imaginary Indian: The Image of the Indian in Canadian Culture.* Vancouver: Arsenal Pulp
Grant, Agnes. 1994. 'Reclaiming the Lineage House: Canadian Native Women Writers.' *SAIL* 6 (1):43-62
Green, Heather. 1994. 'This Piece Done, I Shall be Renamed.' In Carol Camper, ed., *Miscegenation Blues,* 291-303. Toronto: Sister Vision
Green, Rayna. 1975. 'The Pocahantas Perplex: The Image of Indian Women in American Culture.' *Massachusetts Review* 16 (4):698-714
Hauptman, Lawrence M. 1981. *The Iroquois and the New Deal.* Syracuse: Syracuse University Press
–. 1985. 'Designing Woman: Laura Minnie Cornelius Kellogg, Iroquois Leader.' In Raymond Wilson and L.G. Moses, eds., *Indian Lives,* 159-86. Albuquerque: University of New Mexico Press
–. 1986. *The Iroquois Struggle for Survival: World War II to Red Power.* Syracuse: Syracuse University Press
Jasen, Patricia. 1995. *Wild Things: Nature, Culture, and Tourism in Ontario 1790-1914.* Toronto: University of Toronto Press
Johnson, E. Pauline (Tekahionwake). 1900. 'One of Them [Pauline Johnson].' 'The Iroquois Women of Canada.' *Women of Canada. Their Life and Work.* Ottawa: National Council of Women of Canada
–. 1913. *The Shapganappi.* Toronto: William Briggs
–. 1926 [1911]. *Legends of Vancouver.* Toronto: McClelland & Stewart
– 1972 [1911]. *Flint and Feather. The Complete Poems of E. Pauline Johnson.* Toronto: Paperjacks
–. 1987 [1913]. *The Moccasin Maker.* Introduction, Annotation, and Bibliography by A. LaVonne Brown Ruoff. Tucson: University of Arizona Press
Johnston, Charles M. Brant. 1967. *Brant County: A History 1786-1945.* Toronto: Oxford University Press
Keller, Betty. 1981. *Pauline. A Biography of Pauline Johnson.* Vancouver and Toronto: Douglas and McIntyre
Kidwell, Clara Sue. 1992. 'Indian Women as Cultural Mediators.' *Ethnohistory* 39 (2):97-107
Koss, Stephen. 1973. *The Pro-Boers: The Anatomy of an Anti-War Movement.* Chicago:

University of Chicago Press
Landsman, Gail. 1992. 'The "Other" as Political Symbol: Images of Indians in the Woman Suffrage Movement.' *Ethnohistory* 39 (3):247-84
Larson, Charles R. 1978. *American Indian Fiction*. Albuquerque: University of New Mexico Press
Leacock, Stephen. 1973. 'Greater Canada: An Appeal.' In A. Bowker, ed., *The Social Criticism of Stephen Leacock*, 3-11. Toronto: University of Toronto Press
Lighthall, William D. 1892. *Canadian Songs and Poems: Voices from the Forests and Waters, the Settlements and Cities of Canada*. London: Walter Scott
Lundgren, Jodi. 1995. '"Being a Half-Breed": Discourses on Race and Cultural Syncreticity in the Works of Three Metis Women Writers.' *Canadian Literature* 144 (Spring):62-79
Mcbride, Bunny. 1995. *Molly Spotted Elk: A Penobscot in Paris*. Norman and London: University of Oklahoma Press
McClung, Nellie L. 1915. *In Times Like These*. Toronto: Thomas Allen
–. 1945. *The Stream Runs Fast*. Toronto: Thomas Allen
MacDonald, Mary Lu. 1990. 'Red & White; Black, White & Grey Hats.' In W.H. New, ed., *Native Writers and Canadian Writing*, 92-111. Vancouver: UBC Press
Martin, Christopher. 1967. *The Russo-Japanese War*. London and New York: Abelard-Schuman
Owram, Douglas R. 1972. 'European Savagery: Some Canadian Reaction to American Indian Policy, 1867-1885.' MA thesis, Queen's University, Kingston, Ontario
Page, Robert. 1987. *The Boer War and Canadian Imperialism*. Ottawa: Canadian Historical Association
Petrone, Penny. 1990. *Native Literature: From the Oral Tradition to the Present*. Toronto: Oxford University Press
Poignant, Roslyn. 1993. 'Captive Aboriginal Lives: Billy, Jenny, Little Toby and Their Companions.' *Captured Lives: Australian Captivity Narratives. Working Papers in Australian Studies*, 85, 86, 87. The Sir Robert Menzies Centre for Australian Studies and the Institute for Commonwealth Studies: University of London
Prentice, Alison, et al. 1996. *Canadian Women: A History*. 2nd edition. Toronto: Harcourt Brace
Prucha, Francis P. 1986. *The Great Father: The United States Government and the American Indians*. Lincoln and London: University of Nebraska Press
Ramusack, Barbara, and Antoinette Burton. 1994. 'Feminism, Imperialism and Race: A Dialogue Between India and Britain.' *Women's History Review* 3 (4):469-81
Said, Edward. 1994. *Culture and Imperialism*. New York: Vintage
Saywell, John T., ed. 1960. *The Canadian Journal of Lady Aberdeen, 1893-1898*. Toronto: Champlain Society
Shimony, Annemarie Anrod. 1994. *Conservatism among the Iroquois at the Six Nations Reserve*. Syracuse: Syracuse University Press
Shoeman, Karel. 1992. *Only an Anguish to Live Here: Olive Schreiner and the Anglo Boer War, 1899-1902*. Cape Town: Human and Rousseau
Silvera, Makeda, ed. 1995. 'Maria Campbell Talks to Beth Cuthand: "It's the Job of the Storyteller to Create Chaos."' In *The Other Woman: Women of Colour in Contemporary Canadian Literature*, 264-70. Toronto: Sister Vision
Smith, Donald. 1987. *Sacred Feathers: The Reverend Peter Jones (Kahkewaquonaby) and the Mississauga Indian*. Toronto: University of Toronto Press
–. 1990. *From the Land of Shadows: The Making of Grey Owl*. Saskatoon: Western Producer Prairie Books
Strong-Boag, Veronica. 1976. *The Parliament of Women: The National Council of Women of Canada*. Ottawa: National Museums of Canada
Tennant, Paul. 1990. *Aboriginal Peoples and Politics: The Indian Land Question in British Columbia, 1849-1989*. Vancouver: UBC Press
Titley, E. Brian. 1986. *A Narrow Vision: Duncan Campbell Scott and the Administration of Indian Affairs in Canada*. Vancouver: UBC Press
Tooker, Elisabeth. 1996. 'Women in Iroquois Society.' In Wendy Mitchinson et al., eds., *Canadian Women: A Reader*, 19-32. Toronto: Harcourt Brace

Turner, Margaret E. 1995. *Imagining Culture. New World Narrative and the Writing of Canada*. Montreal and Kingston: McGill-Queen's University Press

Valverde, Marianna. 1991. *The Age of Light, Soap, and Water: Moral Reform in English Canada, 1885-1925*. Toronto: McClelland & Stewart

Van Kirk, Sylvia. 1976. '"The Custom of the Country": An Examination of Fur Trade Marriage Practices.' In L.H. Thomas, ed., *Essays on Western History*, 49-68. Edmonton: University of Alberta Press

Van Steen, Marcus. 1965. *Pauline Johnson: Her Life and Work*. Toronto: Musson

Wagner, Sally Roesch. 1990. 'The Root of Oppression Is the Loss of Memory: The Iroquois and the Earliest Feminist Vision.' In W.G. Spittal, ed., *Iroquois Women. An Anthology*, 223-8. Ohsweken, ON: Iroqcrafts

Walden, Keith. 1982. *Visions of Order*. Toronto: Butterworths

Weaver, Sally M. 1972. *Medicine and Politics among the Grand River Iroquois: A Study of the Non-Conservatives*. Publications in Ethnology, No. 4. Ottawa: National Museums of Canada

–. 1994. 'The Iroquois: The Grand River Reserve in the Late Nineteenth and Early Twentieth Centuries, 1875-1945.' In E.S. Rogers and Donald B. Smith, eds., *Aboriginal Ontario: Historical Perspectives on the First Nations*, 213-57. Toronto and Oxford: Dundurn

Wilson, Stephen. 1982. *Ideology and Experience: Anti-Semitism in France at the Time of the Dreyfus Affair*. London: Associated University Presses

Encountering Anomalies:
A Cultural Study of Chinese
Migrants to Early Canada
Lisa Chalykoff

There is perhaps still some wisdom left in the old adage 'home is where the heart is.' Home is one of those concepts in which individual and collective constructions intermingle with varying degrees of harmony. Whether it signifies a nation-space, a region, an architectural dwelling, or a sphere of intersubjectivity, home cannot be fully understood without reference to political, historical, geographic, economic, and sociological factors. But neither can home be realized without some final and ineffable participation of the heart.

In an attempt to encompass its multidimensionality, I provisionally theorize home as a sort of mirage that opens for the subject a psychic space of – seemingly – unalienated being. I figure home as a mirage in order to acknowledge that no subject can carve out for herself a dwelling on which social constructions do not perform much of the psycho-architectural work; rather, in contexts of profound social inequality, people suffer from differing degrees of alienation and, thus, enjoy differing degrees of at-home-ness. One of the ways that I attempt to take the measure of a subject's success at constructing an efficacious sense of at-home-ness is to investigate the extent to which she can exercise definitional power within this multidimensional site.

Though I make my own disciplinary home in English studies, I stray afield in my specific approach to analyzing Sky Lee's *Disappearing Moon Cafe* and Denise Chong's *The Concubine's Children: Portrait of a Family Divided,* the two literary works this chapter considers. One useful theoretical tool for prosecuting such an interdisciplinary foray is Michel Foucault's concept of discourse analysis. Certainly, the text-based language analysis so prevalent within English studies affords an excellent means of demonstrating the instability of epistemological categories such as race, gender, and class insofar as they operate within a single text. But because textual analysis demands that we fix our attention exclusively upon the text, it addresses only intratextual authority and operates, seemingly, outside other systems of power. Foucauldian discourse analysis can help us to expand the breadth of our foci and to encounter the machinations of extra-textual power because it asks that we question how it is 'that one particular statement appeared rather than another' (Foucault, 27).

Asking Foucault's question not only of Lee's and Chong's works, but also of scholarly texts that rely on official state documents for information on early Chinese immigrants to Canada, has called my attention to certain important differences in emphasis. These differences separate explicitly fictional or personal representations of immigrant experiences, such as are found in Lee's and Chong's texts, from representations governed by more fact-based epistemes.[1] Unlike the former, the latter tend to focus predominantly upon the experiences of those Chinese immigrants who sought to make Canada their permanent home.

The texts governed by fact-based epistemes come from the disciplines of traditional history and sociology and rely centrally on official state sources for their evidence. Collectively, they create a narrative that traces the struggles of Chinese immigrants to achieve equal citizenship in Canada, as Canadians. That texts generated within Canada addressing the experience of early Chinese immigrants to Canada should focus upon their struggles to achieve equal citizenship seems only natural. But is it? Had I not read these traditional historical and sociological sources on early Chinese immigration to Canada in conjunction with *Disappearing Moon Cafe* and *The Concubine's Children*, I might not have noticed what the former narratives tend to miss. What my reading of *Disappearing Moon Cafe* and *The Concubine's Children* suggests is that a considerable proportion of the Chinese citizens who came to Canada as contract labourers had little interest in making Canada their home.[2]

I am not arguing that the relative silencing of those Chinese immigrants who were not interested in receiving Canadian citizenship results from insensitivity on the part of traditional historians and sociologists. More simply, this silence may be largely explained by the relative unavailability of unofficial, personal documents conveying the points of view of early Chinese migrants. As historian Patricia Roy suggests about Chinese contract labourers brought to complete the Canadian Pacific Railway, 'diaries, reminiscences and letters home could tell us what members of Chinese work gangs thought [felt?] about their toils' if only such documentation were available (13).

I argue that the relative absence of documentary evidence conveying the feelings of early Chinese immigrants to Canada has itself been productive, though not necessarily in a positive sense. This absence has had ideological ramifications; it powerfully reinforces the hegemonic notion, so zealously repeated by Canada's current prime minister, that Canada is the best of all possible nations – a country to which all of the world's potential migrants yearn to belong. The documentary silencing of those Chinese migrants who did not yearn for Canadian citizenship helps the nationalist insistence on Canada's desirability to remain unquestioned.

Other voices are also absent from the traditional historical and sociological studies of early Chinese migration to Canada. Because so few women immigrated from China in the late nineteenth and early twentieth centuries, their experiences have been largely ignored by mainstream scholarly literature.[3] Though the presence of Chinese women is almost always referred to, such references are either confined to presentations of the relevant statistical evidence (see Li, 61; Con and Wickberg, 14) or, alternatively, the significance of these women's presence is bounded within a patriarchal discourse of 'family life' (see Li, 57-60; Bolaria and Li, 95; Tan and Roy, 4-5).

By tracing the discursive record backward, I have found that virtually all contemporary studies of the early Chinese experience in Canada depend significantly on the 1885 *Report of the Royal Commission on Chinese Immigration*. The commission's *Report* becomes, in these accounts, the key source for information concerning the means by which Chinese migrants arrived in Canada, for relevant statistics, and for discerning the parameters that informed the early debates concerning the Chinese presence in Canada.[4] What is perhaps most interesting about this use of the 1885 Royal Commission is that the text itself is not interrogated. It is invoked as a means of explaining *something else* rather than as a target for scholarly questioning. Excepting records of parliamentary debates, the Royal Commission's *Report* was the first official state discourse to address the topic of Chinese immigration. Thus, both the *Report*'s temporal primacy and its acceptance as *factual* by subsequent commentators have informed my decision to place it in interrogative contact with Sky Lee's *Disappearing Moon Cafe* and Denise Chong's *The Concubine's Children*.

I juxtapose fictional and (auto)biographical with 'official' statements concerning the experiences of early Chinese immigrants to Canada's west coast for three reasons. First, such a juxtaposition helps to highlight the sheer complexity of the relationship between subjectivity and the concept of home (and the roles race, class, and gender play in this multidimensional relationship). Second, it provides an illustration of the means by which rules of discursive formation operate to delimit the kinds of information that are deemed relevant to the pursuit of knowledge. Third, my specific use of literary texts is intended to show how fictional and (auto)biographical texts, which are not bounded by fact-based epistemes, can provide a means of reconstructing histories rendered invisible within official documents. In other words, the freedom that literary texts have to convey not fact but feeling makes them an excellent tool for discovering wrinkles upon the surfaces of official state documents, whose rules of formation work to naturalize their contents by representing them as polished, rational, and complete.

The *Report of the Royal Commission on Chinese Immigration* legitimates its authority through claims to thoroughness. Chairman Chapleau begins his *Report* by stating, 'We were directed by our Commission to enquire into all the facts and matters connected with the whole subject of Chinese immigration. We have accordingly made ourselves – as far as possible through books – acquainted with it' (xi). This same insistence on the commission's thorough knowledge of written documents is revealed when Chapleau states in his preliminary remarks that he and his assistants 'have availed ourselves of much that is documentary ... We have further read all the literature bearing on Chinese immigration, and the issues raised in connection therewith, which the Library of Parliament and the most diligent search elsewhere placed within our reach' (x).

Such emphases upon encyclopedic knowledge help the commission to inscribe its discourse as unquestionable. The obvious preference accorded written statements – documents and books – is also a means of delegitimizing the statements of oral contributors, which are sometimes interpreted and at all times transcribed in the *Report*. By contrast, *Disappearing Moon Cafe* makes no such attempt to be encyclopedic; the discontinuous jumps in time, place, and narrative perspective that shape or, rather, resist shaping Lee's novel protect it against any temptation she may have had, or her readers may have, to tie up loose ends within a totality – a pressure toward closure that few narratives can resist.

Yet to suggest that the very structure of *Disappearing Moon Cafe* ensures its freedom from a centripetal pull toward a centre is not to say that Lee's text lacks order and the meaning such order engenders; rather, there are *orders* at work. These orders could be articulated in any number of configurations. One such articulation would posit three forces that drive the novel's voices toward some form of resolution. The first force is a genealogical drive to complete the Wong family tree – a force that arises from Kae's desire to invest Suzie Wong's death with meaning. The second is a feminist drive to subvert a misogynist economy of reproduction that focuses on both Fong Mai's and Kae's sexualities. And the third is a sociological drive to understand the relationship between race, community, and nation that develops from Wong Gwei Chang's search for the bones of contract labourers who died building the CPR and Chinatown's response to the Janet Smith murder. Each of these thematic directives informs the others, yet none can be seen as the novel's motivating centre.

By deploying interdependent motivating foci instead of a unitary, totalizing centre, *Disappearing Moon Cafe* participates in what Foucault terms 'general history.' In *The Archaeology of Knowledge*, Foucault contrasts this concept with 'total history.' Jeffrey Weeks's explanation is helpful here:

'Total history, [Foucault] observes, attempts to draw all phenomena around a single causative centre or spirit of a society or civilisation. The same form of historical influence is then seen to operate at all levels. General history, on the other hand, is concerned with "series, segmentations, limits, differences of level, time lags, anachronistic survivals, possible types of relation"' (110). General histories, like *Disappearing Moon Cafe*, posit only contextual truths; total histories, like the Royal Commission's *Report*, claim to have mastered all contexts and, therefore, to speak the truth. Because a text such as Sky Lee's *Disappearing Moon Cafe* is not constrained by the mastering impulse of total history, it can provide not only the details conveyed by more official or factual accounts of reality, but also the details that the rules of formation banish from rational discourse – those that ground the emotional realities of subjecthood.

Disappearing Moon Cafe begins by situating us in 'the village at the mouth of two rivers,' somewhere along the route of the CPR in 1892, seven years after the publication of the Royal Commission's *Report* (8). We first encounter young Wong Gwei Chang, 'fresh off the boat from China,' newly arrived in a new 'Canada,' on a mission to uncover old bones at the behest of the 'Benevolent Associations' (12, 10). Wong Gwei Chang's task is not only to pursue the past by uncovering the remains of the Chinese labourers left in unmarked graves along the route of the 'iron road,' but also to participate in correcting the past by returning these bones 'home' to China (2).

After losing his way amidst the mountainous terrain of British Columbia's coastline, Wong Gwei Chang is rescued by Kelora, the daughter of Chen Gwok Fei and his deceased Native wife. Because Wong Gwei Chang has lost not only his sense of direction, but also his sense of how to begin his search for bones, Chen Gwok Fei offers his assistance to the young and naive Wong. Chen eschews the official maps, 'with sections of the railroad numbered,' that the Benevolent Association has acquired for Wong, most likely from the CPR (11). Instead, he leads the young man to 'the first of many leftover work camp gangs' (11). To Wong Gwei Chang the men composing these gangs seemed initially 'strange ... maybe because of the shadow of loneliness and isolation that hovered over them' (11). He 'saw the loneliness in the brothers, toiling, poor ... they hankered for news of their villages' (12). As Wong Gwei Chang becomes familiar with these men and labours at their side, he experiences a deep sense of community that enables him to see that 'their shadows walk ahead of them, homesick' (13). Through Wong Gwei Chang's eyes we see that the labourers work 'unceasingly, as if they would fall apart if they ever stopped' (11). But these remarkable efforts do not reflect that, as a contributor to the Royal Commission fearful of competition from Chinese workers explained, 'on physiological principles [the Chinese are] especially fitted for such employment' (XXIV); rather, Sky Lee, through Wong Gwei Chang, allows us to see that these men's bodies laboured, as their hearts yearned, to return 'home' to China.[5]

My interdisciplinary journey began when I asked myself why Sky Lee inscribes China as *home* to the Chinese labourers who participated in perhaps the most epic project of nation-building in Canada's history – the construction of the CPR (2, 1). The men who came to Canada to work on the CPR were granted no citizenship rights; thus, China remained their legal home. Yet, ill-paid for their life-threatening labour, and forgotten after its completion, Canada remained their physical home. Juxtaposing Lee's depiction of the workers who remained in Canada after the completion of the CPR with that of the 1885 Royal Commission indicates the importance of considering fictional accounts of those absent from official history.

The first instructive peculiarity in the commission's *Report* is that no Chinese men or women living within Canada were asked to give evidence; instead, the Chinese voices in the *Report* are those of two men living in San Francisco. One of these men was Huang Tsun Hsien. Huang's testimony did not focus on the issues of emotional alienation and geographical displacement that Sky Lee stresses. He emphasized instead the extent to which one's legal relation to place defines one's sense of it as home. Huang asked the commission to 'recollect that the Chinese immigrants coming to this country are denied all the rights and privileges extended to others in the way of citizenship: the laws compel us to remain aliens' (XII). Huang goes on to report, 'I know a great many Chinese who will be glad to remain here permanently with their families, if they are allowed to be naturalized and can enjoy privileges and rights' (XII). It seems relevant to question what motivated the Royal Commissioners to invite a Chinese man living in the United States to participate in a federally sponsored study investigating Chinese immigration into Canada, when the *Report* includes no testimony from Chinese men or women living in Canada.[6] To extract at least a partial answer to this question, Huang's statement must be interpreted within the larger sociopolitical context in which it was deployed.

It is no coincidence that the *Report of the Royal Commission on Chinese Immigration* appeared in 1885, the same year the CPR was completed. As Bolaria and Li suggest, the combination of the perceived necessity for inexpensive Chinese labour to finish the CPR and the extreme anger directed by white workers against the perceived Asian competition meant that 'legislative control of the Chinese was inevitable, as soon as major projects of development were completed in British Columbia, and Chinese labour became dispensable' (86). Thus, it was something of a foregone conclusion that the Royal Commission would recommend that measures be taken to limit Chinese migration to Canada.

Commissioner Gray and Chairman Chapleau – the men appointed to resolve, through a federal government discourse, a BC controversy – had a

delicate agenda to negotiate. Their chief task was to reestablish the legitimacy of federal authority in British Columbia, which was threatened by
the widespread perception among white British Columbians that Ottawa's
intransigence was the reason for continued Asian migration to 'their'
province. At the same time, however, simply pandering to racist sentiment
could create another set of problems. To encourage white racism in a
province with a significant non-white population would threaten public
order, public safety, and the accumulation of capital.[7] Gray and Chapleau
opted for a compromise, the ambiguity of which is easily detected in
Commissioner Gray's concluding remarks. While Gray admitted to finding no evidence that the Chinese presence threatened either public safety
or morality, he tells us that 'nevertheless, there is another element to be
considered, that is Public sentiment ... The public in British Columbia
have almost unanimously, in the evidence, expressed a wish that some legislation should be had on this subject. Therefore, though there be not any
actual immediate danger, it may be and is desirable that sufficient legislation to meet existing evils, or what may augur the future advent of
supposed greater evils, should be had' (LXXXII). To speak plainly, Gray
attempted to calm racist white voters in British Columbia by assuring them
that there was no problem while, simultaneously, drawing them into the
rule of law by recommending that legislative action be taken against this
non-existent problem on their behalf.[8]

Bringing some knowledge to bear upon Huang Tsun Hsien's words concerning the agenda that drove the Royal Commission enables the
recognition of a significant oddity. Huang's message to the commission
evokes a condition in the present tense that would more accurately have
been posed in the future conditional; namely, the presence of families: 'I
know a great many Chinese who will be glad to remain here permanently
with their families,' his statement reads. Yet the very issue being discussed
by the Royal Commission – whether Chinese immigration into Canada
ought to be continued – would determine whether the predominantly
male population of Chinese living within Canada would be allowed to
bring their families (if they so desired). It was not, as Huang Tsun Hsien
represents it, a matter of whether the workers and their families would
choose to stay if granted full citizenship. Although such a claim may have
reflected accurately the realities of Chinese immigrants to the United
States, it can in no way be said to have represented the realities of Chinese
living in Canada in 1885 – at least not if we understand 'family' along
patriarchal, heterosexist lines. Statistics from the commission's own *Report*
tell us that 'out of a total of 10,550 Chinese in the Province there are altogether only 154 Chinese women' (LIX).

We are not told of the methods by which Huang Tsun Hsien's testimony
was conveyed to the Royal Commission, whether he spoke English,

whether his knowledge of the language was thorough, or whether his speech was translated (and, if so, by whom). We are, however, given reason to question the degree to which Huang Tsun Hsien's words can be said to represent his perspective accurately. A brief note, which Chairman Chapleau includes after documenting 'A Nevada Miner's View,' informs us that 'this language used is clearly not the language actually used by any miner. But it nonetheless expresses the miner's sentiments' (xv). We are left to determine independently the extent to which Huang Tsun Hsien's statement was similarly *reinterpreted* – and to what ends.

There are three reasons we can infer, from the commission's agenda, that it is possible, if not probable, that Huang Tsun Hsien's words were 'interpreted' to better fit a specific rule of discursive formation; namely, that any statements reported by Chinese participants should blur, rather than highlight, the very different circumstances of Chinese and Caucasian peoples in British Columbia in the 1880s. The first reason is Commissioner Gray's and Chairman Chapleau's desire to mitigate British Columbians' hostility toward Chinese immigrants. Some of this racist hostility was founded on complaints that the Chinese in Canada had no vested interest in nation-building but, instead, returned to China with the economic fruits of their labours in Canada (Royal Commission, XI, XXI). The second reason is the precedent of interpretive liberty Chairman Chapleau established with the statements of the 'Nevada Miner,' and the third reason is the presence within the *Report* of two sections addressing the public's fear of gambling and prostitution within Chinatown – concerns Bolaria and Li link directly to 'the deprivation of a conjugal family life' (95).

The questions that must be asked regarding the truth value of Huang Tsun Hsien's speech arise because Gray and Chapleau, unlike Huang, acted under the state's aegis to execute an official power of definition. It is this power that was deployed to extract the 'sentiment' from the speech of the anonymous Nevada miner. As a writer, Sky Lee can also be said to have a power of definition but, unlike that of Commissioner Gray and Chairman Chapleau, hers has not been legitimized by the Crown as authoritative.

Disappearing Moon Cafe provides a portrait of the Chinese immigrants brought to complete the CPR that flatly contradicts the priorities of Chinese immigrants as represented to the Royal Commission by Huang Tsun Hsien: Wong Gwei Chang's more emotional perspective suggests that these men were not preoccupied by a desire for fuller citizenship. Juxtaposing the representations of these two mens' respective experiences allows us to see that the presence of Huang Tsun Hsien's statement within the *Report* conveniently allowed the government to efface, in the interests of capital, a rather embarrassing fact that would surely have emerged if the Chinese who built the CPR had also been given a voice in the *Report*. Wong Gwei Chang learns that these men dream of returning to China and that they remain in Canada because they have been 'left behind to rot because the CPR had reneged on its contract to pay the Chinese railway workers' passage home' (12).[9] It seems that a mutually informing combination of state and corporate deceit operated to alientate these men from their power to define their homes both personally and geographically.

Further evidence to counter the hegemonic credo that Canada was the desired home of early Chinese migrants is provided by Denise Chong's *The Concubine's Children*. Chong's text is a narrative reconstruction that tells the story of her maternal grandparents: Chan Sam and his third wife, or 'concubine,' Leong May-ying. Included within the monologic narrative that runs from May-ying's childhood in China to Chong's current subject-position is a representation of Chan Sam's perspective on the attitude of Chinese migrants who came to 'Gold Mountain' in search of employment (7). Chong's foreword reveals the source of her information. She tells us that 'to recover the family's past in Canada, I myself was not enough of a living link. I had known my grandfather only as a young child, and my memories of him were fragmentary. I had known my grandmother longer, but by the time I was either interested in the past or had the necessary courage to ask her about it, she was long gone. And so, I had to rely upon my mother's memory' (x).

Through a thrice-mediated process, then, Chong tells us that 'Chan Sam and his friends all said the same thing: "In earlier times, ninety-nine of one hundred overseas Chinese here wanted to go home. Now, because of all the fast changes in China, not one in ten thousand wants to go back"' (189). It was not changes within Canada but, rather, the 1949 communist revolution in China that affected Chan Sam's dream of returning to his 'home' (189). Though the adjectives 'early' and 'now' lack precise dating, we do know that Chan Sam arrived in Vancouver in 1913 and died there in 1957 (11, 214).

Chan Sam's situation challenges Huang Tsun Hsien's contribution to the Royal Commission even more fundamentally than does that of Wong Gwei Chang. Though Chan Sam was naturalized as a Canadian citizen, his granddaughter reports that he never felt at home in Canada (189). This emotional reality impeded Chan Sam's enjoyment of his citizenship; he felt not only alienated from, but indeed indifferent to, the Canadian political process. Chong tells us that her grandfather 'had little interest in the [Chinese-Canadian] newspapers' campaigns for equal access to unemployment relief and welfare for whites and Chinese in Canada, or for other rights due them as residents and citizens. The future that preoccupied Chan Sam was China's; he cared only about developments at home that might affect his house, his *mau tin* [property] and his kin left behind' (61).

Denise Chong directly links Chan Sam's allegiance to China with the signifiers of his prestige there – his home, his property, and his second wife and two children. Any money Chan Sam was able to make in Canada was sent to China to further the construction of his home and to increase his store of property; these were the things that assured Chan Sam of an elevated status in the Chinese community to which he hoped to return.

It is social and economic class location that most clearly separate Chan Sam's experience of home from that of Sky Lee's fictional character, Wong Gwei Chang. The connection Chong establishes between a man's socio economic status and his emotional relation to place is corroborated by contrast with Wong Gwei Chang. When Lee catapults Wong from 'the village at the mouth of two rivers' in 1892 to Vancouver's Chinatown in 1924, we find him installed comfortably as a 'patriarch' within his community (8, 70). Because he was able to alter his status from that of a labourer to that of a merchant, Wong could afford to pay the 'head tax' necessary to bring his first wife, Mui Lan, to join him in Canada. Wong does not dream of geographical relocation and enhanced social status but of Kelora, the 'second wife,' whom he abandoned and whom, from his new postion of respectability, he never acknowledges. Comparing Wong Gwei Chang's and Chan Sam's relations to their legal homeland suggests that a man's relation to power – both economic and symbolic – has everything to do with his understanding of home.

Returning to the *Report of the Royal Commission on Chinese Immigration* with the lives of Mui Lan and Denise Chong's maternal grandmother, May-ying, in mind reveals a new dimension within the hierarchy marking subjects' relations to the power of definition. In the Royal Commission's *Report* the one instance in which Chinese women are addressed relates to prostitution. Commissioner Gray states that 'out of a total of 10,550 Chinese in the Province there are altogether only 154 Chinese women, of whom 70 are prostitutes, scattered throughout the Province entirely among their own countrymen many as concubines, that relationship being among them deemed no offense, and no discredit' (LIX). It is interesting to note that the blurred line between a Chinese woman's legally ambiguous status as a concubine and her strictly illegal status as a prostitute is here left to stand as it is; Commissioner Gray leaves the power to define a woman's relation to a man in the hands of the Chinese community – or so his statement suggests.

The case of May-ying belies Commissioner Gray's easy acceptance of the role concubines played in early twentieth-century Chinese (and Chinese-Canadian) culture. In narrating her maternal grandmother's life, Denise Chong tells us that, being born female, May-ying was held to be a burden to her family. Within May-ying's cultural context, 'a girl [was] "someone else's," a mouth to feed until she marrie[d]' (6). To release themselves from this financial burden, May-ying's parents sold her as a servant at age four. May-ying remained in this capacity until her seventeenth year, at which time her owner informed her that a man had offered to purchase her. This man was Chan Sam, who already had a wife: 'he wants a *chip see* [concubine] in *Gun San* [Gold Mountain],' May-ying's owner tells her (8). Chong reports: 'the effect was more cruel than if May-ying had been told no family would have her ... May-ying knew it would be taken as a mark against herself. No decent girl became a concubine, married off in shame without wedding or ceremony. On the other hand, the more concubines a man had the more prestige and social status he garnered' (8).

May-ying's feelings about being sold as a concubine, though mediated both through Denise Chong's mother's memories and through Chong's narrative interpretation of them, seem strong enough to suggest another rule according to which Commissioner Gray's discourse regarding Chinese prostitutes and concubines was formed. When Commissioner Gray states that the status of a concubine is 'among them no offense,' the Chinese subject-position the pronoun 'them' signifies could only be that of the Chinese *men* whose prestige increased as that of the women they purchased decreased. Perhaps not surprisingly, Commissioner Gray's discourse, when juxtaposed with that of Denise Chong, reveals his *Report* to have been driven by a phallocentric understanding of Chinese subjectivity.

The blurry line Commissioner Gray draws to distinguish between prostitutes and concubines within the community of early Chinese immigrants to Vancouver demonstrates two things. First, when viewed in conjunction with what we know of May-ying's feelings, it exemplifies the way in which a discourse informed by the juxtaposition of two patriarchal cultures can serve not only to alienate women from their powers of self-definition but also to erase all traces of women's self-perceptions. Second, the commissioner's blurry line reveals the lack of anxiety informing his understanding of the distinction between prostitutes and concubines. This lack of anxiety itself tells us that the issue was not in need of the Royal Commission's governance – Gray could assume that it was being effectively 'managed' by the community of Chinese 'countrymen' whom the prostitutes were assumed to be 'scattered entirely among' (LIX).

The patriarchal values that were common to Canada's non-Native population have operated so as to all but erase the productivity of Chinese women who immigrated to early Canada. Though the work some of these women performed as prostitutes is acknowledged in the Royal Commission's *Report*, any other labour they performed is unrecorded in a document that legitimated its authority via a rhetoric of thoroughness. It will be recalled that, for both Chan Sam and Wong Gwei Chang, the economic success their labours in Canada brought them informed profoundly the power they had to define their relations to place. The power of self-definition that economic success afforded these men was denied their female counterparts. Both Sky Lee and Denise Chong trace the circumstances and attitudes that combined to render the productivity of Chinese women invisible.

Examining the respective situations of Wong Gwei Chang and Chan Sam shows that, although these two men reaped benefits for whatever economic gains they made, these gains did not result from *their* labours alone.

When Janet Smith's murder joins the plot of *Disappearing Moon Cafe*, a pall of fear is seen to fall over Vancouver's Chinatown. This community's fear spurs it to action, and Wong Gwei Chang is the 'patriarch' called in to manage the crisis (70). A narrative voice that cannot be identified tells us that Wong Gwei Chang's status as a patriarch was 'given to him when he became one of the privileged few who could hire his fellow chinese ... His business thrived, and he was able to hire more and more. As a result, in chinatown, Gwei Chang was both well-respected as a fair and honest boss to toil under, and very much admired for being a ten-parts smart and reliable businessman' (75). Wong Gwei Chang's success is linked directly to his prosperous business: it is the success of 'Disappearing Moon Cafe' that enables Wong to 'hire his fellow chinese' and, thus, to gain repute as a businessman. The gaze of admiration directed at Gwei Chang by his fellows blinds them to the work of Mui Lan. When Mui Lan arrives in Vancouver she finds herself one of the only women in Chinatown. For a time she lacks both female community and personal direction in her new location. A narrative voice reports that, 'Before long, she found other interests. She found she was very good at a lot of things, especially good at making money. At night, after she finally turned off the restaurant's lights and locked its doors ... she'd finalize the daily accounts with the old man ... Mui Lan enjoyed adding up the day's take, energetically organizing the money into neat rubber-bound bundles' (28).

The only aspect of Gwei Chang's success that can be fairly attributed to him alone is his generous treatment of his workers. Though an admirable characteristic, given the nature of capitalism, it is Mui Lan's harder-edged frugality, efficiency, and ambition that are more likely responsible for the success of *Wong Gwei Chang's* enterprise. As her 'entry papers' tell us, Lee Mui Lan arrives in Canada marked patriarchally as 'a merchant's wife' (28). No amount of successful toil enables her to reappropriate her own powers of self-definition and to alter her categorization as her husband's dependant. Her business acumen is instead projected onto Gwei Chang.

Denise Chong writes of how the labour of her grandmother, May-ying, was never acknowledged by those who benefited most from it because of the patriarchal premise that the husband is a household's chief source of income. Chong's writing is a response to this injustice. May-ying arrived in Vancouver to find that her husband, Chan Sam, had contracted her to work as a waitress at a Chinese tea house to recover the price of her ticket. Because Vancouver's post-CPR demographics were marked by an excess of male labour-power and an insufficiency of female labour-power, May-ying's services were in high demand: she worked steadily as a waitress until her old age. Chan Sam worked sporadically. As a result, it was largely May-ying's earnings that allowed Chan Sam to build the house and purchase the land that brought him such status in his home village. Denise Chong and her mother visited the family Chan Sam never returned to in China and found that he was worshipped for his unfailing efforts on their behalf. Chong tells us that 'in the face of such devotion to her father's memory, Mother held back the truths dawning in her own mind ... [t]hat the house they cherished as a monument to her father had been built on her mother's back, on the wages and wits of waitressing and the life that came with it' (254). In *The Concubine's Children*, Denise Chong finally reaches a point in cultural time and space where her voice can speak into the vacuum created by her mother's, and by her grandmother's, silences.

Denise Chong and Sky Lee are two writers who have brought histori-cally informed imaginations to the respective genres of the novel and (auto)biography. Lee and Chong deploy the power of definition that pub-lication has allotted them in very different ways. Sky Lee's *Disappearing Moon Cafe* is written multiperspectivally and, thus, represents its truths as partial and contextual. Denise Chong's *The Concubine's Children* is written uniperspectivally; in her foreword she tells us that, 'in plumbing the depths of [her mother's] memory, [she] was able to find [her] way into those of May-ying and Chan Sam' (x). Chong's is an authoritative narra-tive stance, separated from that of Commissioners Gray and Chapleau only by the absence of Crown-granted legitimacy, and from that of traditional historians and sociologists by its dependence upon personal rather than *official* documentation. Denise Chong acknowledges that she has taken the lived history of a family and 'press[ed] it flat onto the pages of a book' (xi). But both Lee and Chong have laboured for the same end: their works ret-rospectively introduce representations of the lives of Chinese immigrants to Canada into the narrative record. These labours put a fresh spin on a very old cliché – better late than never.

When one asks the Foucauldian question, how is it 'that one statement appears rather than another?' of texts from a selection of disciplinary sources, a number of instructive answers emerge (Foucault, 27). These answers tell us about the construction of Canada; about subjects consti-tuted by default as 'statistical anomalies'; about disciplinarity; and about the roles race, class, and gender play in the relationship between the con-cept of home and the power of definition. Juxtaposing statements made by Sky Lee, Denise Chong, and Huang Tsun Hsien concerning Chinese migrants' perspectives on national belonging has shown the Royal Commission's *Report* to be premised on an extremely reified understand-ing of Chinese subjectivity. This discovery suggests that scholars using official documents should be aware that the uncritical use of such docu-ments as *factual evidence* to explain the experience of their subjects carries with it a considerable risk – that of being unwittingly complicit in reproducing harmful assumptions (in the case of the Royal Commission's *Report*, those of patriarchy and hegemonic nationalism).

Though a dependence on *official* state documents is not necessarily wrong in itself, such dependence should be predicated on the understanding that state documents rely on reified representations of identity-categories – in this case, the category of 'Chinese immigrants.' To draw the lines demarcating identity positions too widely is to risk effacing the diversity of human experience. Such effacement is demonstrated by the *Report*'s treatment – replicated in those scholarly works that make extensive use of it – of those migrant Chinese labourers who had no interest in Canadian citizenship and, in particular, of Chinese women migrants. The importance of the former's feelings, and the diversity and productivity of the latter's lives, are silenced by the *Report*.

In conclusion, the concept of home has been shown to be extremely complex. Home, however, can be rendered more understandable by considering factors of race, class, and gender. These categories have been shown to inform most profoundly the power a subject has to construct for herself a sense of *at-home-ness* by exercising the power of definition within this site. Though the power of racial definition was left in the hands of the white civil servants who administered the Royal Commission's *Report*, those Chinese men who gained economic power in Canada appear to have been far more *at-home* here than were their female and poor male counterparts. The power of racial definition penetrated into but did not eclipse that of patriarchy: Chinese men were allotted the power to define Chinese women as prostitutes or concubines. Those who emerge from this study as most alienated from the power of definition are Chinese women. It is these women whose histories are only now being caught in the more pliant net of fictional and (auto)biographical representation, not surprisingly, by the Chinese women authors whose lives have been most marked by this alienation.

Notes

1 The texts that have informed my analysis of these disciplinary tendencies include sociologists B. Singh Bolaria and Peter Li's *Racial Oppression in Canada*, Peter Li's *The Chinese in Canada*, historians Jin Tan and Patricia Roy's study of the same name, Roy's 'A Choice Between Evils,' and Con and Wickbert's *From China to Canada*.

2 Though some of the texts I have examined refer in a sentence or two to this feeling among the population of male Chinese contract labourers (Tan and Roy, 4; Li, 21), the import of these brief references is easily lost among the far more detailed and defended arguments that document the sociopolitical nature of these immigrants' physical presence as opposed to their feelings about location.

3 About this silencing, Canadian historian Veronica Strong-Boag argues that unless historians redress the overrepresentation of bourgeois white male subjects in Canadian historical writing, historians will 'become fundamentally irrelevant to the construction of a meaningful memory for all Canadians' (17).

4 For a sampling of current historians' and sociologists' dependence upon the *Report* of the 1885 Royal Commission, see Bolaria and Li, 104-9; Li, 16, 22, 24, 26-7; Tan and Roy, 7-8; and Roy, 15, 17, 21.
5 For reasons of clarity it should be noted that Commissioner Chapleau's report is paginated using lower-case Roman numerals, while Commissioner Gray's is paginated using upper-case Roman numerals.
6 In *Racial Oppression in Canada*, Bolaria and Li quote from Huang Tsun Hsien's statement to the 1885 Royal Commission (114), but they do so without either stipulating or problematizing his location in San Francisco. Li also invokes Huang's testimony to the Royal Commission in *The Chinese in Canada* (22) (again without encountering Huang's location) to bolster his argument that enfranchisement, and not human feeling, has influenced the tendency for Chinese migrants to leave Canada with their earnings rather than to make this nation-space their permanent home.
7 On the history of federal-provincial conflict over Chinese immigration to British Columbia, see Bolaria and Li, 107-9.
8 The Act to Restrict and Regulate Chinese Immigration into Canada was passed as a result of the *Report of the Royal Commission on Chinese Immigration* (1885). This act limited cargo ships to carrying 'one such immigrant for every fifty tons of its tonnage' and instigated a head tax of $50 upon every Chinese immigrant entering Canada (*Statutes of Canada* [1885], Ch. 71, 209).
9 Sky Lee's status as a writer of 'fiction' lends her the licence to take a deliberately interested stance in assessing responsibility for the fates of the Chinese labourers who had no choice but to remain in Canada after completion of the CPR. Because Andrew Onderdonk, the CPR's railway contractor, had subcontracted out the task of supplying Chinese labour for the building of the railway line from Eagle Pass to Port Moody, the allocation of responsibility for the fates of thousands of labourers who had not earned enough money to pay for passage 'home' to China was highly contested. Patricia Roy notes that there was a shared sentiment among the white population of British Columbia that the workers who were no longer deemed necessary should be returned to China but that 'newspaper editors and legislators ... could not decide whether the cost should be borne by the Chinese contractors, Onderdonk, the federal or even the provincial government' (34). Sky Lee suffers from no such problem in pointing her finger at the CPR (who likely earned the greatest profit from these mens' labours). These bickerings eventually died out, and the labourers themselves, bereft of both gainful employment and the money to leave, remained stranded along British Columbia's coastline.

Works Cited
Bolaria, B. Singh, and Peter S. Li. 1985. *Racial Oppression in Canada*. Toronto: Garamond
Canada. Parliament. 1885. *Report of the Royal Commission on Chinese Immigration*. Ottawa: Printed by Order of the Commission
Chong, Denise. 1994. *The Concubine's Children: Portrait of a Family Divided*. Toronto: Penguin
Con, Harry, and Edgar Wickberg. 1982. *From China to Canada*. Toronto: McClelland & Stewart
Foucault, Michel. 1972. *The Archaeology of Knowledge*. Trans. A.M. Sheridan Smith. Scranton: Tavistock
Lee, Sky. 1990. *Disappearing Moon Cafe*. Vancouver: Douglas and McIntyre
Li, Peter S. 1988. *The Chinese in Canada*. Toronto: Oxford University Press
Roy, Patricia E. 1984. 'A Choice Between Evils: The Chinese and the Construction of the Canadian Pacific Railway in British Columbia.' In *The CPR West: The Iron Road and the Making of a Nation*, 13-34. Vancouver: Douglas and McIntyre
Strong-Boag, Veronica. 1994. 'Contested Space: The Politics of Canadian Memory.' Presidential Address. *Journal of the Canadian Historical Association* 5:3-17
Tan, Jin, and Patricia Roy. 1985. *The Chinese in Canada*. Ottawa: Canadian Historical Association
Weeks, Jeffrey. 1982. 'Foucault for Historians.' *History Workshop* 14 (Autumn):106-19

Part 3: Toward a New Canada

The Mountie and the Nurse: Cross-Cultural Relations *North of 60*

Linda Warley

The visibility of images of Native people in the popular media has increased over the past few years, especially on both big and small screens. Movies such as *Dances With Wolves, The Last of the Mohicans, Black Robe, Clear Cut, Dance Me Outside, The Indian in the Cupboard,* and Disney's mega-movie and marketing event *Pocahontas* have attracted large audiences as well as much debate. In both the United States and Canada, mainstream television shows such as *Northern Exposure, Star Trek, The X-Files, Liberty Street, The Rez,* and, of course, *North of 60,* incorporate, to varying degrees and with different effects, Native characters and Native themes. In the spring of 1995, the American television networks launched two documentaries, *500 Nations* and *The Way West,* both revisionist histories intended to address (if not necessarily *re*dress) the negative consequences of European conquest of and settlement in the Americas. These movies and television shows are part entertainment, part self-scrutiny. Considered in a generous light, it might seem that, as one response to growing political pressure from Native groups concerning unsettled land claims and treaty rights, as well as the deplorable poverty in which many Native people continue to live, non-Native North Americans are engaged in a process of consciousness-raising. A more cynical view would be that commodified images of Native peoples are once again fulfilling a white consumer hunger for the exotic. As bell hooks argues, representations of ethnic and racial otherness are easy to sell because 'within commodity culture, ethnicity becomes spice, seasoning that can liven up the dull dish that is mainstream white culture' (1992, 21). And Joel Monture reminds us that the popularity of all things Indian peaks in twenty-year cycles (121). Perhaps we are only once again at one of those peaks.

The success and popularity of the CBC television drama series *North of 60* is surely testament to the appeal of Native content. But I am not cynical about this program's success; rather, I am delighted by it, because this program has brought images of Native people into Canadian homes in a way that is unprecedented, and it has opened up a venue for debating not only the content of those images but also how they are received by Canadian viewers. *North of 60* is something of a phenomenon. According to one estimate, it attracted an audience of a million and a half viewers every week (Bell, C7). Running for an impressive six seasons, the series attracted a loyal following and was nominated for nine 1995 Gemini awards (Feindel, 32). At the first Aboriginal Awards Banquet at the 1996 Dreamspeakers Festival (a showcase for Native filmmakers and video artists held annually in Edmonton), Tina Keeper, who plays the Dene RCMP officer and is one of the show's stars, received the award for Best Actor in a Dramatic Role ('Dreamspeakers' 6). This chapter is about the appeal of *North of 60*. It asks what this program does for its audience. My readings and discussions tell me that it is generally well received by both Native and non-Native viewers, and part of my purpose here is to elucidate why it seems to work – though differently – for both constituencies. My argument is this: *North of 60* offers a complex but ultimately positive representation of contemporary Native life – one with which Native viewers are motivated to identify. Further, it makes space for non-Native viewers by incorporating white characters into its narratives and by portraying relations among white and Native characters which, though fraught with the legacy of settler colonialism, are not necessarily limited by it.[1] While it might be true that *North of 60* provides white viewers with an opportunity to taste the world of the 'other' – the exotic spice that bell hooks talks about – this program also requires white viewers to reflect on the assumptions and attitudes that they carry with them into that world.

North of 60 is set in the present and it is about people, mostly Dene people, who live in Lynx River, an imaginary community in the Northwest Territories. The program deals with issues that are relevant to contemporary Native life, issues such as community management of land, resources, and businesses; the role of government and white people generally in local projects; alcohol and solvent abuse; adolescent struggles over identity; unemployment; the legacy of residential schools; and the role of the RCMP and the judicial court system in policing Native communities and resolving local disputes. Importantly, the program also addresses issues that have little if anything to do with white people, including feuds between families, generational tensions, and the political wranglings of the band council. *North of 60*, however, is not solely defined by the problems and crises that inform its storylines; rather, this is a program that depicts Native people as survivors, as competent human beings. And this, in itself, is appealing.

Native people have long argued that either they are not represented in the media at all or media representations of them are usually misrepresentations. In a 1988 study conducted by the Ad Hoc Committee for Better

Race Relations, Native people, when asked on a questionnaire, 'What do you dislike the most about media coverage of your community and other minorities?' overwhelmingly responded that the coverage was 'too negative' (Khaki and Prasad, Appendix 4). While stories about Native people may appear in the mainstream media, those stories are generally either focused on and contained by a distant past – which is either romanticized or characterized by genocide and cultural breakdown – or they show contemporary people in a state of crisis. Think of Davis Inlet. While no one is denying that problems exist in Native communities, consistent representations of Native people as a doomed, or lost, or degenerate race have profoundly damaging effects on the people who consume those images, perhaps especially on young Native people. For Native artists and cultural workers, one important task might be to represent and affirm what keeps their people and their communities strong (King, 4). In this respect, *North of 60* accomplishes four things: it represents Native people not as passive players in sensationalized stories, but as people living in a community where conflicts are explored and solutions negotiated; it considers the sources of social and individual problems, putting issues such as alcohol abuse and unemployment in context; it affirms the continuity of culture, which is depicted as dynamic and changing – rooted in the past but not fixed there; and, importantly, it shows some Native people succeeding in life.

North of 60 functions as a realist visual text. Although it is obviously a representation of a Native community, it relies on viewers being able to accord that representation a certain credibility. As Ella Shohat and Robert Stamm note, 'Spectators (and critics) are invested in realism because they are invested in the idea of truth, and reserve the right to confront a film with their own personal and cultural knowledge ... That films are only representations does not prevent them from having real effects in the world' (178). Realist texts represent alternative perspectives and can function as counter-narratives that challenge official versions of truth. Plus, they carry emotional (as well as political) weight in that they can confirm and validate the experiences of individuals who belong to disempowered groups. Bell hooks, in addressing the importance of the concept of 'the real' to Black people and other minority and oppressed peoples, argues that 'the history of colonization, of imperialism is a record of betrayal, of lies, and deceits. The demand for what is real is a demand for reparation, for transformation. In resistance, the exploited, the oppressed work to expose the false reality – to reclaim and recover ourselves' (1989, 3). The television viewer's ability to identify with particular representations is an important aspect of realism. And if realist visual texts are powerful, it is *because* they are believable.

North of 60 expressly aims for accuracy. Each episode is subject to a number of reality checks, with scripts being reviewed by a panel of insider experts, including representatives from the Dene community and the RCMP (Bell, C7; Dudley, A13). Part of the program's credibility also certainly comes from the identities of the people who make it. Although the creators and producers are not Native, many of the people who work on the show are, including members of the production and technical crew. Positions of senior story editor, writer, and director have been held by the likes of Jordan Wheeler, Thomas King, and Gil Cardinal, respectively, and all of the actors playing Native characters (who constitute 90 percent of the characters) are Native, though not necessarily Dene. Thus, the program seeks to correct an old wrong: the media industry's habitual practice of creating images of Native people in the absence of consultation with or involvement of Native people themselves. It provides both opportunity and training for Native people who wish to work in the media arts. And, by ensuring that Native people have access to one powerful image-making machine, this television program also creates the possibility for Native people to have at least some control over the images produced by that machine.

I wish to be absolutely clear about this: Native people do not have complete creative or production control over this program, as many would wish (see Farmer; Wagamese); however, they are involved to an unprecedented extent in Canada and not at all in the United States. One commentator reported to me that she was impressed by the fact that the program was an hour-long weekly drama based on Native issues and starring Native actors. Even on PBS in the United States there is no comparable program; therefore, this effort by the CBC could be interpreted as a Canadian attempt to inform the Canadian public about contemporary Native issues. It is important to recognize what Canadians do differently and do well.

The concept of authenticity that I am invoking has been much debated and remains problematic. It seems to me, however, that it is a concept that means different things in different contexts. Notions of authenticity and truth have been thoroughly discredited by the European-derived poststructuralist theories that currently circulate in academic institutions. To suggest that *North of 60* is a more accurate representation of northern Native experience than is generally seen on the mainstream media, as I am doing here, might be to reinscribe the false assumption that the relationship between text and world is a stable one. As poststructuralists would argue, there is no way for a representation, whether visual or literary, to get it 'right.' All representations are artificial, shaped according to the biases and investments of those who make them as well as of those who receive them.

Furthermore, authenticity can be a hegemonic concept, even when invoked by members of marginalized groups, for such a concept often partakes of a discourse of essentialism and suggests that identity categories such as 'Native' are homogenous and unchanging. Insisting on authenticity often means predetermining the constituent features and characteristics of the authentic and then requiring subjects within the group not only to conform to but also to *perform* those features and characteristics. As commentators such as Trinh T. Minh-ha have noted, minority subjects are constantly required to enact such performances, which are not only limiting but which also reinscribe incommensurable differences between minority and dominant groups, thus forestalling efforts to move beyond those differences (82). Moreover, as Marilyn Dumont points out, 'authentic' images of Nativeness tend to overvalue the traditional and negate the experiences and artistic productions of Native people who are at various removes from traditional forms and practices. Dumont argues that 'there is a continuum of exposure to traditional experience in native culture, some of us have been more exposed to it than others, but this does not mean that those who have been more exposed to it are somehow more Indian, as if we are searching for the last surviving Indian. Because this notion of *Indians vanishing* is the effect of nineteenth century ideas about culture as static, this notion of culture as something immutable compounded by the Indian Act affects images of ourselves as either *too Indian or not Indian enough'* (47, emphasis in the original).

While it might be true that images of Native people created by Natives are not necessarily more accurate or representative of Native reality and experience than those created by non-Natives, they at least provide a point of comparison. Perhaps more important, they contribute to a plethora of diverse images of Native peoples that challenge and subvert stereotypes. If, as Ward Churchill argues, 'the handling of American Indians and American Indian subject matter within the context of commercial US cinema is objectively racist on all levels, an observation which extends to television as well as film' (231), then countering racism in the media is a vitally important artistic and political undertaking – one in which those who have been the *objects* of racist representations have the greatest stake. To refuse to accept the possibility that Native image-makers might do a better job of representing their experiences, their histories, and their communities than non-Native image-makers, that Native writers, actors, editors, technicians, and consultants might get things more 'right' than a non-Native crew, strikes me as inappropriate. *North of 60* may not be an absolutely accurate representation of northern Native life. Indeed, distortions are inevitable. The fact that characters speak in English and not Slavey or another Dene language is already a distortion, as Jordan Wheeler points out (cited in Dudley, A13). But this does not mean that the program is not credible or that it does not effectively present reality from a Native point of view. If one common experience of Native people in Canada has been the conflict between Native truth and white truth, then *North of 60* provides an important occasion for such conflicts to be foregrounded and explored. Furthermore, it does so on mainstream television before a million or more viewers, weekly during the fall/winter season and also during summer reruns.

Of course, not all Native viewers like *North of 60*, although many do endorse it. In the absence of a broad-based statistical study, I report what I have gleaned from media reports and my own efforts to canvas responses from viewers. Significantly, if Native viewers do like *North of 60*, it is generally because it rings true to them. In media reports (which must be regarded with some suspicion, not least because they can function as advertisements), some of the actors who work on the program have commented that either they identify with the characters they play or they recognize their friends and relatives in other characters (Quill, F6; Dudley, A13; Zimmerman, A14). When I posted a request for reviews of *North of 60* on two Internet listservs, Natchat-L and Nativelit-L, Native people who had seen the program[2] often evaluated it in terms of its credibility. Amelia Davisson wrote that she thinks the show is successful because of 'the reality behind it ... *North of 60* is an accurate representation of tribal community life. Also, I feel that the actors and actresses featured on *North of 60* are extremely human and likable ... not to mention believable.' April Lindala, who used to work in television, did not think that the acting or the camera work were particularly remarkable, and she would like to see the crew taking more risks; however, she also commented that she was pleased that it was 'not filled with gratuitous acts of spirituality. You don't see someone smudging all the time for whatever reason (I have seen this in other programs). If there is a need for healing such as the youth talking circle, then they do it. The program is also not filled with fakes. Part of the charm of the program is the fact that these people seem like people. While the calibre of acting is not high, you still feel for these characters. The youth especially, seem like kids you would see wandering at a powwow. The grandma in the one episode was very real. She felt like the quiet power before a thunderstorm. I don't even know if she had two lines. It was just real.'

When I asked Emma LaRocque during the question period of a session at the 1995 Learned Societies Conference at the Université du Québec à Montréal what she thought of *North of 60*, she answered that she liked it because it represents Native people as fully developed, well-rounded human beings rather than as stereotypes. As LaRocque also noted, the particular value of a serialized television drama series is that it provides both time and space in which characters can change and develop.[3] Perhaps a comment by Tina Keeper's father sums up the reason many Native viewers like *North of 60*: 'They [the characters] are Indians as people, not people as

Indians' (cited in Bell, C7). *North of 60*, then, provides Native viewers with the opportunity to see themselves, in all of their complexity, reflected in *and* validated by a realist visual text. And there can be little doubt that the program offers Native viewers representations of Native characters that can serve as positive and credible role models.[4]

But why does this program work for white viewers? After all, if we think in terms of simple demographics, white viewers must make up a significant portion of the audience in order for it to score so well in the ratings. Perhaps *North of 60* is only warmly received by a mainstream Canadian audience because it presents a picture of 'Nativeness' that is easy for non-Native viewers to consume. Dale Blake comments that she finds *North of 60* 'too air-brushed,' and she worries that viewers will forget about other Native communities, such as Davis Inlet, that are a lot harder to look at. Marilyn Dumont suggests that *North of 60* reinscribes familiar images of Native people as rural, thereby perpetuating the stereotype of the Indian as close to nature, living a simple life based on a subsistence economy and distanced from the urban wage economy (48). Richard Wagamese, noting that 'the test pattern Indian' remains a pervasive primetime television image, remarks that 'even the much bally-hooed *North of 60* fails to represent us accurately. Who among us has been to an aboriginal community so completely lacking in dogs and laughter, for instance?' (50). Regina Harrison notes that the program avoids really tough legal and constitutional issues, specifically the issue of Native sovereignty, thereby effacing the threat to Canadian unity that Native political subjectivity represents. And I would add that because the program is set in the Northwest Territories, it is possible for southern Canadian viewers to continue to locate Native people as *out there*, up North or on a reserve, and not *right here* as immediate neighbours with whom they share both physical and social space. Images of the North are foundational to the Canadian national imaginary, and part of this program's appeal surely has to do with the repeatability of images of northernness that confirm, but do not challenge, particular constructions of the nation.[5] If a program focused on the lives of Native people were to be truly radical, it would probably be about Native people living in the city. Certainly the image of Nativeness represented on *North of 60* is a safe and comfortable one. It has to be in order to sell.

But is that all there is to say? Are white viewers only passive consumers of images that feed their own hunger for the exotic? Does this program simply function to confirm white subjectivity within Canadian social space? I would like to suggest that *North of 60* might appeal to Canadian viewers of European descent because they, too, can see themselves reflected in the world it represents. Lynx River is home to several white characters; it is also regularly visited by a host of white people with various missions and agendas. Whether they be RCMP officers, lawyers and judges,

Department of Indian and Northern Affairs bureaucrats, anthropologists, or European businesspeople, white people are very much part of this representation of a northern community. As a realist visual text, then, *North of 60* presents a mirror to white Canadians too, but what it frequently reveals is how white arrogance and interference continue to affect the lives of Native people and to sustain the colonial relationship between mainstream society and the First Nations. In other words, while white viewers can also find points of identification in this text, those points of identification are often unsettling. One of the strengths of *North of 60* is its careful treatment of the tensions created by the simultaneous and paradoxical integration and non-integration of white characters. Often it is a white character who is 'othered' in this visual text. Such a reversal of the conventional cinematic and television paradigms creates a subject position that is unfamiliar and uncomfortable for the white viewer.

In order to explore this point further, I will now analyze one particular cross-racial, cross-cultural relationship: the friendship between Michelle Kenidi, the Dene RCMP officer (played by Tina Keeper), and Sarah Birkett, the white nurse (played by Tracey Cook). The Mountie and the Nurse. Clearly *North of 60* toys with conventionalized images, in this case, those that come from Mountie movies. As critics such as Daniel Francis and Pierre Berton have documented, the Mountie is an iconic figure in media (especially Hollywood) representations of the North, and the relationship between the men in scarlet and the Indians they 'cared for'[6] is an essential ingredient of Canadian national identity. The Hollywood Mountie always had to get his man, but he also had to get his girl. In the first season, *North of 60* introduced the conventional Mountie/Nurse romantic plot. Sarah was involved with Eric Olsen, the white Mountie who comes to Lynx River from Vancouver; however, since the removal of Eric from the program, this emblematic relationship has been transferred to Michelle and Sarah. It has also, through transference, been transformed. For this is no longer a heterosexual love relationship but a friendship between women. Same nurse; different Mountie.

Both characters are partly drawn from a complex set of stereotypical images. Michelle may be an RCMP officer – one of the few Native (let alone female) ones around – but she is also a recovering alcoholic, a survivor of residential school, and a single mother. If Michelle's alcoholic past had been represented, the program could be criticized for creating images of Native women that confirm negative stereotypes, but it is not. It functions mainly as a reminder of how far she has come, although it has also been used against her by other Native characters who accuse her of feeling superior to them. Indeed, how Michelle negotiates her loyalties to her people, her past, and her position as a representative of the Canadian state is one of the most fascinating aspects of *North of 60* and probably deserves a separate study. Some might find the character of Michelle to be sanitized, too good to be true, but she is not a Pocahontas-style Indian Princess. Neither is she the flip side of the stereotypical representation of Native women, a dirty squaw (see Acoose; Green). The character of Michelle partakes of stereotypes but is not constrained by them.

Sarah's character is also partly constructed through the evocation of stereotypes. Her story repeats a conventional imperialist narrative: white man/woman wants to understand a meaningless or troubled past and goes north to find him/herself. As Margery Fee has shown in her study of English-Canadian literary texts, such white characters often accomplish their quest and resolve their confusion through contact with an object, image, or person associated with Native cultures (16). Sarah goes to Lynx River to escape the limitations of life in Windsor, Ontario, and to avoid a troubled relationship with her family. In fact, as one of the white characters once commented, all of the white residents are there because it is the end of the line for them in some way. The North is different. The North is away. The North is anonymous, unmarked. You can become someone new there. But the North is also dangerous, especially to white people (another stereotype), and Sarah 'goes crazy' in Lynx River. Because of a series of misdiagnoses that Sarah makes in her capacity as community nurse, she is eventually fired by the band council, and, at her lowest moment, she ends up in a psychiatric institution being treated for a nervous breakdown.

A recurrent theme in the program is the outsider status of white characters, and, throughout, Sarah has been a focus of debates about how welcome she and others like her are in Lynx River. This issue came to a head with the birth of Sarah and Albert's child and Sarah's request for a house and, by implication, permanent residency in Lynx River. While her daughter is a band member and thus has a right to band property, Sarah, because she is not Native and not married to Albert, is not. The people debated – in the coffee shop and in their homes as well as in band council and town meetings – how connected Sarah was to the community, what that connection might be based on, and whether or not she should be allowed to stay among them.

Every relationship that Sarah has with Native people in the community is, in some way, complicated by the historical fact of white settler colonialism. This is perhaps especially true of her relationships with women, including Michelle. A telling early episode concerns the birth of Ellen's child. Ellen, a psychologist with whom Sarah has professional contact but whom she also at one point regarded as her 'best friend,' refuses to accept Sarah's professional opinion that she should be medi-vacced out to a hospital in Yellowknife. Ellen insists that she will have her baby at home.[7] Elsie, an elder in the community, acts as midwife; Sarah is the helper, her white 'expertise' unwelcome. Her presence in the room is tolerated by the other two women, but only just. The conflict is partly between white and Native responses to and practices of childbirth, but the episode complicates this issue by showing how hurt Sarah is not to be included in her friend's decision-making process or in the actual birth. She is on the outside, and she knows it.

Although Sarah does establish strong personal relationships with Native women in Lynx River, racial and cultural differences between them are not cited. In the episode just described, what might have become a sentimental television moment that portrays women overcoming their differences in order to participate in and help one another during a universal female experience of childbirth turns out to be a moment where a politically loaded tension, due both to different world-views and to the long history of white society discrediting and outlawing Native cultural beliefs and practices, remains in the room with them. Any simplistic notions of female bonding at such a moment are, importantly, denied. Moreover, women can (and sometimes do) use the fact of racial and cultural difference against other women. For example, while Sarah eventually does have a relationship with Eric, the white RCMP officer, she is also aware of competing with Michelle for his attention. In an act of pure jealously, Sarah reports to the RCMP commander what she perceives to be inappropriate fraternizing between the two. But this is not just simple tale-telling. The consequence of Sarah's phone call to Yellowknife is that Michelle risks being transferred out of Lynx River. Because Lynx River is Michelle's home, and because her ties to both place and people are central to her identity as a Dene woman, this would be an extremely destructive outcome. Sarah's act is motivated by sexual jealousy, but this is more than a fight between women over a man. This is a situation inflected by unequal relations of power (Sarah assumes that she has a right to 'tell' on Michelle) *and* the historical dispossession of First Nations peoples. The threat of Michelle's transfer out of the community implicitly recalls the fact that she was sent to residential school as a child as well as the larger issue of the removal of First Nations peoples from their traditional territories.

The treatment of the relationship between Sarah and Michelle, then, does not buy into the myth of universal sisterhood; instead, it emphasizes how racial and cultural differences between them, as well as unequal relations of power that result from settler colonialism, underlie any dealings women have with one another. As feminists of Colour have long argued, women's experiences – including the experience of patriarchal oppression – are not all alike. Rather, women are variously positioned in relation to one another, as well as to society as a whole, by multiple factors that constitute their subjectivities. Furthermore, women frequently experience their lives in terms of complex and sometimes paradoxical interrelationships between their multiple subject positions. Considering why many

Aboriginal women either reject or feel alienated by the mainstream (read white) women's movement, for instance, Patricia Monture-Angus succinctly states her position: 'Some Aboriginal women have turned to the feminist or women's movement for solace (and solution) in the common oppression of women. I have a problem with perceiving this as a full solution. I am not just woman. I am a Mohawk woman. It is not solely my gender through which I first experience the world, it is my culture (and/or race) that precedes my gender. Actually if I am the object of some form of discrimination, it is very difficult for me to separate what happens to me because of my gender and what happens to me because of my race and culture. My world is not experienced in a linear and compartmentalized way. I experience the world simultaneously as Mohawk and as woman' (177-8).

Monture-Angus states that her culture and/or race *precede* her gender; other feminists of Colour would not necessarily prioritize their affiliations with different identity categories. Most would insist on their mutual imbrication, for there is no way of separating out factors such as race or gender and treating them as discrete markers of identity (see Bannerji, 49-50; Brand, 10-11). The crucial point here is that gender cannot transcend racial, cultural, class, or other differences. A white woman and a Native woman cannot *assume* common ground on the basis of their gender. All the more reason, then, for the relationship between the characters Michelle and Sarah to be portrayed in all of its complexity and allowed to develop over time. If these women are to develop a strong bond of love, then they must learn how to understand, respect, and accept (not just tolerate) each other's differences. Such negotiation and learning might not be necessary in the imaginary world of television, but it is crucial in real life, and the fact that the makers of *North of 60* do not simplify the issues that shape the friendship between a particular white woman and a particular Dene woman adds to its reality effect. Indeed, one of the strengths of the program is that it does not go for easy depictions of complex situations.

At first, Sarah and Michelle do not have much to do with one another; however, as the program has developed, so too has their relationship. On two occasions Sarah leaves Lynx River: first, because she is sent out for treatment after her nervous breakdown and later, after the birth of her child and Albert's abandonment, because she wants to see if she can still live in Windsor. On both occasions Sarah returns, and the process of her reentry into the community is partly facilitated by her friendship with Michelle. Motivated by her own need for connection with another woman, a female friend, it is Sarah who seeks Michelle out. A breakthrough of sorts occurs over Eric's death. The two women admit to each other that they both loved him (although the nature of each woman's love is different), and this brings them closer together. They mourn his death as a common loss. Increasingly, Sarah and Michelle have become more and more involved in each other's lives. Significantly, they continually offer one another emotional support. Michelle is there when Sarah's relationship with Albert breaks down, letting her stay at her house and eventually inviting her (although Sarah refuses) to move in on a permanent basis. When Sarah decides to go back to Windsor, it is Michelle's voice on the answering machine saying 'I miss you' that prompts Sarah to recognize where her emotional home is. And when Michelle's daughter dies, it is Sarah who knows that Michelle must be left alone to deal with her grief in her own way. While the relationship between Sarah and Michelle has certainly deepened, it is by no means smooth. Each challenges the other. For example, Sarah questions Michelle's morals when Michelle has an affair with a married white anthropologist. Michelle, in turn, questions Sarah's morals (as well as her intelligence) when Sarah refuses to believe that Albert continues to oversee the family bootlegging operation. Sarah and Michelle are not friends just because they are both women. Cultural and personal differences continually complicate their relationship. They have to work at it.

One of the things I like best about *North of 60* is how Sarah (other white characters too, but especially Sarah) is often shown with a confused or angry look on her face after having just encountered a situation or a response that she either does not fully understand or that goes against her own cultural knowledge and background. Yet Sarah does not run at the first sign of difficulty or non-communication; rather, she pays attention and she learns not only how to listen but also how to hear – at least most of the time. If Michelle and Sarah are friends, it is because they have found ways of knowing each other; but they both recognize that knowing each other is a long and sometimes difficult process. Both have to acknowledge and cope with a historical mistrust that informs their relationship, yet they are shown working with and against that historical mistrust in order to move beyond it.

North of 60 investigates the legacy of European settler colonialism and its effects on present-day relationships between Native and white people, but it does not remain stuck in the past; instead, it offers a model of how individuals might work with one another in order to form both effective political alliances and deeply meaningful human relationships. Although racism against and oppression of First Nations peoples living within the social space of Canada is systemic and structural, the attitudes, behaviours, and actions of individuals can make a difference. Confrontations between First Nations and white communities at Oka, Ipperwash, and Gustafsen Lake (to name only a few examples) have been widely reported in the media and are generally characterized by violence and mutual animosity, if not outright hatred. Given the persistence of such negative media images, the kind of positive representation of cross-racial and cross-cultural relationships that *North of 60* offers – relationships that are based on mutual learning, accommodation, and respect – take on extra urgency.

Acknowledgments
This chapter has been revised partly to reflect developments in the television series *North of 60* since the Race, Gender, and the Construction of Canada Conference. I would like to thank members of the audience and the organizing committee for their helpful comments and suggestions, which have constituted an integral part of the revision process, as well as Dale Blake and Renée Hulan for critiquing an early draft. I gratefully acknowledge the financial support of the Social Sciences and Humanities Research Council, which assisted with the research and writing of the chapter as well as with travel expenses.

Notes

1 My exclusive concern with representations of relationships between Native and white characters is based on the fact that, up to this point, no significant characters from other racial groups have been introduced into the plots of *North of 60*. The program focuses on white/Native relations in their historical and contemporary contexts.
2 Members of these listservs form a particular constituency of Native television viewers. They are generally (though not exclusively) people who either hold academic positions or work in other large institutions, such as libraries. Members of these listserves also tend to be Americans; thus, responses to my post were from Canadians or those Americans who live close enough to the border to pick up CBC on their television sets. I received twelve responses: ten from people who identified themselves as Native; two from North Americans of European descent. Quoted by permission.
3 Cited with permission.
4 The *Wawatay News* reports that Tina Keeper was invited to visit Wabaseemoong Independent Nation School 'in the hope of offering inspiration to the lives of local youths' (Henry, 6). Whether or not she is an inspiration because she is an actor or because of her role as an RCMP officer is difficult to tell and probably unimportant.
5 Sherrill Grace demonstrates just how pervasive and long-lasting images of the North are in Canadian cultural productions of all kinds and argues that they constitute a 'master narrative' of the nation.
6 This formulation distinguishes the Canadian Mountie from the American Sheriff, the latter being constructed as more oppressive. The story of the benevolent and just Mountie is, as Francis points out, one of the great romances of Canadian history.
7 Ironically, Sarah also decides to have her baby in Lynx River. While Ellen's wish to have her baby in her home community is at least partly based on her sense of tradition and the necessity of continuing cultural practice (at this time her husband, Peter, is chief, and it could be that she thinks that she should set an example), Sarah's decision is motivated by her unwillingness to deliver her child alone in a strange environment.

Works Cited
Acoose, Janice/Misko-Kìsikàwihkwè (Red Sky Woman). 1995. *Iskwewak – Kah' Ki Yaw Ni Wahkomakanak: Neither Indian Princesses nor Easy Squaws*. Toronto: Women's Press
Bannerji, Himani. 1995. 'Introducing Racism: Notes Towards an Anti-Racist Feminism.' In *Thinking Through: Essays on Feminism, Marxism and Anti-Racism*. Toronto: Women's Press
Bell, Katherine. 1994. 'Accidental Actor Thrives in Real Role.' *Winnipeg Free Press*, 19 October 1994: C7
Berton, Pierre. 1975. *Hollywood's Canada: The Americanization of Our National Image*. Toronto: McClelland & Stewart
Blake, Dale. E-mail to the author. 29 July 1995
Brand, Dionne. 1994. 'Bread Out of Stone.' In *Bread Out of Stone: Recollections Sex, Recognitions Race, Dreaming Politics*. Toronto: Coach House
Churchill, Ward. 1992. 'Fantasies of the Master Race: Categories of Stereotyping of

American Indians in Film. In M. Annette Jaimes, ed., *Fantasies of the Master Race: Literature, Cinema and the Colonization of American Indians*, 231-41. Monroe: Common Courage

Davisson, Amelia. E-mail to the author. 8 July 1995

'Dreamspeakers.' 1996. *Aboriginal Voices* 3 (3):6

Dudley, Wendy. 1993. 'TV Writer Still Feels the Pain of Racism.' *Calgary Herald*, 6 February 1993: A12-13

Dumont, Marilyn. 1993. 'Popular Images of Nativeness.' In Jeannette Armstrong, ed., *Looking at the Words of Our People: First Nations Analysis of Literature*, 45-50. Penticton: Theytus

Farmer, Gary. 1996. 'From the Editor.' *Aboriginal Voices* 3 (3):4

Fee, Margery. 1987. 'Romantic Nationalism and the Image of Native People in Contemporary English-Canadian Literature.' In Thomas King, Cheryl Calver, and Helen Hoy, ed., *The Native in Literature*, 15-33. Toronto: ECW

Feindel, Pat. 1995. 'What Makes This Show Different? "North of 60."' *Pacific Current* (June):32-4

Francis, Daniel. 1992. *The Imaginary Indian: The Image of the Indian in Canadian Culture*. Vancouver: Arsenal Pulp

Grace, Sherrill. 1996. 'Kroetsch and the Semiotics of North.' *Open Letter* 9th ser. 5/6 (1996):13-24

Green, Rayna. 1984. 'The Pocahontas Perplex.' *Sweetgrass* (Jul-Aug):17-23

Harrison, Regina. E-mail to the author. 2 August 1995

Henry, Anthony. 1995. 'Keeper Inspires Youths in Wabaseeemoong.' *Wawatay News* 4 (May):6

hooks, bell. 1989. 'Introduction: Some Opening Remarks.' In *Talking Back: Thinking Feminist, Thinking Black*. Boston: South End

–. 1992. 'Eating the Other: Desire and Resistance.' In *Black Looks: Race and Representation*, 21-39. Toronto: Between the Lines

Khaki, Aziz, and Kam Prasad. 1988. *Depiction and Perception: Native Indians and Visible Minorities in the Media*. Vancouver: Ad Hoc Committee for Better Race Relations

King, Thomas. 1994. 'Interview.' By Jeffrey Canton. *Paragraph* 16 (1):2-6

Lindala, April E. E-mail to the author. 11 July 1995

Monture, Joel. 1994. 'Native Americans and the Appropriation of Cultures.' *ARIEL* 25 (1):114-21

Monture-Angus, Patricia. 1995. 'Organizing Against Oppression: Aboriginal Women, Law and Feminism.' In *Thunder in My Soul: A Mohawk Woman Speaks*, 169-88. Halifax: Fernwood

Quill, Greg. 1994. 'Show's Grasp of Native Life Pleases *North of 60* Star.' *Toronto Star*, 10 November 1994: F6

Shohat, Ella, and Robert Stamm. 1994. *Unthinking Ethnocentrism: Multiculturalism and the Media*. London: Routledge

Trinh, T. Minha-ha. 1989. *Woman, Native, Other: Writing Postcoloniality and Feminism*. Bloomington: Indiana University Press

Wagamese, Richard. 1996. 'The Final Word.' *Aboriginal Voices* 3 (1):50

Zimmerman, Kate. 1993. 'Teevee's TV Career Came as a Surprise.' *Calgary Herald*, 6 February 1993: A14

A Lesbian Politics of Erotic Decolonization

Becki Ross

> Nation: A people, usually the inhabitants of a specific territory, who share common customs, origins, history and frequently language or related languages; an aggregate of people organized under a single government; citizens united ... over a long period by common cultural and social ties, not necessarily by racial and national bonds.
>
> *– Houghton-Mifflin Canadian Dictionary*

> Lesbian Nation: The totally woman committed woman, or lesbian, who shares this consciousness with other women, is the political nucleus of a woman's or lesbian state – a state that women cannot achieve by demand from the male bastion but only from within from exclusive woman strength building its own institutions of self support and identity.
>
> *– Jill Johnston, Lesbian Nation*

Throughout the twentieth century, the discourse of nation, nationhood, and nationalism has worked powerfully to articulate and mobilize sentiments of community with complex results. In the 1930s, Adolf Hitler used the eugenic construct 'Aryan race' to galvanize the 'right kind' of German national around the methodical persecution of Jews, Gypsies, homosexuals, 'anti-social' women (prostitutes, lesbians, unwed mothers), and the mentally and physically disabled. The contemporary incarnation of Aryan Nation, with its neo-fascist, youth-based constituency, has chapters across North America and Europe and is one of a number of groups dedicated to white supremacy.[1] In the 1990s, nationalisms in the former Yugoslavia, India, Sri Lanka, Rwanda, Somalia, Burundi, and elsewhere have spawned cruel battles, vicious ethnic cleansings, and the deepening of ideological factions and historic hatreds within and across state borders. Ethnic nationalists appeal to blood loyalty and, if necessary, to violent struggle as a way of keeping enemies in their place or overthrowing some legacy of cultural subordination.[2]

That nationalisms have been repositories of male hopes, male aspirations, and male privileges has been a central discovery of feminist inquiry into the gendered processes of nation-making. Nira Yuval-Davis, Floya Anthias, Anne McClintock, Valentine Moghadam, and others have shown that women often play a symbolic role in nationalist narratives, carrying in their reproductive bodies the 'honour of the nation' and the embodiment of cultural identity as the custodians of time-honoured values. Dubravka Zarkov points out that rape has always been used as a 'natural' strategic weapon of nationalist wars: 'raped women often become flags waved by the warring parties' (106). Indeed, nation and citizenship have been largely premised within parameters of hegemonic masculinity and naturalized heterosexuality.[3] As M. Jacqui Alexander and Chandra Talpade Mohanty note, 'Certain women, prostitutes, and lesbians are now being disciplined and written out of the nation's script; they have been invested with the power to corrupt otherwise loyal heterosexual citizens, positioned as hostile to the procreative imperative of nation-building, and, therefore, invested with the ability and desire to destroy it' (xxiv). Whatever their sexual identity, women around the world have found themselves the objects of both protection *and* violation in the context of hetero-gendered and class-bound ideologies and practices of nationhood.

Given long-standing linkages between nationalism and colonialism, nationalism and heteropatriarchal dominance, and nationalism and genocide, one is left to wonder why, and under what conditions, the construct of nation has appealed to subordinated, subaltern groups whose disenfranchisement propels their own search for community, belonging, and security. What positive resonance does it have for the dispossessed? In this century, national liberation struggles have been mounted in South Africa, Vietnam, China, India, the former Eastern Bloc, Ireland, Mexico, Nicaragua, Cambodia, the Philippines, and elsewhere. In Canada, First Nations peoples have stepped up their claims for land, self-government, and an end to the racist, sexist, and paternalistic rule of the federal government. And yet contradictions have permeated nationalist movements. Quebec sovereignists continue to lobby fiercely for independence from English Canada, but their aspirations have at times led to racism toward immigrants and Québécois(es) of Colour, and their pro-natalist policies have encouraged Francophone women to become fecund breeders of *'pure laine'* children.[4] National Aboriginal associations in Canada have tended to adopt a masculinist view of Aboriginal nation-states, which has meant the exclusion of Aboriginal women's organizations, such as the Native Women's Association of Canada (NWAC), from negotiations at the constitutional table.[5] In the US, African-American Louis Farrakhan, the Muslim leader of the Nation of Islam, remakes the ideology of black self-determination in response to systemic racial inequalities and, at the same time, is known for his anti-Semitism and misogyny.

In the early 1990s, chapters of 'Queer Nation' across Canada and the US – prefigured by the advent of 'Lesbian Nation' in the 1970s – were emboldened by a direct action mandate to address the AIDS crisis, to oppose gay-bashing, and to dismantle all manifestations of heterosexism, though lesbians, bisexuals, and queers of Colour were often critical of the white male leadership (Maggenti, 20-3; Berlant and Freeman, 149-80).[6] As Helma Lutz, Ann Phoenix, and Nira Yuval-Davis observe, 'Wherever a delineation of boundaries takes place, processes of exclusion and inclusion are in operation' (4). Nationalist projects have always involved processes whereby populations are divided into racialized, sexualized, and gendered categories of 'belonging' and 'otherness.' Exploring the ways in which people construct their 'imagined communities' can tell us much about how they locate themselves in relation to others and where they draw lines between groups (B. Anderson, 5).

In this chapter, I endeavour to historicize and theorize the construct of Lesbian Nation as it was discursively and materially deployed in the 1970s by lesbian feminists in English Canada.[7] Though not marked by military, ethnic, or religious fervour, the predominantly white, middle-class lesbian nationalism of that decade invoked shared properties of custom, language, dress, ethics, and the urban and rural territories of 'amazon acres.' What were the political, ideological, and economic conditions in English Canada under which 'lesbian nationhood' came to serve as a flashpoint for a generation of feminist activists? What distinguished the ideology and practice of 'lesbian nationals' in the 1970s from the lives of gay women who routinely hid, lied about, and feared reprisals for their same-sex desire in the 1940s, 1950s, and 1960s? To what extent did Lesbian Nation have the same potency and gravitational force in Canada that it did in parts of the US? Why was this originally American designation imported in the first place? Did it operate as one example, among many, of American intellectual imperialism? From the vantage point of the late 1990s, what gains were made under the banner of Lesbian Nation? At the same time, how did the ideological operations of Lesbian Nation work, however temporarily, to homogenize difference, displace plurality, and put forward faith in an illusory and totalizing unity? What or who got erased or bracketed in the universalizing move of nationhood? And how might we compare the formation and eventual dissolution of 1970s lesbian nationalism to women's involvement in other nationalist discourses and mobilizations in North America and around the globe? Indeed, how does a focus on the metaphor of Lesbian Nation invite us to extend our gaze broadly to the configuring of gender, (hetero)sexuality, and citizenship in regimes of national identity?

My attempt to answer these questions is organized into three roughly chronological sections: (1) before the Stonewall rebellion in New York in 1969; (2) the emergence of Lesbian Nation in the mid-1970s; and (3) its collapse a decade later. The answers are intended to contribute to the larger project of integrating sexuality with variables of gender, race, class, and region in Canadian historical sociology.[8] By queering our various stories of the past, we complicate narratives of Canadian nation-building. By specifying the emergence of lesbian activism north of the forty-ninth parallel, we establish a basis for comparative analysis of lesbian nationalism and community formation in transnational contexts. And finally, we enlarge our sociohistorical grasp of the powerful nature of nationalisms and myth-making in the twentieth century.

Female Homosexual Identities and Practices, pre-1969

Before European colonization, there was a vast range of gender, social, and sexual relations among Aboriginal peoples across North America. Although there was significant regional variation, First Nations peoples who cross-dressed, cross-worked, and enjoyed same-sex erotic pleasures were embraced as the visionaries, the medicine people, and/or healers of their nation.[9] Because 'two-spirited' people were integrated into a number of indigenous communities, they experienced no need to defend their existence. However, with the expansion and domination of the British Empire in Canada, the culture of two-spirits – what colonial anthropologists termed *berdache* – was destroyed through subordination to white, Anglo-Saxon norms of gender and (hetero)sexual propriety and familism. According to white politicians, social scientists, and missionaries, there was no room for gender and sexual 'savages,' 'heathens,' and 'redskins' in the developing nation called Canada. Not only were 'Indians' seen to exhibit bizarre sexual practices, they did not treat women and children as property or endorse other Euro-patriarchal and materialist norms, all of which meant that they needed to be 'civilized,' Christianized, and stripped of all claims to identity, land, and community in order to be assimilated into the nascent Canadian nation state.

Beginning in the late nineteenth century, there is some evidence that female homoerotic culture and communities emerged gradually, unevenly and yet steadily, across English-speaking Canada. 'Romantic friends' such as Victoria Hayward, a journalist, and her companion Edith Watson, a photographer, lived and worked together recording the scope and shape of women's work in rural Canada from 1912 to 1943, the year of Watson's death (Rooney 1995a, 185-94; Rooney 1995b, 2-31). The American-born sculptors Frances Loring and Florence Wyle happily shared their craft, their income, their converted church/home, and a 'Boston marriage' in Toronto from 1917 to 1968 (Rooney 1983, 18-29; McDonald, 8-9). Canadian writer

Mazo de la Roche, who gained fame through her Jalna novels, was involved in a very intimate relationship for over seventy years with her adopted sister, Caroline Clement (who was a first cousin once removed). British-born Elsa Gidlow grew up in Montreal and her book of homoerotic love poems, *On a Grey Thread*, was published in 1923. Constance (Conti) Grey Swartz, who grew up as a member of the white elite of Victoria, British Columbia, was known to have passionate relationships with both women and men (Duder, 17-8).

Though there is no evidence that any of these women suffered discrimination or hardship as lesbians or bisexuals, public discourse on the topic of female homosexuality was nevertheless virtually non-existent. For most of the twentieth century, homosexuality was listed as a crime in the Canadian Criminal Code and was primarily used to prosecute men who engaged in gross indecency and sodomy. Women who loved women were not targeted by state law as 'deviants' or 'criminals' in the same way; however, 'independent women' (including romantic friends, prostitutes, and single heterosexual women) who eschewed their patriotic obligation to motherhood and wifedom were widely perceived as disorderly, amoral, and a threat to foundations of civil society and 'laws of nature.' As historian Veronica Strong-Boag notes, turn-of-the-century anti-feminists in Canada like Goldwin Smith (1823-1910) 'grouped independent women, together with Jews and Blacks, as a menace to the progress of the "human" race' (1996, 6). Smith and other Victorians caricatured first-wave feminists and suffragists as lonely, bitter, and desexed creatures, 'spinsters' who weakened the heteropatriarchal sinews of Anglo-Celtic Canada; they embodied national deterioration (10, 12). Attacks on independent women, the surge of popular sexological discourse that pathologized homosexuality in the early twentieth century, and the economic barriers faced by non-married women, made living outside 'traditional families' impracticable to all but the wealthy.

Against considerable odds, subterranean gay networks began to flourish across Canada in the 1930s. Gay women found each other by frequenting downtown bars in the major urban centres; by placing personal ads in pulp tabloids *Flirt* and *Frivolo* in Montreal and *Tab*, *Flash*, and *Justice Weekly* in Toronto; and by joining competitive baseball, basketball, ice hockey, and curling leagues (Higgins and Chamberland, 422; Setliff 1994, 10-15; 1995, 30-1). Canadian women made up approximately 10 percent of the players in the All-American Girls Professional Baseball League (1943-54), and a number were known to be lesbians (Browne, 10). In the post-Second World War period, with increasing numbers of women seeking paid employment and independence from their families, gay women across Canada met in boarding houses, straight jazz clubs and speakeasies, women's hotels, nurses' residences, teachers' colleges, and at suburban house parties. Those 'in conflict with the law' met in training schools, in hostels for street women (such as Toronto's Street Haven), in provincial prisons, and in the federal penitentiary – the Kingston Prison for Women (Ross 1997a, 561-95; Hinojosa Baker, 49-67). Lesbian mothers, often in isolation, raised children conceived in heterosexual marriages (Arnup, in press). Gay women socialized where they found small queer colonies: on the islands of the Gulf Stream off the west coast of British Columbia; at summer resorts on the shores of Lake Winnipeg, Lake Erie, and Lake Huron; on the islands in the Toronto harbour; in Hogan's Alley, a turn-of-the-century African-Canadian settlement in Vancouver; and in the small farming hamlets of Nova Scotia's Annapolis Valley.[10]

Often introduced to the 'demi-monde' via the notorious lesbian pulp novels of the 1950s, adventurous gay women with money travelled across the Canada/US border to Provincetown, Martha's Vineyard, New York City, Syracuse, Rochester, Buffalo, Detroit, and Seattle. Many left remote towns and villages, agricultural communities, and mining outposts in search of employment and sexual partners in growing cities from St. John's, Newfoundland, to Victoria, British Columbia. Butches, femmes, and nicknacks (bisexuals) in the 1940s, 1950s, and 1960s defied gender and heterosexual prescriptions by defending queer spaces, sporting tattoos, and raising children together while battling with Children's Aid Societies. Some of the butches assumed male identities and sought out gender-reassignment operations at Toronto's Clarke Institute of Psychiatry (O'Brien, 1-25).

Whether as working-class women employed in offices and factories or as middle-class teachers, secretaries, and nurses, gay women in Canada lived with the fear of losing friends, jobs, families, and housing. They faced enormous risks and there was no political movement within which to agitate for social change. Homosexual practices remained illegal, including sex with a minor of the same sex under the age of 21 (Kinsman 1996, 222). Gay women lived with medico-moral 'expertise' of the mid-twentieth century, which targeted male and female homosexuality as a major 'social problem.' In 1952, the Canadian Immigration Act was revised to bar homosexuals (treated as 'subversives' in the Act) from entry into the country – a tactic similarly used at different times to prohibit others from becoming legitimate members of the Canadian nation; namely, Chinese, Japanese, and South Asian immigrants. Also in 1952, an Ottawa judge declared the depictions of lesbianism in the pulp novel *Women's Barracks* (1950) by Tereska Torres to be 'exceedingly frank' hence 'obscene'; the bookseller was fined for corrupting the morals of impressionable youth (Adams, 89-117). Between 1958 and 1964, some gay women were purged from their jobs in the federal Civil Service, including the National Film Board, because they were suspected or confirmed homosexuals and were classified as 'national security threats' (Kinsman 1995, 133-61). Throughout the 1950s and 1960s, female civil servants (especially the 'good-looking girls') were urged to compete in beauty contests sponsored by the Recreation Association (RA) in ways that reinforced normative codes of femininity, masculinity, and heterosexuality (Gentile, in press). In effect, postwar homosexual identities and communities were organized as much by lesbians and gay men as by the police, medical profession, the mass media, and state discourses.

Homosexuals, positioned outside the parameters of what experts termed 'normality,' were not and could not be included as fully fledged members or citizens of the Canadian nation. Rather, they were perceived as dangerous, sick, potential criminals and improperly socialized deviants. In effect, lesbians and gay men figured in Canadian narratives of nation-making only insofar as homosexuality itself was defined as anathema to national harmony, law, order, and the 'public good.' How significant and ironic, therefore, that in the 1970s, some Canadian lesbian activists would appropriate the metaphor of 'nation' for themselves.

Lesbian Solidarity in the Making

The mid- to late-1960s marked a time of optimism for many Canadians, who were, as Monique Bégin remembers, 'elated at the memory of [Canada's] Centennial celebrations and at the spirit of generosity of the Montreal Expo '67: "Man and His World"' (22). At the same time, students across Canada were beginning to attack the establishment politics of major institutions: the military-industrial complex, the education system, corporations, and the mass media. The New Left, in particular the Student Union for Peace Action (SUPA), the Company of Young Canadians (CYC), the Canadian Union of Students (CUS), and the militant Left of the New Democratic Party (NDP), seeded the ground for the emergence of feminist and lesbian political action and consciousness (Kostash, 3-55). Quebec's renewed nationalist emphasis on French culture and language in the 1960s, heightened by the Front de Libération du Québec (FLQ) crisis in 1970, also raised awareness among Anglophone activists, including lesbians, of the historic struggles waged by Francophones against Anglophone domination. Some Canadian feminists, both straight and lesbian, sharpened their political teeth in the course of Third World solidarity work with Latin American, Algerian, Vietnamese, Chinese, and Cuban Canadian organizations. Under the banner of 'Red Power,' Canada's First Nations intensified their fight for economic, spiritual, and cultural self-government against the historic racism and sexism of the federal government's Indian Act, 1869 (Satzewich and Wotherspoon, 1-41; Long 118-34). In general terms, those oppressed by gender, race, and ethnicity began to articulate the necessity of organizing autonomously on the basis of what held them together – their 'minority' identity status and their collective experiences of inequality and discrimination. Because the population of activists in Canada was quite small in comparison to that in the US, groups overlapped to reinforce awareness of oppression in ways that opened up unique opportunities for both collaboration and conflict.

The hopeful and unsettled tenor of the 1960s was captured in the 1970 *Report of the Canadian Royal Commission on the Status of Women* (RCSW), which the mainstream press named a 'call to revolution' (Westell, 4). Its 167 recommendations championed women's equality, including access to abortion, the rewriting of schoolbooks, and sweeping law reforms. In the late 1960s, largely white, middle-class women in large Canadian cities had already captained the second-wave women's liberation movement, putting abortion rights, sex-stereotyping, equal pay, birth control, and day care atop their grassroots agenda. The groundbreaking popular anthology *Women Unite!* (1971) outlined goals remarkably similar to those proposed in the *RCSW*. Neither the anthology, nor the *RCSW,* mentioned lesbianism, nor, for that matter, women of Colour or First Nations women (Arscott, 110-14). The absence surrounding lesbian lives reflected heterosexist and homophobic assumptions: lesbians did not exist or were not worthy of inclusion and had no 'status' as Canadian women. Indeed, there was some speculation that they (especially the butches) were not women at all.

By the late 1960s and early 1970s, the women's movement and gay liberation in Canada had supplied a context within which lesbians could come out and name their sexuality as a site of public, political action, though their reception was not always hospitable. For the first time in Canadian history, largely white, middle-class lesbians began organizing to address the legacy of their subjection to psychiatric control, to criminalization in the country's legal code, to moral condemnation by religious leaders, to stereotypic myths about 'queers' in popular media (both Canadian and American), and to the painful, debilitating condition of invisibility. As angry outsiders, they formed independent lesbian groups to defeat decades of pathologization and to better confront both gay men's sexism and straight feminists' heterosexism (Ross 1995, 23-40). Lesbian activists across English Canada sought out and created new identities and new communities, a new vocabulary and political focus, all the while navigating vexed tensions among loyalties to feminism, gay liberation, the New Left, and, in Quebec, the struggle for sovereignty.

Lesbians began to organize systematically *as lesbian feminists* in Canada shortly after the start of the American lesbian movement.[11] The CUNTS was a group of lesbians who splintered from the Community Homophile Association of Toronto (CHAT) in 1971; Montreal Gay Women exited the male-dominated Gay McGill in the spring of 1973; in the fall of 1973, the group Lesbian Feminists was formed in Saskatoon; and lesbian drop-ins were held at women's centres from coast to coast early in the 1970s. Lesbian activists in English Canada turned to American lesbian writings and cultural production – magazines, book publishing, record companies, and large-scale music festivals – for insight and direction. Texts like Radicalesbians' 'Woman Identified Woman' (1970); *off our backs, Lesbian Connection*, and *The Furies*; Sidney Abbott and Barbara Love's *Sappho Was a Right-On Woman* (1972); and Jill Johnston's *Lesbian Nation: The Feminist Solution* (1973) instructed Canadian readers in the norms, ideas, and strategies of lesbian activism in the US (Taylor and Whittier, 111-13). Gradually, networks in Canada were built, discussions were fostered, and lesbian feminists became linked *through texts* across diverse geographical settings in Canada and in the US.[12]

In the mid-1970s, small numbers of lesbian activists in Winnipeg, Montreal, London, St. John's, Victoria, Saskatoon, Vancouver, Halifax, and Toronto began to voice their right to equality, justice, and freedom from persecution.[13] Some of these women, like Nancy Adamson, Rosemary Barnes, and Judith Bennett, were American expatriates who had emigrated to Canada but maintained contact with friends in social movements south of the forty-ninth parallel. They launched their own newsletters and periodicals, such as *Long Time Coming* (Montreal), *Lesbian Canada Lesbienne* (Halifax), *The LOOT Newsletter* (Toronto), *The Pedestal* (Vancouver), and *Web of Crones* (Hornby Island, BC). Inside, they routinely reprinted the Collective Lesbian International Terrors (CLIT) statements, the 'Woman Identified Woman,' and articles by The Furies (CLIT, 3-38). In 1973, a seventeen-point lesbian-feminist statement was published in a special lesbian issue of *The Other Woman*. In 1979, Canadian sociologist Dorothy E. Smith captured the power of texts published in the context of the women's movement: 'They mobilized people, put things in place, got things going, redefined goals and above all built the general exchange of practical understanding and knowledge of how to go about it' (12). Like members of other 'imagined communities,' lesbian feminists did not all know one another, and yet the texts they consumed communicated images of their shared communion and oriented them to local, collective action (B. Anderson, 15). American ideas and plans were read, reprinted, and tested by Canadian lesbians in their own milieux. The Canadian nationalists among them were openly leery of American imperialism, although they were inspired and informed by the first lesbian-authored tracts.

In American writings and analysis, references to 'Nation,' armed struggle, and warfare appeared and rapidly assumed currency. Rita Mae Brown described 'the lesbian movement' as an 'army of lovers that cannot fail' (1971);[14] the Radicalesbians defined lesbianism as the 'rage of all women condensed to the point of explosion' (1970), which suggests its bomb-like properties. The labyris – a double-headed axe – became a venerated lesbian symbol (Radicalesbians, 240). A cadre of separatist lesbians in Washington, DC, named themselves 'The Furies' – 'Goddesses of Vengeance and protectors of women' (Berson, 19). Theorist Ti-Grace Atkinson defended lesbianism as the vanguard of the women's movement and drew a startling parallel: 'Can you imagine a Frenchman, serving in the French army from 9:00 am till 5:00 pm, then trotting "home" to Germany for supper overnight?' (11). Lesbian activists used the language and signs of national defence, of allies and enemies, to describe and mobilize their new movement. In a much reprinted article, former Furies member Rita Mae Brown intoned: 'You can't build a strong movement if our [straight] sisters are out their fucking with the oppressor' (14). A quote from Brown graced the publicity pamphlet for the Lesbian Organization of Toronto (LOOT) in 1977: 'Becoming a Lesbian does not make you instantly pure, perpetually happy and devotedly revolutionary. But once you have taken your life into your own hands, you will find you are no longer alone ... you will be part of that surge forward and you will leave your fingerprints on the shape of things to come' (Brown, quoted in LOOT 1977, 1). In a statement informed by Brown's vision, Karol published 'Dyke Power' (1973) in the Toronto-based newspaper *The Other Woman*: 'Little has been heard from the radical, man-hating dyke simply because we will not allow ourselves to be Liberalized ... [but] I want to repeat that Dykes are organizing: this being the only group of Females who are threatening to the male structure, and who can create agony within' (7). And Judith Quinlan contributed to lesbian feminist discourse in the Canadian feminist journal *Broadside*: 'Whenever we try to make our love grow outside the mind-binding institutions of marriage, monogamy and sado-masochistic ritual, we are whirling into a life-loving vortex that will eventually level the towers of patriarchal babble' (8).

Canadian lesbian activists did not have an actual army to enable its goals or defend its territory, though at times their uniform of cropped hair, jeans, flannel shirts, and Kodiak boots conveyed a militaristic message. Unlike the gun-toting young males between the ages of 18 to 25 who perpetrate most of the nationalist violence around the world,[15] lesbian feminists did not resort to violence, nor did they own or control any real territory beyond small residential enclaves and community spaces, such as those occupied by the Lesbian Organization of Toronto (LOOT), Montreal Gay Women – an anglophone group, Coop femme – a lesbian Francophone collective in downtown Montreal, the Lesbian Organization of Ottawa Now (LOON), the Atlantic Provinces Political Lesbians for Equality (APPLE) in Halifax, and the Lesbian Caucus of the British Columbia Federation of Women (Vancouver). Small clusters of lesbians chose to homestead on 'wimmin's land' near the major cities of Toronto, Winnipeg, Vancouver, and Montreal. A farm in British Columbia set up under the banner of 'Amazon Acres.' Women-Only Rural Land Development (WORLD) was a lesbian communal experiment in egalitarian living near Peterborough,

Ontario. Other initiatives included co-ops in rambling, old downtown houses in a host of cities, critical refuges of safety and solidarity, love and allegiance, in the midst of urban chaos and anonymity (Ross 1995, 96-9).[16] Dedicated to sharing, hand-making, and recycling consumer goods, members of the co-ops undermined North American corporate capitalism and the patriotic duty of every Canadian citizen to keep the economy strong (on the brink of a late-1970s recession) by purchasing endless varieties of products stamped 'made in Canada.'

In Toronto, a kind of radical lesbian praxis – living collectively in 'gomer' (male-free) space, zapping public venues, becoming vegetarian, privileging non-monogamy, and distrusting 'the man' and the male Left – co-existed with competing ideological currents (Ross 1995, 85-140). For a number of radical dykes, their links to anarchism, gay liberation, and/or versions of socialism informed by Marx, Lenin, Trotsky, or Mao made their desire for and dedication to a lesbian nationalist project ambivalent but did not extinguish the visceral appeal of all that lesbian nation-making symbolized. Depth of attachment to the metaphor of Lesbian Nation varied regionally, and much more empirical study is required to address the variations. In Toronto, it seemed to possess mythological mystique: it promised belonging, heightened self-confidence, shared identity, and vision. Not unlike the nationalist rhetoric of African-American Muslim Malcolm X, it captured lesbian feminist anger, brash indignation, and ardent commitment to a kind of anti-assimilationist chauvinism that intended the interruption, if not the overthrow, of ruling discourses of fear, (self)hatred, and shame. Lesbian Nation signified the tantalizing possibility of both stabilizing what it meant to be lesbian warriors and withdrawing from the dominant culture in order to reinvent both it and themselves.

By naming lesbian as a badge of pride, hence displacing the malicious, common-sense epithets of queer, variant, and sex deviate in the 1950s, lesbian feminists paraded their need to be recognized and their need for what Adrienne Rich has called 'a common language' (1). As such, the quest for Lesbian Nation in some ways resembled the quest for traditional nationalisms. According to writer Michael Ignatieff, the desire for recognition and understanding pervades nationalist campaigns world-wide: 'To belong is to understand the tacit codes of the people you live with; it is to know that you will be understood without having to explain yourself. People, in short, "speak your language"' (7). As a method of recognizing each other as 'insiders,' some lesbians created the new language of 'wimmin,' 'womyn,' 'womon'; they elaborated a new vocabulary connected to 'womon-identification'; they invented names for themselves and rejected the use of paternal surnames. For others, the metaphor of Lesbian Nation invited a revivalist, genealogical focus on matriarchal traditions, amazonian warriorhood, and the ancient writings of the Greek poet Sappho.

Canadian lesbian activists in the 1970s yearned to differentiate themselves from what they envisaged as a past steeped in retrograde, degenerate butch/femme role-playing, secretive double-living, denial, despair, and silence. In opposition to what they condemned as 'depoliticized' bar culture (heretofore the only public lesbian space), activists argued for 'being out' in all aspects of their lives. They were primarily students, they held part-time 'shit-jobs,' they worked for state-funded feminist projects, or they started up lesbian-run small businesses. They did not have professional reputations to protect, few had children to lose in custody battles, and the romantized ethos of downward mobility worked to solidify the collectivity and to varnish over class and race differences in much the same manner as it did for Canadian Left nationalists and Quebec sovereignists at the time. In large cities across Canada, lesbian feminists' most successful initiatives were coffee houses, dances, lesbian music, poetry, film, counselling collectives, coming-out support groups, and small-scale publishing – the fruits of a kind of lesbian social and cultural endogamy. In ways that resonate with Alberto Melucci's analysis of 'new social movements,' what became known as lesbian feminist living acted as a 'cultural laboratory in the production of new meanings and forms of relationships within civil society' (60).

Dedicated to non-hierarchical decision making and power-sharing, lesbian feminists attempted to nurture unity by consent and consensus rather than by force. They used their status as economic and ideological outsiders to claim vanguard status within the larger (white, middle-class) women's movement. The unofficial leaders among them professed a brand of radical feminism uncompromised by attachments to men and patriarchal artifice. In effect, a politicized lesbian identity, like other identities forged in the heat of nationalist contestation, was determined by what it was not – it was shaped by what it opposed (P. Anderson, 3; Breuilly, 380). Initially, bar-goers, straight feminists, and gay men were 'the other,' alongside everything and anything that smacked of 'male identification.' It was the intoxicating combination of passion, anger, and urgency that enabled lesbian feminists to articulate and display the power of 'womon-identification' in urban centres across the country. For the first time in Canadian history, autonomous lesbian organizing permitted lesbians *to speak for themselves*, to collectively defy strictures of heteronormative familial relations, to combat internalized homophobia, and to set the terms for self-determined identity and community.

In the 1970s, Anglo-lesbian activists in Canada did not want a place alongside 'normal' Canadians; they did not want responsible civic membership in the ways that they felt the closeted, suburban, tax-paying, law-abiding, middle-class gay professionals did. The majority were suspicious of 'human rights' organizing within gay liberation that targeted policy reform at the level of municipal, provincial, and federal governments; they argued that these reforms would solely benefit economically advantaged gay men and long-term, monogamous coupling. They did not seek tolerance or even acceptance by mainstream religions, legal structures, the mass media, or the military. They did not lobby for legal recognition of same-sex marriage. Grappling with the state in order to transform its complex processes and to secure their own status as 'officially' Canadian was neither the initial nor the primary objective; instead, the desire was to propagandize the specificities of radical lesbian politics – the need for visibility and affirmation of a newly emancipated identity, the radical redefinition of femininity and womanhood, the attainment of economic independence and women-only space. To borrow from Benedict Anderson, members of the Lesbian Nation shared a 'deep, horizontal comradeship' (16). Not only did they seek to reveal the contours of their own oppression, but they materialized what Teresa De Lauretis has called erotic space where women recognized each other 'as subjects and as objects of female desire' (155). The lesbian vision aroused a deep psychic investment in personal change as political action; in the mid-1970s across English Canada it was founded on prescriptions for purity of principle and practice that resembled exclusivist elements of other nationalist struggles around the world.

The Discourse of Lesbian Nation as Both Liberatory and Prescriptive

Intrinsic to lesbian feminism in English Canada in the 1970s was a set of ideas designed to promote allegiance based on what counted as a 'real,' 'true,' 'authentic' lesbian identity: how to dress, with whom to make love, what to eat, where to live, how to organize and with whom. And, as I've argued elsewhere, the boundary markers that delineated who was 'in' and who was 'out' had regulatory effects (Ross 1995, 197-218). Most urban Canadian lesbian activists in the 1970s were critical of sex trade workers, male-to-female lesbian transsexuals, bisexuals, femme and butch bar-goers, and those who did not devote full-time energy to lesbian activism. Few women of Colour were pro-actively recruited into lesbian political communities; activist women of Colour were more likely to channel their energy into anti-racist protest. Though lesbian groups initially pledged openness to 'all lesbians,' intrinsic to the 'nationalist fantasy' was an intolerance for departure from codes that led to self-scrutiny and judgment of others. Conflicts about membership and mandate inside lesbian organizations meant that the much-craved goal of lesbian unity was forever chimerical. As Chela Sandoval observes, 'Even the most revolutionary communities come to prohibit their members' full participation; every marginalized group that has organized in opposition to the dominant order has imported

[the] same desire to find, name, categorize and tame reality in a way that ultimately works to create marginalized positions within its own ranks' (244). It is as if the very unity upon which nationalist struggles depend is made mandatory at the expense of any plausible manifestation of 'unity in diversity' – a seemingly irreconcilable paradox. Avtar Brah notes that the nationalist struggle for independence in India required an emphasis on the common condition of being a colonized people, 'but this nationalism became internally fractured when religion emerged as a focus for mobilization in the political movement for the creation of Pakistan' (15). Similarly, in North America, the critique developed by African-American feminists of the sexism structuring the Black Panther Party and the Black Power movement in the 1960s, and the challenge posed by women's liberation in North America to the male-centred agenda of the New Left, suggest that splits specific to lesbian feminism were not unique.

By the late 1970s in English Canada, the construct of Lesbian Nation and its utopian promise of escape from a homophobic world had begun to break apart and dissolve, albeit peacefully. For lesbian feminists across Canada, although Lesbian Nation had at first carried enormous ideological cachet, it proved to be neither durable nor elastic enough to last. Deepening ideological ruptures and unmet needs within organizations could not be accommodated; smaller numbers of activists than were evident in large American cities meant that building a vigorous separatist culture was more difficult. In Vancouver, for example, lesbian nationalism never took root in the ways it did in the American north-east. The strong presence of working-class lesbians with greater suspicion of nationalism, and a powerful provincial organization – the British Columbia Federation of Women – promoted the collaboration of lesbian and straight feminists (Creet, 183-97). In Toronto, socialist and gay liberationist lesbians became frustrated that the discourse of lesbian feminism did not include a detailed political agenda beyond naming institutionalized heterosexism as a social problem of immense scale. Lesbians who identified as radical feminists were drawn to anti-violence campaigns (e.g., Women Against Violence Against Women, anti-pornography, and anti-rape organizing). As skirmishes broke out beyond the borders of Lesbian Nation, lesbian organizers were increasingly called upon to rethink separatist leanings.

Turning Outward

From the early 1970s, brutal collisions with police forces made lesbian feminists increasingly aware of the power of state repression. The pressing need for mixed-gender coalitions began to make Lesbian Nation unworkable as either philosophy or practice. In 1974, four lesbians were arrested at a Toronto bar for 'causing a public disturbance' and later roughed up in police custody. During violent police raids on gay men's bars and bath houses in Montreal (1975, 1976, 1977), Edmonton (1980), and Toronto (1978, 1981), hundreds of men were arrested as 'found-ins' and 'keepers' of a common bawdy house. In 1977 in Toronto, the office of *The Body Politic*, a monthly gay newspaper with an international readership of 10,000, was raided by Project P, an anti-pornography morality squad, and charged with distributing scurrilous materials. *The Body Politic* (1971-87) figured prominently in the education of many lesbians who worked on the paper as volunteers and, later, as paid staff, and it provided a context for friendships between politicized dykes and fags in ways that had no American equivalent. After the 1977 raid, lesbian journalists and activists across Canada catalyzed a defence campaign that persevered until the paper's eventual acquittal in 1983. In addition, blatantly anti-gay/lesbian policies at the *Vancouver Sun*, *Toronto Star*, and Vancouver's YWCA, and the high-profile firings of lesbian and gay workers and armed forces personnel in the mid-1970s, exposed the depth of discrimination and societal hostility.[17]

Across Canada, numerous constituencies – 'Canadians for Decency,' 'Positive Parents,' 'Campaign for Life,' the 'League Against Homosexuals,' 'Renaissance International,' and Anita Bryant's 'Save Our Children' – stoked their nationalist, anti-homosexual, racist, and 'pro-family' crusades in the 1970s. The names of the organizations reveal that members did not believe that lesbians and gays could be successfully assimilated into the nation-forming project: 'queers' were indecent, a negative influence, anti-life, and simply non-Canadian.[18] At the same time, lesbians and gay men in every major Canadian city formed alliances to protest the spectrum of Right-wing injustices – a development that both strengthened liberationist muscle and hastened the collapse of Lesbian Nation.[19]

In less than five years, the ideal of a Lesbian Nation had flared and sputtered. By the late 1970s, primarily socialist feminist lesbians in Vancouver, Kitchener, Toronto, Saskatoon, Halifax, and Winnipeg had abandoned lesbian nationalist hopes in order to build links with labour unions and members of anti-imperialist liberation struggles, anti-nuclear activism, the sex trade, reproductive rights, anti-poverty, and anti-free trade groups. This coordinated shift differs from the dominant strand of lesbian-led cultural feminism that reigned in parts of the US following the decomposition of lesbian nationalist dreams there (Echols, 243-86), and it distinguishes socialist lesbianism as a dynamic current north of the forty-ninth parallel. Across Canada, socialist dykes had never entirely deserted the Left, though many had been seduced temporarily by the magical euphoria of a discourse that pledged to metamorphose women-loving bodies into a radical movement. As lesbians committed to broad social change and influenced by the long tradition of Canadian socialism, they would later strive to introduce analyses of heterosexism and homophobia into movement politics that were counter-hegemonic but not lesbian-specific. Sociologists

Roberta Hamilton and Michèle Barrett have observed that 'in Canada, the task [of apprehending diversity without becoming totally distracted by it] has been undertaken with greater solidarity and less suspicion among activists and intellectuals, academics and reformers than has been the case in Britain or the United States' (2, 11). Indeed, by the early 1980s, many Canadian lesbian feminists recognized that embracing 'difference' was both imperative and fruitful. Lesbians of Colour, Jewish and disabled lesbians, rural and working-class dykes, lesbian transgenders, older lesbians, lesbian youth, and activist bisexuals began to produce new knowledge about how sexuality is complexly inflected by race, ethnicity, age, and gender (see Stone 1997, 180-93).

Lesbian Organizing in the 1990s and Beyond

Challenges to the restricted meanings of lesbianism have been made by the lesbian caucus of the DisAbled Women's Network of Canada, OWLS (Outrageous, Wiser Lesbians), Lesbian Youth Peer Support, YouthQuest, Asian Lesbians of Toronto, Nice Jewish Girls, Two-Spirited Peoples of the First Nations, Lesbian Mothers Network, and Bamboo Triangle, among countless others. While each of these groups holds on to the value of identity-based organizing, they have relinquished the dream of a unified (white, middle-class) lesbian subject and all illusions of a coherent Lesbian Nation. Bisexual women in groups like Bi-Face, and lesbian- and bi-identified transgenders and transsexuals, are pioneering the need to deconstruct the constrictive, binary discourses of homo/hetero and masculine/feminine on the road to gender and sexual pluralism. These complex developments have operated to de-essentialize the singular category 'lesbian' by insisting on diversity; they have widened the conceptual grasp of oppression, and they have specified claims on resources in ways similar to claims made by 'visible minorities' inside 'multicultural' Canada (Bannerji, 103-28).

Organized lesbian activity across Canada in the 1970s contained both progressive *and* conservative tendencies. While endeavouring to meet the emotional, political, recreational, and cultural needs of every lesbian, lesbian feminists deployed criteria that restricted membership – a paradoxical set of contradictions that has structured virtually every liberation movement. In the late 1990s, the leaders behind lesbian political and cultural projects eschew being 'all things to all lesbians.' Today, lesbians across Canada continue to work for social change in the context of feminist, anti-racist, anti-censorship, labour, environmental, cooperative housing, and anti-poverty politics as well as in lesbian-centred initiatives, as shown above. Their presence and influence attests to the impressive 'mainstreaming' of lesbian-inspired critiques of homophobia, sexism, and heterosexism within the broader progressive community.

One instrumental arm of lesbian and gay activism has sought to redress legal inequalities through inclusion within anti-discriminatory statutes and the extension of social benefits (medical, health, survivor, inheritance, and pension) to lesbian and gay couples. Coalition members, including a small number of lesbian feminists, rejected the rhetoric of a Lesbian Nation; instead, they looked to make legal gains within arenas of law-making and public policy via dramatically recast definitions of 'spouse' and 'family.' Using existing discourses of minority civil rights, these reformers appealed to the state to secure the status of lesbians and gays as a sexual minority who deserve equality, fairness, and respect as Canadian citizens. This has involved lobbying for the admission of 'sexual orientation' as a protected category equivalent to sex, religion, creed, ability, race, ethnicity, and language group in the Canadian Charter of Rights and Freedoms. In effect, over the past twenty-five years, human rights strategies have been mobilized by strong provincial coalitions (such as the Ontario Coalition for Lesbian and Gay Rights, Saskatchewan Gay Coalition) and national bodies (such as National Gay Rights Coalition [NGRC] and Equality for Gays and Lesbians Everywhere [EGALE]).

In 1986, George McCague, a Conservative member of the Ontario legislature, publicly rejected an amendment designed to include sexual orientation in the Ontario Human Rights Act: 'Homosexual marriage would be harmful to family life and would be socially undesirable. The family remains the essential building block of society, and its continued resilience in the face of impossible economic and social tensions is a hallmark of its preservation ... Homosexuality, on the contrary is essentially anti-family. The law has every right to discourage people from entering into paths that are demonstrably destructive, physicially and psychologically, first to the homosexual and then to society' (cited in Ross 1990, 136). If, according to McCague (and millions of sympathetic others) in the mid-1980s, 'the family' is the definitive Canadian institution and homosexuality is anti-family, then, by extension, lesbians and gay men are not fully Canadian and can never be accepted as healthy, productive contributors to Canadian society.[20] Beneath this century-old heterosexist nationalism lies the figure of the repellent queer whose claims to dignity, security, and equality must be understood as dangerous, illegitimate, and liable to precipitate Canada's complete undoing.

In spite of ongoing backlash, in 1998 a majority of provinces and territories enshrine anti-discrimination protection for lesbians and gay men in their human rights codes: the exceptions are Newfoundland, Alberta, Prince Edward Island, and the Northwest Territories. Other legal victories include a 1992 Supreme Court decision to ban discrimination against homosexuals in the Canadian Armed Forces and the Supreme Court's 1995 decision to grant refugee status to those immigrants who fear homosexual-based persecution in their home countries. In 1995, an Ontario judge ruled that non-biological lesbian parents have the legal right to adopt the child/ren they co-parent; in 1996, British Columbia followed suit. At the same time, child custody decisions remain uneven, and recent concessions unfold against the historical backdrop of myriad rulings whereby lesbian mothers were declared 'unfit.' In 1995, in *R. v. Egan*, the Canadian Supreme Court ruled that same-sex couples did not have the right to spousal pension benefits under the Old Age Security Act. Lesbian/gay marriage is not legal, and Canadian immigration policy does not permit the sponsor of a same-sex partner in ways available to heterosexuals. However, in May 1996, Bill C-33 – an amendment to the Canadian Human Rights Act designed to prohibit discrimination on the basis of sexual orientation – was passed by the House of Commons. Reformers have steadfastly applied tactics of lobbying, letter-writing, direct-mail campaigns, and educational drives – all in an effort to advance lesbian and gay legal equality in a context of Right-wing backlash. At the same time, queer critics in the 1990s, such as Ruthann Robson (975-96), Cynthia Peterson (118-37), and Carol Allen (101-8), have lamented the assimilationist and privatizing tendencies of lesbian and gay 'we are family' campaigns and mass 'marriages.'

Though decisions overall have been contradictory, there is agreement among Canadian activists that legal gains in Canada have been more numerous and substantial than have those in the US and outside North America (Rayside, 308-14). In part, they point to a much less powerful Christian fundamentalist Right-wing in Canada, the pro-gay efforts of the Left-leaning New Democratic Party (NDP) both provincially and federally, the cross-provincial coordination of lesbian/gay lobbying via EGALE, and a long-standing socialist-inspired tradition of wresting provisions from the state. However, notwithstanding victories in legal protections, law reform remains a limited avenue for social change. British sociologist Jeffrey Weeks argues that, 'Within the terms and processes [of liberal rights claims], there is little scope for challenging the normative assumptions within law, legal processes and social practices' (120). Moreover, in recent court rulings, the white, straight male adjudication of lesbian/gay pornography under obscenity law has punished bad queers (and their fantasies) as nasty, deviant, and un-Canadian, all the while reinscribing the polite, patriotic, and governable body as purely heterosexual.[21] According to Crown Prosecutor Charles Granek in the obscenity case *R. v. Scythes* (1992), s/m lesbians belong to a community 'whose rights are, thankfully, not protected by the Canadian Charter of Rights and Freedoms' (cited in Ross 1997b, 175). Granek, who curiously professed knowledge of who s/m lesbians are and what they do, consigned all members of this 'violent' sexual subcommunity to a netherworld far beyond the colonial-liberal essence of a naturally heterosexual and non-s/m Canada.

Agents of the brutal, coercive arm of state regulation, members of the Montreal police force are more fantastically zealous about raiding local gay men's sex clubs and prosecuting gay leathermen than they are about solving the murders of ten gay men in the city's gay village over the past six years. On the education and media fronts, there is still no high school curriculum anywhere that integrates histories of queer Canadians alongside stories of heterosexual Canadians. Groups like Citizens United for Responsible Education in Ontario (CURE), similar to their 1970s precursors, target the 'homosexual menace' as responsible for the corruption of children's minds and bodies.[22] The Canadian Broadcasting Corporation (CBC) and National Film Board (NFB) have largely tokenized 'queer realities' and lag behind independent queer film-making, fearful of alienating already ornery Canadian taxpayers. Again, lesbians (as well as gays and bisexuals) are cast as dubious members of Canada's 'representative' democracy.

Queer Postnationalism?

In times of social, moral, and political upheaval, contradictions abound. In 1996, Toronto's Lesbian and Gay Pride Day Parade attracted 750,000 people, reportedly the largest of its kind in the world. Cities from coast to coast host pride celebrations, film and video festivals, and are home to queer theatre companies, anti-censorship groups, art collectives, and counselling centres. The Canadian Lesbian and Gay Studies Association was formally constituted as a national 'learned society' in 1994, when it began meeting alongside all other academic disciplines. The Toronto Centre for Lesbian and Gay Studies sponsors numerous events, awards, and community-based courses and operates a country-wide journal, *Centre/Fold*, for queer research and scholarship. The contribution made by a Canadian contingent to international negotiations around 'sexual orientation' and women's sexuality at the 1995 Women's Conference in Beijing, China, indicates one direction of robust lesbian feminist energy at work both inside and outside Canada. And still, against the backdrop of sociocultural, political, and intellectual resources unimaginable in the 1950s, most queers who are HIV+, queer street youth, sex trade workers, and transgenders live precarious, endangered lives on the fringes of Canadian society, their own sense of national belonging both compromised and insecure.

In the 1970s, Canadian lesbian feminists did not galvanize a large, broad-based following. In late capitalist culture, they held no real economic or political power; they were suspicious of mainstream media in ways that lesbian aficionados of popular culture (both producers and consumers) in the 1990s have trouble comprehending. They had no blood ties to each other and only sketchy information about their homosexual ancestors. And yet without historical precedent they collectively contested the terrain of representation – the images and meanings attached to queer and lesbian – and they fought, on the ground, to constitute themselves as agents of social struggle. They put into question conventional divides between the public and the private, the individual and the social (Weeks, 101-23). They seized the vocabulary of the day – (lesbian) nationalism as liberation – with no foreknowledge of the human wreckage that global nationalisms would inflict in the 1990s. They wanted to achieve erotic autonomy from the state by imagining a Lesbian Nation that affirmed lesbians as a powerful group.

Comparing and Contrasting Nationalisms

Comparing lesbian nationalism to women's involvement in other nationalist struggles in the twentieth century yields rich insights into the nature of political community-making. Women function both practically and symbolically to guarantee a variety of nationalisms. Suruchi Thapar explains how middle-class Indian women were active in the independence movement against British rule: they spun and wove *khadi*, educated other women, contributed to nationalist literature, and held meetings and demonstrations (81-96). At the same time, however, they took instructions from the exclusively male leadership, and they were circumscribed discursively by heteropatriarchal rhetoric as 'defenders of civilization' whose maternal honour 'had to be protected' (88). Moreover, according to Ketu Katrak, the spiritual leader Mahatma Ghandi drew on Hindu mythology to reinscribe Indian women in the ideology of marriage, wifehood, motherhood, and domesticity – a reinscription pivotal to his political strategy for liberation (396). Commenting on the Iranian and Afghan revolutions in the late 1970s, Valentine Moghadam says: 'Sexual politics are at the centre of Islamist movements which seek the reordering of society and the construction of a new moral and cultural order based on rigid sex roles and the exaltation of the (patriarchal) family. To the typical Afghan Mujahid, self-determination and autonomy (vis-à-vis the state or the Soviets) are not privileges extended to females. To the Iranian Islamist ideologue, "freedom" and "independence" – slogans of the Revolution – were not to be construed as personal freedoms for women' (426). Similarly, in Zionist discourse, Israeli Jewish women have been 'recruited' in the 'demographic race' between Jews and Arabs 'to bear more children as their national duty to the Jewish people in general and the Israeli Jewish people in particular' (Davis, 100). As Nira Yuval-Davis explains, it is this discourse that co-exists with the failure in Israel to guarantee women's overall equal constitutional rights (104). In their 1993 issue on 'Nationalisms and National Identities,' the editors of *Feminist Review* conclude that, in nationalist ideologies, women are the *symbol* of the nation while men are its *agents* (1). In my view, women have never been entirely stripped of agency; however, they have been constrained to embody virtue and honour in the context of heteronormative, nationalist practices and policies. To quote M. Jacqui Alexander, 'No nationalism could survive without heterosexuality – criminal, perverse, temporarily imprisoned, incestuous or as abusive as it might be, nationalism needs it. It still remains more conducive to nation-building than same-sex desire, which is downright hostile to it, for women presumably cannot love themselves, love other women, and love the nation simultaneously' (83).

The framework of lesbian nationalism in the 1970s broke sharply from the heteropatriarchal traditions that have underpinned and shaped women's relationship to most nationalist projects. By defying essentialist constructions of woman as natural caretaker inside the family – what Nora Räthzel calls 'the cornerstone of the stability of the nation state [in Western societies]' – lesbian feminist agents enacted their disloyalty, their disobedience to the Canadian state (168). Unlike ethnic nationalisms that privilege blood connections and kinship, being of good lesbian 'stock' was based in the soundness of one's ideology rather than in the 'proof' of one's genes. Belonging was earned by adherence to political principles of lesbian feminism rather than by rights of inheritance. The fact that few activist lesbians in the 1970s were raising children further contradicted nationalist and racist discourses that sutured together nation and reproduction and figured (heterosexual) mothers as moral guardians of 'the (white) race.'[23] Importantly, lesbian feminists rejected not only the heterosexual social contract of marriage, but also all directives to reproduce biologically the next generation of (white, middle-class) Canadian citizens.[24] In effect, lesbians' disengagement from and disdain for heterosexual intercourse, mothering (especially boy children), and nuclear families, combined with their refutation of patriarchal political leadership, distinguishes them from women in other nationalist struggles.

In the 1970s, lesbian feminists in English Canada were courageous risk-takers, but their lives stood in stark contrast to the millions of women in developing nations who were non-literate, exploited labourers both inside and outside the domestic sphere, who lacked the time and resources to mount their own anti-patriarchal and anti-colonial initiatives. By the same token, women's access to resources has never guaranteed the pursuit of a progressive path: some women in privileged First World nations have been advantaged by their roles in reactionary, sometimes bloody, nationalisms. Anne McClintock reveals that white Afrikaner women throughout the twentieth century 'were complicit in deploying the power of motherhood in the exercise and legitimation of white domination ... Clutching this small power, they became complicit in the racism that suffused Afrikaner nationalism' (72).[25] Research by Kathleen Blee shows that female members of the Ku Klux Klan in the US were highly active in advancing a platform of racist hatred toward African Americans and Jews. And a number of first-wave maternal feminists in English Canada, such as Nellie McClung and Emily Murphy, believed in Anglo-Saxon racial superiority and the degeneracy of the 'feeble-minded,' immigrants of Colour, and unwed mothers (Bacchi, 104-116; McLaren, 129; Valverde, 3-26). In her book *The Black Candle* (1922), Murphy warned that women in western Canada were being lured into the 'white slave trade' (prostitution) by Chinese men addicted to opium (17). In Murphy's widely shared view, Canada was a white settler nation in need of defence against the encroaching 'yellow peril' and all that threatened its rightfully British roots. In other words, women worldwide have had complicated, contradictory relationships to the manufacture and direction of nationalist regimes.

On the cusp of the twenty-first century in Canada, debates and disagreements persist about what 'lesbian' means; what the content of a 'lesbian' novel, film, play, or lyric should be; how best to thwart heterosexism and homophobia where we live; and how best to reach those secreted in the closet. At the same time, there is fierce, hard-won satisfaction among lesbians who have built and witnessed the steady growth of queer networks and communities (still structured by differences of class, race/ethnicity, ability, and generation) in rural towns, inner cities, and urban enclaves all across the country (Bouthillette, 213-32; Ingram, 95-126; Grube, 127-46; Riordan, 2-15). And there is some tentative evidence that gay and lesbian commercial and political spaces are emerging internationally, particularly in Southeast Asia, South and Central America, and Eastern Europe, though they habitually co-exist with the reality of discrimination and violence (Altman, 77-9).

Today, while numerous nations around the world continue to grind out hardhearted, nationalist warfare, there are some lesbians, bisexuals, gay men, and transgenders in Canada who have realized some modicum of safety, love, and hope for a transformed future. For them, and for myself, the dream of an independent Nation no longer works as a unifying metaphor; it no longer supplies the necessary ideological glue (if it ever truly did). And though queer relationships to the patriarchal, racist, and heterosexist Canadian nation remain strained and conflicted, the battle for erotic liberation proceeds doggedly, without mass torture, systematic rape, or the blood spilled on killing fields.

Acknowledgments

I am grateful to Veronica Strong-Boag for inviting me to write this chapter, for believing that I had something more to say, and for her keen editorial eye. Sherrill Grace supplied much-appreciated tidying up. I also want to thank Leslie Roman for rich, stimulating conversations, references and ideas, and for reading the manuscript.

Notes

1 See the National Film Board documentary, 'Hearts of Hate' (1995), which captures the emergence and intensification of white supremacists organizing across Canada in the 1990s.

2 Here I borrow from Michael Ignatieff's analysis of civil and ethnic nationalisms (5-6).

3 On the complex ways in which citizenship is heterosexualized, see B.S. Turner (1-22), David T. Evans (89-113), and M. Jacqui Alexander (63-100).

4 For more on this subject, see Patrice LeClerc and Lois A. West (220-46), and Roberta Hamilton on pro-natalism, feminism, and nationalism (135-52). For a thoughtful, theoretically inspiring yet somewhat depoliticizing account of the gendering and heterosexualizing of Quebec nationalism via popular Francophone television and film production, see Elspeth Probyn (65-91).

5 See Teressa Nahanee on Aboriginal justice in Canada (1993), Liliane Ernestine Krosenbrink-Gelissen on the Native Women's Association of Canada (1991), and Marlene Brant Castellano and Janice Hill (232-51) and Jo-anne Fiske on the Indigenous Women's Movement in Canada (65-95).

6 On criticism of queer nationalism by lesbians and gays of Colour, see Sagri Dhairyam (25-46), Gloria Anzaldua (249-63), and Barbara Smith (12-16).

7 There are many other stories to be told about the complex relationship that Francophone and Anglophone lesbians developed to Quebec nationalism beginning in the late 1960s. On lesbian history in Montreal, see Andrea Hildebran (2-25).

8 In her otherwise thoughtful, pointed assessment of recently published Canadian history textbooks in the *Journal of Canadian Studies*, Gail Cuthbert Brant elects to disregard contributions to the 'history of sexuality' in Canada (184-7). In the same issue of the journal, Kathryn McPherson does not make the same mistake in her reading of the same texts (187-94). Reporting on the 'Gender, Nationalism and National Identities' symposium in Bellagio, Italy, in 1992, Catherine Hall notes that there was no talk about the 'kind of national identities which have been available for lesbians and gays' (97). On a promising note, Gillian Creese and Daiva Stasiulus invite contributors to the field of Canadian political economy to practise 'intersectional forms of analysis' that provide a 'more complex sense of the multidimensional nature of power, privilege, and inequality in contemporary societies' (5-14).

9 For a selection of writings on two spirits within Aboriginal societies, see Susan Beaver (197-8), Evelyn Blackwood (27-42), Paula Gunn Allen (106-17), Jonathon Goldberg (3-18), and Will Roscoe (48-76).

10 See 'Hogan's Alley,' a half-hour video by Andrea Fatona and Cornelia Wyngaarden (Video Out, 1994) which features Leah 'Curt' Curtis, an African-Canadian lesbian who reminisces about her relationship to Vancouver's black community in the 1950s and 1960s.

11 American writers who have explored politicized lesbian communities in the US include Deborah Wolf, Susan Krieger, Alice Echols, Verta Taylor, Nancy Whittier, Sarah Schulman, Arlene Stein, Shane Phelan, and Lisa Walters.

12 American lesbian and gay magazines published before 1970, such as *The Ladder, One,* and *Mattachine Review*, all had a small circulation in Canada.

13 Histories of lesbian and bisexual activism in these cities remain sketchy. I look forward to more research projects devoted to fleshing out the particulars of each city and each region of the country.

14 For her reflections on the American lesbian membership and mandate of the Lavender Menace almost thirty years ago, see Rita Mae Brown (1995, 40-7).

15 In *Blood and Belonging*, a book that incorporates, unacceptably, no gender analysis, Michael Ignatieff concludes by noting that young males not only accomplish violent nationalist warfare, many of them 'loved the ruins, loved the destruction, loved the power that came from the barrels of their guns' (187).

16 The metaphor of Lesbian Nation did not have the same meaning, resonance, or relevance to lesbian groups across the country. Andrea Hildebran reports that Francophone lesbian activists in Montreal were influenced by Quebec nationalist discourse, and, at the same time, some of them recall ambivalence toward the racist elements of le mouvement

indépendentist vis-à-vis First Nations and non-Francophones (55).

17 On the refusal of the *Vancouver Sun* to print a two-line classified ad submitted by the Gay Alliance Toward Equality (Vancouver), which marked the beginning of one of the most famous legal cases in Canada involving lesbian and gay rights, see Donald McLeod (144, 188-98).

18 Here I have adapted Himani Bannerji's cogent description of state exclusions practised on 'visible minorities' in Canada.

19 These first tentative bonds formed the infrastructure of what would later emerge as lesbian/gay/bisexual HIV/AIDS activism in response to government neglect and profit-driven pharmaceutical empires.

20 I am grateful to Michelle Swann for pointing out that my earlier analysis (Ross 1990, 133-96) of the legislative debate regarding sexual orientation could be reframed around questions of citizenship.

21 See Becki Ross's discussion of lesbian bodies as they figured in prosecutorial discourse during the *R.v. Scythes* obscenity trial in Toronto, 1992 (1997b, 152-98).

22 As Veronica Strong-Boag points out, Canadian anti-feminist Betty Steele has explained what she sees as the dangers of lesbianism and feminism in *Together Again: Reuniting Men and Women: Love and Sex, Mothers and Children* (Toronto: Simon and Pierre 1991).

23 For more on (heterosexual) women as 'national reproducers,' see Nira Yuval-Davis (1993, 621-32), Floya Anthias and Nira Yuval-Davis (1992, Chapter 4), and the case studies on Australia, South Africa, Italy, Turkey, Iran, Uganda, Israel, Cyprus, and England in Nira Yuval-Davis and Floya Anthias, eds., *Women-Nation-State* (New York: St. Martin's 1989). Also see Strong-Boag (1997, 128-45) for discussion of challenges by feminists, First Nations, and workers to the rhetoric of citizenship in post-Confederation Canada.

24 Lesbian feminists did not begin to pursue motherhood via artificial insemination (or alternative fertilization) until the late 1970s, and they did not do it in large numbers until the 1990s. There were lesbian mothers who had conceived children heterosexually, and their high-profile custody battles mobilized considerable local and national protest. On the 1974 example of Darlene Case in Saskatchewan, see Christine Boyle (129-45) and see numerous references to Case's struggle for custody in the lesbian and gay press in McLeod (176-7). On this history of activism in support of lesbian mothers, see Stone (1990, 198-208).

25 See also the comparative analysis of nation, race, and motherhood in Afrikaner nationalism and in the African National Congress by Deborah Gaitskill and Elaine Underhalter (58-78) as well as Zengie Mangaliso on nationalism in South Africa (130-46).

Works Cited

Adams, Mary Louise. 1995. 'Youth, Corruptibility, and English Canadian Postwar Campaigns against Indecency.' *Journal of the History of Sexuality* 6 (11):89-117

Alexander, M. Jacqui, and Chandra Talapde Mohanty. 1997. 'Introduction: Genealogies, Legacies, Movements.' In M. Jacqui Alexander and Chandra Talpade Mohanty, eds., *Feminist Genealogies, Colonial Legacies, Democratic Futures*, xiii-xlii. New York: Routledge

Allen, Carol. 1993. 'Who Gets to Be Family: Some Thoughts on the Lesbian and Gay Fight for Equality.' In Linda Carty, ed., *And Still We Rise: Feminist Political Mobilizing in Contemporary Canada*, 101-8. Toronto: Women's Press

Allen, Paula Gunn. 1989. 'Lesbians in American Indian Cultures.' In Martin Duberman et al., eds., *Hidden from History: Reclaiming the Gay and Lesbian Past*, 106-17. New York: Meridian

Altman, Dennis. 1996. 'Rupture or Continuity: The Internationalization of Gay Identities.' *Social Text* 14 (3):77-94

Anderson, Benedict. 1983. *Imagined Communities: Reflections on the Origin and Spread of Nationalism*. London: Verso

Anderson, Perry. 1991. 'Nation States and National Identity.' *London Review of Books* (May 9):3

Anthias, Floya, and Nira Yuval-Davis. 1989. 'Introduction.' In Nira Yuval-Davis and Floya Anthias, eds., *Woman-Nation-State*, 1-15. New York: St. Martin's

–. 1992. *Racialized Boundaries: Race, Nation, Gender, Colour, Class and the Anti-Racist Struggle*. London and New York: Routledge

Anzaldua, Gloria. 1991. 'To(o) Queer the Writer – Loca, escritora y chicana.' In Betsy Warland, ed., *Inversions: Writing by Dykes, Queers and Lesbians*, 249-63. Vancouver: Press Gang

Arnup, Katherine. In press. 'Invisible Women: Lesbian Mothers in the 1950s and 1960s.' In Becki Ross, ed., *Forbidden Love: Unashamed Lives of Postwar Canadian Lesbians*. Vancouver: Press Gang

Arscott, Jane. 1996. 'Thinking Straight about Public Policy in the '70s and '90s.' *Canadian Woman's Studies Journal* 16 (2):110-4

Bacchi, Carol. 1983. *Liberation Deferred? The Ideas of the English-Canadian Suffragists, 1877-1918*. Toronto: University of Toronto Press

Baker, Kathryn Hinojosa. 1992. 'Delinquent Desire: Race, Sex and Ritual in Reform Schools for Girls.' *Discourse* 15:49-67

Bannerji, Himani. 1996. 'On the Dark Side of the Nation: Politics of Multiculturalism and the State of Canada.' *Journal of Canadian Studies* 31 (3):103-28

Beaver, Susan. 1991. 'Gays and Lesbians of the First Nations.' In Makeda Silvera, ed., *Piece of My Heart: A Lesbian of Colour Anthology*, 197-8. Toronto: Sister Vision

Bégin, Monique. 1992. 'The Royal Commission on the Status of Women in Canada: Twenty Years Later.' In C. Backhouse and D. Flaherty, eds., *Challenging Times: The Women's Movement in Canada and the United States*, 21-38. Montreal and Kingston: McGill-Queen's University Press

Berlant, Lauren, and Andrea Freeman. 1992. 'Queer Nationality.' *Boundary* 19 (1):149-80

Blackwood, Evelyn. 1984. 'Sexuality and Gender in Certain American Indian Tribes: The Case of Cross-Gender Females.' *Signs* 10 (1):27-42

Blee, Kathleen. 1991. *Women of the Klan: Racism and Gender in the 1920s*. Berkeley: University of California Press

Boyle, Christine. 1976. 'Custody, Adoption and the Homosexual Parent.' *Reports of Family Law* 23:129-45

Brah, Avtar. 1993. 'Re-Framing Europe: En-gendering Racisms, Ethnicities and Nationalism in Contemporary Western Europe.' *Feminist Review* 45:15-24

Brant, Gail Cuthbert. 1996. 'Comment: New Wine or Just Old Bottles? A Round Table on Recent Texts in Canadian History.' *Journal of Canadian Studies* 30 (4):184-7

Breuilly, John. 1982. *Nationalism and the State*. Chicago: University of Chicago Press

Browne, Lois. 1992. *Girls of Summer*. Toronto: HarperCollins

Castellano, Marlene Brant, and Janice Hill. 1995. 'First Nations Women: Reclaiming Our Responsibilities.' In Joy Parr, ed., *A Diversity of Women: Ontario 1945-1980*, 232-51. Toronto: University of Toronto Press

Collective of Lesbian International Terrorists. 1995. 'CLIT Statement.' *Long Time Coming* (January 1995):2-36

Creese, Gillian, and Daiva Stasiulus. 1996. 'Introduction: Intersections of Gender, Race, Class and Sexuality.' *Studies in Political Economy* 51:5-14

Creet, Julia. 1990. 'A Test of Unity: Lesbian Visibility in the British Columbia Federation of Women.' In Sharon D. Stone, ed., *Lesbians in Canada*, 183-97. Toronto: Between the Lines

De Lauretis, Theresa. 1988. 'Sexual Indifference and Lesbian Representation.' *Theater Journal* 40 (2):155-77

Dhairyam, Sagri. 1994. 'Racing the Lesbian, Dodging White Critics.' In Laura Doan, ed., *The Lesbian Postmodern*, 25-46. New York: Columbia University Press

Duder, Karen. 1994. 'Dykes in the Dumpster? The Recovery of Lesbian and Bisexual Women's Sources.' *Centre/Fold* 7 (Fall 1994): 17-8

Echols, Alice. 1989. *Daring to Be Bad: Radical Feminism in America, 1968-1975*. Minneapolis: University of Minnesota Press

Evans, David T. 1993. *Sexual Citizenship: The Material Construction of Sexualities*. London and New York: Routledge

Fatona, Andrea, and Cornelia Wyngaarden. 1994. 'Hogan's Alley.' Videorecording. Vancouver: Video Out

Feminist Review Editors. 1993. 'Editorial.' *Feminist Review* 44:1-5

Fiske, Jo-anne. 1996. 'The Womb Is to the Nation as the Heart Is to the Body:

Ethnopological Discourses of the Canadian Indigenous Women's Movement.' *Studies in Political Economy* 51:65-95

Gaitskill, Deborah, and Elaine Unterhalter. 1989. 'Mothers of the Nation: A Comparative Analysis of Nation, Race and Motherhood in Afrikaner Nationalism and the African National Congress.' In Nira Yuval-Davis and Floya Anthias, eds., *Woman-Nation-State,* 58-78. New York: St Martin's

Gentile, Patrizia. In press. '"Mirror, Mirror on the Wall": Beauty Contests, Femininity and Sexuality in the Canadian Civil Service, 1950-1973.' In Becki Ross, ed., *Forbidden Love: Unashamed Lives of Postwar Canadian Lesbians*. Vancouver: Press Gang

Goldberg, Jonathon. 1993. 'Sodomy in the New World: Anthropologies Old and New.' In Michael Warner, ed., *Fear of a Queer Planet: Queer Politics and Social Theory*, 3-78. Minneapolis: University of Minnesota Press

Hall, Catherine. 1993. 'Gender, Nationalism and National Identities: Bellagio Symposium, July 1992.' *Feminist Review* 44:97-103

Hamilton, Roberta. 1995. 'Pro-natalism, Feminism and Nationalism.' In Francois-Pierre Gingras, ed., *Gender and Politics in Contemporary Canada*, 135-52. Toronto: Oxford University Press

Hamilton, Roberta, and Michele Barrett. 1986. 'Introduction.' In *The Politics of Diversity*, 1-31. Montreal: Book Center

Higgins, Ross, and Line Chamberland. 1992. 'Mixed Messages: Gays and Lesbians in Montréal Yellow Papers in the 1950s.' In Ian Mckay, ed., *The Challenge of Modernity: A Reader on Post Confederation Canada*, 421-38. Toronto: McGraw-Hill Ryerson

Hildebran, Andrea. 1997. 'Lesbian Activism in Montréal, 1970-1980.' MA thesis, Department of History, Université du Québec à Montréal

Johnston, Jill. 1973. *Lesbian Nation: The Feminist Solution*. New York: Simon and Shuster

Katrak, Ketu H. 1992. 'Indian Nationalism, Gandhian "Satyagraha," and Representations of Female Sexuality.' In Andrew Parker et al., eds., *Nationalisms and Sexualities*, 395-406. New York: Routledge

Kinsman, Gary. 1995. 'Character Weaknesses and "Fruit Machines": Towards an Analysis of the Social Organization of the Anti-Purge Campaign in the Canadian Federal Civil Service, 1959-1964.' *Labour/le travail* 35 (Spring):133-61

–.1996. *The Regulation of Desire: Homo and Hetero Sexualities*. 2nd ed. Montreal: Black Rose

Kostash, Myrna. 1980. *Long Way from Home: The Story of the Sixties Generation*. Toronto: James Lorimer.

Krieger, Susan. 1983. *The Mirror Dance: Identity in a Women's Community*. Philadelphia: Temple University Press

Krosenbrink-Gelissen, Lilianne Ernestine. 1991. *Sexual Equality as an Aboriginal Right: The Native Women's Association of Canada and the Constitutional Process on Aboriginal Matters 1982-1987*. Saarbrucken: Verlag Breitenbach

LeClerc, Patrice, and Lois A. West. 1997. 'Feminist Nationalist Movement in Québec: Resolving Contradictions?' In Lois A. West, ed., *Feminist Nationalism*, 220-46. New York and London: Routledge

Long, David. 1992. 'Culture, Ideology and Militancy: the Movement of Native Indians in Canada.' In William Carroll, ed., *Organizing Dissent: Contemporary Social Movements in Theory and Practice*, 118-34. Toronto: Garamond

Lutz, Helma, Ann Phoenix, and Nira Yuval-Davis. 'Introduction: Nationalism, Racism and Gender: European Crossfires.' In Helma Lutz et al., eds., *Crossfires: Nationalism, Racism and Gender in Europe*, 1-25. London: Pluto

McClintock, Anne. 1993. 'Family Feuds: Gender, Nationalism and the Family.' *Feminist Review* 44 (Summer):61-80

McDonald, Ingrid. 1987. 'Frances Loring and Florence Wyle, Sculptors.' *Broadside* (November):8-9

McLaren, Angus. 1986. 'The Creation of a Haven for "Human Thoroughbreds": The Sterilization of the Feeble-Minded and the Mentally Ill in British Columbia.' *Canadian Historical Review* 67 (2):129-50

McLeod, Donald. 1996. *Lesbian and Gay Liberation in Canada: A Selected, Annotated*

Chronology, 1964-1975. Toronto: ECW

McPherson, Kathryn. 1996. 'Comment: New Wine or Just Old Bottles? A Round Table on Recent Texts in Canadian History.' *Journal of Canadian Studies* 30 (4):187-94

Maggenti, Maria. 1991. 'Women as Queer Nationals.' *Out/Look: National Lesbian and Gay Quarterly* 11 (Winter):20-3

Mangaliso, Zengie. 1997. 'Gender and Nation-Building in South Africa.' In Lois A. West, ed., *Feminist Nationalism*, 130-46. New York: Routledge

Melucci, Alberto. 1989. *Nomads of the Present: Social Movements and Individual Needs in Contemporary Society*. Philadelphia: Temple University Press

Morris, William, ed. 1980. *Houghton Mifflin Canadian Dictionary of the English Language*. Markham, ON: Houghton Mifflin

Murphy, Emily. 1922. *The Black Candle*. Toronto: Thomas Allen

Nahanee, Teressa. 1993. 'Dancing with a Gorilla: Aboriginal Women, Justice and the Charter.' *Aboriginal Peoples and the Justice System: Report of the Round Table on Aboriginal Justice Issues*, 1-66. Ottawa: Royal Commission on Aboriginal Peoples

O'Brien, Kelly. 1996. 'Discourses of Gender and Sexual "Dysphoria" at the Clarke Institute, 1950-1965.' Paper presented at the University of Toronto

Phelan, Shane. 1989. *Identity Politics: Lesbian Feminism and the Limits of Community*. Philadelphia: Temple University Press

Probyn, Elspeth. 1996. *Outside Belongings*. New York: Routledge

Radicalesbians. 1973. 'The Woman Identified Woman.' In Anne Koedt, Ellen Levine, and Anita Rapone, eds., *Radical Feminism*, 240-45. New York: Quadrangle

Räthzel, Nora. 1995. 'Nationalism and Gender in West Europe: the German Case.' In Helma Lutz et al., eds., *Crossfires: Nationalism, Racism and Gender in Europe*, 161-89. London: Pluto

Rayside, David. 1998. *On the Fringe: Gays and Lesbians in the Political Process*. Ithaca and London: Cornell University Press

Rich, Adrienne. 1978. *Dream of a Common Language: Poems 1974-1977*. New York: Norton

Riordan, Michael. 1996. *Out Our Way: Lesbian and Gay Life in the Country*. Toronto: Between the Lines

Robson, Ruthann. 1994. 'Resisting the Family: Repositioning Lesbians in Legal Theory.' *Signs* 19 (4):975-96

Rooney, Frances. 1983. 'Loring and Wyle, Sculptors.' *Pink Ink* 1 (1):18-20

–. 1995a. 'Edith S. Watson: Photographing Women in Rural Canada.' *International Journal of Canadian Studies* 11 (Spring/Fall):185-94

–. 1995b. *Working Light: The Working Life of Photographer Edith S. Watson*. Ottawa: Carleton University Press

Roscoe, Will. 1988. 'Strange Country This: Images of Berdaches and Warrior Women.' In Will Roscoe, ed., *Living the Spirit: A Gay American Indian Anthology*, 48-76. New York: St. Martin's

Ross, Becki L. 1990. 'Sexual Dis/Orientation or Playing House: To Be or Not to Be Coded Human.' In Sharon D. Stone, ed., *Lesbians in Canada*, 133-46. Toronto: Between the Lines

–. 1995. *The House That Jill Built: A Lesbian Nation in Formation*. Toronto: University of Toronto Press

–. 1997a. 'Destaining the (Tattooed) Delinquent Body: Moral Regulatory Practices at Toronto's Street Haven, 1965-1969.' *Journal of the History of Sexuality* 7 (4):561-95

–. 1997b. '"It's Merely Designed for Sexual Arousal": Interrogating the Indefensibility of Lesbian Smut.' In Brenda Cossman et al., eds., *Bad Attitude/s On Trial: Feminism, Pornography and the Butler Decision*, 152-98. Toronto: University of Toronto Press

Sandoval, Chela. 1985. 'Comment on Krieger's "Lesbian Identity and Community: Recent Social Science Literature."' In *The Lesbian Issue: Essays from Signs*, 241-4. Chicago: University of Chicago Press

Satzewich, Vic, and Terry Wotherspoon. 1993. *First Nations: Race, Class and Gender Relations*. Scarborough, ON: Nelson Canada

Setliff, Eric. 1994. 'Sex Fiends or Swish Kids: Gay Men in the Toronto Tabloids, 1946-1956.'

MA Thesis, University of Toronto
–. 1995. 'Between the Scandal Sheets (1949).' *Centre/Fold* (Spring):30-1
Smith, Barbara. 1993. 'Queer Politics: Where's the Revolution.' *Nation* 5 (July):12-16
Smith, Dorothy E. 1979. 'Where There Is Oppression There Is Resistance.' *Branching Out* 5 (1):10-5
Stone, Sharon D. 1990. 'Lesbian Mothers Organizing.' In Sharon D. Stone, ed., *Lesbians in Canada*, 198-208. Toronto: Between the Lines
–. 1997. 'From Stereotypes to Visible Diversity: Lesbian Political Organizing.' In William Carroll, ed., *Organizing Dissent*, 2nd ed., 171-96. Toronto: Garamond
Strong-Boag, Veronica. 1996. 'Independent Women, Problematic Men: First- and Second-Wave Anti-Feminism in Canada from Goldwin Smith to Betty Steele.' *Histoire sociale/Social History* 57 (Spring):1-22
Taylor, Verta, and Nancy Whittier. 1995. 'Collective Identity in Social Movement Communities: Lesbian Feminist Mobilization.' In Aldon Morris and Carol McClurg Mueller, eds., *Frontiers in Social Movement Theory*, 104-29. New Haven and London: Yale University Press
Thapar, Suruchi. 1993. 'Women as Activists; Women as Symbols: A Study of the Indian Nationalist Movement.' *Feminist Review* 44:81-96
Turner, B.S., ed., 1993. *Citizenship and Social Theory*. London, Newbury Park and New Delhi: Sage
Valverde, Mariana. 1992. '"When the Mother of the Race Is Free": Race, Reproduction, and Sexuality in First Wave Feminism.' In Franca Iacovetta and Mariana Valverde, eds., *Gender Conflicts: New Essays in Women's History*, 3-26. Toronto: University of Toronto Press
Weeks, Jeffrey. 1995. *Invented Moralities: Sexual Values in an Age of Uncertainty*. New York: Columbia University Press
Westell, Anthony. 1970. *Toronto Star*, 3 December:5
Wolf, Deborah. 1978. *The Lesbian Community*. Berkeley: University of California Press
Yuval-Davis, Nira. 1989. 'National Reproduction and the "Demographic Race" in Israel.' In Nira Yuval-Davis and Floya Anthias, eds., *Woman-State-Nation*, 92-109. New York: St. Martin's
–. 1993. 'Gender and Nation.' *Ethnic and Racial Studies*. 16 (4):621-32
Zarkov, Dubravka. 1995. 'Gender, Orientalism and the History of Ethnic Hatred in the Former Yugoslavia.' In Helma Lutz et al., eds., *Crossfires: Nationalism, Racism and Gender in Europe*, 105-20. London: Pluto

Hegemonic Nationalism and the Politics of Feminism and Multiculturalism in Canada

Jo-Anne Lee and Linda Cardinal

In Canada, feminism and multiculturalism are often accused of preventing Canadians from having a sense of belonging and a common set of values.[1] As political movements, they are held responsible for fragmenting and hindering the development of a strong national identity (Gairdner; Bissoondath). Paradoxically, within multicultural and feminist circles in English-speaking Canada, there is also a corresponding lack of critical consciousness around the politics of nationalism (Cardinal and Lee).[2] This failure to recognize English or Anglo-Canadian nationalism's mediation of feminist and multicultural political cultures has left movement activists without the conceptual tools and political strategies needed to respond to neo-conservative attacks.[3] Although the popular media and neo-conservative critics regularly portray feminism and multiculturalism as related 'interest groups,' in reality, as diversely constituted movements, there is little organized collaboration between the two on matters of political strategy.

This chapter focuses on the effects of nationalism on the Canadian feminist movement, its political culture, and strategies as a way of understanding the separation between feminism and multiculturalism in Canada. There are many competing nationalisms in Canada that generate multilayered conflicts; however, this chapter addresses only Anglo-Canadian nationalism outside of Quebec, since it is the nationalism of the dominant groups that concerns us. Anglo-Canadian nationalism, while endlessly contested, has now achieved a more or less stable hegemonic status that encircles and subsumes power relations among other contending bases for Canadian nationalism. In its dominance, Anglo-Canadian nationalism claims for itself inclusive universalism and sees itself as 'natural,' 'true,' and 'authentic.' Anglo-Canadian nationalists see themselves as singularly without artifice. Unlike advocates of other competing nationalisms, Anglo-Canadian nationalists generally do not perceive themselves as being 'nationalistic' when they appeal for 'Canadian' (meaning an Anglo or English) unity or when they suggest that 'Canadian' identity is threatened.

Anglo-Canadian nationalism views itself outside of ethnic particularities – the bases of those 'other' competing nationalisms.

Feminism, Multiculturalism, and Nationalism
To begin mapping nationalism's complex effects on the political culture and strategies of the feminist movement, we examine three different analytical moments: the separation between feminism and multiculturalism as distinct arenas of political struggle; strategies of inclusion, such as affirmative action and pay equity programs; and racialized and ethnicized women's participation in government multicultural programs. Two case studies drawn from a larger study of racialized and ethnicized women's engagements with multicultural policies are presented to illustrate how boundaries across mothering, teaching, and volunteering, widely understood as gendered activities, are also formed through the effects of state-organized national identity formation. The larger ethnographic study was conducted in Saskatchewan between 1990 and 1995 (Lee).

Our analyses point to the need for mainstream feminism to achieve a clearer understanding of hegemonic nationalism and its effects. Mainstream feminism's myopia regarding nationalism as a force that structures relations among women and men has resulted in political strategies remaining centred on mainstream Anglo-Canadian women's issues. This narrow vision marginalizes issues viewed as not 'belonging' to the 'national' feminist agenda. For example, national feminist organizations, such as the National Action Committee on the Status of Women (NAC), have not viewed multiculturalism and multicultural policies as an arena for political struggle. The approach adopted in this essay situates present feminist debates over 'difference' as a political project of national identity formation. Because present painful struggles over identity and difference, a reaction to exclusion, have not been successful in reformulating Canadian feminism's political agenda, we hope to shift present debates over identity and difference to a place where it might also be possible to transform feminist strategies for change. Much work needs to be done in linking feminist struggles to nationalism, and the framework presented here should only be considered a tentative point of departure, not a final destination.

Anglo-Canadian Nationalism as a Hegemonic Formation
Hegemony is achieved when ideas and beliefs are no longer questioned but are taken for granted and assumed as natural (Gramsci). However, Gramsci also observed that hegemony is never total. It is constantly challenged and contested through counter-hegemonic ideas and practices, such as those initiated by feminist and multicultural activists. A hegemonic formation is an outcome of ongoing processes of counter-hegemonic challenges and

hegemonic reformulations in the political, economic, and civil spheres of life. Language and cultural practices are central to Gramsci's idea of hegemony because of their role in unifying people into a common consciousness. According to Gramsci, hegemony is not imposed from above but is constantly being produced, challenged, and reproduced in our everyday struggles. The constant shifts and changes in cultural practices of hegemonic dominance help to maintain in people an ongoing willingness to be governed. In this sense, Anglo-Canadian nationalism has not only accommodated and recognized feminist and multicultural demands, it has also been central to the development of these movements' political cultures. Thus, the feminist movement is not situated outside Anglo-Canadian hegemony but, as a hegemonic project itself, is located within discourses and practices of hegemonic nationalism.

Historically, the Canadian feminist movement has exhibited a nationalizing desire to unify all women under a single Anglo-Canadian banner. Although a national voice for women has achieved gains for many Anglo, middle-class women seen as 'belonging' to the national community, these gains have come about by ignoring differences among women and excluding women who stand outside the imagined national community.[4] Until recently, the complicity of the mainstream feminist movement in maintaining Anglo-Canadian nationalism as a hegemonic formation has been overlooked. Increasingly, the Canadian women's movement has been forced to address issues around the politics of diversity, pluralism, and difference. It has been the voices and actions of marginalized women, including those of Aboriginal, refugee, migrant, and immigrant women in the women's movement, that has helped to accelerate a realignment in the cultural boundaries of Anglo-Canadian nationalism. And it is precisely for these reasons that neo-conservatives attempt to portray feminist activists as threats to 'the' nation.

The incorporation of the Canadian women's movement into the nationalizing project has been fostered by the Canadian state. The state is one of the main instruments for asserting and reasserting hegemonic dominance.[5] Through its institutions and administrative apparatuses, the state plays a central role in organizing the conditions for hegemony.[6] State policies and programs offer resources for both hegemonic dominance and counter-hegemonic struggles. By accepting and lobbying for state funding, feminist and multicultural groups face the dilemma of negotiating between co-optation and the need for resources. While these contradictory effects have been recognized by feminist analysts, less recognized is their effect in structuring relations among social movements. Elsewhere in this chapter we offer a closer analysis of state mediation of the feminist movement's political culture. Here we wish to draw the link between hegemonic nationalism and state actions by showing how state mediation establishes parameters around multiculturalism and feminism as separate policy fields.

State policies and programs help to divide issues, groups, and individuals into separate fields for policy treatment. Through different institutional discourses, bureaucracies, and administrative structures, state policies and programs reinforce and perpetuate assumptions that multiculturalism and feminism are two different arenas of political struggle. State intervention into the feminist movement has contributed to its failure to create alliances with parallel struggles, such as those undertaken by racialized and ethnicized women who attempt to engage with multiculturalism as official government policy and as social reality. State intervention reinforces already existing cultural assumptions concerning Anglo-Canadian nationalism that have been inculcated into the consciousness of movement members. These assumptions are found in the principles, philosophies, political strategies, and actions of the organizations making up the feminist movement.

A view of the nation imagined as naturally white, male, Christian, middle and upper class, English-speaking, British, and, more recently, Northern European in cultural heritage is now more or less synonymous with the idea of 'Canadianess.' We use the term 'hegemonic nationalism' to describe this dominant view. The term 'non-national' refers to an analytical framework and a set of practices that is critical of 'Anglo-Canadianness' as the one 'true,' 'natural,' universal, and foundational national identity of Canada. A non-national analytical framework makes problematic the assumption that the universal basis for Canadian national identity should be Englishness – unproblematically referred to in the media as 'English-speaking Canada.' But it does not imply an ontological stance outside of nationalism. The consciousness of feminist activists and scholars, including the authors', is also shaped by nationalistic discourses and practices. However, feminists can develop a position from which to critique hegemonic nationalism as a structuring dynamic by engaging in the everyday struggles of racialized and ethnicized women and others who stand outside the idealized Anglo-Canadian identity. Feminists can also draw upon personal marginalized and submerged identities in order to critically examine the effects of hegemonic nationalism on their consciousness and practice.

A non-nationalistic framework rejects a conception of Anglo-Canadianness as the inevitable outcome of coherent intentions that are objectively knowable; rather, Anglo-Canadianness is seen as socially constructed, historically emergent, and open to change in response to, among other dynamics, hegemonic and counter-hegemonic struggles over national identity formation. Questioning the present territorial division between the multicultural and feminist movements in Canada entails departing from a functional analysis that takes the division between the two movements as a 'function' of naturally different interests. Using a non-nationalistic framework, we ask why, despite their similar political goals, the two movements are politically separated and isolated. We posit that multiculturalism and feminism are, in fact, linked. There are several reasons for this claim. They both challenge questions of identity, representation, equality, and justice. They both address issues surrounding identity categories and practices of representation. As 'new social movements' they both counterpose a politics of transformation based solely on 'class.' Both movements advocate more equal distribution of opportunities in order to achieve the ideals of liberal democracy. Although these are not separate issues, one movement challenges practices of representation by questioning how 'woman' is constructed as different from 'man,' while the other questions why some groups are considered 'ethnic' and 'raced' and others are not. Despite similarities and intersections in their goals, the feminist and multicultural/anti-racist movements have as yet failed to locate their emergence and, more important, their mutual distancing within the context of state-organized, hegemonic nation-building.

At present, the feminist movement in Canada has only narrowly addressed multicultural concerns. The national feminist organization in Canada, NAC, has focused on anti-racism within its own political organizations as a result of challenges by racialized and ethnicized women to the dominance of white, middle-class, Christian, English-speaking women, but it has not addressed other multicultural concerns (Gottlieb; Vickers, Rankin, and Appelle 1993, 166-7). Anglo-Canadian nationalism helps to structure a myopic view of multiculturalism as a feminist political issue. This has prevented feminists from recognizing that women's cultural labour is mediated by the state in the interests of hegemonic nation formation and that racialized and ethnicized women are engaged in important cultural resistance to hegemonic nationalism through their engagements with official multicultural policies and programs.

Anglo-Canadian nationalism within the feminist movement has led to a truncated political agenda and flawed strategies for change. We argue that political strategies and visions of possibilities for political action in the feminist movement have been contained and constrained within a nationalistic discursive formation that frames what is taken up, and what is not taken up, as central issues. There is an urgent need for feminist activists to fully recognize how this process of inculcation takes place as well as its effects on feminist strategies for change. An imperial feminism cannot continue unchallenged if the feminist movement is to achieve its goal of equality and justice for all.

The responsibility for developing a dialogue across social movements does not, however, lie solely with feminist activists. Multicultural and other movement activists need to consider how to integrate a feminist perspective into their analyses, discourses, and practices so that a mutually informed dialogue becomes possible.[7] Failure to do so will continue the exclusion and blindness toward, for example, racialized and ethnicized women engaged in the work of 'non-national' cultural production. Racialized and ethnicized women who undertake so-called 'heritage,' 'ethnic,' or 'multi' cultural production and reproduction in the family and/or community have been ignored and excluded from the agendas of both feminist and multicultural movements as a consequence of unacknowledged masculinist and 'nationalistic' assumptions. This oversight has led to a misrecognition of racialized and ethnicized women's participation in official government multicultural programs. Their participation in government multicultural programs is not without political agency, as is generally thought; rather, we must understand their participation as a form of democratic resistance to hegemonic nationalism.

Multiculturalism is often seen to be a policy for immigrants, refugees, and 'ethnics' – in other words, those who stand outside of the imagined nation. Mainstream feminism's absorption of this view is reflected in the generally unproblematic use of the terms 'visible minority women,' 'immigrant women,' and 'refugee women' to describe marginalized women. But according to many cultural critics of nationalism (see Gilroy; Goldberg 1990, 1993), the ongoing unproblematic use of categories based on citizenship continues the same historical projects of power and domination as do colonialism and imperialism. A continuing unproblematized use of citizenship categories and discourses based on assumptions of national belongingness helps to support hegemonic strategies of nation-building. Categories such as 'visible minority,' 'Third World,' 'immigrant,' 'non-English-speaking,' and so on are based on cultural, racial, ethnic, linguistic, and other markers that are socially constructed as meaningful in the course of nation formation.

By using a non-nationalistic framework, our analyses uncover and acknowledge the work of cultural resistance undertaken by racialized and ethnicized women. At present, their contributions and struggles are invisible in the platforms and on the agendas of the two social movements. Furthermore, their struggles in the multicultural sphere demonstrate the artificiality of the gulf between feminist and multicultural activists – an artificiality that has resulted in an inability to 'see' the struggles and 'hear' the voices of women engaged in making a multicultural nation a reality. Most Canadian feminists have failed to recognize the extent to which official government multicultural policies are a feminist issue because they do not understand the gendered basis of multicultural policies and programs. The fact that this lacuna has gone unrecognized for so long is evidence of the extent to which hegemonic conceptions of the nation have been absorbed into the Canadian women's movement. The lack of recognition of multiculturalism as a feminist issue feeds into tactics employed by neo-conservatives to maintain the dominance of Anglo-Canadian nationalism. Recognizing nationalism as a structuring dynamic allows feminists to respond to neo-conservatives who have attempted to locate 'Canadian' nationalism outside of multiculturalism and feminism and to position feminist and multicultural advocates as 'enemies' of the nation. Movement activists have been subjected to dismissal as disloyal, unpatriotic, dangerous, and destructive of 'our' nation. This 'othering' justifies the exclusion of feminist and multicultural groups from meaningful discussions in reshaping the cultural and material content of the nation. The logic that leads to defining feminists and multiculturalists as not 'Canadian' must be refused. This mode of thinking ultimately abandons discourses about 'the nation' to the Right, who define the nation in their own image as a means of retaining power and authority. But feminists need to do more than simply reject neo-conservative discourses. This, in itself, will not shift the discourse onto more productive grounds. Feminists must first recognize the Trojan horse of 'Canadian' nationalism.

Neo-conservatives incorrectly portray multicultural and women's movements as standing outside and against nationalism. They argue that official multiculturalism prevents the formation of a unifying Canadian identity because it nurtures an excessive tribalistic identification with 'ethnic roots' among 'those' ethnics. Neo-conservatives also see feminism's demands for recognition of 'difference' as destroying the possibility of realizing a universal and universalizing citizenship that disregards differences. In contrast, we argue that multiculturalism and feminism are locatable not *outside* but *inside* a hegemonic 'Canadian' nation-building project for two reasons. First, the meanings, problems, and possibilities considered legitimate for political action are *already* situated and framed within a 'nationalistic' master narrative. We must remember that the women's movement in Canada emerged within an already existing geographical, political, and cultural space imagined first as British and then, begrudgingly, as French. The second reason follows directly from the first. It is simply that assumptions of Anglo-Canadianness as natural and given have been internalized and naturalized within the minds of actors as well as the political culture of the women's movement. This double lack of consciousness with regard to its inherent Anglo-Canadianness helps to explain why neo-conservatives have so easily subverted the transformative possibilities of the feminist movement.

One example of this dictum is the present fragmented 'politics of difference' – a politics that has been delimited and shaped by Anglo-Canadian national hegemony. Current preoccupations with and confusions over the 'politics of difference' impede the development of a pluralist politics of citizenship because disputes over authority and authenticity prevent the feminist and multicultural movements from addressing issues of power redistribution and conflict. These movements have been territorialized by the state, which keeps them focused on interior concerns, leaving their frontiers and boundaries assumed and unexamined. It has resulted in divisions among community groups, issues, campaigns, and so on. Questions concerning how, whose, and which issues appear on which 'terrain of struggle' can only be fully answered if state mediation is taken into account. Why do issues concerning so-called 'ethnic' identity 'belong' to the multicultural movement, while women's lives and experiences and gendered and sexualized identities 'belong' to the feminist movement? Uncritical acceptance of such boundaries results in ethnicized and racialized women occupying the sidelines of political agendas. A case in point is the impossibility of discussing, at this particular historical moment, a critical multicultural feminist politics.[8] An understanding of racialized women's struggles in the multicultural arena will help to broaden feminist political action by making clear how the dynamics of hegemonic nationalism operate as a structuring dynamic of gender, race, and ethnic inequality.

Rethinking Nationalism and Feminism

The conceptual tools available through social scientific discourse have also helped to obscure the effects of state-organized hegemonic nationalism. Until recently, nationalism was thought of as an evolutionary stage of development through which all politically organized territories would ultimately pass. The European model of politically unified nation-states was viewed as the highest, most advanced stage of political organization. Conceptually, nationalism was seen as an abstract construct and an ideology of peoplehood. From a positivistic perspective, nationalism was thought to exist as an objective reality out there, knowable by comparing a political unit to preexisting and predefined attributes. Ideas of nationalism have been deconstructed and denaturalized by many authors (see Hobsbawm 1983, 1990; Anderson; Gilroy; Yuval-Davis and Anthias). These writers argue that nationalism is a liberal modernist project arising out of the humanist, enlightenment philosophies and European imperial projects of the eighteenth and nineteenth centuries. Nationalism's rise was coterminous with the ascendancy of European colonization and racism (Amin). Nationalistic discourses allowed the European groups in the eighteenth and nineteenth centuries to claim universal dominance over the colonized others. In the Anglo-European world, nationalism led to exclusion and marking the 'other' as inferior. Political struggles for equality meant equality among other Anglo-Europeans, not with or for the colonized 'others.' A consciousness of 'us-ness,' of common citizenship, was used to unify 'the people' against those constituted as 'other.' Citizenship in the nation was analyzed in terms of access to universal rights. But recently, the concept of citizenship has also been rethought. The myth of a universal citizenship equally available to all citizens has been contradicted by the reality that citizenship categories are used to regulate the boundaries between 'us' and 'them.' The concept of citizenship has been reformulated in terms of categories of identities and linked to nationalism, which deploys race, gender, ethnic, linguistic, cultural, and other markers to classify and organize peoples into different hierarchically structured categories of citizenship, thereby justifying and allowing for differential treatment of groups seen as 'non-national.'[9]

Paradoxically, the birth of the nation has been linked to the emergence of democratic politics, individual rights, equality, and 'fraternity' (Anderson; Gauchet; Touraine; Schappner). Nationalism is a phenomenon linked fundamentally with the emergence of liberal-democratic regimes. Democracy was intended to be pluralist by virtue of its rejection of a former politics of unity. But liberal democracy has also failed to achieve its promise largely because of the compromises in democratic principles of pluralistic representation demanded by nationalistic discourses of universalism founded on a single, common, and masculinist identity of belongingness. Therefore, what needs to be addressed more fully when analyzing nationalism is the contradiction between democratic ideals of pluralism and state-organized nationalism based on unity and universalism. Democratic nationalism claims the power to unify disparate groups into a single unity, but in reality it involves a new form of politics. In Canada, democratic nationalism was inspired by an Anglo-Saxon state project of unilingual and homogeneous nation-building concerned, first, with status in the British Empire and, second, with geographic consolidation and anti-Americanism (see Miller). This tradition of nation-building formed the ground from which the Canadian feminist movement emerged.

Feminism in Canada remains a largely institutionalized form of politics, well integrated into the day-to-day functioning of the state and its bureaucracy (Findlay; Pal 1993). As the principle organizer of hegemony, the state employs explicit policies to ensure the conditions for hegemonic dominance (Breuilly). To achieve this purpose, the state funds and supports community-based organizations. Through its funding programs, the state can and does intervene and mediate the politics of grassroots women's and multicultural groups. But the nature of state mediation shifts and changes over time in response to multiple determinations. Recent events in the 1990s illustrate the tenuousness of the state's commitment to the feminist movement. Although the feminist movement, through NAC, was involved in the recent constitutional debates at Charlottetown and Meech Lake and contributed to the development of the Charter of Rights and Freedoms, the state still moved to reduce its financial commitments to support women's organizations. After almost a decade of state funding support, the Liberal government's 1995 budget abolished some important government services for women. Across Canada, conservative and socialist provincial governments facing economic pressures eliminated or severely restricted programs and services to women, workers, the poor, and racialized and linguistic minorities. The failure of the women's movement to defend its gains against drastic cuts by a previously sympathetic state can be linked to its political culture, which identifies 'national' crises as its own. This self-identification with 'national' concerns occludes its perception of other issues. The feminist movement's participation in national constitutional fora precisely when the restructuring of global capitalism was having devastating effects on women's lives demonstrates the extent to which state-organized hegemony mediates the Canadian women's movement. These actions prompt a questioning of the so-called 'gains' of the women's movement; their fragility signals a need to seriously reexamine the movement's political culture.

Today, the Canadian women's movement is fragmented. It has had the illusion of strength because of constitutional guarantees and a strong institutionalization of feminist politics (Vickers 1992; Findlay). Moreover, it has developed neither a complex, radically pluralized strategy nor an organizational structure capable of going beyond a narrow agenda delimited by feminist national 'elites.' Many of these elites adopt a celebratory view of Canadian feminism. For example, Sylvia Bashevkin (1994) claims the women's movement in Canada was able to resist neo-conservative politics because of the strength of its politics and its organizational structure. But it is precisely these elites who, despite their rhetoric, are unwilling to address the privileges conferred by an Anglo-Canadian nationalism constructed upon a British/European colonial heritage (Bannerji; Carty 1993).

It is in this context that present political strategies of inclusion need to be examined. Inclusion strategies have been adopted by many Canadian feminist groups, ranging from NAC to the Canadian Research Institute for the Advancement of Women (CRIAW) to the National Organization for Immigrant and Visible Minority Women (NOIVM). Inclusion strategies have been promoted in an attempt to unify a movement now fragmented around the 'politics of difference,' but they have only reinforced fragmentation. Whether they be in the form of employment equity, affirmative action, or other types of programs, they fail to question the context in which identity categories have been produced as meaningful. Strategies of inclusion are not inherently transformative. When implemented on their own, these strategies leave the structuring institutional dynamics of inequality untouched, while they reinforce hierarchical categories of difference. The failure of inclusion strategies to bring about equality is, in part, an effect of an underlying norm of Anglo-Canadianess in the feminist movement's political culture.

The call of 'unity in diversity,' identical to the nationalist call, is centred in the experiences of mainly white, Anglo-Saxon, European women. Ethnocentric liberal feminists have invoked a universal model contiguous with hegemonic nationalism as a means of promoting unity in feminist politics. They thus reinforce their role at the centre of power while articulating a political strategy that claims to achieve the opposite. Universalism based on the notion of 'sisterhood,' or solidarity, keeps white, European women as the norm to which others must conform. This strategy has opened only limited space for marginalized women's political struggles to attempt to decentre the power of those who have defined the political agenda of the Canadian women's movement in their own image. These political struggles have proven incapable of generating an alternative to a liberal form of pluralism that ignores power and inequality. We now examine feminist experiences with strategies of inclusion to demonstrate the ineffectiveness of a politics located within the liberal pluralist framework of Anglo-Canadian nationalism.

Strategies of Inclusion or Oppressive Inclusion?

Strategies of inclusion bear closer examination because feminists have adopted them to increase democratic participation within their own organizations as well as in the wider public arena. Underlying many well-meaning attempts to increase representation in feminist organizations is the dogma of 'inclusion.' However, the desire to include necessarily focuses on 'differences,' those so-called 'objective,' observable characteristics that allow individuals to be slotted into their respective categorical containers for administrative treatment. Inclusion transfers attention onto those who 'need' to be included and away from practices of exclusion. Responsibility for 'absence' is shifted onto those 'not here.' Actual exclusionary practices that need to be identified, named, and dismantled remain untouched.

The biggest problem with affirmative action programs based on categories of group identity and 'quotaism' is that they pit one group against another. Inclusion has been defined in a limited way to mean the numerical inclusion of individuals as members of categories of difference and the establishment of quotas for categorical differences. Filling quotas replaces real, meaningful change. 'Quotaism' has produced painful competition among those whom the strategy of inclusion was designed to assist (see Charbursky; Abella). Based on the concept of 'categorical difference,' the strategy of 'inclusion' may have helped some individuals, in some specific institutional contexts – for example, white, middle-class, able-bodied women in the world of employment (see Cuneo; Fudge and McDermott).

But its greater legacy has been to obscure ongoing practices of exclusion and subordination by reproducing common-sense notions of the 'realness' of race and gender categories, thereby leaving these initiatives open to racist, sexist attacks (Cuneo, 156-61). The strategy of inclusion has relativized and trivialized differences by taking for granted different categories of women: immigrant, refugee, Third World, black, migrant, Asian, First Nations, and so on. How these categories are produced as meaningful is seldom questioned. They are assumed and seen as self-evident. By not recognizing hierarchies in categorical difference, strategies of inclusion contribute to the erasure of inequality by pluralizing differences and ignoring power and resource differentials.

At the level of implementation, another dynamic operates. Individuals with decision-making powers are able to avoid personal responsibility by delegating day-to-day management to 'the administrative system.' But the administrative system alone is not able to make strategies of inclusion work as they were intended to because these systems were constructed on the sedimented accumulation of earlier historical practices and logics of exclusion. Under the guise of 'simplicity,' 'efficiency,' and 'objectivity,' administrative routines perpetuate practices of inequality through everyday practices. There are also the deliberate efforts on the part of employers to circumvent the principles of equity programs. Employers circumvent, manipulate, and avoid the legislative requirements around equity programs with seeming impunity and often with implicit support from government officials (Cuneo). In Canadian jurisdictions where there is equity legislation, it is so weakened and compromised by 'negotiations' that these laws fail to achieve equity in either wages or jobs (Cuneo; Fudge and McDermott). Political strategies of inclusion exist as a means of 'buying' off the feminist and multicultural movements without disrupting existing arrangements. Programs are designed to assist employers and not those most in need. These programs serve to satisfy well-meaning people until the next round of challenges and resistance from excluded individuals and groups. At present, under quotaism and categoricalism, individuals from underrepresented groups are prevented from being whole, complex persons because the administrative system reminds them that their presence is categorical in origin. In advocating inclusion strategies, women wanted equality. What we obtained is, at best, an administrative system to manage differences.[10] Within feminist political organizations and other organizations, affirmative action, employment, education, and other equity initiatives have resulted in conflict and divisiveness.

The dynamics of 'quotaism' in affirmative action programs warrant closer examination still. When quotas, explicit or implicit, are established on the bases of so-called 'natural' distributions of particular characteristics in the wider population, the absence of individuals holding these characteristics can then be subjected to 'scientific' management techniques that remove these issues from the political domain. A numerical threshold is established for a 'category,' and the problem of absence can be managed by the administrative system, which is responsible for enumerating and tracking the numbers of people belonging to a specific category. The category is now taken as a real and meaningful concept that 'stands in' for the population (see Rutherford). 'Success' in many programs implemented to achieve inclusion is measured through the 'filling' of categories. Categoricalism supplants real, meaningful change. Structural practices of exclusion can be ignored. In advocating for inclusion, Canadian liberal feminists have merely reproduced assumptions regarding the meaningfulness of categories derived from nationalist, imperialist, and colonialist thought.[11] The irony is that under the authoritative protection of multiculturalism and feminism, the political strategy of 'inclusion' has become another system of race and gender classification. As Foucault might have observed, the political strategy of 'inclusion' has been transformed into a technology of disciplinary power. The strategy of inclusion has resulted in 'quotaism' and 'categoricalism,' neither of which challenges the reproduction of national categories of citizenship and identity as the basis for signifying 'difference.' The liberatory potential of multiculturalism and feminism is thus reinscribed within a nationalist framework. Liberal-democratic nationalism reestablishes the centre by appeals to unity and consensus. Liberal discourses that encourage inclusion 'do not adequately theorize "oppressive inclusion" and tend to interpret "inclusion" as a sign of "fairness" and "equality"' (Dhaliwal, 43). Without a reflective understanding of these dynamics, we argue, feminist and multicultural strategies will fail to achieve their ideals. The politics of inclusion must be problematized because

> the privileging of inclusion politics does not account for the ways inclusion can still oppress or fail to alter structures of domination. The inability of radical democratic inclusion politics to deal with inclusion retaining peripheralization is a key limitation, especially given that, in many liberal democratic societies, many democratic groups have been 'included' by being accorded certain formal rights like the right to vote. If inclusionary attempts often reaffirm a 'hegemonic core to which the margins are added without any significant destabilization of that core' or continue to valourize the very centre that is problematic to begin with, then it is clear that the motivation to include needs questioning. (Dhaliwal, 43)

Dhaliwal's insights can be applied to the Canadian feminist movement, which emerged historically as an exclusionary movement dominated by Anglo women (Vickers, Rankin, and Appelle). Women from Anglo-Canadian backgrounds continue to form the core of the women's movement in Canada, and this situation has remained more or less unchanged despite attempts by marginalized women to destabilize it. To further understand the resilience of this hegemonic core, we must examine the feminist movement's institutionalization in the state. Engagement with the state helps to maintain Anglo-Canadian hegemony, partly because hegemonic conceptions of the nation already underlie government policies, and partly because these assumptions penetrate into the heart of women's organizations through contractual and administrative requirements attached to funding programs.

Nationalism and State Policy

Anglo-Canadian nationalism mediates and shapes government policies and state agents' views of feminism and multiculturalism as different fields for policy treatment. This bicameral perspective allows the state to be structurally selective in its deployment of strategies to reinforce 'common sense' boundaries of difference. State policies may be implicit or explicit in operationalizing assumptions of national cultural identity. Very often these strategies are disguised so as not to undermine the hegemonic construction of Anglo-Canadian nationalism as 'true,' 'natural,' and rooted in a foundational moment of history. Among the most obvious examples of cultural identity formation through national policies are cultural, education, official language, citizenship, immigration, women's, and multicultural policies. Their common concern with citizenship formation is not merely ideological or symbolic; it takes material form through everyday documents, procedures, regulations, administrative practices, and so on. Bureaucratic routines are not devoid of political content. Indeed, it is through everyday, administrative routines and procedures that hegemonic assumptions of Anglo-Canadian identity are transmitted as normal, natural, and perennial by innumerable state agents.

For example, the bureaucracy established to manage the federal government's multicultural and women's programs can be traced to the federal Nationalities Branch of the Department of the Secretary of State, which was created during the Second World War. This branch was established to address the federal government's concern with resident 'aliens.' In this period, it was believed that Anglo-Britishness, as the basis for national identity, was being threatened. The need for citizens to support the war effort prompted the government to develop specific programs to foster loyalty and patriotism (Pal 1993). After 1945 the Citizenship Branch took responsibility for these programs, and the administrative routines developed during that period, along with their nationalist assumptions about unity and assimilation, persist in today's Department of Secretary of State programs, which provide funding to multicultural, women's, and official minority language programs. Pal (1993) argues that current federal women's and multicultural programs and policies continue to be framed around issues of identity, citizenship, and national unity. Anglo-Britishness as the core of Canadian national identity is the silent partner of state funding programs.

The implicit hegemonic assumptions of national identity underlying government multicultural policies amplify Homi Bhabha's comments on the problematic endorsement of cultural diversity:

> Although there is always an entertainment and encouragement of cultural diversity, there is always also a corresponding containment of it. A transparent norm is constituted, a norm given by the host society or dominant culture, which says that 'these cultures are fine, but we must be able to locate them within our own grid.' This is what I mean by a *creation* of cultural diversity and a *containment* of cultural difference. The second problem is ... that in societies where multiculturalism is encouraged racism is still rampant in various forms. This is because the universalism that paradoxically permits diversity masks ethnocentric norms, values and interests. (208)

The Gendered Bases of Multicultural Policy

Although Bhabha's observations are helpful in unmasking ethnocentric universalism and racism in Western celebrations of cultural diversity, they fail to uncover the close relationship between multiculturalism and gender. Gender is central to Canadian multicultural policy. From its inception, the principles, practices, and policies of multiculturalism were gendered, ethnicized, and racialized, but the liberalism inherent in multicultural principles and practices have obscured the origins of their construction. The liberal tenet of 'choice' suggests that minority ethnic individuals should be free to *choose* to 'preserve' their cultural practices in the family and the community if they so wish. In a liberal democracy such as Canada, this principle results in the state expressing support for 'non-national' 'ethnic' practices, while simultaneously reasserting so-called 'national' cultural practices as fundamental, natural, and core. This is achieved through multicultural polices that perpetuate the relegation of so-called 'ethnic' cultural practices to the 'private' sphere of community and family life, where they usually become the responsibility of women.[12] The liberal myth of free choice hides the serious implications of state organized liberal multiculturalism for racialized and ethnicized women. It is they who carry the burden of transforming Canada into a multicultural nation at the level of everyday practice under official multicultural policy.

The omission of gender in current debates about multiculturalism dismisses and devalues women's roles in producing identities through cultural practices, but, more important, it also fails to acknowledge their role in destabilizing the hegemonic core of Canadian nationalism. In their roles as mothers and volunteers, 'ethnic' minority women pose a potential threat to hegemonic conceptions of citizen identities and nationalism by making available 'other' bases for identity formation through transmitting 'ethnic' cultural knowledge, language, and skills to children. The field study used in this chapter, and conducted in Prairieville,[13] Saskatchewan, found that the state responds to multiple demands such as those arising from nationalism, trade globalization, and community-based resistance in contradictory ways (Lee). These often conflicting demands result in policies and programs that structure unequal opportunities for racialized and ethnicized women. Government policies and programs work to segregate, divide, and hierarchically organize women into different categories depending upon their perceived value to the nation.

The study concluded that the occupational distinctions of 'mother,' 'community volunteer,' and 'teacher' – normally taken as given – are, in fact, socially constructed through state boundary regulating processes that employ language, culture, ethnicity, race, and national origin as markers of difference. Government policies and programs do not differentiate women's cultural labour simply on the objective grounds of demographic prevalence of language or ethnic background. Certain world or trade languages, regardless of their minority status, are deemed to be in the national interest and, therefore, worthy of increased government support and a place in the formal education system. However, very few languages, no more than five or six, fall into this category. The majority of languages are left to the ethnic groups themselves to support, primarily through women's cultural labour in the 'private sphere.'

Therefore, the widely held assumption that 'non-official,' 'non-national' languages and cultures should be transmitted by ethnic and racial minority women who are 'mothers' and 'community volunteers,' while official languages and national cultures should be transmitted in schools by 'teachers' (preferably indigenous to the national culture) who have undergone extensive training needs to be critically reexamined. Feminists need to question the popular belief that the state-supported education system should pay wages to teachers who transmit the 'national' culture, whereas the teaching of 'ethnic' culture should be relegated to community-based, non-profit, voluntary organizations in which (mainly) women teach as unpaid volunteers. Failure to consider the cultural content of occupational categories means that mechanisms of nationalistic boundary positioning (between mothering and teaching, for example) remain undertheorized.[14] Teaching and mothering, as sets of activities, cannot be unproblematically counterposed as separate and autonomous. The content of one defines the content of the other. The roles of mothering and teaching must be viewed as socially constructed, at least partly, in the interests of hegemonic nationalism. We argue that taking these distinctions as 'normal' obscures the reality that all women do cultural work and that whether they do it as teachers, volunteers, or mothers is determined by the state.

The two case studies that follow illustrate some of the tactics used to maintain the cultural boundaries between 'national' and 'non-national' as well as women's responses to these tactics. Cultural practices are effected in and through women's lives, and minority ethnicized and racialized women's bodies have become critical sites for regulating the cultural boundaries of the nation. State policies and hegemonic nationalism regulate the appearance and non-appearance of 'non-national' women and their cultural practices to particular places, spaces, and times that are located outside of formal, mainstream, institutional sites. From the perspective of those who stand outside the national community, the multicultural myth of 'choice' is often experienced as containment. Multicultural policy is more than symbolic: its material effects are primarily experienced by women who shoulder the responsibility of transmitting cultural practices in the 'private' sphere of community and family.

One of the most effective mechanisms of regulation found in the Saskatchewan field study was the use of credentialling to exclude racialized and ethnicized women from mainstream educational institutions. Credentials were marked by national origin. Agencies such as the Ministry of Education, professional bodies, and local school boards viewed teaching credentials acquired outside of Canada, especially if they were from developing countries, with suspicion. Foreign credentials were rarely recognized as equivalent to Canadian credentials.[15] Another exclusionary tactic signified non-official minority languages as 'not academically worthy' of inclusion in the officially sanctioned curriculum. This judgment helped to justify treating the speakers, teachers, and students of minority languages as inferior, illegitimate, and unimportant (see Skutnabb-Kangas). The perceived inferior status and 'non-official' status of minority languages also justified relegating non-official language instruction to surplus schools and after-hour access to public school buildings. The heritage language schools were 'confined' to one wing of the school building so that they would not 'disrupt' the rest of the school. Treating these cultural practices as 'second class' reinforced the resentment felt by some regular classroom teachers over having to share their classrooms with 'those ethnics.' Many racist assumptions underlie complaints by teachers and janitors about the behaviour of children from certain (non-European) language schools.

Language was not only the object of regulation, it was also a technique of regulation. Heritage language teachers were required to read and write in English before they were allowed to enrol in a university and community-sponsored heritage language certificate program meant to improve their skills in teaching heritage languages. Since many teachers were immigrant women who could not speak English fluently, the majority of heritage language teachers had to enrol in ESL (English as a Second Language) classes before they could participate in a heritage language certification program offered by the university. Institutional processes ensured that women's suspected non-national consciousness was further mediated by teaching them about 'Canadian' methods and principles of curriculum development, classroom management techniques, timetabling and scheduling, and other forms of student control.[16] These examples demonstrate that racialized and ethnicized women's engagements with government multicultural programs must be understood as occurring not only within a liberal context of individual choice vis-à-vis the preservation of an ethnic heritage, but also within a context of subordination. At stake are children's subject identities and their formation within a hegemonic national culture. The state is concerned with who, what, when, where, and how the national subject identities in children are shaped, and for what purposes.

Yet feminist theorizing and activism around mothering has rarely integrated an understanding of ethnic practices in the context of nation formation. Mothering as a form of cultural work concerned with shaping collective and individual identities has been overlooked (Collins). Viewing racial and ethnic minority women as cultural workers helps to reveal the relationships between mothering and teaching and how they are related to discourses and practices of nationalism. By examining minority ethnic and racialized women's participation in multicultural programs through the lens of nationalism, the significance of their engagement with government multicultural programs becomes much clearer. Too often, writers have overlooked minority women's efforts to expand the cultural boundaries of the nation. Their participation in multicultural programs should not be interpreted as co-optation or naivité. Racial and ethnic minority groups may be able to work from within multicultural programs to resist the erasures of 'other' identities. Women participate in these programs not only to assist 'cultural preservation,' but also to build stable individual and community identities for themselves, their children, and their 'new' and developing communities. In organizing the material conditions for minority ethnic language and cultural transmission, women support collective identities of community and nurture individual identities (Collins). Organizing skills are developed and networks are established. From these bases, racialized communities are better able to resist racism and marginalization in mainstream Canadian society. Participants in multicultural programs are involved in reshaping the nation by working concretely to enlarge the cultural resources through which the nation is imagined.

Michiko's Story

The first case study taken from the larger Saskatchewan field study, that of a Japanese language teacher named Michiko, illustrates how state multicultural policies shape women's lives. Michiko's occupational roles shifted as her labour moved through different state-constructed categories of representation determined by differing demands on the nation-state. As the ability to speak Japanese became more valuable through trade globalization, the state moved to incorporate Japanese language instruction into the 'public' sphere of formal schooling. When the Japanese language began to be viewed as a 'human resource skill' to be learned to enhance skills for global economic competitiveness and not merely as an ethnic heritage language to be preserved for cultural purposes, Michiko's occupational category changed from mother, to volunteer, to community organizer, to heritage language teacher, and finally to teacher in a public high school. Depending on where the state positioned the boundaries between public and private, formal and informal, and national and non-national, Michiko was inserted into different categories of representation. For example, the categories of heritage language volunteer or paid teacher should not be taken as a given, but need to be understood within a broader context of the state's interest in regulating the cultural content of work. When her cultural labour was considered to be of little value to the nation, it was seen as 'volunteer work' and was not considered to be legitimate. Michiko received no professional recognition and financial compensation for her work until the state determined that learning Japanese was in the 'national' interest. At that point, only after a series of cultural transformations and local political struggle, did she enter into the formal education system as a regular teacher (although she continued to fill an 'ethnic' category). Her professional qualifications had not substantially changed, although she had received a certificate from the university to teach heritage languages.[17] What had changed was the school board's perception of the value of Japanese to 'national' development. Michiko's experiences demonstrate that women's lives are affected by shifting cultural boundaries of inclusion and exclusion in the nation.

Michiko's story, and those of many other women, serve to illuminate the point that racial and ethnic minority women's voluntary, unpaid participation in community-based heritage language programs should not be taken for granted. The category of 'heritage language teacher' is socially produced within the context of nation formation.[18] Multicultural policies reinforce, naturalize, and normalize existing assumptions about nationalism and gender. Such nation-building strategies have racializing and gendering effects because they not only mark boundaries of difference but also mark boundaries of value and worth. They help to construct hierarchies of difference.

The Swahili Language School

The second case study, that of the Swahili language school in Prairieville, illustrates racialized and ethnicized women's creative resistance to hegemonic nationalism through engagement in multicultural programs as well as the need to de-territorialize feminism and multiculturalism. Although multicultural policies have regulatory effects, they also provide a space of possibility for those who transmit minority languages and cultures. The women who were observed in the Swahili language school used the resources made available through multicultural programs for transformative purposes. Their attempts to create positive identities through heritage language education can be understood as a form of resistance to the erasure of a linguistic base for identity formation. Moreover, their efforts demonstrate important differences among women who taught European languages and those who taught non-European languages.

In the minds of the parent group who began the Swahili language school, the available cultural models of Afro-Canadian and Afro-American identities were seen to be contaminated with traces of racism. The North American concept of 'black' was not an identity they wanted to adopt. They did not identify with blackness based on skin colour, since some families were Ismailli Muslim who identified themselves as African rather than 'black' in the North American sense of the word. Blackness as a form of identity did not reflect an African identity that would fit their collective experiences. They deliberately chose to construct a 'new' African-centred identity that reflected the heterogeneity of their community. Their motherwork involved creating and devising new cultural ways of living, speaking, and interacting that were inclusive and capable of bridging the huge cultural differences of life in Canada and memories of a life in Africa – a life that their children might never directly experience. By working together on an 'identity-building community project,' they were nurturing a more secure self-identity for themselves and their children. They attempted to build a more stable community within which a new and evolving cultural identity could flourish. As mothers/teachers/volunteers/organizers doing cultural work, these women were inventing and creating new cultural content. They were not simply reliving or recreating an ethnic past in Canada; they were trying to find a balance across cultures, ethnicities, and languages. They were doing the cultural and political work of building new structures and practices that recognize multinational and multilocational realities.

White, European, ethnic minority mothers, on the other hand, seemed to be interested in teaching their 'home' language as a prevention, an inoculation against forgetting. For these women, the multicultural discourse of preservation of cultural heritage and learning the language for a healthy self-identity seemed to work quite well. For racialized, non-

European, non-white mothers, the reasons for teaching language were more complicated. Teaching the 'home' language was not simply a means of guarding against forgetting one's cultural heritage but also a form of defence against the negative effects of societal racism. For racialized women, motherwork as cultural work included reconciling contradictory needs concerning identity, 'finding a balance,' and preparing children to cope with and survive within systems of racial oppression. Not only did women involved in the Swahili language school address issues of marginalization in Canadian national culture, they also confronted nationalisms arising out of their colonial past in East Africa. Parents' choice of language for identity construction was a strategic political decision. Swahili was selected, despite its checkered past linked to the slave trade and colonization, for the same reason it was chosen in East African nations as an official, national language – its usefulness in building a sense of solidarity and mobilizing people around a common sense of community. As a trading language it was the vernacular language of the marketplace, widely spoken and understood. By strategically selecting Swahili over any one family's tribal language, parents in the Swahili language school demonstrated their concern with organizing and mobilizing individuals around a new sense of community.[19]

Mainstream feminists need to understand that racialized and ethnicized minority women do not necessarily all have the same investments in multiculturalism. Women's investments in ethnic cultural heritage preservation differ depending on different trajectories of incorporation into the nation and different demands made on cultural and linguistic practices. The two case studies discussed here, though limited, demonstrate that the conceptions of teaching, mothering, and motherwork that have dominated explanatory frameworks of teaching, family, and mothering have been based on an idealized middle and upper middle class, white, English-speaking, Canadian national identity. Clearly, when examining the activities of teachers and mothers outside of this narrow range, what constitutes mothering and teaching work, and other forms of 'reproductive labour' for racial and ethnic minority women, goes beyond the physical and emotional care of one's biological children or family network to include community-building and expanding the cultural bases of nation formation (Glenn).

Reprise: Toward a Framework for a Non-Nationalistic Feminist, Multicultural Politics in a Multinational Space

In closing, we wish to address the possibility of a 'non-nationalistic,' multicultural, feminist politics that recognizes the changing multinational context of Canada. It seems clear from the case studies that dominant forms of nationalism do not disappear when groups relocate to Canada; rather, traces of earlier hegemonic nationalisms from other times and other places intersect and collide with dominant Anglo-Canadian nationalism as well as with other contending nationalisms. It seems futile, given our analysis, either to envision a future without nationalisms or to consider shedding one's constructed national identity in order to put on a new one. Therefore, feminism must embrace the cultural construction of citizen identities and national identity as feminist issues because nationalizing forces are central to understanding women's lives. This means placing nationalism and multiculturalism more centrally on the feminist movement's political agenda. It will require the Canadian feminist movement to become more aware of its own hegemonic assumptions around Canadian nationalism. At present, the women's movement, as a nationally organized social movement, is structured to exclude the lives, concerns, acts of resistance, and will to survive of subaltern groups. Ignoring the consequences of an uncritical and unconscious internalization of nationalistic assumptions within its political cultures will continue to hinder the transformative potential of feminism.

Several findings arise from our application of a non-national analytical framework to the boundary-making dynamics that delimit the 'feminist' terrain of struggle. We have shown that gender is presupposed in the process of constructing citizen's national identities through nationalistic tactics that deploy race, ethnicity, national origin, and language as cultural markers of difference. By examining the logics and practices of exclusion through ethnicized and racialized minority women's lives, the gendering of multiculturalism is exposed, making it no longer possible to conceive of feminism and multiculturalism as inherently separate terrains of political struggle. Another important finding is that feminist conceptual understandings of resistance must be reformulated to include the non-national cultural work of racialized and ethnicized women. We have also shown that the lives of these women must be accorded analytical and theoretical significance. Once this is done, it becomes possible to see how a politics based on nationalized, categorical 'difference' denies minority women the opportunity to live full, complex lives as transnational and multinational hybrid subjects. A politics claiming cultural diversity without simultaneously addressing inequality and power will necessarily be reinscribed into dominant forms of nationalism. Thus, feminist and multicultural politics must integrate an analysis of nationalism as a unifying, homogenizing force that destroys difference and diversity and that precedes democratic movements.

This is an urgent project if we are to move beyond present models of oppression based on the 'colonial' model of the oppressor and the oppressed, and the 'transgression model' of oppression and resistance, and toward a model of articulation or 'transformative practice.' Present models of oppression are inappropriate to contemporary relations of power.

Moreover, they are incapable of creating alliances 'because they cannot tell us how to interpolate fractions of the "empowered" into the struggle for change in something other than a masochistic (guilt-ridden) way' (Grossberg, 95).

Finally, returning to the argument that feminism and multiculturalism threaten national unity, what is really threatened is a hegemonic form of Anglo-Canadian nationalism that sees itself as the only true, natural, and superior basis for nation formation. The full transformative potential of this challenge can only be realized if multicultural and feminist movements shift to a 'non-nationalistic' model of politics. It will require acknowledging that individuals hold multiple national identities; that the myth of British identity and Canada's position in the British Empire as the country's pre-eminent historical tradition of nation formation needs to be dismantled; and that it is impossible to objectively assign individuals into gendered, ethnicized, linguicized, and racialized categories around which democratic oppositional struggles are to be organized. Even the current politics of 'multiple intersecting differences' is only a partial basis for a politics of transformation. Old approaches remain mired in an acceptance of categorical differences shaped by larger forces.

A 'non-nationalistic' form of politics will require confronting the effects of 'pathological' nationalism in state-organized policies. Such a politics would no longer be founded on the fear of the 'other' or even the need to construct 'otherness' as the basis of commonality. As the lives of transnational, ethnicized, and racialized women show, nationalism, as a mode of subjectification linked to relations of power, is not always oppressive and subordinating (as it is in dominant Anglo-Canadian nationalism's treatment of its competitors). It can also be potentially liberating and oppositional (as when it is used to oppose the subordinating practices of hegemonic nationalisms). Democratic movements seeking to achieve diversity and equality must take up this challenge and understand the relations of power operating through nationalism as a dynamic structuring force.

To conclude, the Canadian feminist movement has failed to fully recognize its emergence on a nationalist terrain and to interrogate the influence of hegemonic nationalism on its political culture. Moreover, the continuing silence of the feminist movement around multiculturalism has resulted in a truncated agenda for political action and a misrecognition of minority women's engagements in multicultural programs.[20] There is an urgent need for feminists to develop a more critical and self-reflective awareness of the mediating effects of nation formation, Canadian or other, on our praxis. A conjoined politics of equality/inequality and diversity/difference is possible. Such a 'non-nationalistic' politics requires feminism and multiculturalism to acknowledge both their embeddedness and emergence within the politics of nationalism. Until multiculturalism and feminism as political movements understand their location within the metanarrative of a totalizing and dominating Anglo-Canadian nationalism, their full transformative potential will remain unrealized.

Acknowledgments
An earlier version of this chapter was presented at the Canadian Women's Studies Association Annual Meeting in June 1995, at the Learned Societies Meetings at the Université du Québec à Montréal, by Linda Cardinal and Jo-Anne Lee. The ideas discussed in this chapter arise out of an ongoing intellectual collaboration between Linda Cardinal and Jo-Anne Lee. As the senior author of this essay, Jo-Anne Lee takes responsibility for any errors and omissions. She would like to acknowledge the support and many conversations about this issue with Nayyar Javed, Christine Lwanga, and Kathryn Poethig.

Notes

1 In the United States, multiculturalism is an umbrella discourse around pluralism and diversity. There is no official government policy on multiculturalism. However, in Canada there has been an official multiculturalism policy since 1971. Although its emphasis has shifted several times, a state bureaucracy is firmly in place to manage funding to community organizations, research and publication programs, consultative committees, and other programs.

2 Nationalism has always been an important structuring force in Canada. From its European inception in the 1800s until today, nationalism, both in English and French Canada, has influenced the way in which individuals were formed as citizens. It has meant, until the 1960s, assimilating into a white Anglo-Saxon model of a homogeneous society, which at times accommodated some demands from the French-Canadian group – as long as it did not unduly disrupt the British colonial lineage as the 'natural' cultural and historical birthright of Canadians. Anti-Americanism has also been deployed to strengthen and defend this narrative of nationalism. For a deeper discussion of the roots of Canadian nationalism, see D. Francis and D. Smith, in particular the chapter by J.R. Miller. See also Ramsey Cook.

3 Neo-conservative attacks constantly shift and take new forms. Some of the shifting loci include attacks on the abortion rights movement, gay and lesbian rights, immigration, affirmative action, multiculturalism, and feminism. Neo-conservatives are also proactive in pushing patriarchal family values, Christian fundamentalism, and European/British cultural heritage as 'national' issues.

4 See Backhouse and Flaherty for a discussion of the dynamics underlying the rise of the contemporary women's movement in Canada. See especially the chapters by C. Backhouse and J. Vickers, and Part 4, 'Racism and the Women's Movement.'

5 I use the term 'the state' to refer to a complex formation including all levels of government, institutions and agencies, policies, procedures, and regulations as well as state agents who initiate, implement, manage, and represent the state. My use of this short-hand term is not meant to imply a monolithic cohesive entity that acts with logic and coherence. The state is also historically emergent, changing, contested, and a site of struggle.

6 Nationalism has been incorporated into state policies since the formation of the nation, but especially since the period of J.A. Macdonald (in the form of the National Policy). Historians identify the period between 1890 and 1920 as the period of nation formation. Lee shows how nationalism operated in the development of an English-only common schooling system in Saskatchewan.

7 We are not advocating the merging of two separate movements into one fully integrated, collective struggle or a single, unified, collective, political organization; rather, we are problematizing the extent to which this territorial separation should be assumed as 'natural' and the effects of this separation on political strategies for change.

8   This is not unique to Canada and/or Canadian experiences.

9   Feminist authors have examined how nationalism is inherently gendered and gendering (Yuval-Davis and Anthias; Ng). Gilroy has noted that race is used to form nationalism and national identity among citizens. Roxanna Ng has argued that seeing race, gender, and class as *relations* allows an analysis of how racism and sexism were deployed to subordinate particular groups of people in the colonization of Canada and in the development of the Canadian nation-state.

10 Eyraud et al. conclude, in an overview of pay equity programs in fifteen countries, that although pay equity programs have made some progress in reducing wage disparities they have relied on legislative enforcement. The complex process of bringing in and enforcing legislation with many social actors produces very weak, compromised results that favour employers. Fudge and McDermott caution activists about the complexity of pay equity processes. Cuneo documents other reasons for less than satisfactory results, including the inclination of employers to interpret, manipulate, and take advantage of loopholes in regulations to avoid paying for wage discrepancies. Many writers note that pay equity strategies are principally concerned with gender inequities; they do not address race-based or race/gender-based inequality. Indeed, as Fudge and McDermott note, there is not even adequate statistical data available to document a race/gender wage gap.

11 See Balibar's discussion on the modernity of democracy and the rise of racism and nationalism and their interrelations within modernity.

12 Although there were community-sponsored ethnic language schools in existence prior to 1978, when the government instituted a program to support community-sponsored 'heritage' language teaching, there was a dramatic increase in the number of these schools. At this time the government introduced the name 'heritage' to describe this field of activity. See Lee for a further discussion of the implications of naming this field of activity 'heritage' language teaching.

13 This is an invented name used to protect the identity of those individuals involved in the case studies.

14 There is a rich conversation about mothering, but in this chapter we are concerned with the cultural content of mothering and the intersection of race, gender, and mothering. For other discussions see Ruddick. Also see O'Barr, Pope, and Wyer.

15 See Wotherspoon for a discussion of how credentials and foreign qualifications were used to control the teaching force at earlier periods of Canadian national development.

16 See Gaskell and McLaren's book on Canadian women and education. Except for one article on minority women teachers by Roxanna Ng, Gaskell and McLaren's book ignores how race, ethnicity, and language structure women's experiences in teaching as a form of cultural transmission.

17 The heritage language certificate was developed by the Prairieville Multilingual School Association to upgrade the skills of heritage language teachers, many of whom had no formal background in teaching. It was also developed as a way of providing support to heritage language teachers and as a way to increase the legitimacy of this marginalized activity. Although the university offered university-level credits for the courses, under pressure from the multilingual school association and other multicultural groups, the university would not permit these credits to be used toward a regular degree program in teaching; yet another example of how 'the centre' remains centred.

18 As we have previously argued, the cultural work of women is organized by the state in the context of nationalism and citizenship (Glenn; Yuval-Davis and Anthias 1993; and Juteau-Lee). In reality, the burden of transmitting by themselves the ethnic or home language is beyond the ability of most parents. Statistics Canada data show that ethnic languages generally decline past the second or third generation (Canada RCBB 1970; Bourbeau). There are some notable exceptions, but these languages belong to ethnic groups that still enjoy strong immigration. Clearly, then, language transmission is only one of several reasons racial and ethnic minority women remain involved in heritage language education.

19 Only one parent could teach Swahili, as none of the other parents had been educated in that language. But because she was unavailable to teach in the school, parents hired two

teenagers who had been educated in Swahili in Tanzania. Although parents tried to see this as an opportunity for the children, it was clear that language learning was not the primary objective of the language school and that there were many problems related to hiring youthful, inexperienced teens as teachers.

20 Some of the issues that could be advanced collaboratively include several ethnic groups' claims for redress and apology for past discrimination and mistreatment, media racism, and issues around racism and violence. The women's movement could also begin analyzing the discriminatory gender and race effects of multicultural policies that are based on the logic that 'national' cultural practices are different from 'heritage' or 'ethnic' cultural practices.

Works Cited

Abella, R. 1984. *Report of the Commission on Equality in Employment.* Ottawa: Supply and Services

Amin, S. 1989. *Eurocentrism.* Trans. R. Moore. New York: Monthly Review

Anderson, B. 1983. *Imagined Communities.* London: Verso

Backhouse, C. 1992. 'The Contemporary Women's Movements in Canada and the United States: An introduction.' In C. Backhouse and D.H. Flaherty, eds., *Challenging Times: The Women's Movement in Canada and the United States,* 3-20. Montreal and Kingston: McGill-Queen's University Press

Backhouse, C., and Flaherty, D.H., eds. 1992. *Challenging Times: The Women's Movement in Canada and the United States.* Montreal and Kingston: McGill-Queen's University Press

Balibar, E. 1991. 'Racism and Nationalism.' In E. Balibar and I. Wallerstein, eds., *Race, Nation and Class: Ambiguous Identities,* 37-68. London: Verso

Bannerji, H., ed. 1993. *Returning the Gaze: Essays on Racism, Feminism and Politics.* Toronto: Sister Vision

Bashevkin, S. 1994. 'Confronting Neo-Conservatism: Anglo-American Women's Movements under Thatcher, Reagan and Mulroney.' *International Political Science Review* 15 (3):275-96

Bhabha, H. 1990. 'The Third Space: Interview with Homi Bhabha.' In J. Rutherford, ed., *Identity: Community, Culture, Difference,* 207-21. London: Lawrence and Wishart

Bissoondath, N. 1994. *Selling Illusions: The Cult of Multiculturalism in Canada.* Toronto: Penguin

Bourbeau, R. 1989. *Canada: A Linguistic Profile.* Ottawa: Supply and Services

Breuilly, J. 1993. *Nationalism and the State.* 2nd ed. Chicago: University of Chicago Press

Cardinal, L., and Lee, J. 1995. 'Feminism, Nationalism and Citizenship Policies in Canada.' Paper presented at the Canadian Women Studies Association Annual Meetings in June 1995, at the Université du Québec à Montréal

Carty, L., ed. 1993. *And Still We Rise: Feminist Political Mobilizing in Contemporary Canada.* Toronto: Women's Press

Charbursky, L. 1992. 'The Employment Equity Act: An Examination of Its Employment and Direction.' *Revue de droit d'Ottawa* 24 (1992):305-65

Collins, P.H. 1994. 'Shifting The Center: Race, Class, And Feminist Theorizing about Motherhood.' In E.N. Glenn, G. Chang, and L.R. Forcey, eds., *Mothering: Ideology, Experience and Agency,* 45-66. New York: Routledge

Cook, R. 1977. *The Maple Leaf Forever: Essays on Nationalism and Politics in Canada.* Toronto: Macmillan

Cuneo, C.J. 1990. *Pay Equity: The Labour-Feminist Challenge.* Toronto: Oxford University Press

Dhaliwal, A. 1994. 'Reading Diaspora.' *Socialist Review* 4 (24):13-43

Eyraud, F. et al. 1993. *Equal Pay Protection in Industrialised Market Economies: In Search of Greater Effectiveness.* Geneva: International Labour Office

Findlay, S. 1988. 'Feminist struggles with the Canadian state.' *Resources for Feminist Research* 17 (3):5-9

Francis, D., and D. Smith, eds. 1986. *Readings in Canadian History: Post Confederation.* 2nd ed. Toronto: Holt Rinehart and Winston

Fudge, J., and P. McDermott. 1991. *Just Wages: A Feminist Assessment of Pay Equity.*

Toronto: University of Toronto Press

Gairdner, W.D. 1991. *The Trouble with Canada*. Toronto: General Paperbacks

Gaskell, J., and A.T. McLaren, eds., 1991. *Women and Education*. 2nd ed. Calgary: Detselig

Gauchet, M. 1993. 'Le mal démocratique.' *Esprit* (novembre):67-89

Gilroy, P. 1987. *There Ain't No Black in the Union Jack*. London: Hutchinson

Glenn, E.N. 1994. 'Social Constructions of Mothering.' In E.N. Glenn et al., eds., *Mothering: Ideology, Experience and Agency*, 1-32. New York: Routledge

Goldberg, D.T., ed. 1990. *Anatomy of Racism*. Minneapolis: University of Minnesota Press

–. 1993. *Racist Culture: Philosophy and the Politics of Meaning*. Oxford: Blackwell

Gottlieb, A. 1993. 'What About Us? Organizing Inclusively in the National Action Committee on the Status of Women.' In L. Carty, ed., *And Still We Rise: Feminist Political Organizing in Contemporary Canada*, 371-86. Toronto: Women's Press

Gramsci, A. 1971. *Selections from the Prison Notebooks*. Q. Hoare and G. Nowell Smith, eds., and trans. London: Lawrence and Wishart

Grossberg, L. 1993. 'Cultural Studies and/in New Worlds.' In C. McCarthy and W. Crichlow, eds., *Race, Identity and Representation in Education*, 89-108. New York and London: Routledge

Hobsbawm, E. 1983. 'Introduction: Inventing Traditions.' In E. Hobsbawm and T. Ranger, eds., *The Invention of Tradition*, 1-14. Cambridge: Cambridge University Press

–. 1990. *Nations and Nationalism since 1780*. (Canto ed.) New York: Cambridge University Press

Hobsbawm, E.J., and T. Ranger, eds. 1983. *The Invention of Tradition*. Cambridge: Cambridge University Press

Juteau-Lee, D. 1979. 'The Evolution of Nationalism in Quebec.' In J.L. Elliot, ed., *Two Nations, Many Cultures*, 60-74. Scarborough, ON: Prentice-Hall

Lee, J. 1996. 'Constructing the Nation Through Multiculturalism, Language and Gender: An Extended Case Study of State Regulation and Community Resistance.' PhD dissertation, University of Saskatchewan, Saskatoon

Miller, J.R. 1986. 'Unity and Diversity, the Canadian Experience: From Confederation to the First World War.' In D. Francis and D. Smith, eds., *Readings in Canadian History: Post Confederation*. 2nd ed., 147-56. Toronto: Holt Rinehart and Winston

Ng, R. 1989. 'Sexism, Racism and Canadian Nationalism.' In J. Vorst et al., eds., *Race, Class, Gender: Bonds and Barriers*, 10-29. Toronto/Winnipeg: Between the Lines/Society for Socialist Studies

O'Barr, J., O. Pope, and M. Wyer. 1990. *Ties that Bind: Essays on Mothering and Patriarchy*. Chicago: University of Chicago Press

Pal, L. 1989. 'Identity, Citizenship And Mobilization: The Nationalities Branch and World War Two.' *Canadian Public Administration* 32 (3):407-26

–. 1993. *Interests of the State: The Politics of Language, Multiculturalism and Feminism in Canada*. Montreal, Quebec: McGill-Queen's University Press

Ruddick, S. 1990. *Maternal Thinking: Towards A Politics of Peace*. New York: Ballantine

Rutherford, J. 1990. *Identity, Community, Culture, Difference*. London: Lawrence and Wishart

Schappner, D. 1994. *La communauté des citoyens*. Paris: Gallimard

Skuttnab-Kangas, T. 1990. *Language, Literacy and Minorities*. London: Minority Rights Group

Touraine, A. 1994. *Qu'est-ce que la démocratie?* Paris: Fayard

Vickers, J. 1992. 'The Intellectual Origins of the Women's Movement in Canada.' In C. Backhouse and D.H. Flaherty, eds., *Challenging Times: The Women's Movement in Canada and the United States*, 39-60. Montreal and Kingston: McGill-Queen's University Press

Vickers, J., P. Rankin, and C. Appelle. 1993. *Politics as if Women Mattered*. Toronto: University of Toronto Press

Wotherspoon, T. 1989. 'Immigration and the Production of a Teaching Force: Policy Implications for Education and Labour.' *International Migration* 27 (4):543-62

Yuval-Davis, N., and F. Anthias, eds. 1989. *Woman-Nation-State*. New York: St. Martin's

Constructing Nation:
The Gendering and Racializing of the Canadian Health Care System

Joan Anderson and Sheryl Reimer Kirkham

On 17 June 1996, a headline in the *Vancouver Sun*, 'Women's group elects black leader' (A3), announced Joan Grant-Cummings as the newly elected president of the National Action Committee on the Status of Women (NAC). Grant-Cummings, who has declared her commitment to social justice, is the executive director of the Women's Health in Women's Hands Community Health Centre in Toronto. Her aim is to make NAC more relevant to 'minority' women; she is promising to lobby against the contributors to poor health among women: poor housing, high unemployment, and violence against women (*Vancouver Sun*, 17 June 1996, A3). This news story is noteworthy for at least two reasons. First, it alerts us to issues that are centre stage in Canada. Why, one might ask, is the election of a 'black woman' as president of a national committee seen as newsworthy in a country committed to multiculturalism? We suspect that the election of a white woman would have been seen as natural. That the rise of a black woman to a position of leadership is seen as newsworthy informs us of the ways in which the construction of Canada is raced (and how the construction of gender is raced) and points to fundamental contradictions in Canadian society. A society that espouses multiculturalism treats as extraordinary the inclusion of people of Colour in so-called positions of power and privilege. What is the meaning of multiculturalism, we might ask, in a country that has always defined itself in terms of 'Two Founding Peoples'?

This news story also highlights the factors that influence the health of Canadian women. It is to these two issues – the racing and gendering of Canada and the issue of health as located within a gendered, classed, and raced society – that we turn attention in this chapter. We focus, in particular, on Canada's health system, recognizing that, in so doing, the influences on health, such as poor housing and high unemployment, will not receive our full attention. This is not an oversight; rather, these issues, while they cannot be separated from the discourse on health, deserve separate attention.

We need to be aware that the construction of Canada's health care system is not an entity in itself; it is enmeshed in a racialized and gendered construction of nation and the capitalist world-view that organizes women's everyday lives. In other words, the health care system cannot be neatly separated from broader social, economic, and political contexts. Canada's health care system is one of the best in the world, yet there are fundamental contradictions in our health system (and in our society, in general) that are inextricably intertwined with the construction of nation. We want to unmask some of these contradictions; through this process we hope to reflect on some of the issues that are often glossed over but that are pivotal in the lives of people.

The expectation that people should be self-sufficient and resilient in the management of their own care is deeply embedded in the ideological frameworks that underpin the construction of the Canadian nation (Anderson 1990). The ideologies of egalitarianism and individualism result in the assumption that all citizens have an equal opportunity to achieve optimum health because all have equal access to health care services. Thus, a level playing field is assumed and individuals are seen as being largely independent of social constraints. The ideologies of individualism and egalitarianism make it easier for those charged with providing resources for preventive health services to consistently avoid examining the sociostructural impediments to maintaining and protecting people's health (Alonzo). These ideologies, then, lead to a rhetoric of equality, even in the face of inequities and discrepant policy statements.

Crichton points out that social policies in Canada, though having similar historical roots in Britain and Australia, have emerged differently because of different resources as well as different environmental and social pressures. Nonetheless, the 1601 Poor Law legislation in Britain guided social welfare provision in that country and its colonies for the next three centuries insofar as people were expected to help themselves to survive and to seek out family and community resources if they could not manage by themselves (160, 161). The notion that equal opportunity is available to all, and that individual effort is responsible for success (Li), is as much a part of the ideology of health care as it is a part of the ideology of other institutions, and it leads to contradictions between what may be seen as a problem and what is proposed as a solution. For example, now that equity and the social determinants of health have become entrenched in the discourse of governments, documents such as *Achieving Health for All: A Framework for Health Promotion* (Canada 1986) state emphatically that reducing inequities is the first challenge we face. We are told there is disturbing evidence that, 'despite Canada's superior health services system, people's health remains directly related to their economic status' (Canada 1986, 4). Low-income people, including older people, single women supporting children, and people from 'minority groups' (such as Aboriginal people and immigrants), we are told, face health problems and risks that high-income people do not face. 'Poverty affects over half of single parent families, the overwhelming majority of them headed by women. These are the groups for whom "longer life but worsening health" is a stark reality' (Canada 1986, 4). Yet, in the very same document we are told that to meet the challenge of reducing inequities, we must have health promotion mechanisms such as self-care:

> We believe that the three *mechanisms* intrinsic to health promotion are:
> - self-care, or the decisions and actions individuals take in the interest of their own health;
> - mutual aid, or the actions people take to help each other cope; and
> - healthy environments, or the creation of conditions and surroundings conducive to health (7).

We are told that the public sector and others are already engaged in encouraging people to care for themselves (9). At one level, then, issues of poverty are seen as a challenge to health; however, the solutions that follow do not seem to recognize the measures that would be necessary to alleviate poverty; namely, ways of redistributing wealth and the role of governments in this process.

In order to understand these contradictions, we begin by providing a brief outline of the evolution of Canada's health care system and the social forces that have contributed to the construction of a Canadian health care system that is raced, classed, and gendered. We go on to examine the factors that have sustained systemic inequity by drawing attention to the disjuncture between the discourses of the state and the actual practices in health care institutions. We argue that these disjunctures are located in the historical construction of Canada and the notion of two founding peoples, which has produced the politics of exclusion in our institutions. These exclusionary practices, sometimes invisible, influence the lives of those who are marginalized in profound ways.

Next we discuss the competing discourses on multiculturalism, culture, and ethnicity. We believe that these discourses have unwittingly produced stereotypic notions that have essentialized and marginalized groups that have already been marginalized, and have reinforced the construction of Canada as white and Eurocentric. We conclude by pondering directions for the future, and we advocate the production of transformative knowledge from a critical feminist and anti-racist perspective to inform health and social policy. This kind of knowledge, we believe, will allow for an examination of structural inequities that transcend the health care system and will provide the basis for praxis within Canada's health care system that extends toward the broader social system.

Evolving Health Care System: Constructing Nation

Robert Evans, one of Canada's leading health care economists, makes the point that health care systems reflect the cultural values and the status of individuals within nations. As such, a health care system is a product of a country's history and culture. We would argue that, not only is a health care system a product of a country's history and culture, but it is also instrumental in constructing nation by shaping identities and experiences, institutions and policies, oppressions and inequities. Thus, an examination of the history of the Canadian health care system reveals the dialectical evolution of nation and health care system. It is not within the scope of this chapter to discuss the entire history of Canada or the health care system; instead, we point to several key examples that illustrate the constructing of nation and health care system as racialized and gendered.

Frideres observes that many social scientists have rejected the colonial analysis as misleading because Canada's social and political patterns are different from those experienced by colonized peoples in Africa and India. Nonetheless, he maintains that the indigenous peoples of Canada were unquestionably colonized and that their position in Canada today is a direct result of this colonization process. This period of colonization was crucial in constructing the indigenous peoples of Canada as savage, other, and inferior, and it had disastrous effects on their health, beginning with early pandemic infectious diseases (such as smallpox and typhus brought by European explorers and settlers) and continuing to today's higher morbidity and mortality rates.

The colonization and othering of Aboriginal peoples demonstrates the iterative process of constructing a vision of 'native' that carries devastating influences on their health and that, in turn, reinforces stereotypical ideas of Aboriginal peoples. Today, these populations are marginalized in a health care system that appears unable to deal with their complex health problems and often resorts to stereotyping and victim-blaming.

The practice of othering Aboriginal populations also extended to othering immigrants coming into Canada. Immigrants were needed to fill the vast spaces, to provide labour for the building of the railway, and to farm the land; they were recruited from China, India, and Eastern Europe. Both British and French-Canadians, critical of immigration policies that allowed in people whom they regarded as foreigners, made efforts to establish themselves at the head of a racial and cultural hierarchy in the new land (Whittaker). Immigrant labourers were discouraged from becoming permanent citizens of Canada through various means, such as the head tax on Chinese labourers and a prohibition against them bringing their wives and families into Canada. Immigration policies became increasingly exclusionary during the early part of the twentieth century on the grounds of physical and medical disability. Medical and character examinations of entrants were often a cover for ethnic discrimination (Whittaker). Policies demonstrating the explicit preference for white immigrants continued with regulations enacted in 1956 that established a hierarchy of 'most-to-least-welcome' national origins. These overtly racist policies were replaced in the 1960s with legislation that ranked potential immigrants according to criteria such as education, skills, and resources. The point system, while appearing to make immigration policy more equitable, in effect continued to prevent poorer immigrants from gaining entry. Today's immigration program, which favours people from the business class, could similarly be understood as being classist.

The theme of a gendered health care system and nation is further exemplified by considering who has provided the majority of health care throughout the years. Early government health care services were limited to care for the insane, lepers, and orphans, and to public health measures, including public health laws and quarantines, during epidemics (Di Marco and Storch). Social problems were handled by families, the church, or by local government. By and large, women carried the responsibility for health care, providing care and medicines for their families. This practice of women providing health care has been maintained throughout Canadian history, both in family settings and in formalized health care. For example, the recent *Closer to Home* health reform policies (British Columbia 1991) have resulted in women providing an increasing amount of health care to their families, often without the support of community services.

Along with these practices of othering Aboriginal peoples and immigrants and the provision of care by women, a third issue in tracing the gendering and racializing of the health care system is that of the dominance of biomedicine, a largely patriarchal system, in the establishment of health institutions and policies. The emergence of scientific medicine in the first half of the twentieth century was critical in influencing the construction of Canada's health care system. Until the early 1900s, health care had been seen as both curative and preventative, and the origin of disease was generally understood to be multifactorial (Waitzkin). Among the most important factors in causation were the material conditions of people's everyday lives.

In 1910, the esteemed Flexner report, *Medical Education in the United States and Canada*, was published. One underlying assumption of the report was that scientific medicine, oriented especially to teaching the biological basis of disease, produced a higher quality and more effective medical practice. Although the comparative effectiveness of various medical traditions (including homeopathy, traditional folk healing, chiropractic, and so forth) had never been subjected to systematic testing, the report argued that medical schools not oriented to scientific medicine fostered mistreatment of the public in the form of quackery. The uncritical support of the report by the medical profession and large private philanthropies contributed to its widespread influence (Waitzkin).

Several other developments followed to entrench the dominance of biomedicine within the health care system. The breakthroughs and expansion of diagnostic and therapeutic capabilities between the 1920s and 1950s (e.g., antibiotics, surgical technique, radiology, and laboratory analysis) focused attention on curative, interventive aspects of disease treatment rather than on prevention. Legislation also reinforced the place of biomedicine; the federal Hospital Insurance and Diagnostic Services Act, 1957, made publicly funded hospital care a reality. The sequence of hospital insurance preceding other forms of health insurance firmly established the physician's practice around the hospital bed. Services and diagnostic services formerly provided in a physician's office now took place in hospitals, where they were publicly funded (Armstrong and Armstrong). Thus, through a complex interplay of legislation, the influence of key stakeholders, and scientific advancements in an era of commitment to empiricism, the dominance of biomedicine was established. The predominantly male medical profession was 'expert' in diagnosing and treating disease, while nurses (women) took on the subservient 'assistant to physician' role.

The pre-eminence of biomedicine and the dominance of physicians played a central role in the establishment of Medicare, the system of public health insurance in Canada. Although a publicly funded health system would not be implemented until the 1960s, the notion had been a part of Canadian consciousness for a long time. Interestingly, as early as 1919, Mackenzie King began lobbying for a national, publicly insured health care system. The Rowell-Sirois Commission, known as the Royal Commission on Dominion-Provincial Relations, commissioned in 1937 by the government of Prime Minister Mackenzie King to clarify federal and provincial jurisdictions, recommended that the provinces take basic responsibility for matters of health while Dominion involvement should be the exception rather that the rule (Canada, 1940). During this time, several proposed health insurance bills at federal and provincial levels were defeated, typically due to opposition from physicians, insurance companies, and manufacturing associations. Finally, Saskatchewan, under the leadership of Tommy Douglas, established the first universal public health insurance plan in 1947. Other provinces followed by developing similar plans, which they found difficult to finance from provincial revenues alone (Rachlis and Kushner). The responsibility for health was being carried by the provinces, but the majority of revenue came from the federal government. Pressure resulting from this discrepancy led to federal response in the form of the Hospital Insurance and Diagnostic Services Act, 1957. With this act, Ottawa agreed to pay for half the costs, while provinces had to meet the five criteria of comprehensiveness, accessibility, universality of coverage, public administration, and portability of benefits in order to qualify for funding.

The next step in the implementation of a national insurance program, the introduction of medical coverage, was controversial because physicians were opposed to government-sponsored insurance (Taylor). Once again, Saskatchewan took the lead in introducing a government-sponsored plan in 1962. Despite widespread public support for the plan, the majority of the province's physicians went on strike in an effort to maintain their autonomy. As part of the negotiations to end the strike, the provincial government abandoned the plan to put many doctors on salary and agreed to a fee-for-service payment scheme based on private practice and autonomy (Armstrong and Armstrong). Other provinces implemented voluntary medical insurance plans, and then, in 1966, the federal government enacted the Medical Care Bill. Once again, the federal government promised to pay half of provincial expenditures on the understanding that the conditions of comprehensiveness, universality, portability, and public administration be met. In 1984, Ottawa passed the Canada Health Act in response to concerns over the erosion of Medicare through user charges. This act reaffirmed the basic principles of the earlier hospital insurance and diagnostic services and medical care acts. More recently, revisions to the Established Programs Financing Act have reduced the transfer payments to the provinces, with significant ramifications for health care, involving health care reform, fiscal restraint, restructuring, and shifting care from the hospital to the community. This move has had far-reaching consequences for women, who are usually the primary caretakers, and for other groups who, for the reasons discussed below, are at a disadvantage in accessing resources that would alleviate the difficulties of caring for ill family members in the home.

The Rhetoric of Equality: Systemic Inequity and the Health System
Canada's Immigration Act, 1952, reflected earlier notions about who should constitute the Canadian nation and permitted the refusal of potential immigrants on the basis of their nationality and ethnicity. The Immigration Act, 1976, was meant to change these discriminatory practices and embodied principles of non-discrimination, family reunion, and humanitarian concern for refugees (Canada 1978). As the ethnic, racial, and cultural composition of the population changed over the ensuing years, Canada called for recognition of the cultures of different groups and the protection of the human rights of all individuals. We have, therefore, seen legislation such as the Multiculturalism Act passed in 1988, which 'commits the Government of Canada to assist communities and institutions in bringing about equal access and participation for all Canadians in the economic, social, cultural, and political life of the nation' (Canada

1991, 1). In 1960 the Canadian Bill of Rights, which is a constitutional document designed to protect the rights of all Canadians and to ensure equality of opportunity for all, laid the groundwork for the 1982 Canadian Charter of Rights and Freedoms. The Charter ensures 'equal protection and equal benefit of the law without discrimination and, in particular, without discrimination based on race, national or ethnic origin, colour, religion, sex, age or mental or physical disability' (s. 15(1)). In addition to federal legislation, there are provincial multiculturalism and human rights acts (e.g., British Columbia 1993a; British Columbia 1984; British Columbia 1993b).

Health legislation in Canada echoes some of the principles that are to be found in other legislation. For example, the principles of comprehensiveness, universality, and reasonable access to health services are key principles in the Canada Health Act, 1984. Canada appears to have ample legislation, both at the federal and provincial levels, to protect human rights and to ensure equality of opportunity and access to services, including health care services. Not only is Canada credited as having one of the best health care services in the world, but Canada's humanitarian services for immigrants and refugees have also been internationally recognized. In 1986, Canada was the recipient of the United Nations Nansen Award for humanitarian behaviour, for which the country can be rightfully proud.

Yet, it has been widely argued that there is a gap between the ideal and the reality, in particular, as noted by Li, between the multicultural ideal and institutional realities (9). Li has observed that 'despite a widely shared ideology of equality, which is best represented by the popular version of the mobility dream, social inequality remains well entrenched in Canadian society' (129), and he goes on to show the ways in which ethnic origin has been a source of inequality.

A gap is visible between different groups, not only in terms of the distribution of privileges within the wider society, but also within specific sectors, such as health care delivery. In fact, as noted earlier, government reports such as *Achieving Health for All: A Framework for Health Promotion* (1986) and the *Report of the British Columbia Royal Commission on Health Care and Costs* (1991) draw attention to inequities in health and systemic inequities and issues of accessibility in the health system. This latter report has provided the impetus for an extensive plan for health reform in the Province of British Columbia (British Columbia, 1993c), which is aimed at making the health system more equitable as well as more effective.

Yet, for health reform to work, we must go beyond recognizing that there is inequity to grasping the *historical factors* that have shaped our institutions, and we must rewrite our history to be more *inclusive* of all Canadians. Unless we *recognize* and *unmask* the unquestioned and taken-for-granted notions that are embedded in our institutions, health reform may build on the ideological structures that form the substratum of our current theorizing, policy decisions, and health care practices. Were this to happen, we would fail to address some of the very issues that might have been the impetus for health reform in the first place. The issues that underlie inequity need to be understood and addressed by governments and policy makers as well as by health professionals; they must form the background against which administrative and clinical decisions are made, practitioners educated, and programs of research implemented.

In this section, therefore, we want to interrogate the unspoken and implicit notions that are woven into the fabric of the Canadian state, that have shaped our health care institutions and the institutionalized practices within these institutions, and that have provided the lenses through which Canada has come to construct the multicultural other. We begin by arguing that the notion of 'two founding peoples' that has permeated the construction of Canada – a notion that is exclusive rather than inclusive – and that constructs as other those who are not of the so-called 'mainstream,' remains embedded within our institutions and organizes the ways in which health care systems are structured and priorities established. It is in the context of 'two founding peoples' that the concept of multiculturalism has come to be interpreted, even though the Multiculturalism Act is specific in referring to multiculturalism as an essential part of what it means to be Canadian. The dissonance between what might have been intended in the act and how it is interpreted may be due not to ambiguities in interpretation but, rather, to a fundamental ideology about who is 'Canadian' and who can rightfully be a Canadian.

As we have discussed at the beginning of this chapter, a theme that has been recurrent in Canada's nationalist thought is that of Canada as a northern country for a 'northern race' (Berger). 'The first coherent Canadian statement of the idea of the northern race,' Berger points out, 'came from an associate of the Canada First Movement ... Robert Grant Haliburton ... The peculiar characteristic of the new dominion, he asserted, "must ever be that it is a Northern country inhabited by the descendants of Northern races" (5, 6). Canada's immigration policies prior to the new Immigration Act (which was tabled before Parliament in 1976 and became law in 1978 [Canada 1978]), attest to the ways in which this notion of Canada was put into effect. According to Calliste, 'Race and gender ideologies were used to justify the ... domination, exclusion, and restriction of blacks and other people of colour, particularly women ... The ideology of racism ... perpetuated the belief that different racial and ethnic groups had inherent attributes which suited them to particular jobs' (138).

In writing about the history of the Chinese in Vancouver, Griffin has discussed the restrictions that were put on Chinese people coming into Canada, noting in particular the special head tax that was imposed on them and the legalized discrimination that was enforced (34). Several scholars have brought to our attention the dominant ideologies that underpin Canada's historical development, and they have explicated the ways in which gender, race, and class relations have shaped Canada's history (e.g., Li; Ng; Bannerji; Calliste).

Despite the Charter of Rights, and, in particular, Section 15, which speaks to equality rights of all Canadians, the notion (often implicit) that Canada is a northern country peopled by northern races still lingers, and it might be recalled that the Meech Lake Accord 'was premised ... on the notion that Canada consisted of two "founding peoples"' (Bliss, 16), thus excluding First Nations peoples and other groups who are not part of the 'two founding peoples.' Historians such as Bliss have argued for a renewal of our appreciation of the history of Canada, but as he points out, 'we must not do it at the cost of leaving out those Canadians who were excluded from old history' (16).

What is striking today is the invisibility of so-called 'visible minority groups' within the public arena in Canada. In commenting on this phenomenon, especially as it relates to the construction of scholarly work, Bannerji argues that this invisibility could lead readers and scholars elsewhere to conclude, from published evidence, that 'a) Canada does not or did not have a significant non-white population; or b) if they at all existed, women or (men) among them were/are incapable of writing or not significant enough to be written about; and c) understanding Canadian society is possible without any consideration of colonialism and (sexist) racism' (xiii).

It is this construction of Canada, and the absence and marginal positions of some groups within the so-called Canadian mosaic, that needs to be examined if we are to understand why some people do not find the health care system accessible to them. Whereas the need for recognition of different groups is voiced, the *fundamental structures* of society have not changed so as to be inclusive and representative of the different groups that make up Canada; and institutions, including health care institutions, remain Eurocentric and classist. If one asks 'Who is the health care system designed for?' it is likely that one would be told that the health care system is accessible to all; however, on closer scrutiny it becomes obvious that these institutions are, in fact, designed for middle-class Canadians who are fluent in English (in English-speaking Canada) and who have Euro-Canadian backgrounds. For, as noted in the *Report of the British Columbia Royal Commission on Health Care and Costs* (1991), 'many people of minority ethnic background are not using existing services because those services are not culturally responsive or *accessible* to them' (C-36).

Experiences Seeking Help

To explicate the ways in which the gendering and racing of health care institutions shape the experiences of women and people from racialized groups who seek help, we conducted a field research study with men and women who are both health care providers and users of health services.[1] We interviewed eight people who were involved with health and social agencies serving populations from different cultural backgrounds. To further elaborate upon the experiences of people who seek help, we draw upon other research studies that we have conducted over the past ten years with women from different ethnocultural communities, and with nurses, regarding the provision of intercultural health care (Anderson 1990, 1991, 1992, 1993; Anderson, Blue, and Lau; Anderson, Blue, Holbrook, and Ng; Anderson, Elfert, and Lai; Reimer; Reimer Kirkham).

In all of these studies we have been struck by the ways in which health care institutions announce themselves to their users as gendered, raced, and classed. Those who speak neither English nor French will find that basic communication between health care provider and patient is sometimes not possible because interpreter services that would make health care more accessible to non-English people (in English-speaking Canada) are sometimes lacking or inadequate. This leads to a situation in which cultural meanings and the everyday realities that have a profound impact on health and illness management are obscured.

There are other issues that make visible the classed, raced, and gendered construction of the health system. In some institutions, the scheduling of clinic hours makes it difficult for people from some groups to attend.[2] These are people who do not have the privilege of taking time off from work (with pay) to seek out health care services. Many immigrant people, women in particular, in the lower echelons of the workforce, who speak neither English nor French, have jobs in which they get paid for the actual hours worked. If they take time off from work to go to a clinic or to consult with a health professional, they do not get paid. Many cannot afford this loss of pay. Furthermore, some are hesitant to tell their employers about their health care problems and their need to go to a clinic for fear of losing their jobs (many of these women are without labour market protection and depend on their income to support themselves and their families). Many are taking care of small children and must coordinate responsibilities for home, child care, and job along with managing an illness. Getting to a clinic or a doctor's appointment becomes a major undertaking, especially when they are required to take an interpreter, who might be a family breadwinner, and who will also lose pay for taking time off from work. These issues all speak to the ways in which the health care system is organized to serve people from particular social groupings and to exclude those who cannot communicate in the dominant language and are in the lower echelons of the workforce, where time off means loss of pay or even loss of the job.

Even when women are able to attend a clinic and find someone to interpret for them, they may not receive the help they need. Instructional styles and materials may not be geared to these women. Their frameworks of meaning and interpretation may differ significantly from those of the health professionals who provide care to them and whose explanatory frameworks are usually steeped in the culture of Western biomedicine. Racial stereotypes may organize the ways in which health care providers interact with women, thereby erasing any possibility of mutual understanding. As this person puts it:

> People who are capable of the language will benefit the most, but people who can't manage the language may suffer from this system. And also the relationship between the professional and the patient is another issue. There's a lot of improvement needed in cross-cultural understanding in health professionals. I feel there are a lot of professional people, they have their own cultural superiority sense, and this has done a lot of harm to the relationship between the care people and people being cared ... Even though you are using the same kind of medicine, the same kind of prescriptions, the same kind of diagnosis, but if you have a different perspective from a certain culture you look down upon some patients, or you create some sort of feeling among the patient. You look superior. I dare not tell you some bad habit I have.

Another person in another interview puts the problem this way: 'I think that a fair number of people of colour communities perceive that they can't get decent health care from the dominant community because there's just so many things they perceive that the current medical model doesn't understand and accept.'

Organizational practices in the health care system reveal institutionalized ideas and stereotypes about 'race,' gender, power relations, and the eminence of biomedicine; they are not just matters of 'cultural insensitivity' on the part of health care providers. In fact, popularized notions of what it is to be culturally sensitive have not been without the pitfalls of using stereotypic cultural assumptions to interpret complex life issues (Anderson, Elfert, and Lai; Anderson 1990; Anderson, Blue, and Lau; Anderson, Blue, Holbrook, and Ng).

The structure of the health care system and the absence of resources, such as basic interpreter services, also have an effect on front-line health professionals, who are usually women (such as nurses, occupational therapists, physiotherapists) placed in the untenable situation of not being able to provide the care they believe their clients need. As women within these particular occupational categories, they seldom have a voice in health care decision making concerning the setting of priorities and the allocation of resources. Yet they must live with the decisions that are handed down to them and the stresses created when the resources available are inadequate to meet the demands of the workplace.

Health care institutions themselves are microcosms of a raced, classed, and gendered society. In hospitals most positions of power and privilege are occupied by white males, although males constitute less than 20 percent of paid health care workers (Sherwin). Although many people of Colour[3] are health care workers, they are relegated primarily to the non-professional ranks of cleaners, kitchen staff, porters, and so forth. There is increasing evidence of racism in professions such as nursing, whereby nurses of Colour experience various forms of discrimination on an ongoing daily basis and face considerable barriers to advancement (Das Gupta). Yet, even those health professionals who appear to be in decision-making positions experience structural constraints. As one physician with whom we have spoken puts it,

> It's not a health care system, it's a medical industry, and that's all it is. It's got some applications of some business principles but there is no sense of greater social responsibility or accountability and I guess part of the difficulty of all the health care professions – on one hand we have the medical professions having gone to the point of having the CMA code of ethics confirming that the role of the physician is to be the absolute advocate for the patient for everything. You have the cadre of bright, powerful people within the system who are there to advocate absolutely everything for the individual patient who are being challenged all the time to step away from that, and come to one or two or three steps back, to talk about ... what are the priorities that help us decide where we are going to spend the money or put the resources.

From what this physician has to say, one might argue that decisions about providing health care are not solely in the hands of physicians; instead, the practice of Western biomedicine needs to be seen in the context of a capitalist world system wherein the priorities that drive the larger economic system filter down into institutional practices (Baer, Singer, and Johnson; Navarro) and, in turn, determine what each health professional is able to do. In other words, priorities within the health care system at any given time must be understood within the complex system of economic and political relationships underpinned by Eurocentric assumptions and capitalist interests.

The Discourse on Multiculturalism, Ethnicity, and the Construction of the 'Other'

We argue, then, that even though the principles of multiculturalism have been articulated by governments in legislation, institutional structures have not changed to reflect these principles. Ideologies propagated within a Eurocentric and capitalist world-view continue to organize the processes and everyday operations of our institutions, including dictating the boundaries of professional practice. But our analysis cannot stop here. It would be naive to conclude that adhering to the principles of multiculturalism will ensure equitable health care to people from racialized groups. The concept of multiculturalism must itself be problematized.

'One difficulty with a concept of multiculturalism,' according to Margaret Lock, is that 'in establishing boundaries as to what exactly is a culture or an ethnic group ... a 19th century style of thinking is usually drawn upon in which nation states, or large regional areas, language, religion, and even skin color or other physical features are taken as the relevant immutable markers' (240). She goes on to discuss the ways in which people from a geographical region are often lumped together without regard for local conditions and intra-group differences.

Other scholars have raised questions about what exactly is meant by an ethnic group and whether people from a designated ethnic group would have a common culture. Li argues that 'there is no reason to believe that people of the same ethnic label necessarily come from a uniform culture. Indeed, whatever cultural homogeneity may have existed among different peoples of the world, the capitalist world-economy ... that has been operating since the sixteenth century has long transformed it ... There are substantial cultural diversities within an ethnic group, so much so that in many instances the *intra*-ethnic cultural variation is as great as the *inter*-ethnic one' (28-9).

Lumping people together into ethnic categories is not the only issue. People have also been lumped together into the more all-encompassing category of visible minorities, a term that has become a primary marker for those thus categorized while, at the same time, glossing over differences among people. Carty and Brand suggest that this term, developed by the Canadian state, 'is void of any race or class recognition and, more importantly, of class struggle or struggle against racism. It is therefore ahistorical and serves to reduce to meaninglessness the specific parts it purports to elevate' (169). Carty believes this term marginalizes people by erasing their different histories and cultures and their significance (18).

The present discourses of multiculturalism, ethnicity, visible minority, and the like overlook the social relations inherent in the production of these categories, mask the processes that determine people's experiences, and create stereotypes that keep people marginal and excluded. These stereotypes extend into what is assumed to be people's beliefs and practices concerning health and illness. Therefore, the difficulties that people encounter in accessing health care and in managing health and illness may be attributed to their cultures and to their difference from the 'mainstream.'

At least two things need to be considered. First, in our focus on culture and cultural sensitivity, there is a real risk of oversimplifying the concept of culture, with the concomitant cultural stereotypes that this produces. Second, while understanding the culture of the client is a crucial dimension of competent health care, it is only one aspect of the complex nexus in which people's experiences are located. When 'difference' is reduced to the culture of the individual or to ethnicity, the structural factors that shape inequity may be overlooked, and 'Western culture,' taken as the norm against which others are judged, goes unquestioned and unscrutinized. Furthermore, Schiller argues that while the concept of culture 'allows us to understand that the primary source of differences among different groups of humans is learned, socially patterned behavior' and is, therefore, a 'liberating concept,' 'in point of fact, the concept of culture can be used to subordinate as well as liberate ... Anthropologists have come to recognize that colonized peoples have been constructed as the cultural other, reinforcing political subordination with cultural domination' (247).

We believe that the discourses of multiculturalism, ethnicity, and culture can be marginalizing discourses; the stereotypic, essentializing images produced through these discourses reinforce the notion of the gendered, classed, and racialized other. These images set the stage for health care providers to relate to patients as the 'objectified other' with alien beliefs and practices. The actual everyday experiences of racism, classism, and sexism and other forms of oppression that organize the everyday lives of patients may be glossed over, not to mention that the process of essentializing, itself, creates racist/sexist/classist interactions between health care provider and patient.

Moving toward a health care delivery system in which all people might be equitably served will require no less than a shift to a framework for practice that, instead of starting from the essentializing and marginalizing discourses of the state on multiculturalism, visible minority, and the like, would start from the everyday life experiences of people and unmask the many layers of contexts that organize their experiences. We suggest that a critical feminist and anti-racist perspective might facilitate this process, foster the development of transformative knowledge through emancipatory research, and help us to realize a more inclusive and equitable health care system.

Toward a Critical Feminist Anti-Racist Perspective in Health Care

Within the last two decades a small number of nursing scholars (see, for example, Anderson 1991, 1993, 1996; Campbell and Bunting; Chinn; Hall and Stevens; MacPherson; Thompson, Allen, and Rodriques-Fisher) have drawn upon anti-racist and postcolonial feminist discourses as a way of challenging the dominant discourses in health care and the politics of gender, race, and class relations. This has meant the introduction of praxis-oriented paradigms into the discipline. Such paradigms, concerned with both producing emancipatory knowledge and empowering the researched (Lather), have heightened awareness that research is political insofar as it unmasks relations of domination and, through this process of unmasking (a reciprocally educative process between researched and researcher), offers a new vision of generating knowledge for freedom and social justice (see MacPherson; Anderson 1991; Lather). Allen suggests that the voice of critique in nursing is not just a way of mastering theory and applying it to nursing practice; instead, it is 'learning to speak, think, see, and be in the world from those places that are elsewhere, other than the dominant, center, colonizing, hegemonic world order' (xii).

It is striking that the emerging emancipatory discourses in nursing are taking place at the intersection of interdisciplinary dialogue. By this we mean that nursing scholars have drawn upon knowledge from other disciplines (such as the humanities and social sciences), not to apply it unquestioningly in their practice, but to help them to see and be in the world from elsewhere, as Allen puts it. Speaking from elsewhere rather than from the dominant, colonizing centre, we believe, broadens the lens through which we can make sense of human life and experiences and opens up the possibility of understanding the genesis of oppression and generating knowledge that prescribes ways of eliminating oppression. Such knowledge, created at the intersection of different disciplines, is not additive (e.g., sociology + medicine + nursing + anthropology, etc.). Nor does it emerge by simply building upon past knowledge and categories (such as visible minority). It destabilizes the categories to which we have become accustomed; it implies reformulating ideas and reconceptualizing issues using, as the starting point, the voices and experiences of those who have been oppressed and marginalized. By challenging fundamental structures and ways of organizing reality, and providing the understanding necessary for addressing the complex issues that are encountered in health care practice, it provides a means of transforming deeply entrenched institutional practices.

While the emergence of a feminist and anti-racist perspective in nursing holds promise, it would be misleading to call it a groundswell. Yet, the complex problems in health care today suggest some urgency for health care professionals to become more fully cognizant of the intersectionality of different forms of oppression and the ways in which the historical positioning of some groups influence health. If they are to do this, then interdisciplinary education may be key. This would mean engaging with different disciplines in developing knowledge that is not bound by the past but that transcends the boundaries of particular disciplinary perspectives.

Embarking upon this course of action will mean a critical examination of the boundaries of professional practice. It would be naive to assume that enlightened health care professionals will make a substantial difference to the health of those who have been marginalized and oppressed if they choose to work in isolation from policy makers and decision makers. We believe that a critical feminist anti-racist perspective means a commitment to change and a commitment to the political struggle that accompanies change. Neither research nor practice can be apolitical if we are truly committed to improving the health of the population.

Conclusion

We began by asking why the election of a black woman as president of the National Action Committee on the Status of Women made headline news. Such an event becomes news because it destabilizes the taken-for-granted notions about those who are *entitled to power and privilege*. At the same time, it exposes multiculturalism as a myth and as empty rhetoric. With this as a starting point, we have attempted to unmask the ways in which dominant discourses in Canada shape health care delivery systems and, therefore, organize the lives of ordinary people. For example, the discourse on multiculturalism provides interpretive lenses that operate in health care delivery and that influences the ways in which 'problems' are constructed and solutions negotiated. Ironically, in failing to unmask the ideologies that underpin hegemonic systems of domination, these discourses further marginalize those they are intended to include. They may therefore result in policies that are ineffective, and they may contribute to the very problems they purport to alleviate.

In turning attention to the health care system, our focus has been on the institutionalized practices and the many layers of contexts that shape people's experiences of health and illness. While we have not explored the complex nexus of social and economic relationships that influence health, we have nonetheless provided a glimpse into the relations of power that structure health care relationships and that profoundly affect the everyday experiences of those who seek help.

We have proposed a critical feminist anti-racist perspective as one way of developing transformative knowledge that would help us to go beyond the biomedical framework and traditional health and social science perspectives. This would move us toward recognizing the institutionalized practices that have shaped the wider social, political, and economic processes that influence health and toward attending to the relations of power within the hierarchy of health care delivery systems. Above all, it would enable us to unmask injustice and to join in the struggle for social justice so that all people can be equitably served.

Acknowledgments
We thank the Social Sciences and Humanities Research Council of Canada for supporting the research upon which this chapter is based, and we are deeply indebted to the people who have allowed us the privilege of entering into their lives, and who have shared their thoughts and experiences with us. We thank Sherrill Grace for her thoughtful reading of an earlier draft of this chapter and for her insightful comments. We alone must take responsibility for whatever shortcomings are present in this manuscript.

Notes

1 We are indebted to the people who participated in these conversations. We have received permission from some of these people to acknowledge them either by name or by organization. Others did not give their permission to have their own names or the names of their organizations included, so they are not mentioned here: Beverly Nann; Sadie Kuehn; United Chinese Community Enrichment Services Society (SUCCESS); Ruth Coles, Dianne Doyle, Providence Health Care; Mount Saint Joseph Hospital; Shashi Assanand, Vancouver and Lower Mainland Multicultural Family Support Services; Guninder C. Mumick, Multicultural Health Education Consultant, Vancouver/Richmond Health Board.

2 It should be noted that since these studies were conducted, considerable efforts are being made to improve interpreter services and access to clinics in some institutions. However, the issues discussed remain pertinent.

3 We use the term 'colour' as it has been use by Carty: 'Within the Canadian context, those of us doing political work have been insistent on naming ourselves: First Nations, Black, South Asian, Chinese, Filipino, East Asian, Latin American, Korean and so on. In reference to our collectivity, we have resisted terms such as "visible minority" which were developed by the state in its attempt to ignore our heterogeneity and to marginalize us by erasing our different histories and cultures and their significance. My usage of the term "women of Colour" acknowledges our ethnic differences which is why Colour is capitalized, denoting more than different shades of skin colour. Further, I use it indicating a common context of struggle based on shared systemic discrimination in the Canadian social and political context. In this chapter, therefore, the term has a particular political relevance' (Notes 1, 17-8).

Works Cited

Allen, David. 1992. 'Introduction.' In J. Thompson, D.G. Allen, and L. Rodriques-Fisher, eds., *Critique, Resistance and Action: Working Papers in the Politics of Nursing*, xi-xvi. New York: National League for Nursing

Alonzo, A. 1993. 'Health Behavior: Issues, Contradictions and Dilemmas.' *Social Sciences and Medicine* 37 (8):1019-34

Anderson, J.M. 1990. 'Home Care Management in Chronic Illness and the Self-Care Movement: An Analysis of Ideologies and Economic Processes Influencing Policy Decisions.' *Advances in Nursing Science* 12 (2):71-83

–. 1991. 'Reflexivity in Fieldwork: Toward a Feminist Epistemology.' *Image: Journal of Nursing Scholarship*. 23 (2):115-8

–. 1992. 'Using Research to Change Social and Health Policy.' Proceedings of Canadian Council on Multicultural Health 2nd National Conference. *Multicultural Health* 11: Towards Equity in Health, 84-9. Whistler, BC

–. 1993. 'Ethnocultural Communities as Partners in Research.' In R. Masi, L. Mensah, and K. McLeod, eds., *Health and Cultures Exploring the Relationships. Policies, Professional Practice and Education*, vol. 1, 319-28. Oakville, New York, London: Mosaic

–. 1996. 'Empowering Patients: Issues and Strategies.' *Social Science and Medicine* 43 (5):697-705

Anderson, J.M., C. Blue, and A. Lau. 1991. 'Women's Perspectives on Chronic Illness: Ethnicity, Ideology and Restructuring of Life.' *Social Science and Medicine* 33 (2):101-13

Anderson, J.M., C. Blue, A. Holbrook, and M. Ng. 1993. 'On Chronic Illness: Immigrant Women in Canada's Workforce: A Feminist Perspective.' *Canadian Journal of Nursing Research* 25 (2):7-22

Anderson, J.M., H. Elfert, and M. Lai. 1989. 'Ideology in the Clinical Context: Chronic

Illness, Ethnicity, and the Discourse on Normalization.' *Sociology of Health and Illness: A Journal of Medical Sociology* 11 (3):253-78

Armstrong, P., and H. Armstrong. 1994. 'Health Care in Canada.' In P. Armstrong et al., eds., *Take Care: Warning Signals for Canada's Health System*, 15-30. Toronto: Garamond

Baer, H., M. Singer, and J.H. Johnson. 1986. 'Toward a Critical Medical Anthropology.' *Social Science and Medicine* 23 (2):95-98

Bannerji, H., ed. 1993. *Returning the Gaze: Essays on Racism, Feminism and Politics.* Toronto: Sister Vision

Berger, C. 1966. 'The True North Strong and Free.' In P. Russell, ed., *Nationalism in Canada*, 3-26. Toronto: McGraw-Hill

Bliss, M. 1991. 'Privatizing the Mind: The Sundering of Canadian History, the Sundering of Canada.' *Journal of Canadian Studies* 26 (4):5-17

British Columbia. 1991. *Closer to Home: The Report of the British Columbia Royal Commission on Health Care and Costs.* Vol. 2. Victoria: Crown Publications

–. 1993a. *Bill 39 Multiculturalism Act.* Victoria: Queen's Printer

–. 1993b. *Bill 33 Human Rights Amendment Act.* Ministry of Education and Minister Responsible for Multiculturalism and Human Rights. Victoria: Queen's Printer

–. 1993c. *New Directions for a Healthy British Columbia.* British Columbia: Ministry of Health and Ministry Responsible for Seniors

Calliste, A. 1991. 'Canada's Immigration Policy and Domestics From the Caribbean: The Second Domestic Scheme.' In J. Vorst et al., eds., *Race, Class, Gender: Bonds and Barriers* (2nd rev. ed.), 136-68. Toronto: Garamond

Campbell, J.C., and S. Bunting. 1991. 'Voices and Paradigms: Perspectives on Critical and Feminist Theory in Nursing.' *Advances in Nursing Science* 13 (3):1-15

Canada. 1940. *Report of the Royal Commission on Dominion-Provincial Relations.* Ottawa: King's Printer

–. 1978. *New Directions: A Look at Canada's Immigration Act and Regulations.* Ottawa: Supply and Services

–. 1986. *Achieving Health for All: A Framework for Health Promotion.* Ottawa: Supply and Services

–. 1990. *Canadian Multiculturalism Act: A Guide for Canadians.* Ottawa: Supply and Services

–. 1992. *Charter of Rights and Freedoms: A Guide for Canadians.* Ottawa: Supply and Services

Canada Health Act. 1984. Ottawa: Queen's Printer

Carty, L. 1991. 'Women's Studies in Canada: A Discourse and Praxis of Exclusion.' *Resources for Feminist Research* 20 (3/4):12-8

Carty, L., and D. Brand. 1993. 'Visible Minority Women: A Creation of the Canadian State.' In H. Bannerji, ed., *Returning the Gaze: Essays on Racism, Feminism and Politics*, 169-81. Toronto: Sister Vision

Chinn, P.L., ed. 1981. 'Women's Health.' *Advances in Nursing Science* 1 (1):1-125

Crichton, A. 1981. 'Development of Rehabilitation Policies in Britain, Canada, and Australia: A Comparison.' In G.L. Albrecht, ed., *Cross National Rehabilitation Policies: A Sociological Perspective*, 157-84. London: Sage

Das Gupta, T. 1996. *Racism and Paid Work.* Toronto: Garamond

Di Marco, M., and J. Storch. 1995. 'History of the Canadian Health Care System.' In D. Wilson, ed., *The Canadian Health Care System*, 5-15. Edmonton: Faculty of Nursing, University of Alberta

Evans, R. 1992. '"We'll Take Care of It for You." Health Care in the Canadian Community.' In D. Kindig and R. Sullivan, eds., *Understanding Universal Health Programs: Issues and Options*, 159-72. Ann Arbor, MI: Health Administration Press

Flexner, A. 1910. *Medical Education in the United States and Canada.* New York: Carnegie Foundation

Frideres, J. 1993. *Native Peoples in Canada: Contemporary Conflicts.* Scarborough, ON: Prentice Hall

Griffin, K. 1993. *Vancouver's Many Faces: Passport to the Cultures of a City.* Vancouver/ Toronto: Whitecap

Hall, J.M., and P.E. Stevens. 1991. 'Rigor in Feminist Research.' *Advances in Nursing Science*

13 (3):16-29

Lather, P. 1991. *Getting Smart: Feminist Research and Pedagogy with/in the Postmodern*. New York: Routledge

Li, P. 1988. *Ethnic Inequality in a Class Society*. Toronto: Thompson Educational Publishing

Lock, M. 1990. 'On Being Ethnic: The Politics of Identity Breaking and Making in Canada, or *Nerva* on Sunday.' *Culture, Medicine and Psychiatry* 14 (2):237-54

MacPherson, K. 1983. 'Feminist Methods: A New Paradigm for Nursing Research.' *Advances in Nursing Science* 5 (2):17-25

Navarro, V. 1976. *Medicine Under Capitalism*. New York: Prodist

Ng, R. 1991. 'Sexism, Racism, Canadian Nationalism.' In H. Bannerji, ed., *Returning the Gaze: Essays on Racism, Feminism and Politics*, 182-96. Toronto: Sister Vision

Rachlis, M., and C. Kushner. 1994. *Strong Medicine: How to Save Canada's Health Care System*. Toronto: Harper Perennial

Reimer, S. 1995. 'Nurses' Descriptions of the Experience of Caring for Culturally Diverse Clients.' MA thesis, University of British Columbia, Vancouver

Reimer Kirkham, S. 1998. 'Nurses' Experiences of Caring for Culturally Diverse Clients.' *Clinical Nursing Research* 7 (2):125-46

Schiller, N. Glick. 1992. 'What's Wrong with This Picture? The Hegemonic Construction of Culture in AIDS Research in the United States.' *Medical Anthropology Quarterly: International Journal for the Analysis of Health* 6 (3):237-54

Sherwin, S. 1992. *No Longer Patient: Feminist Ethics and Health Care*. Philadelphia: Temple University Press

Social Planning and Review Council of British Columbia. 1980. *The History and Present Status of the Health Insurance System in British Columbia*. Vancouver: Social Planning and Review Council of British Columbia

Stern, L. 1996. 'Women's Group Elects Black Leader.' *Vancouver Sun*, 17 June:A3

Taylor, M. 1990. *Insuring National Health Care*. Chapel Hill, NC: University of North Carolina Press

Thompson, J.L., D.G. Allen, L. Rodriques-Fisher, eds. 1992. *Critique, Resistance and Action: Working Papers in the Politics of Nursing*. New York: National League for Nursing Press Pub. no. 14-2504

Waitzkin, H. 1983. 'A Marxist View of Health and Health Care.' In D. Mechanic, ed., *Handbook of Health, Health Care, and the Health Professions*, 657-82. New York: The Free Press

Whittaker, R. 1991. *Canadian Immigration Policy Since Confederation*. Ottawa: Canadian Historical Association

Building Transdisciplinary Standpoints: An Integrative Bibliography

Gabriele Helms, Matt James, and Patricia Rodney

An important initiative on the part of the research team that generated this book was to create a bibliographic resource for our own use during the project, for readers making of our findings, and for future scholars undertaking similar endeavours (Helms, James, and Rodney, 16-17). As graduate student research assistants, the three of us applied ourselves to this task from the outset of the project. For each of us, it was the first opportunity to do interdisciplinary work on this scale. This chapter is the culmination of our bibliographic work. Within it, we discuss the process of making bibliographic choices oriented toward promoting interdisciplinary collaboration, and we present the resources that we found to be most useful.

As research assistants, our initial task was to see whether scholars had studied the interconnections of gender, race, and class in the construction of Canada in an interdisciplinary manner. This initial search was almost fruitless. The research team then agreed that before our disciplines could come together, hybridize, and dialogize each other in order to help realize more progressive visions of social relations in Canada, we needed to identify and interrogate the various ways in which our respective disciplines had helped to build the unequal construction 'Canada' that we now know. We then each surveyed the literature in our respective fields with three questions in mind: How have our disciplines constructed their notions of Canada? Have scholars attempted to reflect on this process critically in order to understand the nation's past and/or to participate in bringing about changes in its present and future? Has anybody approached the question of construction from an interdisciplinary perspective, and how have they proceeded? With a number of extensive bibliographies on disks, we decided that the next step was to compile our separate (selected) sources and make them available to all members of the research team.

Out of the original purpose of generating a bibliographic resource for our own use during the project came the idea to present a selection of the material as an introductory bibliography to future readers, who would find themselves in the same situation as we did; that is, looking for a guide that would introduce them to the field by suggesting useful references from a number of relevant disciplines. The bibliographic resource that we have subsequently compiled is, therefore, not encyclopedic and does not claim to be exhaustive.

We have selected sources that, for us, reflect concepts that are central to building connections within and between our various disciplines (Helms, James, and Rodney, 16-17). In particular, we have included studies that try to investigate the *interconnections* of race, gender, and class in the Canadian context. Our selection criteria are necessarily subjective, and our bibliography shows a strong emphasis on material that either comes from or overlaps with our respective disciplines. It was also important to us to include material only if it was accessible to us. As a result, we are aware that we have constructed our own critical lens regarding how to approach the problem of Canada's construction.

Some of our most important bibliographic choices were methodological. We needed to decide what theoretical lenses we would bring to bear on questions about race, gender, and class as they affect the construction of Canada. In particular, we required theoretical lenses that would work against naturalized disciplinary categories such as literary criticism, political science, and nursing. This search led us to sources in the philosophy of social science; critical, literary, and political theory; and feminist theory. In addition, we surveyed methodological works concerning interdisciplinarity in order to help us think more clearly about the process in which we were engaging.[1]

To explain our search for concepts and source materials that would promote interdisciplinary collaboration, we may begin with Julie Thompson Klein's helpful unpacking of the range of potential scholarly approaches that can be called 'interdisciplinary.' One important distinction Klein draws is that between 'additive' and 'integrative' interdisciplinary work (1990, 56-73). Additive interdisciplinarity describes work that involves, from a particular disciplinary standpoint, the borrowing of analogies or general approaches from one or more disciplines. Thus, additive interdisciplinarity seeks not to transcend disciplinary boundaries so much as to develop insights and approaches unavailable from the standpoint of one particular discipline alone. By contrast, key to integrative interdisciplinarity is the notion of hybridization. In integrative interdisciplinarity, particular disciplinary standpoints (concepts, methodologies, data, etc.) become merged so as to foster the development of approaches to particular problems that respond more to the exigencies of the problem in view than to the traditions and concepts specific to particular disciplines. It is important to keep in mind that the distinction between additive and integrative interdisciplinarity is drawn for heuristic purposes; that is, to emphasize important differences in the way interdisciplinary inquiry can be approached rather than to suggest that one form of interdisciplinary work is necessarily more valuable than the other.

In the case of our specific problem – to examine the reciprocal impact of raced, classed, and gendered identities and processes of nation construction – we began with the additive approach but, finally, decided that the integrative interdisciplinary method was more suitable. Initially, we selected concepts central to our disciplines to help us choose the material for our bibliographies and discussions. The political scientist, for example, focused on the concept of 'state,' the literary critic chose 'language,' and the scholar in nursing suggested 'health policy.' In this way, we produced specialized bibliographies, but we were unable to integrate our work because these concepts were not equally relevant in all our fields; at times, they even interfered with communication. We realized that the additive approach was promoting the pursuit of agendas internal to our respective disciplines rather than focusing us, as a collective, on developing an integrative bibliography. We then began to search for concepts that had relevance across various disciplines and could help us to synthesize our findings.

Some concepts can help to promote the integration of disciplinary frames of reference so that the object of inquiry becomes 'thinkable' within a new problematic rather than remaining embedded within disciplinary traditions. Disciplinary traditions can be obstacles to integrative interdisciplinarity because they bring with them familiar frames of reference that can keep their practitioners trapped within the comfort of inherited custom. For example, because the notion of 'state' brings with it a range of associated concepts and problems that are habitual for the political scientist, its use as a central organizing category could serve to keep a political scientist within traditional problematics even as she sought to investigate, say, problems of health care delivery in an interdisciplinary manner. Integrative interdisciplinarity, by contrast, requires the discovery of new meeting ground on which to build connections and, hence, new approaches to knowledge construction among scholars from diverse traditions.

An illustration of the advantages of this integrative approach may be seen in considering how to deal with what we call the problem of 'group visibility,' of how it is that some identities become viewed as socially central while others remain submerged. 'Mobilization,' for instance, is a concept that the disciplines of sociology and political science have used to register the ways in which particular groups make their social presence an unignorable reality. However, 'mobilization' may not be a term that helps bring forward the 'visibility/invisibility' problem that other disciplinary perspectives, such as that of literary criticism, might regard as central. A further obstacle is that a more recently politicized discipline, such as health policy studies, may not view visibility/invisibility as relevant. Thus, the importance of developing what we call 'integrative concepts' – concepts that aid the work of building transdisciplinary standpoints. We selected the bibliographic sources that are presented in this chapter because they provided us with useful methodological lenses from which to view our inquiry. Importantly, we also selected them because they helped us to grasp a number of integrative concepts, including class, construction, critique, culture, discourse, gender, hegemony, ideology, race, and representation. Each bibliographic source was mined for a number of these (and other) integrative concepts, and many of the sources simultaneously provided us with a number of helpful methodological lenses. Rather than assigning concepts to sources in a manner that might impoverish the richness of the latter, we have presented the sources in our bibliography alphabetically. As the last point of our introduction, we will illustrate how integrative concepts worked for us in compiling our sources by providing a detailed example: *representation.*

For health services delivery, representation isolates the problem of determining whose input determines appropriate modes of health care. Indeed, it summons up the whole problem of how the cultural embeddedness of particular systems and institutions may perpetuate inequality in health services access. In literary criticism, 'representation' may point to questions of canon formation, the particular work done by processes of linguistic signification, narrative techniques, and so forth. Similarly, 'representation' has been central to political science analysis, conceptually isolating the work that putatively democratic institutions and processes are charged with accomplishing. What the concept of representation can do from a transdisciplinary standpoint is to identify the various social forms and practices that bring particular features of the social world into view, thus making them parts of social reality. We can define representation provisionally as the function of bringing 'into existence in an instituted form ... what hitherto existed only as a serial collection of juxtaposed individuals [or individual standpoints].'[2] Understood in this way, the concept of representation targets the practices governing the social relationship between the visible and non-visible in an integrative, transdisciplinary way – as a concept like 'mobilization' cannot. 'Representation' thus becomes an integrative problematic, a framework for unifying seemingly disparate objects of inquiry. Under this rubric, for example, we can unite a focus on how choices of narrative form in literature either bring into view or submerge marginal identities with, say, a focus on how political institutions and processes select particular types of Canadians as 'representative.' Furthermore, this same conceptual rubric can capture the question of how to make more voices heard in the development of health policy.

Bringing works from particular disciplines under the rubric of an integrative concept is a way to make those works useful for interdisciplinary, collaborative inquiry. For example, literature from the field of health care and nursing, which is usefully considered from within the representation problematic, includes Susan Sherwin's *No Longer Patient* (1992), which critiques the Canadian health care system's insensitivity to women's health care needs, and Joan Anderson's 'Immigrant Women Speak of Chronic Illness' (1991), which articulates the exclusion of immigrant women's voices from health policy development. The voices of marginalized groups have similarly become the focus of a literary criticism that explores the forces of canonical activity in Canada. Many essays in *Canadian Canons: Essays in Literary Value*, a collection edited by Robert Lecker, address the question of whose voices have been excluded from a Canadian canon and why. Paying close attention to formal strategies in writing, Barbara Godard focuses on the work of Native Canadian women in 'The Politics of Representation' to examine in detail how they have begun to challenge an exclusive Canadian literary tradition. This seemingly apolitical and universalist tradition, argues Arun Mukherjee in 'Canadian Nationalism, Canadian Literature and Racial Minority Women,' actually supports a middle-class, Eurocentric Canadian canon that has been reinforced by an equally Eurocentric nationalist criticism. Because the representation rubric focuses attention on how particular parts of the social world are 'selected out' and become social 'reality,' key Canadian political science works are the Royal Commission research studies on women and ethnic and racialized minorities in politics, collected under the editorship of Kathy Megyery in *Ethnocultural Groups and Visible Minorities in Canadian Politics* and *Women in Canadian Politics* (1991). Alan Cairns's 'Constitutional Minoritarianism in Canada' (1990) identifies how the 1982 entrenchment of the Charter of Rights and Freedoms has promoted the representation in citizenship discourse of identities excluded from such discourse prior to 1982.

What follows is the integrative bibliography of English-language references that we have compiled; it is intended to serve as an introductory list of sources that address the interconnections of race, gender, and class in the construction of Canada.

Bibliography

Anderson, J.M. 1990. 'Home Care Management in Chronic Illness and the Self-Care Movement: An Analysis of Ideologies and Economic Processes Influencing Policy Decisions.' *Advances in Nursing Science* 12 (2):71-83
–. 1991. 'Immigrant Women Speak of Chronic Illness: The Social Construction of the Devalued Self.' *Journal of Advanced Nursing* 16 (7):10-7
–. 1996. 'Empowering Patients: Issues and Strategies.' *Social Science and Medicine* 43 (5):697-705
Anderson, J.M., C. Blue, and A. Lau. 1991. 'Women's Perspectives on Chronic Illness: Ethnicity, Ideology and Restructuring of Life.' *Social Science Medicine* 33 (2):101-13

Anderson, J.M., Sherrill Grace, Gabriele Helms, Matt James, and Patricia Rodney. 1995. 'Women Speaking: Heather Rose and the Culture of Health Care.' In Shauna McLarnon and Douglas Nord, eds., *Northern Parallels: 4th Circumpolar Universities Cooperation Conference.* Proceedings, 23-25 February, 84-101. Prince George, BC: UNBC Press

Anderson, Kay J. 1991. *Vancouver's Chinatown: Racial Discourse in Canada, 1875-1980.* Montreal: McGill-Queen's University Press

Andrew, Caroline. 1984. 'Women and the Welfare State.' *Canadian Journal of Political Science* 17

Anthias, Floya, and Nira Yurval Davies. 1992. *Racialized Boundaries: Race, Nation, Gender, Colour and Class and the Anti-Racist Struggle.* New York: Routledge

Armstrong, Jeannette, ed. 1993. *Looking at the Words of Our People: First Nations Analysis of Literature.* Penticton: Theytus

Artibise, A.F.J., ed. 1990. *Interdisciplinary Approaches to Canadian Society: A Guide to the Literature.* Montreal: McGill-Queen's University Press

Ashcroft, Bill, Gareth Griffiths, and Helen Tiffin. 1989. *The Empire Writes Back: Theory and Practice in Post-Colonial Literatures.* London: Routledge

Bannerji, Himani. 1993a. 'Returning the Gaze: An Introduction.' In Himani Bannerji, ed., *Returning the Gaze: Essays on Racism, Feminism and Politics,* ix-xxiv. Toronto: Sister Vision

–, ed. 1993b. *Returning the Gaze: Essays on Racism, Feminism and Politics.* Toronto: Sister Vision

Barer, M.L., and R.G. Evans. 1992. 'Interpreting Canada: Models, Mind-Sets, and Myths.' *Health Affairs* 11 (1):44-61

Barer, M.L., and G.L. Stoddard. 1991. *Toward Integrated Medical Resource Policies for Canada: Report Prepared for the Federal/Provincial/Territorial Conference of Deputy Ministers of Health*

Barrett, Michele, and Roberta Hamilton, eds. 1986. *The Politics of Diversity: Feminism, Marxism and Nationalism.* London: Verso

Bellah, R.N., et al. 1991. *The Good Society.* New York: Vintage

Benhabib, S. 1992. *Situating the Self: Gender, Community and Postmodernism in Contemporary Ethics.* New York: Routledge

Berger, Carl. 1977. 'The True North Strong and Free.' In Peter Russell, ed., *Nationalism in Canada,* 3-26. Toronto: McGraw-Hill

Bernstein, R.J. 1991. *The New Constellation: The Ethical-Political Horizons of Modernity/Postmodernity.* Cambridge, MA: MIT Press

Betkowski, N.J. 1994. 'Public Opinion versus Public Interest.' *Bioethics Bulletin* 6 (3):1-2

Bhaba, Homi K. 1994. *The Location of Culture.* New York: Routledge

Billson, Janet Mancini. 1991. 'Interlocking Identities: Gender, Ethnicity and Power in the Canadian Context.' *International Journal of Canadian Studies* 3 (1991):49-67

Bissoondath, Neil. 1994. *Selling Illusions: The Cult of Multiculturalism in Canada*. Toronto: Penguin

Bliss, M. 1992. 'Privatizing the Mind: The Sundering of Canadian History, the Sundering of Canada.' *Journal of Canadian Studies* 26 (4):5-17

Bolaria, B. Singh, ed. 1991. *Social Issues and Contradictions in Canadian Society*. Toronto: Harcourt Brace

Bolaria, B. Singh, and Peter S. Li. 1985. *Racial Oppression in Canada*. Toronto: Garamond

Bolaria, B. Singh, and Rosemary Bolaria, eds. 1994. *Women, Medicine and Health*. Halifax: Fernwood

Boldt, Menno. 1993. *Surviving as Indians: The Challenge of Self-Government*. Toronto: University of Toronto Press

Boris, Eileen. 1994. 'Gender, Race, and Rights: Listening to Critical Race Theory.' *Journal of Women's History* 6 (2):111-24

Boyd, Susan. 1994. '(Re)Placing the State: Family, Law and Oppression.' *Canadian Journal of Law and Society* 1 (1994):39-73

Boyko, John. 1995. *Last Steps to Freedom: The Evolution of Canadian Racism*. Winnipeg: Watson and Dwyer

Breton, Raymond. 1986. 'Multiculturalism and Canadian Nation-Building.' In Alan C. Cairns and Cynthia Williams, eds., *The Politics of Gender, Ethnicity and Language in Canada*. Vol. 34 of the Royal Commission on the Economic Union and Development Prospects for Canada, 27-66. Toronto: University of Toronto Press

British Columbia Royal Commission on Health Care and Costs. 1991. *Closer to Home: The Report of the British Columbia Royal Commission on Health Care and Costs*. Victoria: Crown Publications

Brodie, M. Janine. 1985. *Women in Politics in Canada*. Toronto: McGraw-Hill Ryerson

Brodie, M. Janine, and Jane Jenson. 1988. *Crisis, Challenge and Change: Party and Class in Canada Revisited*. Ottawa: Carleton University Press

Brodsky, Gwen, and Shelagh Day. 1989. *Canadian Charter Equality Rights for Women: The Step Forward or Two Steps Back?* Ottawa: Canadian Advisory Council on the Status of Women

Bunting, S.M. 1992. 'Eve's Legacy: An Analysis of Family Caregiving from a Feminist Perspective.' In J.L. Thompson, D.G. Allen, and L. Rodrigues, eds., *Critique, Resistance and Action: Working Papers in the Politics of Nursing*, 53-68. New York: National League for Nursing Press

Butler, Judith. 1990. *Gender Trouble: Feminism and the Subversion of Identity*. New York: Routledge

Butler, Judith, and Joan W. Scott, eds. 1992. *Feminists Theorize the Political*. New York: Routledge

Cairns, Alan C. 1977. 'The Governments and Societies of Canadian Federalism.' *Canadian Journal of Political Science* 10 (4):695-725

–. 1990. 'Constitutional Minoritarianism in Canada.' In Ronald L. Watts and Douglas M. Brown, eds., *Canada: The State of the Federation, 1990*, 71-96. Kingston: Queen's University Institute of Intergovernmental Relations

–. 1995. *Reconfigurations: Canadian Citizenship and Constitutional Change.* Toronto: McClelland & Stewart

Cameron, Barry. 1990. 'Theory and Criticism: Trends in Canadian Literature.' In W.H. New, ed., *Literary History of Canada: Canadian Literature in English*, 108-32. Toronto: University of Toronto Press

Campbell, M.L. 1987. 'Productivity in Canadian Nursing: Administering Cuts.' In D. Coburn et al., eds., *Health and Canadian Society: Sociological Perspectives.* 2nd ed., 463-75. Markham, ON: Fitzhenry and Whiteside

Canadian Public Health Association. 1992. *Caring about Health: Canadian Public Health Association Issue Paper on Federal/Provincial/Territorial Arrangements for Health Policy*

Carroll, William, ed. 1992. *Organizing Dissent: Contemporary Social Movements in Theory and Practice.* Toronto: Garamond

Carty, Linda, and Dionne Brand. 1993. '"Visible Minority" Women: A Creation of the Canadian State.' In Himani Bannerji, ed., *Returning the Gaze: Essays on Racism, Feminism and Politics*, 169-81. Toronto: Sister Vision

Casey, B.A. 1986. 'The Quiet Revolution: The Transformation and Reintegration of the Humanities.' *Issues in Integrative Studies* 4 (1986):71-92

Chavkin, W., V. Breitbart, and P.H. Wise. 1994. 'Finding Common Ground: The Necessity of an Integrated Agenda for Women's and Children's Health.' *Journal of Law, Medicine and Ethics* 22 (3):262-9

Chrisjohn, R.D., and S.L. Young. 1994. 'The Circle Game: Shadows and Substance in the Indian Residential School Experience in Canada.' Draft paper submitted to the Royal Commission on Aboriginal People, Canada

Clement, Wallace, and Glen Williams, eds. 1989. *The New Canadian Political Economy.* Montreal: McGill-Queen's University Press

Clifford, James, and George E. Marcus, eds. 1986. *Writing Culture: The Poetics and Politics of Ethnography.* Berkeley: University of California Press

Craig, Terrence. 1987. *Racial Attitudes in English-Canadian Fiction, 1905-1980.* Waterloo, ON: Wilfrid Laurier University Press

Daniels, Jessie. 1997. *White Lies: Race, Class, Gender, and Sexuality in White Supremacist Discourse.* New York: Routledge

Davey, Frank. 1993. *Post-National Arguments: The Politics of the Anglophone-Canadian Novel since 1967.* Toronto: University of Toronto Press

Deber, R.B., and G.G. Thomson, eds. 1992. *Restructuring Canada's Health Services System: How Do We Get There from Here?* Proceedings of the Fourth Annual Canadian Conference on Health Economics. Toronto: University of Toronto Press

Dirks, N.B., G. Eley, and S.B. Ortner, eds. 1994. *Culture/Power/History: A*

Reader in Contemporary Social Theory. Princeton: Princeton University Press

Dufour, Christian. 1990. *A Canadian Challenge/Le défi québécois*. Lantzville, BC: Oolichan

During, Simon, ed. 1993. *The Cultural Studies Reader*. New York: Routledge

Eichler, M. 1992. 'Grasping the Ungraspable: Socio-Legal Definitions of the Family in the Context of Sexuality.' *Transactions of the Royal Society of Canada* 3 (6):3-15

Emberley, Julia V. 1993. *Thresholds of Difference: Feminist Critique, Native Women's Writings, Postcolonial Theory*. Toronto: University of Toronto Press

Epp, J.1986. *Achieving Health for All*. Ottawa: National Health and Welfare

Evans, R.G. 1990. 'Tension, Compression and Shear: Directions, Stresses, and Outcomes of Health Care Cost Control.' *Journal of Health Politics, Policy and Law* 15 (1):101-28

Evans, R.G., M.L. Barer, and T.R. Marmor, eds. 1994. *Why Are Some People Healthy and Others Not? The Determinants of Health of Populations*. New York: Aldine de Gruyter

Findlay, L.M., and Isobel M. Findlay. 1995. *Realizing Community: Multi-Disciplinary Perspectives*. Saskatoon: Humanities Research Unit and Centre for the Study of Co-Operatives, University of Saskatchewan

First Nations Circle on the Constitution. 1992. *To the Source: Commissioners' Report, Assembly of First Nations*. Ottawa: Assembly of First Nations

Fleras, Augie, and John Leonard Elliot. 1992. *Multiculturalism in Canada: The Challenge of Diversity*. Scarborough, ON: Nelson

Fudge, Judy. 1989. 'The Effect of Entrenching a Bill of Rights Upon Political Discourse: Feminist Demands and Sexual Violence in Canada.' *International Journal of the Sociology of Law* 17:445-63

Fuss, Diana. 1989. *Essentially Speaking: Feminism, Nature and Difference*. New York: Routledge

Galbraith, J.K. 1992. *The Culture of Contentment*. Boston: Houghton Mifflin

–. 1996. *The Good Society: The Humane Agenda*. Boston: Houghton Mifflin

Gates, Henry Louis, Jr, ed. 1986. *'Race,' Writing, and Difference*. Chicago: University of Chicago Press

Geertz, C. 1983. *Local Knowledge: Further Essays in Interpretive Anthropology*. New York: Basic Books

Give Back: First Nations Perspectives on Cultural Practice. 1992. North Vancouver: Gallerie

Godard, Barbara. 1990. 'The Politics of Representation: Some Native Canadian Women Writers.' In W.H. New, ed., *Native Writers and Canadian Writing*. 183-225. Vancouver: UBC Press

Goldberg, David Theo. 1993. *Racist Culture: Philosophy and the Politics of Meaning*. Oxford: Blackwell

Goldie, Terry. 1989. *Fear and Temptation: The Image of the Indigene in Canadian, Australian, and New Zealand Literatures*. Kingston: McGill-

Queen's University Press

Greenglass, E.R. 1993. 'Social Support and Coping of Employed Women.' In B.C. Long and S.E. Kahn, eds., *Women, Work, and Coping: A Multidisciplinary Approach to Workplace Stress*, 154-69. Montreal: McGill-Queen's University Press

Guest, Dennis. 1979. *The Emergence of Social Security in Canada*. Vancouver: UBC Press

Harding, S. 1991. *Whose Science? Whose Knowledge? Thinking from Women's Lives*. Ithaca: Cornell University Press

Helms, Gabriele, Matt James, and Patricia Rodney. 1996. 'Multifarious, Pervasive, Processual: Towards an Interdisciplinary Dialogue on Constructions.' *Conference Proceedings: Race, Gender, and the Construction of Canada, October 19-22, 1995*. Vol. 2, paper 15. Vancouver: University of British Columbia, Centre for Research in Women's Studies and Gender Relations

Henry, F., and C. Tator. 1994. 'The Ideology of Racism: "Democratic Racism."' *Canadian Ethnic Studies* 26 (2):1-14

Hillmer, Norman, Bohdan Kordan, and Lubomyr Luciuk. 1988. *On Guard for Thee: War, Ethnicity, and the Canadian State, 1939-45*. Ottawa: Supply and Services

Ho, Rosa. 1994. 'Site-Seeing Vancouver, Positioning Self.' In Paul Delany, ed., *Vancouver: Representing the Postmodern City*, 60-80. Vancouver: Arsenal Pulp

Hoff, J. 1994. 'Gender as a Postmodern Category of Paralysis.' *Women's History Review* 3 (2):149-68

hooks, bell. 1984. *Feminist Theory: From Margin to Center*. Boston: South End

–. 1990. *Yearning: Race, Gender, and Cultural Politics*. Boston: South End

Hopper, S.V. 1993. 'The Influence of Ethnicity on the Health of Older Women.' *Clinics in Geriatric Medicine* 9 (1):231-59

Horowitz, Gad. 1968. *Canadian Labour in Politics*. Toronto: University of Toronto Press

Itwaru, Arnold Harrichand. 1994. *Closed Entrances: Canadian Culture and Imperialism*. Toronto: Tsar

James, S.M., and A.P.A. Busia, eds. 1993. *Theorizing Black Feminisms: The Visionary Pragmatism of Black Women*. London: Routledge

Jameton, A. 1990. 'Culture, Morality, and Ethics: Twirling the Spindle.' *Critical Care Nursing Clinics of North America* 2 (3):443-51

Jenson, Jane. 1989. '"Different" but Not "Exceptional": Canada's Permeable Fordism.' *Canadian Review of Sociology and Anthropology* 1 (1989):69-94

Judd, V., and C. Forgues. 1989. 'Canada's Homeless: Breaking Down the Barriers to Health Care.' *Canadian Nurse* (November 1989):18-9

Kallen, Evelyn. 1995. *Ethnicity and Human Rights in Canada*. Toronto: Oxford University Press

Kaplan, William, ed. 1993. *Belonging: The Meaning and Future of Canadian Citizenship.* Montreal: McGill-Queen's University Press

Ketchum, S.A. 1992. 'Selling Babies and Selling Bodies.' In H.B. Holmes and L.M. Purdy, eds., *Feminist Perspectives in Medical Ethics,* 284-94. Bloomington: Indiana University Press

Kieser, D.M. 1994. 'The Squeeze of Health Care from Hospital to Home: The Impact on Women.' *Bioethics Bulletin* 6 (2):1-3

King, Thomas, Cheryl Calver, and Helen Hoy, eds. 1987. *The Native in Literature: Canadian and Comparative Perspectives.* Edmonton: NeWest

Kjellstrand, C.M. 1992. 'Disguising Unjust Rationing by Calling It Futile Therapy.' *Bioethics Bulletin* 4 (2):1-3

Klein, Julie Thompson. 1990. *Interdisciplinarity: History, Theory, and Practice.* Detroit: Wayne State University Press

–. 1993. 'Blurring, Cracking, and Crossing: Permeation and the Fracturing of Discipline.' In E. Messer-Davidow, D.R. Shumway, and D.J. Sylvan, eds., *Knowledges: Historical and Critical Studies in Disciplinarity,* 185-211. Charlottesville: University Press of Virginia

Kluge, E.H.W. 1988. 'The Calculus of Discrimination: Discriminatory Resource Allocation for an Aging Population.' In J.E. Thornton and E.R. Winkler, eds., *Ethics and Aging: The Right to Live, the Right to Die.* 84-97. Vancouver: UBC Press

Knowles, Richard Paul. 1995. 'Representing Canada: Teaching Canadian Studies in the United States.' *American Review of Canadian Studies* 25 (1):9-26

Kwavnick, David, ed. 1973. *The Tremblay Report.* Toronto: McClelland & Stewart

Labonte, R. 1995. 'Population Health and Health Promotion: What Do They Have to Say to Each Other?' *Canadian Journal of Public Health* 86 (3):165-8

Lather, P. 1991. *Getting Smart: Feminist Research and Pedagogy with/in the Postmodern.* New York: Routledge

Laxer, J. 1996. *In Search of a New Left: Canadian Politics after the Neoconservative Assault.* Toronto: Viking

Lecker, Robert, ed. 1991. *Canadian Canons: Essays in Literary Value.* Toronto: University of Toronto Press

Lee, K.A., et al. 1994. 'Fatigue as a Response to Environmental Demands in Women's Lives.' *Image* 26 (2):149-54

LeFort, S.M. 1993. 'Shaping Heath Care Policy.' *Canadian Nurse* (March):23-7

Lewis, Reina. 1996. *Gendering Orientalism: 'Race,' Femininity and Representation.* New York: Routledge

Li, P.S. 1988. *Ethnic Inequality in a Class Society.* Toronto: Wall and Thompson

Liaschenko, J. 1993. 'Feminist Ethics and Cultural Ethos: Revisiting a Nursing Debate.' *Advances in Nursing Science* 15 (4):71-81

Lock, M. 1990. 'On Being Ethnic: The Politics of Identity Breaking and Making in Canada, or, *Nevra* on Sunday.' *Culture, Medicine and Psychiatry* 14 (92):237-54

Long, B.C., and S.E. Kahn, eds. 1993. *Women, Work, and Coping: A Multi-disciplinary Approach to Workplace Stress.* Montreal: McGill-Queen's University Press

McClintock, Anne. 1995. *Imperial Leather: Race, Gender, and Sexuality in the Colonial Contest.* New York: Routledge

McKague, Ormond, ed. 1993. *Racism in Canada.* Saskatoon: Fifth House

McQuaig, L. 1993. *The Wealthy Banker's Wife: The Assault on Equality in Canada.* Toronto: Penguin

Mandell, N., ed. 1995. *Feminist Issues: Race, Class, and Sexuality.* Scarborough, ON: Prentice Hall

Mann, P.S. 1994. *Micro-Politics: Agency in a Post-Feminist Era.* Minneapolis: University of Minnesota Press

Maroney, Heather Jon, and Meg Luxton, eds. 1987. *Feminism and Political Economy: Women's Work, Women's Struggles.* Toronto: Methuen

Masi, R., ed. 1992. *Canadian Council on Multicultural Health 2nd National Conference: Multicultural Health II: Towards Equity in Health: Proceedings.* Canada: Canadian Council on Multicultural Health

Maxwell, N. 1984. *From Knowledge to Wisdom: A Revolution in the Aims and Methods of Science.* Oxford: Blackwell

Megyery, K., ed. 1991a. *Ethnocultural Groups and Visible Minorities in Canadian Politics: The Question of Access.* Royal Commission on Electoral Reform and Party Financing. Toronto: Dundurn Press

–, ed. 1991b. *Women in Canadian Politics: Towards Equity in Representation.* Royal Commission on Electoral Reform and Party Financing. Toronto: Dundurn Press

Milio, N. 1988. 'Public Policy as the Cornerstone for a New Public Health: Local and Global Beginnings.' *Family Community Health* 11 (2):57-71

Mishler, E.G. 1981. 'Viewpoint: Critical Perspectives on the Biomedical Model.' In E.G. Mishler et al., eds., *Social Contexts of Health, Illness, and Patient Care,* 1-23. Cambridge: Cambridge University Press

Mohr, W.K., and M.M. Mahon. 1996. 'Dirty Hands: The Underside of Marketplace Health Care.' *Advances in Nursing Science* 19 (1):28-37

Monkman, Leslie. 1981. *A Native Heritage: Images of the Indian in English-Canadian Literature.* Toronto: University of Toronto Press

Monture-Okanee, P.A., and M.E. Turpel. 1992. 'Aboriginal Peoples and Canadian Criminal Law: Rethinking Justice.' *University of British Columbia Law Review,* 239-77

Moorhouse, A. 1993. 'User Fees: Fair Cost Containment or a Tax on the Sick?' *Canadian Nurse* 89 (5):21-4

Mouffe, C. 1993. *The Return of the Political.* London: Verso

Mukherjee, Arun P. 1995. 'Canadian Nationalism, Canadian Literature and Racial Minority Women.' In Makeda Silvera, ed., *The Other Woman: Women of Colour in Contemporary Canadian Literature,* 421-44. Toronto: Sister Vision

Mussell, B. 1992. 'Let's Stop Our Oppressive Ways.' *Canadian Journal of Public Health* 83 (5):329

National Forum on Health. 1995. *The Public and Private Financing of Canada's Health System: A Discussion Paper.* Ottawa

Nelson, H.L., and J.L. Nelson. 1992. 'Cutting Motherhood in Two: Some Suspicions Concerning Surrogacy.' In H.B. Holmes and L.M. Purdy, ed., *Feminist Perspectives in Medical Ethics,* 257-65. Bloomington: Indiana University Press

Nelson, M.A. 1994. 'Economic Impoverishment as a Health Risk: Methodologic and Conceptual Issues.' *Advanced Nursing Science* 16 (3):1-12

Neuman, Shirley, and Glennis Stephenson, eds. 1993. *ReImagining Women: Representations of Women in Culture.* Toronto: University of Toronto Press

New Directions Development Division: Ministry of Health and Ministry Responsible for Seniors. 1995. *Policy Frameworks on Designated Populations.* Victoria

New, W.H., ed. 1990. *Native Writers and Canadian Writing.* Vancouver: UBC Press

Ng, Roxana. 1986. 'The Social Construction of Women in Canada.' In Michele Barrett and Roberta Hamilton, eds., *The Politics of Diversity: Feminism, Marxism and Nationalism,* 269-86. London: Verso

–. 1993. 'Sexism, Racism, Canadian Nationalism.' In Himani Bannerji, ed., *Returning the Gaze: Essays on Racism, Feminism and Politics,* 182-96. Toronto: Sister Vision

Oberle, K., and N. Grant. 1994. *Results of the AARN Initiative Regarding the Impact of Health Care Cuts.* Unpublished research report, Alberta Association of Registered Nurses, Edmonton, Alberta

Pal, Leslie. 1993. *Interests of State: The Politics of Language, Multiculturalism, and Feminism in Canada.* Montreal: McGill-Queen's University Press

Palacios, C., and S. Sheps. 1992. 'A Pilot Study Assessing the Health Status of the Hispanic American Community Living in Vancouver.' *Canadian Journal of Public Health* 83 (2):346-9

Palmer, Bryan D. 1983. *Working-Class Experience: The Rise and Reconstitution of Canadian Labour, 1800-1980.* Toronto: Butterworths

Panitch, Leo. 1977. 'The Role and Nature of the Canadian State.' In Leo Panitch, ed., *The Canadian State: Political Economy and Political Power,* 3-27. Toronto: University of Toronto Press

Paulette, L. 1993. 'A Choice for K'aila.' *Humane Medicine* 9 (1):13-7

Pelletier, Alain. 1991. 'Politics and Ethnicity: Representation of Ethnic and Visible-Minority Groups in the House of Commons.' In Kathy Megyery, ed., *Ethno-cultural Groups and Visible Minorities in Canadian Politics: The Question of Access.* Vol. 7 of the Research Studies, Royal Commission on Electoral Reform and Party Financing, 101-59. Toronto: Dundurn

Peterson, V.S. 1993. 'Disciplining Practiced/Practices: Gendered States and

Politics.' In E. Messer-Davidow, D.R. Shumway, and D.J. Sylvan, eds., *Knowledges: Historical and Critical Studies in Disciplinarity,* 243-67. Charlottesville: University Press of Virginia

Petrie, H.G. 1976. 'Do You See What I See? The Epistemology of Interdisciplinary Inquiry.' *Educational Research* 5 (2):9-15

Petrone, Penny. 1990. *Native Literature in Canada: From the Oral Tradition to the Present.* Toronto: Oxford University Press

Philip, M.N. 1992. *Frontiers: Selected Essays and Writings on Racism and Culture: 1984-1992.* Stratford, ON: Mercury

Phillips, S.S., and P. Benner, eds. 1994. *The Crisis of Care: Affirming and Restoring Caring Practices in the Helping Professions.* Washington: Georgetown University Press

Pierson, Ruth. 1986. *'They're Still Women After All': The Second World War and Canadian Womanhood.* Toronto: McClelland & Stewart

Rachlis, M., and C. Kushner. 1994. *Strong Medicine: How to Save Canada's Health Care System.* Toronto: HarperCollins

Radcliffe, S.A. 1994. '(Representing) Post-Colonial Women: Authority, Difference and Feminisms.' *Area* 26 (1):25-32

Rajan, Balachandra. 1990. 'Scholarship and Criticism.' In W.H. New, ed. *Literary History of Canada: Canadian Literature in English,* 133-58. Toronto: University of Toronto Press

Ramazanoglu, C. 1989. *Feminism and the Contradictions of Oppression.* London: Routledge

Razack, Sherene. 1991. *Canadian Feminism and the Law: The Women's Legal Education and Action Fund and the Pursuit of Equality.* Toronto: Second Story Press

Registered Nurses Association of British Columbia. 1990. *Primary Health Care: A Discussion Paper*

–. 1992. *Determinants of Health: Empowering Strategies for Nursing Practice: A Background Paper*

Roman, L.G. 1993. '"On the Ground" with Antiracist Pedagogy and Raymond Williams's Unfinished Project to Articulate a Socially Transformative Critical Realism.' In D.L. Dworkin and L.G. Roman, eds., *Views Beyond the Border Country: Raymond Williams and Cultural Politics.* 322-36. New York: Routledge

Roth, P.A., and J.K. Harrison. 1991. 'Orchestrating Social Change: An Imperative in the Care of the Chronically Ill.' *Journal of Medicine and Philosophy* 16:343-59

Royal Commission on New Reproductive Technologies. 1993. *Proceed with Care: Final Report of the Royal Commission on New Reproductive Technologies.* Canada: Government Services

Said, Edward W. 1978. *Orientalism.* New York: Pantheon

–. 1993. *Culture and Imperialism.* New York: Vintage

Scheier, Libby, Sarah Sheard, and Eleanor Wachtel, eds. 1990. *Language in*

Her Eye: Writing and Gender. Toronto: Coach House

Schwandt, T.A. 1994. 'Constructivist, Interpretivist Approaches to Human Inquiry.' In N.K. Denzin and Y.S. Lincoln, eds., *Handbook of Qualitative Research*, 118-37. Thousand Oaks, CA: Sage

Scott, Joan W. 1986. 'Gender: A Useful Category of Historical Analysis.' *American Historical Review* 91:1053-75

Senate of Canada. 1995. *Of Life and Death: Report of the Special Senate Committee on Euthanasia and Assisted Suicide*. Ottawa: Supply and Services

Sherwin, S. 1992. *No Longer Patient: Feminist Ethics and Health Care*. Philadelphia: Temple University Press

–. 1995. 'Abortion through a Feminist Ethics Lens.' In F. Baylis et al., eds., *Health Care Ethics in Canada*, 441-7. Toronto: Harcourt Brace

Sibbald, B. 1997. 'Delegating away Patient Safety.' *Canadian Nurse* 93 (2):22-6

Simeon, Richard, and Ian Robinson. 1990. *State, Society, and the Development of Canadian Federalism*. Vol. 71 of the Royal Commission on the Economic Union and Development Prospects for Canada. Toronto: University of Toronto Press

Smiley, Donald. 1967. *The Canadian Political Nationality*. Toronto: Methuen

–, ed. 1963. *The Rowell-Sirois Report*. Book I. Toronto: McClelland & Stewart

Smith, D.E. 1987. *The Everyday World as Problematic: A Feminist Sociology*. Toronto: University of Toronto Press

Smith, J. 1994. *Native Blood*. Ottawa: Oberon

Speck, D.C. 1987. *An Error in Judgment: The Politics of Medical Care in an Indian/White Community*. Vancouver: Talonbooks

Spivak, Gayatri Chakravorty. 1987. *In Other Worlds: Essays in Cultural Politics*. New York: Methuen

Squires, J., ed. 1993. *Principled Positions: Postmodernism and the Rediscovery of Value*. London: Lawrence and Wishart

Srivastava, Aruna. 1993. 'Imag(in)ing Racism: South Asian Canadian Women Writers.' In Shirley Neuman and Glennis Stephenson, eds., *ReImagining Women: Representations of Women in Culture*, 299-314. Toronto: University of Toronto Press

Stevens, P.E. 1992. 'Who Gets Care? Access to Health Care as an Arena for Nursing Action.' *Scholarly Inquiry for Nursing Practice* 6 (3):185-200

Storch, J.L. 1988. 'Major Substantive Ethical Issues Facing Canadian Health Care Policymakers and Implementers.' *Journal of Health Administration Education* 6 (2):263-71

Struthers, James. 1983. *No Fault of Their Own: Unemployment and the Canadian Welfare State, 1914-1941*. Toronto: University of Toronto Press

Taylor, C. 1992. *Multiculturalism and 'The Politics of Recognition.'* Princeton: Princeton University Press

Teghtsoonian, Katherine. 1993. 'Neo-Conservative Ideology and Opposition to Federal Regulation of Child Care Services in the United States and Canada.' *Canadian Journal of Political Science* 26 (1):97-121

Thompson, John Herd. 1983. 'The Enemy Alien and the Canadian General Election of 1917.' In Frances Swyripa and John Herd Thompson, eds., *Loyalties in Conflict: Ukrainian Canadians in Canada During the Great War*, 25-46. Edmonton: Canadian Institute of Ukrainian Studies, University of Alberta

Thorne, S.E. 1993. *Negotiating Health Care: The Social Context of Chronic Illness*. Newbury Park, CA: Sage

Trinh T. Minh-ha. 1991. *When the Moon Waxes Red: Representation, Gender and Cultural Politics*. New York: Routledge

Tronto, J.C. 1993. *Moral Boundaries: A Political Argument for an Ethic of Care*. New York: Routledge

Trudeau, P.E. 1968. *Federalism and the French Canadians*. Toronto: Macmillan

Tuana, N., and R. Tong, eds. 1995. *Feminism and Philosophy: Essential Readings in Theory, Reinterpretation, and Application*. Boulder, CO: Westview

Turpel, Mary Ellen. 1990. 'Aboriginal Peoples and the Canadian *Charter*: Interpretive Monopolies, Cultural Differences.' *Canadian Human Rights Yearbook* 6 (1989/90):3-45

Vorst, Jesse, et al., eds. 1991. *Race, Class, Gender: Bonds and Barriers*. Toronto: Garamond

Vosskamp, W. 1986. 'From Scientific Specialization to the Dialogue between the Disciplines.' Trans. J.B. Vahlbusch. *Issues in Integrative Studies* 4:17-36

Watney, S. 1991. 'Citizenship in the Age of AIDS.' In G. Andrews, ed., *Citizenship*, 164-82. London: Wishart

Watson, S.D. 1994. 'Minority Access and Health Reform: A Civil Right to Health Care.' *Journal of Law, Medicine and Ethics* 22:127-37

Waxler-Morrison, N., J. Anderson, and E. Richardson, eds. 1990. *Cross-Cultural Caring: A Handbook for Health Professionals in Western Canada*. Vancouver: UBC Press

Weaver, Sally. 1981. *Making Canadian Indian Policy: The Hidden Agenda, 1968-70*. Toronto: University of Toronto Press

Willms, D.G, et al. 1992. 'A Lament by Women for "The People, the Land" [Nishnawbi-Aski Nation]: An Experience of Loss.' *Canadian Journal of Public Health* 83 (5):331-4

Wilson, Donna M., ed. 1995. *The Canadian Health Care System*. Edmonton: University of Alberta, Faculty of Nursing

Wilson, V. Seymour. 1993. 'The Tapestry Vision of Canadian Multiculturalism.' *Canadian Journal of Political Science* 26 (4):645-69

Wuthnow, R., et al. 1984. *Cultural Analysis: The Work of Peter L. Berger, Mary Douglas, Michel Foucault, and Jürgen Habermas*. London: Routledge

Wylie, A. 1994. 'Reasoning about Ourselves: Feminist Methodology in the

Social Sciences.' In M. Martin and L.C. McIntyre, eds., *Readings in the Philosophy of Social Science*, 611-24. Cambridge, MA: MIT Press

Yeo, M. 1993a. *Ethics and Economics in Health Care Resource Allocation.* Ottawa: Queen's-University of Ottawa Economic Projects

–. 1993b. 'Toward an Ethic of Empowerment for Health Promotion.' *Health Promotion International* 8 (3):225-35

York, G. 1989. *The Dispossessed: Life and Death in Native Canada.* Toronto: Lester and Orpen Dennys

Zapf, K. 1991. 'Educating Social Work Practitioners for the North: A Challenge for Conventional Models and Structures.' *Northern Review* 7:35-52

Acknowledgments

The research team that undertook the project, 'The Construction of Canada: The Changing Meaning of Race and Gender,' at the Centre for Research in Women's Studies and Gender Relations at the University of British Columbia consisted of Joan Anderson (a nurse sociologist), Avigail Eisenberg (a political scientist), Sherrill Grace (a literary critic), Veronica Strong-Boag (a historian), along with four graduate students, Gabriele Helms (English), Matt James (political science), Sheryl Reimer Kirkham (nursing), and Patricia Rodney (nursing). We gratefully acknowledge a research grant from the Social Sciences and Humanities Research Council of Canada (SSHRC), which made the entire project possible. The views expressed in this chapter do not necessarily reflect those of SSHRC.

Notes

1 For a summary of some of the theoretical insights we gained from these sources, see Helms, James, and Rodney.
2 Pierre Bourdieu, 'What Makes a Social Class? On the Theoretical and Practical Existence of Groups.' *Berkeley Journal of Sociology* 32 (1987):14.

Contributors

Yasmeen Abu-Laban is an assistant professor in the Department of Political Science at the University of Alberta. She specializes in Canadian and comparative politics. Her recent publications include articles on race/ethnicity and political representation in Canadian federal politics, multiculturalism policy and globalization, and the role of the melting pot in the American cultural imaginary. She is currently completing a comparative study of gender and the political participation of immigrants.

Joan Anderson, a nurse and sociologist, is a professor in the School of Nursing at the University of British Columbia. She was a Health Canada National Health Research Scholar from 1988 to 1993, during which time she conducted research in the areas of culture, racialization, gender, and health. She has developed a program of research with women living with chronic illness, and she is especially interested in unmasking structural constraints and barriers in the health care system that influence people's experiences of health, illness, and healing. Her research has resulted in a number of publications, invited talks, and workshops for clinicians, policy makers, and educators, and she is developing an anti-racist feminist approach in health research that addresses issues of social justice.

Linda Cardinal is an associate professor in the Department of Political Science and the Women's Studies Program at the University of Ottawa. Her most recent publication is *La pensée de l'engagement: Ecrire en milieu minoritaire francophone au Canada* (1997). She is currently working on reinterpretations of the 'Quebec Revolution' in Quebec as well as on the relationship between rights and politics in Canada.

Lisa Chalykoff, currently in the Department of English at the University of British Columbia, is writing her doctoral dissertation on 'Space and Identity Formation in Canadian Literary Narratives.' Her scholarly interests include interdisciplinarity, theories of identity formation, literary regionalism and nationalism, and the politics and poetics of spatial practice, cultural geography, and critical social theory. She is co-editing a collection of Canadian plays called *Staging the North*.

Peter Dickinson is the author of *Here Is Queer: Nationalisms, Sexualities, and the Literatures of Canada* (University of Toronto Press 1998). He has published several articles on Canadian literature and gay studies and is currently at work on a study of Patrick Anderson's travel writing.

Isabel Dyck is a social geographer and an associate professor in the School of Rehabilitation Sciences at the University of British Columbia. Her current research is concerned with work and identity issues for women with chronic illness, health care practice in multicultural societies, and immigrant women's experiences of the reconstitution of the family in Canada. She has a particular interest in the contributions of qualitative methodology and social theory in analyzing the gendered geographies of women's lives.

Avigail Eisenberg is an associate professor in the Department of Political Science at the University of British Columbia. She has written numerous articles on Canadian politics, constitutional jurisprudence, and democratic theory. Her most recent book is *Reconstructing Political Pluralism* (State University of New York Press, 1995), and she is currently working on a book about theories of colonialism and nationalism.

Sherrill Grace is a professor of English at the University of British Columbia and a Senior Fellow of Green College. She has published widely on Canadian, American, and twentieth-century literature and the arts, with books on Margaret Atwood, literary Expressionism, and Malcolm Lowry. She recently published *Sursum Corda! The Collected Letters of Malcolm Lowry*, two volumes, and guest-edited a special issue of *Essays on Canadian Writing* called *Representing North*. She is currently writing an interdisciplinary book about Canadian culture called *Canada and the Idea of North* and co-editing a collection of plays called *Staging the North*. She is a UBC Killam Research Prize winner (1991) and a Fellow of the Royal Society of Canada.

Gabriele Helms is a lecturer in English at the University of British Columbia. She has published articles on Canadian literature and is currently completing a book on dialogism in contemporary Canadian fiction. Her research interests include the genres of life-writing and cultural studies.

Matt James is currently a doctoral candidate in the Department of Political Science at the University of British Columbia, and his dissertation is on 'Community Politics: Social Movements in Canadian Constitutional Politics, 1940-1993.' His research interests are in strategies of symbolic action in politics, theories of ideology, and cultural studies.

Yasmin Jiwani is the executive coordinator of the FREDA Centre for Research on Violence Against Women and Children. She holds a doctorate in Communication Studies from Simon Fraser University, and in her dissertation she analyzed the representation of race in Canadian television news and the cultural/racial hegemony of mainstream media. She is currently studying the intersection of race and gender in popular media coverage, with particular attention to the representation of violence against women in media coverage and the popular discourse on immigration issues.

Jo-Anne Lee is an assistant professor in the Women's Studies Department at the University of Victoria. She received her doctorate in sociology from the University of Saskatchewan, where she did research on the implementation of multicultural policy at the grassroots level. She has published in the areas of adult literacy, adult education, community development, and immigrant women, and she has been active in many grassroots organizations. Her current research interests include the role of ethnic minority women in urban renewal programs, community wellness for immigrant women, and the relations of gender, citizenship, and democracy.

Sheryl Reimer Kirkham, RN, MSN, is a doctoral candidate in the School of Nursing at the University of British Columbia. Her dissertation, 'Intergroup Relations in Health Care Provision in a Pluralistic Society,' is a critical ethnography with a focus on the processes and consequences of racialization and marginalization. She was formerly a nurse educator at Camosun College, Victoria, and she has published on such topics as intercultural nursing, research methodology, and nursing curriculum.

Patricia Rodney is an assistant professor in the School of Nursing at the University of Victoria and a research associate with the Centre for Applied Ethics at the University of British Columbia. Her feminist ethnographic research focuses on how nurses deal with ethical problems in their practice and on how the culture of the health care system impairs the moral agency of nurses and other members of the health care team.

Becki Ross holds a joint appointment in Women's Studies and Sociology at the University of British Columbia. She teaches in the areas of contemporary gender policy, feminist theory, social movements, qualitative methods, and queer history. Her published works include *The House That Jill Built: A Lesbian Nation in Formation* (1995), a chapter in *Bad Attitude/s On Trial: Feminism, Pornography and the Butler Decision* (1997), and articles on moral regulation in *The Journal of the History of Sexuality* and *Atlantis: A Women's Studies Journal*. Her current research is on the world of sexual entertainment in postwar Vancouver.

Veronica Strong-Boag, former president of the Canadian Historical Association and author of numerous books and articles on Canadian women's history, teaches in Educational Studies and Women's Studies at the University of British Columbia. She was the first director of UBC's Centre for Research in Women's Studies and Gender Relations. In 1988 she won the John A. Macdonald Prize for the best book in Canadian history for *The New Day Recalled: Lives of Girls and Women in English Canada, 1919-1929*, and in 1994 she won the UBC Killam Research Prize. She is currently completing a biography of E. Pauline Johnson with Carole Gerson of Simon Fraser University.

Christl Verduyn is chair of Canadian Studies at Trent University. She has published extensively in the field, and her recent work includes 'Canadian Literary Pluralities' (*Journal of Canadian Studies*) and the books *Dear Marian, Dear Hugh: The MacLennan-Engel Correspondence* (1995) and *Lifelines: Marian Engel's Writings* (1995), which won the Gabrielle Roy Book Prize.

Linda Warley is an assistant professor in the Department of English at the University of Waterloo. She specializes in twentieth-century Canadian literature, read especially from a postcolonial theoretical perspective. She is also interested in First Nations literature and autobiography. She has published articles on these topics in such journals as *Essays on Canadian Writing, Open Letter, Canadian Literature, Kunapipi,* and *a/b:Autobiography Studies.*

Index